ECONOMY HALL

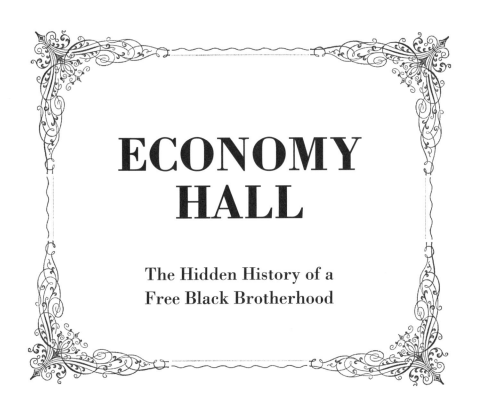

ECONOMY HALL

The Hidden History of a
Free Black Brotherhood

FATIMA SHAIK

THE HISTORIC NEW ORLEANS COLLECTION

THE HISTORIC NEW ORLEANS COLLECTION is a museum, research center, and publisher
dedicated to the study and preservation of the history and culture of New Orleans, the lower
Mississippi valley, and the Gulf South region. The Collection is operated by the Kemper and
Leila Williams Foundation, a Louisiana nonprofit corporation.

533 Royal Street | New Orleans, Louisiana 70130 | www.hnoc.org

Project editor: Cathe Mizell-Nelson
Director of publications: Jessica Dorman
President and CEO: Daniel Hammer
Book design: 10/HALF Studios

LIBRARY OF CONGRESS CATALOGING-IN-PUBLICATION DATA
Names: Shaik, Fatima, 1952– author.
Title: Economy Hall : the hidden history of a free Black brotherhood / Fatima Shaik.
Description: First edition. | New Orleans, Louisiana : The Historic New Orleans Collection,
    [2021] | Includes bibliographical references and index.
Summary: "The Société d'Economie et d'Assistance Mutuelle, a New Orleans mutual aid
    society founded by free men of color in 1836, took a leading role throughout the 19th
    century in the fight for suffrage and education rights for all. Economy Hall, the society's
    meetinghouse, gained renown as a landmark of early jazz"—Provided by publisher.
Identifiers: LCCN 2020047492 | ISBN 9780917860805 (hardcover)
Subjects: LCSH: Boguille, Ludger, 1812–1892.| Economy and Mutual Aid Association—
    History. | African Americans—Louisiana—New Orleans—Intellectual life—19th century. |
    Creoles—Louisiana—New Orleans—Intellectual life—19th century. | Racism—
    Louisiana—New Orleans—History—19th century. | Colorism—Louisiana—New
    Orleans—History—19th century. | African Americans—Louisiana—New Orleans—
    History—19th century. | Creoles—Louisiana—New Orleans—History—19th century. |
    New Orleans (La.)—Race relations—History—19th century.
Classification: LCC F379.N59 N4467 2021 | DDC 305.8009763/35—dc23
LC record available at https://lccn.loc.gov/2020047492

This book has been made possible through a grant from the Louisiana Endowment for the
Humanities, a state affiliate of the National Endowment for the Humanities. The opinions
expressed in this book do not necessarily represent the views of the Louisiana Endowment
for the Humanities or the National Endowment for the Humanities.

Frontispiece: Design from Société d'Economie minutes; 1857–58; by Ludger Boguille;
courtesy of Fatima Shaik

Printed in Canada

I dedicate this book about the past to Lael Naima,
a smart, sweet, strong girl who will thrive in the future.
God bless you. I love you.

—MM

Contents

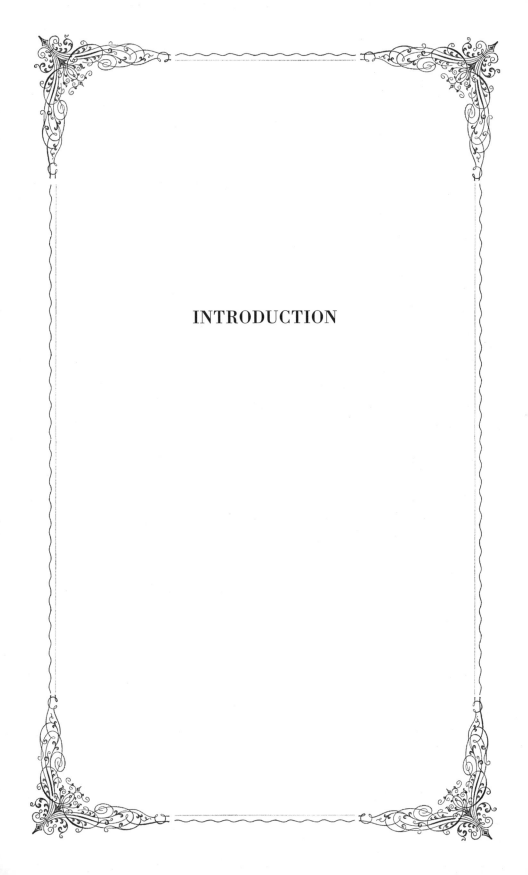

INTRODUCTION

Vous nous voyez, écrivez—les amis sont toujours là!
(You who see us, write—the friends are always there!)

—Cercle Harmonique Séance Registers, 1871

ONE EVENING IN THE 1950s, my father rescued a small library of rare books from the back of a pickup truck. Among them were twenty-four handwritten ledgers, some with marbleized paper covers and spines that were two inches wide. The oldest books had thick, ochre-colored pages made of rag paper. The later ones contained smooth, blue-lined stock. Crammed between thin margins was French script as elegant as a satin-stitched monogram on a linen handkerchief.

From their weight, their tough leather bindings, and my parents' warnings to avoid touching the books, I knew they were important. But they were significant at the time only to us. After all, they had been tossed into the trash.

They were, I later learned, the handwritten records of the Economy Hall from 1836 to 1935. The old wooden building is now known worldwide as one of jazz's most famous incubators. But few people knew its history

Economy Hall; 1939; by Charles E. Smith; *The William Russell Jazz Collection at THNOC, acquisition made possible by the Clarisse Claiborne Grima Fund, 92-48-L.331.133*

in my childhood. Segregation further prevented its story from reaching the mainstream.

The hall's elderly owners were members of the Société d'Economie et d'Assistance Mutuelle (the Economy and Mutual Aid Association). The benevolent organization was disbanding because it had become obsolete. Twentieth-century Black-owned insurance companies and funeral homes took over the society's nineteenth-century functions of providing practical and financial support for families during illnesses and deaths.

Economie member Louis Wilderson Sr. was responsible for selling the hall's contents, collecting the proceeds, and distributing them. He was my father's best friend.

The armoires, desks, chairs, and other furniture were sold off, but nobody wanted the ledgers and library books. So Mr. Wilderson sent them to the garbage dump. Having second thoughts, he told my dad, who hurried that evening to the nearby home of the trash hauler. The books remained in the bed of a pickup, where a rainstorm had drenched them. Some were destroyed. My father retrieved as many books as he could, brought them home in his car, and spread them across our front porch to dry. They promised to be good primary sources for his research.

My dad was in his late thirties then and full of intellectual ambitions, yet he feared that he had reached the zenith of his career. As a boys' counselor at George Washington Carver public school, he modeled professionalism—wearing suits, white shirts, and ties, sometimes in ninety-degree heat. But he was palpably frustrated. He could not go into archives, libraries, restaurants, and other public venues because they barred people then designated as Colored or Negro. The strain frequently sharpened the contours of his face.

Nevertheless, he independently advanced his education. He invited any number of people he met to our home for dinner and conversation in which they exchanged knowledge. He created a library in our house with purchased or found texts like the Economie books.

My dad also listened to Mr. Wilderson's suggestion to take the summers to study, certainly outside of the South, preferably outside of the country. So, in 1957, Mohamed Shaik—a brown-skinned man with a name inherited from his Indian father, and the great-grandson of an enslaved woman—enrolled at the University of Ottawa. Over the next six summers, he drove our family along one- and two-lane highways for four grueling days each way between New Orleans and Canada, where he earned a PhD.

My mother was Lily LaSalle, a native of St. Martinville, Louisiana. French was her first language. In Canada she was able to dip into a cool well of memory as she spoke daily with locals. She also escaped New Orleans's physical and emotional heat. Another benefit of the more than 1,500-mile journey was our relief, for a short time, from the daily scrutiny of the South and one of its consequences—relentless anxiety for people of African descent.

It was around that time that my father rescued the ledgers of the society. He called it "the Economie," using the French pronunciation—"ay-co-no-MEE"—never its English version, Economy. I often heard thoughts expressed in two parlances. But I didn't know the reason that French meant so much to my father. I later realized that his urban community inherited the language and maintained it by choice.

Our neighborhood was the Seventh Ward, a city district drawn in 1852. Living there were many descendants of Louisiana's French speakers. They were also the progeny of the Spanish, Africans, Native Americans, and other people of color who had maneuvered through segregation's maze of regulations and atmosphere of discouragement by becoming doctors, dentists, teachers, and skilled tradesmen. Many of these people also had free colored ancestors—men and women who were not enslaved.

In the first decade of the nineteenth century, two out of three residents of New Orleans were colored. They were already an established community when the Louisiana Purchase occurred in 1803. For the next forty years, almost half of these people were free. Along with the enslaved, these free colored families built and occupied the wood and brick houses of the city. Their children and grandchildren participated in the flowering of the city, which by the 1840s became one of the biggest and most important urban centers in the United States. Their descendants still lived in New Orleans more than a hundred years later.

During my childhood in the 1950s, this community resided primarily in the Seventh Ward and called themselves Creole to remind everyone of their history. The term referred to all people who traced their roots to the earliest New World families—colonial Spanish, French, and West Africans and, often, hybrids of them all.

Others in the city, however, claimed European ancestry without any trace of mixed blood. They, too, were descendants of the city's early settlers. They also called themselves Creole. But during some past decades, they had qualified that designation, using "white Creoles" or "French Creoles" to separate themselves from people with roots in Africa. Or they simply called us "natives" and "Negroes."

The battle for the use of the term Creole had become pitched in the late nineteenth and early twentieth centuries, when white supremacy reigned. Purity was critical. As *The Picayune's Guide to New Orleans* explained in 1903 when it discussed hybrid Louisiana, "Everything 'that is good' in New Orleans is 'Creole.'" The booklet explained that the natural environment of Louisiana had created strains of produce and livestock that local buyers and sellers prized, and they identified these varieties by the term Creole. The guide went on, however, to exclude people of mixed races: "One hears, too, the term, 'Creole negroes,' but it must be remembered always that this is a fine distinction, meaning the Blacks and colored people that are Louisiana bred and born and French-speaking as distinguished from the negroes of other States. 'Creole' means white."

The requisite purity caused southern white historians and writers to extract people of color from books or to ignore them, except for popular stereotypes. From the mid-1850s pamphlets of New Orleans–based Dr. Samuel A. Cartwright, who lectured on racial superiority as a scientific fact, to Margaret Mitchell's *Gone With the Wind* in 1936, to any number of books of fiction and nonfiction until the 1960s, light- and dark-skinned clichés were the norm—quadroon seductresses and tragic mulattos, mammies and bucks. But the facts, especially in Louisiana, showed a range of skin colors, occupations, and economic conditions among African descendants. Nonwhites appeared abundantly in city and state records, though these documents lay fallow. In general, white historians did not concern themselves with the fates of Africans, and the primary sources held in most archives were inaccessible to Blacks. As a result, the published history of New Orleans was always incomplete.

Meanwhile, my community actively maintained a fortress of stories. I grew up learning history on porch steps, in corner groceries, during baptism breakfasts, and especially at the dinner table. At some point in every gathering, family members and friends would bring up their disappeared and deceased relatives, then launch into their history. Each spoke of the past with the passion of a man wrongfully accused of a crime who repeats over and over his account of the moment that proves his innocence. People from our community said their families were once rich, participated in government, fought in the Battle of New Orleans, and appealed to President

Abraham Lincoln for their rights. Ancestors had owned houses and land, traveled to Haiti and France, and lived in Mexico, my relatives claimed. The Creoles were the offspring of white men who loved them, as much as Negro children could be loved in the South, people said. (They did not add that Creoles were also the products of rape.) I nodded and smiled, but I was a skeptic. I thought my family was just trying to give me hope because almost everything I read said that all Negroes were slaves and anyone who mixed with them was inferior.

In 1966 my cousin Elizabeth Moore created an after-school Black empowerment group at Saint Mary's Dominican High School. She was its first president. I held the post the next year. We sought authors to inform us and found James Baldwin, Eldridge Cleaver, Ralph Ellison, W. E. B. Du Bois, and others. But about New Orleans, I could uncover only fiction by Alice Dunbar-Nelson, biography by Charles Barthelemy Rousseve, and a poetry book by my mother and her friends, *Arrows of Gold*. They offered scant support for the stories of our elders. All this time, the historical proof resided in the Economie journals stacked in a cabinet in my family home. The books had traveled only fourteen blocks from the Economie's meeting hall in the Tremé neighborhood. A wealth of unrealized knowledge filled their untouched pages.

By college I was still searching for an explanation of the racial conditions that had formed and still affected me. I attended Xavier University of Louisiana for two years, then transferred to Boston University to study journalism. After graduation, in 1974, I reported for the *Miami News* and the *New Orleans Times-Picayune*. I left again in 1976 for graduate school at New York University and to work as a writer. Over the next two decades, I wrote articles for national and international publications. I also wrote four books of fiction that allowed me to delve into memory and history—a collection of novellas called *The Mayor of New Orleans: Just Talking Jazz*, two picture books titled *The Jazz of Our Street* and *On Mardi Gras Day*, and *Melitte*, a young adult novel in the voice of an enslaved girl in eighteenth-century Louisiana.

All that time, the journals stayed on my mind. I remembered their size (about as big as my childhood suitcases) and heft (dense as the St. Joseph bricks for the sidewalk that my grandfather laid into the mud) and the way that my father had carried the books into the house, blotted the rainwater from their pages and covers, wrapped them in newspaper and Schwegmann grocery bags, and placed them in the red lacquered cabinets he built next to the bricked-up fireplace, across from the photos of his and my mother's parents and grandparents.

My father had received his PhD in 1964 with a dissertation about the education of Negro children in Louisiana. He went on to head the division of education at Xavier University of Louisiana and, later, the division of aeronautics at Delgado Community College—where he had been refused an interview during segregation. He had grown older and more content, and he had left the Economie books alone.

One day in 1997, during a visit home to New Orleans, I looked in the cabinet. Nothing had changed since I was a child. The journals still sat on the shelf. I pulled out the books and arranged them in chronological order on the dining table. I opened the first volume and saw the date, January 1836. By then I knew something of American history as well as Black history, and the ways they had diverged. I realized that not only were these books old, but they told a story about America that few people alive had heard.

THE LEGACY OF THE ECONOMIE JOURNALS

When I began to read the Economie journals, I started to see patterns. I could trace Economie lineages in reverse chronology. Six blocks up my childhood street lived Lionel Dupart Sr. and his family. Before I was born, they resided in a house over my sideyard fence. In 1928, he was the assistant secretary of the Economie and had joined the society in 1910. He had the same surname as Joseph Charles Dupart, who hosted the first Economie meeting in 1836. That founding member had the same last name as Pierre Joseph deLisle, *dit** Dupart, who was living on St. Ann Street in New Orleans in 1727, and Jacques Dupart, who came to Louisiana in 1718 from Condé, France.

---

* A French term used to show that a person was known by more than one surname.

The family name deLisle—also spelled Delille—was familiar as well because Mother Henriette Delille founded the Sisters of the Holy Family in 1842. The nuns were still active during my childhood and resided on Orleans Street in the French Quarter. My family toured parts of the convent and school once when we took a guest to visit the sisters. Now the Bourbon Orleans Hotel, it was then a large wooden building with rickety steps and dark, quiet rooms. The building was similar to the Thomy Lafon Old Folks' Home, which my mother and I had visited regularly. It was within walking distance of my house and a block from the home of Lionel Dupart Sr. Like a child learning to cross the narrow streets, then the broader avenues of her community, I began to make mental notes of the names and places. Eventually, I was able to connect them to the dates and events recorded in the Economie journals.

I found Société d'Economie surnames among my neighbors, such as Rouzan, Bagneris, Boutte, Charbonnet, Barthelemy, and Martinez, and extended family members Bart and Boguille. At once, I saw that the journals corroborated the oral history that my community maintained—and American history excluded.

On subsequent visits to New Orleans, I began to read and research. Twenty-four journals contained about 3,000 handwritten pages, mostly in French. The minutes of meetings, held at intervals from a few days to a month apart, extended from 1836 to 1935. But there were some omissions. I could not find records for 1842 to 1857, except a book with financial reports from 1854 to 1860. There was also a significant gap in one journal, from 1858 to 1864.

I scanned some of the minutes and microfilmed the rest. I bought a small microfilm reader and put it next to the television so that I could continue to work while I spent time with my family in the evenings.

To find context for the material in the Economie minutes, I scoured journal articles and books. I looked at real estate purchases and architectural surveys, delved into notarial acts and census records. I moved between private and public libraries and academic institutions.

I found *Nos hommes et notre histoire*, by nineteenth-century Creole author Rodolphe Lucien Desdunes, which was published in Montreal

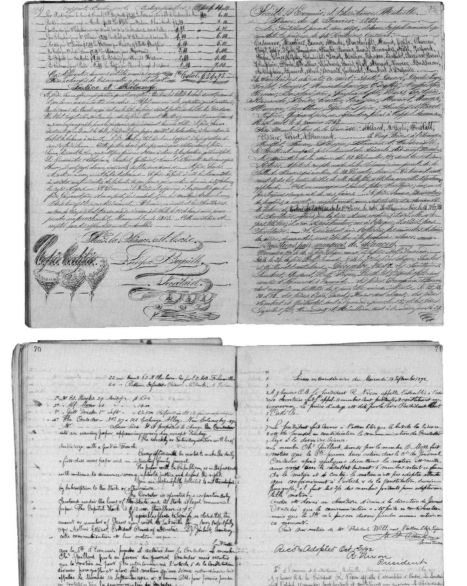

UPPER: Economie minutes, December 28, 1857, and January 4, 1858; *courtesy of Fatima Shaik.* LOWER: Economie minutes, September 7, September 14, and October 1, 1892; *courtesy of Fatima Shaik*

Cabinet card of Basile Barès;
by Pierre Petit; *courtesy of Basile
Barès Collection, Xavier University
of Louisiana Archives and Special
Collections*

in 1911 and in Louisiana in 1973 as *Our People and Our History*, translated
and edited by Sister Dorothea Olga McCants. Desdunes wrote about the
Creole community from memory. He said that the Economie's members
were from "the upper class, composed of professional men, wishing to
distinguish themselves."

The *New Orleans Tribune* newspaper, the first Black daily in the United
States, wrote about the Economy Society in 1867, "The above title is the
name of that society composed of a band of noble-hearted fellows, whose
good work in this community is legend. . . . Since the struggle for equal
rights has begun, the society has kept the doors of its hall open for all
public meetings—to say nothing of the other many acts of generosity on
its part toward all other benevolent societies and the orphans. Were we
to attempt to particularize its good work we would take more room than
we can afford to give at present."

I came to realize that the Economie journals were among the few surviving primary sources written by the community activists themselves. The books contained a history that revealed the multiracial character of New Orleans and a Creole identity that had been prized and debated. The handwritten records affirmed that a liberal-minded society had embraced some Europeans and Anglo-Americans—Black and white—and repudiated others due to their values and politics. In addition, the journals named Economie members who took part in the Battle of New Orleans, the Civil War, Reconstruction, equality movements, and more. The records expanded the narrative of Blacks as active participants in the major social and political events of the United States and offered additional information about their terms of engagement.

The journals also showed that multiethnic and multinational people had thrived in the "colored" Economie community during the nineteenth century in ways that history hardly records. The society's members, who called themselves "Economistes," were part of the African diaspora and Indigenous America. They were also descendants of Germans, Italians, Cubans, Haitians, Mexicans, and other ethnic groups who arrived in this port city. One branch of the Dupart family included a relative from Africa in its household after the Civil War. As Economie member Henry L. Rey said in 1880, the society "should be able to receive Jews and Chinese" if they wanted to join. Joseph Daniel Warburg, the son of a Jewish man, had already been a member for eight years by that time. And near the turn of the twentieth century, when New Orleans was resegregating by violent means, the Economie was headed by Walter L. Cohen, the child of a Negro mother and Jewish father. New York famously absorbed hundreds of thousands of European immigrants, but Creole New Orleans was a much earlier melting pot of America's darker brothers.

I began my work with the Economie journals in 1997, and while I had no plans to slow my career as a fiction writer, the books' content came to absorb me. I deciphered the French handwriting and occasional French-English hybrid sentences. I pored over syntax and word use that my French-speaking friends told me was "Français-Américain." I contextualized the minutes within eras of US history and researched the names of Economie members, their families, and guests. I had long conversations with elderly people who had danced at the hall or lived near it. I combed through oral histories of musicians who had played there. This work brought me to nineteenth-century composers Edmond Dédé and Basile Barès, a French opera company, jazz originators Armand J. Piron and the Eagle Brass Band, and others who had entertained Economie members. The society had also hosted political dignitaries, abolitionists, and mystics at meetings, debates, recitals, séances, parties, and theatrical events.

I began to understand history in a unified way and gained new insight on the methods that the community used to survive. Members continually educated and reinforced other members. I read in the first Economie journal that the society's mission was "to help one another and teach one another while holding out a protective hand to suffering humanity." It had succeeded.

From its original mission in 1836, to the encouragement Mr. Wilderson gave my dad, to the books he gave me, to my childhood neighborhood of intimate friends and loyal families, the Economie had created an environment to sustain us all. An additional reason for the society's cohesion, generation after generation, was its ability to erect and maintain a meeting place at a time when people of color were shut out of public spaces. This venue was la Salle d'Economie—the Economy Hall.

THE ECONOMY HALL

The first connection I made between the Société d'Economie and its hall was in a talk with my father. Economy Hall, as other people called it in English, was in the Tremé neighborhood, near his childhood home. He didn't remember the interior, only the location, so I asked family friends. Mr. Wilderson had died in 1964, but Adrienne Woods Blache and Mildred Meilleur Boissiere were daughters of Economistes and married into Economie families. They told me that as young girls they had danced to Piron's orchestra on the hall's gleaming wood floor. Mrs. Blache's relatives lived nearby and joined her at events. At a party in the hall one night, Mrs. Boissiere met the man who became her husband. I followed this trail of family and jazz back to the building.

Through the journals and property records, I realized that there were three Economie halls in the nineteenth and twentieth centuries. The first was purchased in 1836, and the last was emptied in the 1950s. For at least 114 years, the brothers of the Economie, their families, and friends had come to Ursuline Street between Marais and Villere Streets. Local members walked to the hall from nearby houses, and some voyaged to meetings from France, Italy, and Mexico.

The *Tribune* wrote, "We are compelled to express admiration for the good which has been worked under the roof of that structure which stands on Ursuline street—the hall where the oppressed and the friends of liberty first met in council. Economy Hall, in New Orleans, like Faneuil Hall in Boston, like Carpenters' Hall in Philadelphia, will belong to history."

My interviewees were the latest members of a deliberate community. The first Economie members were free men of color who lived in the French Quarter, the Faubourg* Marigny, and the Tremé neighborhoods of the early nineteenth century. By the mid-nineteenth century the Economistes had settled across Claiborne Avenue, an area that had been called the Seventh Ward since the 1850s. A century later the families migrated toward Lake Pontchartrain, where they prospered in the 1950s and 1960s in Gentilly, Pontchartrain Park, and New Orleans East—the last settlement encouraged by the nearby construction of the NASA complex that manufactured Saturn booster rockets. Other descendants of the Economie were members of the Great Migration to the North from the period after the Civil War through the era of civil rights.

The Katrina diaspora was the biggest disruption to this community. The levee failure and flood after the 2005 hurricane displaced 272,000 African Americans from Orleans Parish, where most Economie descendants resided. More than 92,000 Black people had not returned to the city by 2018. But many had deep roots in the Creole community and came back for baptisms, weddings, and funerals. Their gatherings, where people knew one another through ancestral surnames, were evidence of the community's cohesion. They retold the stories of French and Haitian ancestors, men who

---

* The French term for *suburb*, which is still used today in this neighborhood's name.

served in the Civil War, and mixed-race families who kept silent while their relatives who were passing for white benefited financially. Those were the same oral histories that I had heard when I lived in segregation in the 1950s. They were corroborated now with archival research and DNA evidence.

The downtown faubourgs of Tremé and Marigny, usually associated with French-speaking Creoles, may have been home to the first members of the Economie, but men from throughout the city joined. Over the nineteenth century, Economistes lived in other New Orleans locations, such as Algiers and Jefferson. The society also expanded to include men with Anglo surnames and immigrants who had been born in Mexico, Italy, and Cuba.

Partygoers and members of other organizations—both newcomers and natives—also came through the Economie's doors. One of the first references to the Economy Hall that I found when I began to research was the announcement of an 1873 workers' cooperative meeting in the *Tägliche Deutsche Zeitung*, a German-language newspaper published in New Orleans.

The Economie's reach into so many communities and the interaction of its members with political and military leaders in Haiti, Cuba, Mexico, and the United States—from Louisiana's territorial period through the first civil rights era of the 1860s to the second one in the 1950s—certainly confirm the society as one of the most influential multiethnic Black organizations in the South.

The Economie had a grand impact in one other area—the evolution of jazz. The society hosted local musicians at the hall's inauguration, included the teachers of some of the earliest jazz innovators as members, and rented the ballroom for dances that became legendary.

Economy Hall is known worldwide even now. Millions of people today have heard the repertoire of the society's parties from jazz recordings, and untold thousands have stood under the Economy Hall tent at the New Orleans Jazz and Heritage Festival to hear traditional local music. At least one hundred oral histories in the Hogan Jazz Archive of Tulane University mention the hall as the location of meetings, parties, and parades. Even after the Economie members no longer used the building, several churches leased it, so the location continued to serve as the departure point for marches and second-line funerals. But perhaps only a handful of people alive today know about the society that gave the hall its name. The journals had been hidden away—first by the society and then by my dad.

He evacuated our family home in the Seventh Ward in 2005, just before Hurricane Katrina arrived. All of my relatives "took water," as was the expression after the storm—everyone but my father. Brick piers held the house high off the ground. The aftermath of the levee failures submerged his grass, garden, bushes, and then steps but stopped six inches shy of his porch. Inside, two feet above the floor, the Economie journals sat safely on his shelves.

As a child, I held the can of red stain when my father painted the cabinet doors, and I remember watching him place the books inside. They were too fragile for me to handle, he said, too important. I was too young. Still, I sometimes sneaked into the front room with a flashlight when everyone else was asleep to open the journals and press my fingers to the thick paper, wishing that I understood the secrets they contained.

Many years later, I discovered that several Economie members had met in the dark back room of the Economy Hall to call ghosts through séances, and one night, through a medium, a deceased son came to speak for the dead. The spirit of Victor Lacroix told the séance circle, "*Vous nous voyez, écrivez—les amis sont toujours là!*" (You who see us, write—the friends are always there!) When I read this entry, I felt that his message was also intended for me.

Those words already had resonated throughout my life—on early trips in the car when I was given a small notebook to scribble about my family's adventures, at the bedsides of the elderly who guided my education, and at post-Katrina gatherings, when I listened to the *contes* of friends who encouraged me to write about a disappearing community.

This book is the result—a century of New Orleans history—drawn from my study of the Economie journals and told from the perspective of an important member of the society. As secretary of the Economie for several years Ludger Boguille was a prolific note taker and, in that way, my soul mate. I also chose him because his moral and intellectual growth mirrored his community's evolution. His long life (1812–1892) intersected with the history of America and the Western world as their societies grappled with issues of slavery, equality, and revolution. He was warm, smart, open-hearted, and influential.

In addition, I grew up around the Boguille descendants and their in-laws the Barts. None of us at the time knew that the families were connected for over a century or understood Ludger's role in history. He and Engle Bart were fellow Economistes for over two decades, until 1879, when Bart died. The society's president at the time, Henry L. Rey, identified Bart as a veteran of the Battle of New Orleans and eulogized him as "a gentle and peaceful brother, a respected elder and the one among us who courageously endured the miseries and vicissitudes of existence."

I ran into a Boguille-Bart descendant at the airport shortly after Hurricane Katrina, when I was returning to New York. Steven was a fireman, like three of his cousins and one of mine. He regaled me with stories of his rescues from the dangerous floodwaters. He had pulled many people into boats. He had also commandeered a stray horse and ridden it bareback along the levee to carry an elderly woman to safety. Steven told me that the person I should be writing about was him.

With this book, in a sense, I am. Every generation of Americans has witnessed Black men like Steven and, long before him, Ludger and the radical members of the Economy Society who gave fully of themselves, then disappeared from history or were erased, even though their contributions revealed our common humanity. I hope this book causes us to discover more people like them. The Economie brothers of the nineteenth century were a special group of unknown but aspirational men. This book tells the story of the legacies they created, the obstacles they faced, and their shining moments of courage.

The People Who Disappeared

Divine Providence, may your benediction be spread on this new brother! May he be guided and strengthened by respect to duty, and may his motto be the conversation of union and fraternity with all and for all.

—Economie Minutes, 1857

O̧N DECEMBER 20, 1857, Ludger Boguille arrived at the grand opening party of his benevolent society's new two-story hall. The building sparkled, with copper cornices and fresh white weatherboards. It towered above the small Creole cottages built by brothers of the society and now occupied by immigrants from Europe, South America, and Africa.

The building, on Ursuline Street between Marais and Villere Streets, adjoined a wide, grassy lot. Carriages could park there after delivering luminaries to the front door. They came now, dressed in their most elegant clothes—men in dark, formal jackets and vests, and women in full, cinched-waist skirts. To debark, the ladies had to be lifted and maneuvered away from the muddy aprons of the cabs. As Boguille faced the building, the cabriolets rolled in from the left, the direction of the St. Augustine Church where his friends worshipped on Sundays, and the Place Congo, which had served as a bazaar more than a century earlier, preserved as a few tree-lined blocks where people still gathered.

BALLOU'S PICTORIAL DRAWING-ROOM COMPANION.

ST. AUGUSTINE CHURCH, NEW ORLEANS, LOUISIANA.

St. Augustine Church; 1859; by Samuel S. Kilburn Jr.; *The L. Kemper and Leila Moore Williams Founders Collection at THNOC, 1959.204.2*

The sound of African drums being played in the clearing under the oak trees easily reached Ursuline Street where Boguille stood. The Africans' bamboula beat was already part of the city's repertoire. While local children tapped out the rhythm with sticks on the wooden steps, a Parisian publisher circulated a piano composition called *Bamboula*, opus 2, by New Orleans native Louis Moreau Gottschalk, with the subtitle *Danse des nègres*. Boguille would probably hear the piece played at some point during the gala evening.

As Boguille entered the building, men came to shake his hand and give him a bear hug—called "the official accolade" by his brothers in the Société d'Economie et d'Assistance Mutuelle, a benevolent association known in English as the Economy Society. As secretary of the organization, Boguille knew there were perhaps a few monolingual English guests that night but no such members. In addition, the Economistes were all literate, as their written applications demonstrated. He knew all eighty men in the association intimately.

At least every two weeks, Boguille inscribed their names—surname and initials—in the society ledger when they came to meetings, paid their dues, brought in their doctor bills for reimbursement, and announced the funerals of their dearly deceased. He knew their occupations, the sizes of their families, the state of their finances, and their behavior—due to the periodic reports from the society's committee of investigation. They were the elite of the most prosperous free Black community in the South.

As a scholar and schoolteacher, Boguille had a working knowledge of statistics about the United States. New Orleans was the fifth-largest city in America and home to ten thousand free colored people—those born free and those emancipated—including more skilled workers than New York City. At a time when the United States held four million people in slavery, about half of New Orleans's Black residents were free. That ratio had remained steady for almost as long as Louisiana had been a state.

Boguille imbibed this heady company—possibly peppering his conversations with Latin and proverbs from Saint Domingue, admiring the beauty of the members' wives and daughters, and perhaps passing his hand over the Parisian silk shawls covering their shoulders. The women's variety of earthen skin tones set off their starburst corsages and the bright bouquets that they brought from their gardens as gifts for the hall. All of the Economie families had contributed in some way to the construction of the building, and, like him, they came to celebrate.

Moving indoors with the throng, Boguille passed the Economie's portraits of proud revolutionary presidents: Alexandre Pétion and Ignacio Comonfort. Pétion was the leader of the mulatto faction in the Saint Domingue revolution. He rose to become president of Haiti, the first Black republic in the West. Pétion posed in a long, dark cutaway coat, white breeches, and tall black riding boots. President Comonfort of Mexico wore a close-cut, full-faced beard and a formal white shirt and dark suit. His gentle brown eyes looked out from the portrait at the teeming crowd.

Free woman of color; 1837; by François Jacques Fleischbein;
THNOC, 1985.212

Comonfort had recently invited the men of the Economie to join him in
Veracruz, where they could be free from increasing threats in America.

Men and women with ancestral roots in many nations, but born in
New Orleans, glided along with Boguille through the hallway and past the
Economie's mahogany staircase. As a demonstration of expert carpentry,
the staircase was one of the hall's showpieces.

Guests crowded the polished wood floors of the seventy-foot-long
wainscoted theater. A large, raised bandstand looked over the audience.
The philharmonic of free colored musicians, convened just for this party,
waited for a signal from the hall's master of ceremonies to play the strings,
woodwinds, and piano. Like the other people in the throng, Boguille
anticipated the overture.

That evening, he could finally enjoy the celebration—listen to the inspirational speeches and religious invocations, eat the delicious food and drink the exquisite wines, revel in the beautiful music, and twirl with the other spirited dancers. At that moment, nothing in the outside world mattered.

If Boguille were to consider his place as outsiders did, however, he would have sensed an enormous battle approaching. The Economie's ceremony took place about six months after the Supreme Court's *Dred Scott* decision, which decreed that the Declaration of Independence had not been "supposed to embrace the negro race, which, by common consent, had been excluded from civilized Governments and the family of nations, and doomed to slavery."

To the glittering company that Boguille kept, it was a ridiculous statement. Five days before the opening of the Economie's hall, the society's president had responded to the growing racial prejudice around him by saying, "May our behaviors always strike down our oppressors, so that, in each of us, our miserable enemies may discover the proof that we understand that man was born to live with his equals."

The crowd around Boguille sipped cognac and champagne, and then smoked some of the two thousand cigars bought for the occasion.

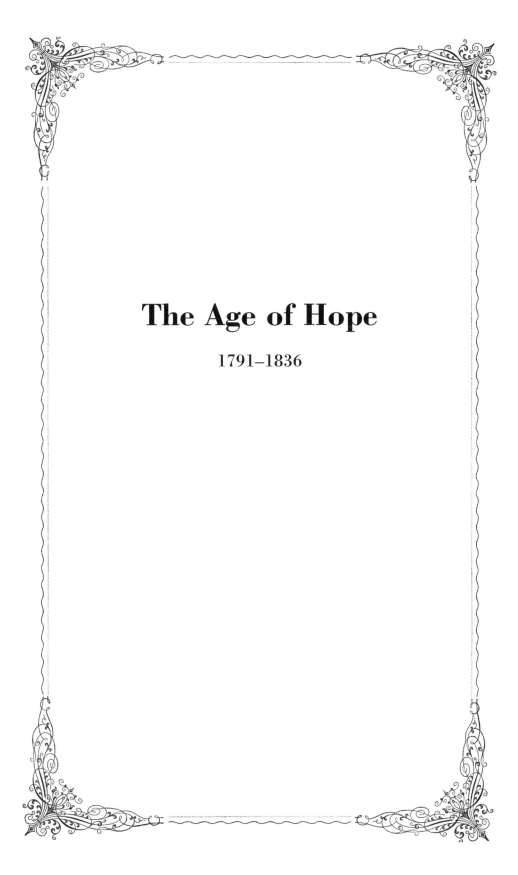

The Age of Hope

1791–1836

In the Beginning: Haiti

1791–1820

The president talked for a long time about politics, the abolition of slavery and the revolution in Haiti, and ended with a prayer.

—Economie Minutes, 1866

MORE THAN A HALF century before the inaugural party, Ludger Boguille's father, François, had abandoned his home on the once-lush island of Saint Domingue. Its port cities were in flames or reduced to smoldering ash. The people in his district of Croix-des-Bouquets had suffered madness.

The revolution began when a free man of color named Vincent Ogé planned in October 1790 to storm the colony's biggest city, Cap-Français. He was defeated and executed five months later. The government displayed his severed head on a stick to warn others against following the same path, but the scare tactic only inspired more revolutionaries.

At thirteen years old, François was living at the center of the Western world's most significant Black revolt when it began in 1791. His upbringing and location beckoned him to the war. His mother was dark-skinned and enslaved. His father was unnamed. Their community included many children of planters and enslaved women. Some of their descendants were now free merchants, farmers, and soldiers in Croix-des-Bouquets as a result of manumission, self-purchase, militia service, and other means. The process of emancipation in the district mirrored the rest of the island of Saint Domingue. François was born into slavery, and if his father did not free him, the coming changes in the nation could.

François's home district was a mountainous area with verdant plateaus. Plantations thrived there through a layered society—profiting the Europeans who owned the farms, the whites who managed them, and the free people of color who supplied them. The backbreaking work of the enslaved supported them all. The darker communities held little hope of mobility, but their people told one another that someday conditions would change. The new government in France, the mother country, had recognized the humanity of all men.

On May 15, 1791, when the French government gave citizenship to the free Blacks born on Saint Domingue, all of its dark children became hopeful. The enslaved saw an opening. The already free people were exhilarated with patriotism, but the whites on the island objected to the changed laws and refused to enforce them.

In François Boguille's home district, the free men of color formed a national guard. Unrepentant followers of Ogé, they recruited enslaved men from the nearby plantations, and the threat of their alliance prompted the whites in the district to act. Still, they granted rights only to the free men and promised their enslaved allies a ship's passage to Central America.

That was in October 1791. By November the whites reneged. In response, the free soldiers of color wrote a declaration of war against "these monsters from Europe": "For far too long have we served as the playthings of their passions and their insidious maneuvering. For far too long we have groaned under the yoke. Let us destroy our oppressors and bury ourselves with them down to the slightest vestige of our shame. Let us tear up by its deepest roots this tree of prejudice."

All around teenaged François, bloody horrors ensued—men eviscerated by sabers and mutilated by cannon fire, and white soldiers burned in the cane fields where they had thought to hide. War engulfed François's adolescence, but he was old enough to join the fighting. The early battles near Croix-des-Bouquets were just the beginning of the revolution that took over the island and touched everyone.

Le jeune Ogé; 1822; by Villain; *THNOC, gift of Dr. and Mrs. Fritz Daguillard, 2017.0003.148*

In other districts as well, the free men of color and enslaved men formed fighting units while their leaders made clever alliances with the Spanish, the British, and whichever faction of French colonial power would help them win a battle. Young François would have been one of the nameless patriots who initiated the revolution in Saint Domingue.

He was also likely a victim of the island's factional wars. Free men and the enslaved fought one another to control the direction of the nation.

François's friend Charles Joseph Savary was one of the fighters whose political vision went contrary to that of the revolution's new and most effective leader, Toussaint Louverture. Savary retreated with his men and their families to nearby Cuba in 1799, remaining there for a decade before continuing on to Louisiana.

Whether François emigrated with Savary is a matter of speculation. He did not write a diary or send a packet of letters to friends to describe his daily life. He had not learned to write. If he did go to Cuba, its searing heat may have reminded him of Saint Domingue, without the mountain breezes. He may have seen Cuba's plantations but missed Saint Domingue's plateaus. He may have heard the romance of the Spanish language but found that it cut his soft French tongue. Even if he could have captured his thoughts about his new environment on paper, war destroyed so many documents of that era that his words would not have survived.

François's movements were never recorded. But this much is known: while the revolution changed Saint Domingue from France's Jewel of the West Indies—its riches created by enslaved laborers—to the first independent Black republic in the West by 1804, François Boguille changed from boy to man. And at some time before 1811, like any number of refugees, he boarded a ship aimed toward an endless northern horizon.

Ten thousand of them arrived in New Orleans.

Jacmel and Jérémie, the first city situated in the South-East, the second in the South-West, are . . . isolated from the rest of the colony by the mountain ranges that surround them and serve as their natural ramparts. In these two regions, more than anywhere else, the insolence and the cruelty of the colonists were extreme. The free people were obliged to flee.

—Joseph Saint-Rémy, *Pétion et Haïti*, 1864

SUZANNE BUTEL LEFT Saint Domingue along with the others escaping the war. Did she regret coming to a new land?

She grew up in Jérémie, a coastal town on the distant southern peninsula of the island, more than one hundred miles from Boguille's home of Croix-des-Bouquets. Jérémie had only 180 residences when she was eleven years old, in 1788. The town was isolated by mountains and rough terrain but faced the open sea. Sailing ships arrived with regularity carrying French colonists, eager to own plantations.

Indigo, cocoa, cotton, and coffee from the nearby farms passed through Jérémie's port legally to France and, occasionally, through smugglers to the British colony of Jamaica. By 1791 the port was busy with sailing vessels moored in the harbor, rowboats gliding out to meet them, and men along the shore making plans for more shipping and building. Butel's hometown boasted upper and lower districts consisting of about fifty oddly configured

DUMAS.

Général des Armées de la Rép.ᵉ

Né à Jeremie en Amerique, le 25 Mars 1762

Thomas-Alexandre Dumas;
between 1790 and 1802;
by François Bonneville;
*THNOC, gift of Dr. and
Mrs. Fritz Daguillard,
2017.0003.76*

residential blocks of triangles, squares, and long rectangles cut by streets with names such as La Marine for seafarers and Les Procureurs for prosecutors. A brutish frontier town with elite French pretensions, Jérémie was home to an amateur theater that reenacted classical plays. Around the time Butel was born, its most famous mixed-race resident, Thomas-Alexandre Dumas—best known as progenitor of a literary dynasty—was leaving Saint Domingue with his white father for the French motherland. The father had sold his other children before leaving.

Important for Butel, however, were the free colored people who remained. Their population had increased to almost half that of whites in Jérémie during her youth. They were the manumitted offspring of planters and enslaved women, or people who achieved freedom through self-purchase and had moved from the hinterlands to her small town. Some free people of color had inherited plantations or bought small farms whose produce they brought to market. Many—both men and women—were selling their rural property to incoming French colonists and leaving to work in Jérémie in the building trades or as artisans and traders. Not as wealthy as most white planters but economically on a par with many whites who had similar skills, the members of the colored elite of Jérémie were part of the culture and the economic life of the colony. Still, their roles were proscribed because they were considered inferiors. Europeans had named at least eleven racial categories of mixes among Africans, Indigenous islanders, and whites—and all natives were granted less legal power than any haggard white immigrant.

As free men of color rallied for citizenship across Saint Domingue in the 1790s, the citizens of Jérémie did too. In 1792 the revolutionaries rose up, but whites armed enslaved Blacks and set them against the free people of color. Free revolutionaries were put to death. Free colored elderly people, women, and children were rounded up, put in chains, and jailed on ships in the harbor. In addition, the mere possibility of Black equality caused the whites in Jérémie and its larger political district Grand'Anse to give up their ties to the French and call in the British army from nearby Jamaica for defense.

Butel may have exited Saint Domingue before the British arrived in September 1793, when she was sixteen years old. Or perhaps she hid in the hills, on a plantation she owned, before dashing to the harbor with a girl named Marie Noel who also lived on the property.

When their dank wooden boat took off, the city's whitewashed houses receded into the dark green forests like the sparse teeth of an old woman. The aquamarine shoals of the harbor changed to the blue glass of the Caribbean.

The old wooden ship could have fallen prey to pirates, storms, or a disaster such as a slow leak that burst into a full-blown hole far out at sea. More than once, ships had sunk amid the chaos of screaming passengers, a scene that turned quickly to an untraceable burial and a crystalline silence.

Butel's vessel, like many departing ships, carried whites, free people of color, and others who were enslaved in Saint Domingue but would be free in every part of Haiti by 1804. In the waters of other nations, however, their status would depend on the jurisdiction.

Butel and Marie Noel headed for Louisiana. They may have been equally frightened, equally lonely, and equally anxious about living in a new country. Still, there was a big difference between them once they arrived in the United States.

Years later, after living with Marie perhaps for decades, Butel needed to buy a house. In 1813 she sold the young woman to Bernard Marigny, the titleholder of a large swath of property just outside the walls of the old city of New Orleans. The land had acquired the name Faubourg Marigny—a suburb named after him. Refugees from Saint Domingue flocked to the area. Butel's new home sat on Washington Square across from a wide park.

Butel received 500 *piastres* for Marie Noel. Written in French, the term *piastre* was used to mean a dollar. The price was equivalent to three years of a laborer's salary. But for Marie Noel, the contract dictated that she would labor without pay for the rest of her life.

*Our militia will never be worth much while our numbers
are so few and scattered over such an extensive country.
They are moreover mingled with those very negroes and free
people of color whom we must necessarily always consider in
a country where slavery exists to the extent it does here as
political enemies.*

—New Orleans Mayor John Watkins, September 6, 1805

FRANÇOIS BOGUILLE WAS NOT welcome in the Louisiana territory, but he never returned to Haiti.

The United States had purchased Louisiana in 1803, and while the female exiles from Saint Domingue were welcome additions to offset the large numbers of frontiersmen and soldiers in the territory, the men who arrived posed a threat. The American government feared that the refugee men would ally with the enslaved people in the territory as they had during the revolution on the island. The exiles might also find common ground with the native free colored Louisianians whose families served in the colonial militias and together establish a volatile, disruptive force. The Americans were correct that the former Saint Domingue soldiers blended into the French-speaking colored community. Many West Indians hid their true origins to avoid expulsion. Some of Savary's men even lived in the swamps at the edge of the city, in an area populated by fugitives from slavery and pirates, among them Jean Laffite.

But the colored community did not pose a menace to the United States anywhere equal to that of its enemy abroad. Great Britain still had not accepted the American Revolution and refused to respect the country's sovereignty. It seized American ships in foreign waters and pressed their sailors into service. Britain also supported Native American uprisings against the US government and settlers in the western territories.

On June 18, 1812, the United States had enough. It declared war on Great Britain and suffered over the next two years in skirmishes across the North American continent. Then, in August 1814, Britain invaded Washington, DC, and set fire to the Capitol, the White House, and other government buildings. A few weeks later, on September 13, 1814, the British attacked Baltimore, Maryland, but this time they failed. Still, the British navy recouped and moved toward the Gulf of Mexico with plans for invading New Orleans.

While the ships and troops were relocating, the British government decided that the war's toll was too painful and moved to negotiate peace. But news of the treaty—signed in the European city of Ghent on December 24, 1814—didn't reach British troops on their way to Louisiana or the Americans ready to defend the city.

By then the United States had sought out colored soldiers. The Saint Domingue fighters and former colonial militia had the skills and sense to help repel the British. In December 1814 General Andrew Jackson came to address the colored community and referred to the Haitian revolutionaries and the men living in New Orleans as "noble-hearted, generous free men of color." He asked them to join the battle and promised them the same pay as white men.

Charles Joseph Savary *père*, now too old and infirm to fight, personally encouraged refugees from Saint Domingue to join this new revolution. He recruited 256 fighters for Major Louis D'Aquin's Second Battalion of Free Men of Color, in which his namesake Charles Joseph Savary *fils* led a company and his son Belton served.

The Saint Domingue troops joined a coalition under Jackson that came to total almost four thousand men—including a First Battalion of Free Men of Color, under Pierre Lacoste, comprising Choctaw Native Americans, Cajuns, Europeans, and Americans. Enslaved men were sent into the war as well, but unarmed. Skirmishing began on December 23, 1814, and continued until January 8, 1815. That morning, under a heavy fog, Jackson's troops and the British faced off some seven miles downriver from New Orleans. Savary *fils*, Belton, and a few other members of the Second Battalion volunteered to take out the British snipers. It was a risky mission, and Belton was mortally injured. But many Englishmen died in the first advance. The second advance showed General Sir Edward Pakenham leading the British troops. A single rifle shot knocked him from his horse, and subsequent bullets killed him. Jackson later wrote a letter to James Monroe saying that he always believed that Pakenham "fell from the bullet of a free man of color." Belton died two days later, on January 10, 1815.

In February 1815 Jackson reassigned Savary's troops to an area outside the city called Chef Menteur and ordered them to do menial work. Savary refused, saying that his men would prefer death to performing the work of laborers. More than a hundred of his men left Chef Menteur and went home to New Orleans and its surroundings. His insubordination went undisciplined, no doubt due to the distinguished efforts of his family during the Battle of New Orleans. Two months later, Jackson wrote a letter attesting to Savary's "patriotism . . . on every occasion by exhorting the Battalion of coulour to a faithful and brave defence of the country that held their wives, their children and their property. It had a very beneficial effect." About a decade later, the Louisiana legislature gave Savary a pension of eight dollars a month because his son Belton was "killed in the defence of the state."

About a year later, the young Savary left Louisiana to lead military expeditions in Texas, where he assisted Mexican insurgents in achieving liberation from Spain.

François Boguille's name appeared on an application for land offered to veterans of the Battle of New Orleans by the federal government, claiming he too had served under Captain Marcelin in D'Aquin's Second Battalion of Free Men of Color. But the application was rejected. Boguille's name appeared on none of the muster rolls.

Whether he fought in Louisiana or simply lived among the other soldiers in New Orleans, Boguille would be closely connected with the elder Savary for decades to come.

Love is a beautiful dream, the aspiration of the known to the unknown, the divine ray ravished by Prometheus. God created the world only because He needed to love.

—Economie Minutes, 1858

FRANÇOIS BOGUILLE COULD WALK about six dark blocks through his neighborhood to the evening dances for men of color held at the Washington Ballroom. The streets captured the music that flowed through the hall's open windows—mostly the sounds of the waltz and quadrille. The men who bought tickets strode up to the wide, two-story building on St. Philip Street. Their tough leather boots were a sign of a comfortable lifestyle in a city where thin shoes and bare feet were the norm. They clunked up the steps fronting the ballroom and entered the open gallery. On warm summer nights, couples lingered there. On cold nights, they cuddled.

Partners danced the quadrille, matching paces across the smooth wooden floor. Skirts and petticoats swayed. Sweat caked the women's powdered necks. When the music stopped, the enveloping humidity of New Orleans in every season brought the dancers, clammy and hot, quickly to the punch bowl. Sweet, cool drinks awaited. Enslaved men and women

served. A few people may have greeted them, while others didn't acknowledge their presence.

More important to the guests was the orchestra, which they could count
on to play a few folk songs they all knew. These were songs brought from
the West Indies. They had sweet melodies and complex rhythms that were
familiar to the enslaved and free alike. *"Chère, mo lemmé toi"*—"Dear, I love
you so"—were the lyrics of one song in which a suitor wanted to declare
his feelings to a beautiful woman but was too shy.

The need for love may have first motivated François Boguille to ask
Suzanne Butel to dance if he saw her at one of these get-togethers. He
would have held her hand to lead her to the floor, then bowed as she curt-
sied. Good manners served to indicate character among strangers when
couples sought homes, children, and stable lives. Perhaps François walked
with Suzanne under the moss-laden oaks. Maybe he whispered to her in
private on an embroidered peacock settee or under the moon near the
white-flowering mayhaw bushes that grew wild and abundant in swampy
areas of the city. At some point, he asked her to marry him.

For a long time, she said no. But not to everything he proposed.

Their fates seemed unpredictable in this era of war. They decided to
become a couple and to live *hors les liens du mariage*—outside the bonds
of marriage. Their love did not need the sanctions of the courts or the
church, in their minds. Their finances did not need to be combined. They
resided circumspectly, off the city records.

In 1820, when the couple decided to marry before the law, François was
forty-two years old, and Suzanne was one year his senior. The contract
notarized by Marc Lafitte on September 27 was a document uniting two
mature and cautious people. Suzanne wrote clearly and without pause. She
inked the tip of her pen appropriately, and she maintained even pressure
against the paper. Boguille could not write, so he didn't sign, and he didn't
make an X, either. Instead, his witness represented his interests. In block
letters was the name Charles Savary, the hero of the Haitian Revolution.

The reason for the contract was contained in a few articles. The couple
admitted that although they were not married, they had been living
together for several years, and during that time Butel had given birth to

a child. The marriage document was necessary to legitimize their son, a smart, wide-eyed boy who was now eight years old. His name was recorded as Heludger. It was a name he never used.

The Early Life of Ludger Boguille

1820–1836

*Before deposition of your votes in the electoral urn to desig-
nate in which hands will be conferred the administration
of your common interests, it would be wise to reflect and
to examine all of your feelings of particular friendship and
to remember to look especially for the man who is able to
demonstrate zeal.*

—Economie Minutes, 1836

KNOWN TO EVERYONE AS Ludger Boguille, the boy grew up during
the 1820s in a city transforming itself. New enterprises bustled all around
him as ideas converged among entrepreneurs and immigrants, Indigenous
people and the enslaved.

His father's cabinetmaking shop on rue Condé was only three blocks
away from the St. Louis Cathedral. Near the church, people from around
the globe congregated, strolled through the square, and climbed the levee.
Ships docked at every pier, carrying goods and travelers from throughout
the world. Descending the levee were shoemakers from Italy, fabric
merchants from France, and traders from South America. People from
Africa debarked from ships that sailed down along the Atlantic seaboard.
They plodded together, blinking at the sunshine after days and often weeks
in the below-deck holds. West Indian women sold prepared food on New
Orleans's streets. Choctaw vendors sat on blankets, offering pelts and fish.

Dark-skinned people of indeterminate origin hawked vegetables as they walked with their baskets from patron to patron.

So many languages were being spoken that Boguille heard no sentences, only a symphony of inflections. Fast, choppy words came like a volley from the northerners carrying their packs off steamboats. Languid verbal melodies emerged from the mouths of migrants walking from rural Louisiana, and phrases squawked through the lips of speakers who rode into New Orleans on rickety carts mottled with dust from towns in Mississippi.

Ludger spoke to everyone in French, at least the Saint Domingue–New Orleans version of the language. It was different from the words the officials used as they walked in clusters out of the nearby buildings on Chartres, Customhouse, and Condé—his father's street. Ludger needed to learn to speak "good French" and to write it well in order to oversee the family finances. His father could not read or write, and customers attempted to cheat him. Typically, they tried to give him worthless foreign coins or to insist that they had agreed on a different type of wood for the furnishings in their homes. But while Ludger's father was not formally educated, he had a good head for business. How else could he have kept a shop in operation?

His neighbors on Condé Street were a planter, an accountant, and a lawyer for whom people made way when he exited his door. Like Ludger's father, Louis Moreau Lislet was a Saint Domingue refugee, but he was a lawyer and a coauthor of the Louisiana legal code. Moreau Lislet was often surrounded by a flock of young clerks in dark, formal clothing. They twittered to one another like sparrows chasing a piece of bread, excited to be so near to a tidbit of celebrity.

On the corner were independent tradesmen more like Ludger's father—a brass founder and a blacksmith. A few steps away was a boardinghouse that Ludger enjoyed observing. He could see people carrying all types of trunks into their temporary home. There were leather-bound document boxes with filigree and brass tacks on the edges, locked to keep out thieves, and ladies' horsehide trunks lugged by stevedores from private cabins on sailing ships directly to Ludger's street. Some trunks were polished wood and crafted so that they were watertight.

Ludger could lean against the stucco walls of nearby buildings, in the shade of their wrought-iron balconies, and watch the visitors arriving on wagons and dragging their bags. But most of the time when he visited his father's shop in the old city, Ludger could work. He was able to sand his father's creations—a new door with decorative carvings for the interior of a house, a dresser whose drawers dovetailed at the corners like fingers in prayer, and the sides of a small jewelry chest. His father might have him buff the wood so that it felt soft to the touch. François's specialty was to bend and shape rigid wood and, without using any nails, make it into small cabinets and armoires, useful and complete. Ludger couldn't help but feel proud when someone came into the shop to admire and buy the work. His father was a good provider for their small family.

In 1820 the Boguilles consisted of only François, Suzanne, and Ludger. Within a few years he would gain two sisters and a brother. But for now, his parents could devote all their energy to him. They arranged for Ludger to spend his time in the best company—boys whose parents came from Saint Domingue and other free people of color who wanted to make the most of their opportunities in Louisiana.

Parents in this community could pay a hefty price for their children to become literate, with school tuition running as much as ten dollars a month—the cost of two barrels of flour. Many families could afford to have a tutor who came to the house. The large dining room table was cleared for the lesson. The tutor walked decisively into the room and handed the child a book published in France so that he could feel the weight of literacy in his hands. The leather binding, embossed pages, and even the smell of the paper inspired the reverie of a growing intelligence. It made him stand straighter and prouder, and challenged him to understand his privilege in a world where other boys his age and complexion lived in bondage.

At eight years old, Ludger could read any one of more than a dozen French newspapers published in New Orleans in the 1820s and find the names of boys for sale—Harry, George, Jean Pierre—and boys who had run away. Little silhouettes—which printers called stereotypes—showed a young man with a walking stick and a bundle of clothes on his back. The images accompanied the ads that filled the pages of the *Courrier de la Louisiane*. Ludger would not have been the only one to observe the $10, $20, and "handsome" rewards promised for capturing a fugitive. Some people called themselves "slave catchers" and made a living returning young-sters as well as adults into bondage.

Louisiana law allowed people to own children and families, just as the other southern states did. But to the west was Mexican territory, a different country, where slavery was not always a given. Some adults argued about whether they should free the people they owned or keep them as property. Ludger could have heard similar discussions in his own home. Although he may not have understood the conversations, he saw the results. He was five years old when his mother went to court and freed Collinette, citing her good behavior, among other reasons. The joy all around was visible. But seven-year-old François and his mother, Dauphine, still lived in bondage at Ludger's house. She very carefully washed the Boguille family's clothes and did not cause problems.

Ludger knew that he was not enslaved, but neither was he the same as the white children who scampered in the streets. They got more smiles and fewer backhand slaps from shopkeepers and passersby than children of color.

A few doors from Ludger's father resided the editor of a newspaper called *Le Louisianais et ami des lois*, published in French and in English as *The Louisianian and Friend of the Laws*. Those laws benefitted men like him. On one day in May alone, his paper ran many ads and collected good revenue supporting the business of slavery—including rewards for runaways such as an enslaved mulatto teenager and a Creole in his twenties as well as the sales of ten people to accompany a sugar plantation.

Ludger could see the editor, John B. Maureau, arriving at his home on rue Condé, his spectacles still balanced on the bridge of his nose, carrying an armful of papers and followed by attentive clerks. Perhaps Ludger over-heard their discussions about justice when they lingered near the corner in the shade and enjoyed a little warm breeze in the afternoon. Ludger might understand from their conversations that even free boys of color could become clerks but not government officials, businessmen but not lawyers, and tradesmen but not doctors.

Perhaps Ludger's father suggested to him that a man who worked with his hands had limited days of employment, but a man who worked with his mind would always be able to earn a living. As his parents knew, revolutions took place all the time. They had experienced two wars in two lands with many nations involved. Maybe the laws would change.

Ludger worked hard to learn proper French and to steady his handwriting, so his facility with a quill would be unmatched, as would his turn of phrase. These abilities might one day elevate him to a more prosperous station in life.

Ludger was able to read Maureau's paper and so many others sold in the city. They were engrossing. They carried ads promoting leeches that had just arrived on a ship, new beaver hats from the manufacturer, and an assortment of shoes from a nearby shop. They told about "the blind man at the corner of St. Louis and Basin Streets" who offered two Negro wet nurses for rent, "both with fine breasts of milk." There was more than enough to compel Ludger to contemplate the activities in his hometown.

Before sundown, a walk of less than a dozen blocks brought Ludger and his father home to another side of New Orleans. Across a wide street called Esplanade was the Faubourg Marigny. Here the roads became less perpendicular, and the corners eased into turns. The creatively named streets crossed in colorful ways—Frenchmen and Victory, Prosper and Elysian Fields. This suburb was full of free people of color, including many from Saint Domingue. In some ways, this part of the city still resembled the rustic villages of his mother and father's island birthplace. Houses were more widely scattered than they were on the other side of Esplanade Street, and the melodic voices of the West Indies surrounded Ludger.

No more than four houses stood on the block where Ludger lived with his parents. Mostly surrounding them were vast stretches of scruffy land and old trees with wrinkled bark. The land sprouted hydrangeas, white and red clover, cinnamon fern, wild fig trees, banana tree clusters, and plentiful sweet oranges and pecans. Also nearby were snakes of every variety, from v-patterned rattlesnakes to ruddy copperheads to black cottonmouths and water moccasins. Wild dogs ran in packs, and birds swept over Ludger's head by the hundreds.

The woods were almost as alive as those in the French fables that Ludger read. In these stories, birds talked. Foxes competed. Wolves and lambs, cats and rabbits had conversations. One of Ludger's favorite authors was François Fénelon, a seventeenth-century French archbishop. He wrote for adults about human rights, and for children about morals. *The Adventures of Telemachus* was Fénelon's epic about the son of the mythological king Ulysses. Telemachus and his teacher, Mentor, were captured and brought to Egypt as slaves, but they still saw beauty in its prosperous cities. Fénelon wrote:

> Mentor then called my attention to the cheerfulness of plenty. . . . The justice which prevented the oppression of the poor by the rich; the education of the youth, which rendered obedience, labour, temperance, and the love of arts, or of literature, habitual; the punctuality in all the solemnities of religion; the public spirit; the desire of honour; the integrity to man, and the reverence to the gods, which were implanted by every parent in every child. He long contemplated this beautiful order with increasing delight, and frequently repeated his exclamations of praise. "Happy are the people," said he, "who are thus wisely governed!"

Ludger heeded Fénelon's descriptions of beauty and saw it around him. He longed for fairness in his hometown. He listened to the authors of his schoolbooks and the voices of his parents, and he began to find his calling. Words would create his virtuous place, perhaps even in opposition to the evidence before his own eyes. He would be a poet, a writer, and, somehow, a leader.

At night, in bed, ideas began to form that Ludger would use later in his drawings and verse. The house he shared with his parents looked out to the corner that shaped him forever. It was located where the street named Love intersected with another called Union.

The town is divided into two "quartiers" or sections, the French and the American. . . . The society, like the town, is divided into two distinct portions, the American and the Creole, and they do not mingle much together.

—Sir Charles Augustus Murray, *Travels in North America*, 1839

THE UNION OF PEOPLE and nature and love did not exist, despite Ludger's childhood dreams. In 1836 the citizens of New Orleans were not getting along. The city separated into three municipalities, each with its own aldermen responsible for governing, maintaining infrastructure, developing business, and more. The Second Municipality contained mostly the English-speaking, newer districts upriver. The First and Third Municipalities, favored by French speakers, incorporated the seventy-odd square blocks of the original city and its suburbs of Tremé and Ludger's childhood neighborhood of Marigny.

Ludger, now twenty-three, lived in the old city near his father's shop. The streets there displayed New Orleans's segregated economy. The poor pattered barefoot on wooden sidewalks while the powdered and privileged rode on horseback or inside surreys. Carriages transported men in tightly woven linen shirts with collars up to the jawline, while mules

Vue d'une rue du Faubourg Marigny, Nouvelle Orléans; ca. 1821; by Félix Achille de Beaupoil, marquis de Saint-Aulaire; *The L. Kemper and Leila Moore Williams Founders Collection at THNOC, 1937.2.2*

pulled creaking wagons with newcomers in homespun cloth and woolen breeches. The transients believed that they were rising in the city's society because they were no longer walking. But they did not understand New Orleans as Ludger did. The city was already a century old and home to a complex social order.

The nature of New Orleans itself came through the windows of Ludger's home. The air contained whiffs of gutted fish and burning wood, aromas that recalled the city's brutal history: in 1718 the French came and claimed the land for their own. The town rose through the efforts of adventurers, soldiers, and enslaved people. At the wrong end of bayonets, the Mandingans, Bambarans, and others born in Africa leveled the cypress forests. Along with half-starved European settlers, they pushed out or killed many of the Chitimacha, Chawasha, Houma, and other natives, unless they joined them in the woods or the swamps as runaways. European men took the available colored women and treated them according to their fear of—or respect for—the afterlife. Unknown thousands of children were conceived through rape, but some men cared for their offspring. Free people of color resulted from a mixture of desperation and progress.

In 1732 there were fewer than ten of them in New Orleans. By 1836 this population was on its way to nineteen thousand—including the children of about three thousand free people who had come from Saint Domingue, an island with a similar colonial history.

Ludger's New Orleans was a city of both conquerors and conquered, the brutal and the hopeful, those who swung between both poles, and those who wanted to make their world civil and new. He was a member of this last group.

Part of a young, privileged community of free people of color, Ludger typically mingled with his peers away from public venues. They visited their friends' homes to drink French wine and smoke Cuban cigars. Frequently Ludger's contemporaries invited visitors who had just come from abroad into their houses for dinner. They entertained everyone with stories of their travels while they feasted on modest, well-prepared meals—fresh grilled fish, an étouffée of tomatoes from the garden served over rice, and desserts of fruit picked from the backyard trees.

After dinner, young and old rose to sing near the piano or to recite poems. Sometimes the children might demonstrate an African dance retained by their neighbors, scandalizing those mothers and fathers whose hopes for the youths' advancement sat on the European horizon. Nevertheless, these slightly risqué *calendas* crept into the family's repertoire for celebrations and stayed. At the end of the night, the patriarchs of the family listened to their wives sing the lullaby "Fais Do-Do Titi" to their babies.

Ludger's generation saw a burgeoning network of family connections. His sister Elizabeth married Louis Clément Sacriste, whose mother had arrived, like François Boguille, from Croix-des-Bouquets. Louis Sacriste's sister married an entrepreneur from Cuba named Barthélemy Rey, and their son Henry L. Rey married Adele Crocker. Her father, Pierre Crocker, would become one of Ludger's mentors.

Among Ludger's contemporaries was a circle of writers who named themselves la Société des Artisans. They wrote verses and stories in the style of Honoré de Balzac, Alexandre Dumas, and Victor Hugo.

As it did for these French authors, romanticism held a deeper meaning for Ludger's peers. It represented their freedom of thought. And because they were colored, romantic poetry also reinforced their status as free men: they had enough liberty to love their women.

Enslaved men kept their feelings hidden out of necessity—a master who suspected alliances among his workers might threaten to scatter lovers to the winds, forcing them to obey under threat of separation. He certainly would sell them away if he suspected that their devotion might inspire a conspiracy to run away.

Free men could write poems and hold their wives in bed and tuck in their children safely in nearby rooms. Free men could act on their plans— saving their money to buy a house or budgeting their few dollars to send a child to school. They might sell their valuables to send a daughter to Europe so she could escape southern prejudice.

Free men could proclaim their love aloud. "Divine one, every day I beseech you, / With passion, / To share the flame that devours / My poor heart," wrote Edmond Dédé, another man whose parents came from Saint Domingue. His songs would come to be known as the classical, heartfelt expressions of Creole New Orleans. A lyricist and composer, Dédé wrote music so beautiful that the neighbors might open their windows and shush their children when his overtures began. Dédé was a young violin prodigy, living in New Orleans and absorbing its culture of romance when Boguille, about fifteen years older, was already a father.

Ludger had met a girl named Andrénette Lamy when he was a teenager, and by the time he was twenty, they had their first child. Suzette was born in 1832. They had a boy, François Fénelon—named for Ludger's father and the seventeenth-century poet—in 1834. And now, in January 1836, Andrénette was ready to deliver again.

While the Americans scrambled to amass tangible fortunes, Ludger put faith in the spiritual realm. At Mass, a verse from the scriptures read, "Where your treasure is, there will your heart be also." It was his duty as a follower of Christ to love others. He focused his energy on love, in both its invisible and its physical manifestations.

Ludger felt empowered: he was enlightened by the ideals of the French Revolution—liberty, equality, and fraternity—passed down to his generation by his father and other refugees from Haiti. Ludger was genteel

Edmond Dédé; between 1857 and 1893; *THNOC, gift of Al Rose, 1985.254.78; original housed in Louisiana Music Collection, Amistad Research Center, New Orleans*

and refined, literate and knowledgeable about the arts and sciences. And he was Creole, born in the New World with roots in the old worlds of Europe and Africa.

New Orleans was not only the site of his birth. The city was his home in every sense of the word—a place of warmth, love, joy, and belonging.

At no distant day, the free people of color of our land will spontaneously and eagerly seek on the shores of their ancestral land those enjoyments and advantages from which, while here, they must be forever debarred.

—*New Orleans Observer*, 1839

NOT EVERYONE WAS AS hopeful for Ludger's community. Many wanted the free people of color to go away.

The American Colonization Society believed people of African descent should be free—just not in the United States. The idea of African repatriation began with a Quaker ship owner who was Black. Paul Cuffee decided to bring men and women back to their ancestral continent, specifically the area of British Sierra Leone. He paid for the first voyage of colonists to Africa in 1816 but died a year later. To pursue his mission, the ACS was formed in Washington, DC, in 1817, with branches in cities throughout the United States. The society collected money to buy freedom for the enslaved and give them passage to Africa. Supporters included ministers, statesmen, and President James Monroe, whose motivations included his belief that repatriation was the best way to prevent Black uprisings and racial mixing. Many white workers in the North as well as the South opposed the abolition of slavery because the sudden abundance of freed people would mean fewer jobs and lower wages for whites. Sending free people of color and formerly enslaved people to Africa appealed to many abolitionists and racists alike. By January 1836 the ACS had already packed off ships full of these colonists to new settlements in an area of West Africa they had named Liberia—"land of liberty." The capital of the new nation was Monrovia, named for the American president.

The ACS was offering the same dubious opportunity for migration to local free people of color. The colored businessmen in New Orleans were not only skeptical, they laughed when they heard this news. The trip was dangerous, possibly life-threatening. Besides potentially killing them, the ACS's creation of "Louisiana in Africa"—the name of the township—would essentially rob them of their incomes and property. Plus, the plan appeared to them to be part of a larger scheme giving American newcomers an advantage in further developing New Orleans by excluding colored people.

The South was on the verge of great prosperity. A steam-powered manufacturing revolution had begun in the northern United States and in Europe. The textile machines now needed raw goods such as cotton from southern plantations. Cotton from the mid-South and north Louisiana fields, sugar from cane grown in south Louisiana, and rice from the marshy Carolina coast all passed through New Orleans. Its port took control of the shipping that had once centered on the now less stable and less trusted West Indies. The port of New Orleans moved goods up and down the Mississippi River to the nation's plains, and out from the Gulf of Mexico to Europe, the Caribbean, and Latin America. The colored businessmen were just as aware of the opportunities as the white ones.

Northerners from the English-speaking United States who came into the city carried *Michel's New Orleans Annual and Commercial Register*, which guided them around the city in English and in French. Men stopped natives like Boguille on the street and used their book-learned translations, asking for the "march-and dee vin" for the wine store, or tapped him on the shoulder in a café to point out that they had ordered a *bière créole*, a Louisiana beer made of rice, pineapple, and brown sugar. European travel guides predicted that because of its sophistication and progress, New Orleans would soon surpass New York. It was "destined . . . to be the greatest and

American Colonization Society membership certificate of President James Madison; 1816; *courtesy of the Library of Congress, Manuscript Division, James Madison Papers*

most important city in North America" if its swampy and "unhealthy" climate didn't slow its progress.

Ships from Hamburg, Liverpool, and many other cities in Europe arrived daily. The cargo holds brimmed with champagne, cutlery, French wine, sugar, tobacco *segars*, embroidered linen, sparkling glass chandeliers, and other wares for trade along America's bustling coastlines and throughout its rapidly developing interior. Steamboats pushed through the river currents. Roughnecks from the Atlantic states and immigrants from Ireland and Italy came to earn some of the money that was circulating in hotels, carriages, construction, and public works.

The new economy attracted businessmen who wished to outfit plantations with machinery, clothing, and furniture. Speculators from New York arrived to make fast money by brokering crops as middlemen between farmers and factories. Pale men in white shirts multiplied on the streets of New Orleans like wild mushrooms after a rain.

New banks opened as fast as the ink dried on their charters. Corporations with Anglo names unfamiliar to the French-speaking natives appeared in the newspapers daily, boasting of the contracts they received from the state. Because they were awarded licenses to operate in Louisiana only if they made improvements to the city, these men now founded the New Orleans and Carrollton Railroad and Banking Company, the New Orleans Gas Light and Banking Company, the New Orleans Improvement and Banking Company, the Merchants' and Traders' Bank, the Union Bank of Louisiana, and the Citizens' Bank of Louisiana. In 1837, Louisiana banks had capital of $36.7 million, compared to $57.9 million in Pennsylvania and $27.1 million in New York. In addition, almost 24 percent of the cash owed by the Louisiana banks was backed by gold and silver, compared to the New York banks' 12 percent.

A few of the businessmen in Ludger Boguille's community tried to take advantage of the growing economy. François Boisdoré, older and well-heeled, bought two hundred shares of stock, about $20,000 worth, when the Citizens' Bank received its charter in April 1833. Boisdoré planned for a financial windfall. His participation, however, like the involvement of all the Americans and Europeans who invested in New Orleans and its booming economy, rested on a tragic foundation.

Some of the new banks of Louisiana were "property banks" that secured the value of deposits through mortgages on either land or enslaved people. In Louisiana, enslaved people were considered real property, like land, so businesspeople could not only earn from their captives' labor but also use them as collateral for mortgages. Banking and industry prospered when the enslaved began to outnumber white people in many parts of the state. The clerks keeping track of financial transactions sat at their thick wooden desks and ciphered into their books an increase of more than 58,000 enslaved people in Louisiana between 1830 and 1840, and an addition of 76,000 more between 1840 and 1850. There would be 331,726 enslaved people living in the state by 1860. Soon after the Louisiana Purchase, a newspaper article had suggested that a planter with an eight-hundred-acre farm and sixty enslaved workers could make $22,000 a year. The profits whetted the appetites of people around the globe.

Slavery's products supported the northern and European fabric mills; filled tables throughout the United States with sugary sweets; employed the shipbuilders, captains, crews, and stevedores who provided transportation; and maintained the retailers who sold clothes and shoes to the farmers and city folk, who were now more prosperous than they ever could have been in their old countries. On southern plantations, enslaved families rose before dawn to break ground on land with an impossible horizon. In Louisiana, they cut cane, fed animals, built houses and furniture, and performed other chores—neither menial nor meaningless but essential to the United States's advancement, Louisiana's economy, and New Orleans's reputation as a center of progress. At the base of this prosperity were the enslaved, like Atlas, holding the international economy on their shoulders.

By mid-century most of the enslaved were Americans, born in the United States, because the African slave trade had been outlawed in 1808. But they were not citizens. Even when they gained freedom and their humanity was acknowledged, the American Colonization Society and its supporters wanted to banish them.

Abolitionists such as William Lloyd Garrison, a founder of the American Anti-Slavery Society, didn't believe that colored Americans should be sent to a continent they did not know just because of their race. They had dreamed of freedom and worked for it. Garrison condemned the ACS and its supporters "for feeling so indifferent to the moral, political and social advancement of the free people of color in this, their only legitimate home."

The free people of color in New Orleans, most of whom were never enslaved, felt that the ACS was part of a movement that was trying to remove them, too, from a city they had helped to create. And Ludger's position in the convergence of escalating international commerce and human cargo? He was a poet, writer, dreamer, father, and intellectual of color, free enough and thoughtful enough to take a stand. But at twenty-three years old, he didn't speak out—not yet.

The Age of Awareness

1836–1857

The Awakening of Ludger Boguille

1836–1846

Always remember those beautiful principles that are in the first books that you opened on the school bench and understand today . . . you must put them into practice.

—Economie Minutes, 1857

IN JUNE 1836, Ludger Boguille held his newborn son swaddled tightly in cotton bands, a French innovation believed to form healthy bones. Ludger whispered his name—Florian—the poet of the eighteenth century who wrote the *History of the Moors of Spain*. This text by Jean-Pierre Claris de Florian recounted the Africans' conquest of the European nation. The author crafted fanciful descriptions of the imperial complex they built in Granada, the Alhambra palace and the gardens of Generalif, "which signifies, in the Moorish tongue, the Home of Love." The grounds were lush with "the interwoven branches of gigantic cypresses and aged myrtles. . . . Then blooming groves and forests of fruit-trees were agreeably intermingled with graceful domes and marble pavilions: then the sweet perfume of the countless flowers that mingled their varied dyes in delightful confusion, floated in the soft air." The book would have sent Ludger into a rapture.

But Florian, the author, also had to face the ugly realities of history. "It is painful to quit the Alhambra and the Generalif, to return to the ravages, incursions, and sanguinary quarrels of the Moors and Christians," he wrote. And so it was for Boguille.

Ludger was busy with his family and his poetry while the city's lawmakers cordoned New Orleans into three separate municipalities at the urging of the American business community and the downtown French-speakers. The systems of taxation, courts, policing, and other administrative tasks functioned differently in the First and Third Districts than in the Second, where more English speakers resided.

Similarly, lines of separation were being drawn between free people of color and whites. When Ludger's parents arrived in New Orleans, documents of their legal transactions only occasionally included their race, at the notary's whim. But after the Americans gained control of Louisiana, the government required their race along with their names on every document. Free people of color became less free. They may have bartered for or purchased their freedom, fought in the military, and been raised in homes that were more prosperous than whites'. No matter how industrious they proved themselves, though, a mention of their race did not bring to mind success. Ancestry now bound free people of color to a history of oppression and made them prey for exploitation every time they bought a house or made a contract. For Boguille and people like him who were supposedly free, race created a world of negative connotations to complicate life's frequent written transactions.

The American government had taken the colored militia out of service, recruiting only white men. A newspaper announcement called the Louisiana militia to muster for a reunion of veterans of the Battle of New Orleans approximately one month before the birth of Ludger's son Florian, on January 8. Ludger could see the notices in German, Spanish, and French—all printed in *L'Abeille de la Nouvelle-Orléans* newspaper—calling for foot soldiers, swordsmen, and horsemen to gather. The organizers did not call either battalion of free men of color.

Deeper emotions justified these actions. The free people of color were once again both needed and feared. A new battery of laws in the 1830s was intended to keep Black minds under siege. The need for enslaved labor to supply sugar cane and cotton plantations had increased. And a new generation of African descendants, born in America, had rebelled. David

Walker, a free colored man, published a pamphlet in 1829 in Boston called *Walker's Appeal . . . to the Colored Citizens of the World, but in Particular, and Very Expressly, to those of the United States*. It told people of color to revolt. Walker rationalized that it was no more unjust for enslaved people to kill their masters than to be killed by their masters. He also expressed the hope that free people would help the enslaved through education so that they could think about ways to break their chains.

Walker wrote, "There is a great work for you to do, as trifling as some of you may think of it. You have to prove to the Americans and the world, that we are MEN, and not *brutes,* as we have been represented, and by millions treated. Remember, to let the aim of your labours among your brethren, and particularly the youths, be the dissemination of education and religion."

The pamphlet had made its way to Louisiana. If Ludger saw *Walker's Appeal*, he would not have admitted it. But rebellion must have crossed his mind. The revolutions of the French, Haitians, and Americans were his cultural heritage. His schoolbooks from Europe had preached freedom, as did the veterans who had fought in the Battle of New Orleans. They lived near his house, knew his father, and likely sat in his parlor talking of bloody battles, weapons, and strategies.

At the same time, Louisiana regulated writing and thinking that might cause people of African descent to consider their oppression. The courts threatened hard labor for up to twenty-one years or even death for "whosoever shall make use of language, in any public discourse, from the bar, the bench, the stage, the pulpit, or in any place whatsoever: or whosoever shall make use of language in private discourses or conversations, or shall make use of signs or actions, having a tendency to produce discontent among the free colored population of this state, or to excite insubordination among the slaves." The law mandated the same punishment for anyone who brought into the state any abolitionist "paper, pamphlet, or book." Another provision of this 1830 law prescribed up to a year in jail for teaching an enslaved person to read or write.

Boguille could not have displayed any radical thinking outwardly. But subtly, metaphorically, he showed his opinions. He named all of his sons but one after writer-intellectuals of Europe. He flourished a grand,

"Your humble and devoted servant": Ludger Boguille's signature; from Economie minutes, April 22, 1842; *courtesy of Fatima Shaik*

powerful signature in an era when a man's handwriting was seen as a mark of his character. Boguille was classically educated at a time when Walker complained that even in the northern schools, Blacks could receive only minimal instruction—enough to scratch out their names. Boguille communicated his identity with broad swirls over a decorative, almost jewel-encrusted script. Sometimes he adorned his name with little knots, diamonds, and flourishes. His oversized capital letters were wide and generous. His sentences were level and clear. Every aspect of his script displayed confidence.

Since childhood he had been drawn to poetry, moved by metaphors about justice in such favorite works as "The Philosopher and the Owl":

> Wrong'd, persecuted, and proscrib'd,
> In foreign lands compell'd to hide,
> For calling things by their right name,
> A sage took with him all his wealth—
> (His wisdom)—which he kept by stealth,
> And to a friendly forest came.
> There, while pond'ring o'er his woes,
> He saw an owl beset by foes—
> An angry crowd of jays and crows.

They peck'd him, curs'd him, call'd him sot,
And said he was no patriot.
"Let's pluck him," said they, "of his plumes—
This rascal who such wit assumes!"
"Let's hang him," said the wrathful birds,
"And judge the villain afterwards!"
[...]
"Wherefore," said [the sage], "is all this strife?
Why do these foes thus seek your life?"
"My only crime," the owl replied,
"Is one which they cannot abide;
The reason why I've rous'd their spite,
Is simply this—I see by night."

The poem's author was the namesake of Boguille's son, Florian.

So, while Andrénette "laid in"—the term for the customary period of bed rest for women after delivery, usually a month or more—and nursed the baby, Ludger had plenty of time to teach the folklore of his Louisiana culture to the two older children. West African tales told of tricksters like the hyena Bouki and the rabbit Lapin who, while small, were shrewd enough to fool the bigger, domineering animals. And there was a children's song from the streets called "Mister Bainjo":

Look at that mulatto, Mister Bainjo, Look how sassy he is.
His hat worn on the side, Mister Bainjo, Look how sassy he is.
His cane in his hand, Mister Bainjo, Look how sassy he is.
His boots tapping "creak, creak," Mister Bainjo, Look how sassy he is.

On the surface, the song described a fashionable free man of color, but *insolent*—the French word for "sassy"—carried meanings ranging from "cocky and impudent" to "incredibly lucky." When he sang the song to his children, Boguille gave *insolent* a positive inflection, even though the enslaved sang the same lyrics with a bitter, satirical edge. The French word used to refer to a mulatto—*mulet*—was an insult because it derived from the Spanish word for "mule," and the enslaved saw some free people of color as impotent beasts, having no real power in society.

In both contexts, however, Mister Bainjo's name referred to the instrument brought from Africa. Singing and playing music was an act of free expression among African descendants at a time when their oppressors thought they had muzzled a population through the law.

Whites would later write that the singers of these songs really didn't understand the words. For example, one scholar noted in 1867 that the lyrics to "Hail, Mary" said, "I want some valiant soldier here, To help me bear de cross." Though they called out for a "soldier" in the refrain, he believed the enslaved surely must have meant "soul" and just added a syllable to fill out the meter. But the tune of "Hail, Mary," another scholar noted, was a variant of "No more peck of corn for me," one line of "Many Thousand Go," a song of rebellion. He called it "a curious illustration of the way in which the colored people make different combinations of their own tunes at different times." But the singers clearly had an intention that didn't suggest religious worship.

Boguille, too, understood the use of subversive metaphors. He possessed a dual consciousness, a type of clandestine comprehension. To avoid punishment, he may never have revealed the double meanings of the stories and songs to anyone outside of his closest circles. But his writing in later years would show that he and his friends communicated in metaphors because their opinions were not welcome and, in some cases, not allowed.

In his early life, Boguille did something else that showed his intentions were similar to David Walker's advocacy of education and religion. Boguille brought his family into the church not only for the sake of racial uplift but as one of the tricks his community used to undermine the Louisiana laws. On June 27, 1836, Ludger took Suzette Elizabeth, François Fénelon, and Florian Joseph to the St. Louis Cathedral, where he had them baptized in the Catholic religion so that God would care for their souls, and the American government would perceive them as upstanding citizens. The church was a recognized authority that could vouch for Boguille's family as a stable, God-fearing unit during an era of slave rebellion. On the same day of the baptisms, for added measure, Ludger married Andrénette in front of the priest.

In the stained-glass alcove of the cathedral, the officiant said the sacred words and blessed the union. Ludger's father could not write, so signing the marriage certificate was Basile Dédé, a veteran of the Battle of New Orleans and the father of Edmond Dédé, the romantic composer. The wedding demonstrated the progress of two generations: the elders were fighters who had paid with blood for the shelter and education of their children, and the younger men now resided in comfort.

In 1836, Boguille played it safe. He raised his daughter and sons, kept his opinions to himself, and thrived in the South, despite its confines. Meanwhile, in Boston, David Walker died unexpectedly at the age of 33. His daughter had died a week earlier of tuberculosis, so perhaps he met the same fate. However, members of the Black community in Boston did not believe it. They said that Walker's radical views had gotten him poisoned. The *Boston Recorder* listed his death among others but added, "the colored man who wrote the pamphlet on slavery, which caused such alarm in the slave holding states."

Above all, Boguille wanted to live.

All the civilized peoples celebrate the memory of the dead! . . . Religion and friendship make it our duty to honor our young brother. . . . Placed in a celestial residence, may he enjoy eternal happiness. Farewell!

—Economie Minutes, 1838

WHEN DID LUDGER BEGIN to understand true compassion for others? His awakening may have come, as it often does, from his own pain. He and Andrénette lost a son.

Etienne Ludger, their fourth child, was born in 1838 and lived only a year. He was buried in the St. Louis Cemetery No. 1, at the edge of the old city. A year and a half later the family lost François Boguille. He was a thirty-eight-year-old enslaved man Ludger's father owned and had named after himself. They buried François in the same cemetery in 1840, not far from the baby, perhaps as a small recognition of their shared humanity.

If this was the case, Ludger would have been ahead of his time. Different social classes did not mix in most parts of the world, even when they were united by skin color. In Russia, serfs who provided crops for the czar shivered through the winters in rags. The British had violently entered the Cape of Africa and were now moving weapons into neighboring Natal. They were also sending opium into China and, in 1842, fought a war for access to Chinese ports. The French were moving slowly from their conquest of Algeria to colonize large parts of Africa. Ludger lived in the Age of Imperialism. People around the world were losing their cultures as they were beaten into submission and killed in wars. Their conquerors were changed, too. They thought they were only providing materially for their nations. But they transformed when they crossed the seas and accepted their roles as superiors. And some assimilated in ways they did not predict, such as adapting to the local cultures, having children who looked just like them with native women, and, sometimes, choosing to remain with these new families while their countrymen continued to wage war in the name of racial hierarchies. The crossing of borders and making the wealth of nations created many human complications.

As he aged, Boguille began to see his life intertwined with the fate of others. He was the eldest son and, at thirty years old in 1842, he became responsible for his increasingly disabled father. François's condition did not improve. For a while, he could stand with the use of a crutch, but soon he couldn't get out of bed. He lay day after endless day—watching as heat from the fireplace caused the smooth plaster walls to sweat in the winter, being transfixed as the spiders embellished the room's corner medallions with webs in spring, and waiting for a summer breeze to pass through the open shutter slats like a last breath.

Adolphe Boyer, François's friend for over a decade, described his condition to others: François "was a joiner by trade & for about three years before his death, he worked no more at his trade, during the year that preceded the two last years of his illness, he done some little work such as varnishing." In his specialized occupation, François once had precisely cut the wooden frames for doors, the shelves of bookcases, tabletops and legs, and the risers of staircases. Then he put them together like puzzles without ever using metal fasteners or nails. Now, the pain held François in bed for so long that he became covered in bedsores. Boyer told people that his skin had "scars from his head to his feet."

The doctor came and prescribed syrups, salts, and pomades. Ludger ordered them from the pharmacy and paid the bills. Other people without such financial resources depended on friends with home remedies or on the concoctions advertised in the newspapers. Herbalists took out ads claiming to cure rheumatism, ringworm, and ulcers with sarsaparilla. Quacks suggested surgery for consumption—the all-encompassing label for tuberculosis or listlessness diagnosed anywhere from the stomach to the lungs.

François had the best physicians in the city. Still, his pain progressed. In the last two weeks of his life, the doctor came every day. A devoted son, Ludger sat at his father's bedside whenever he could. The women and children took turns during the day. François's friend Boyer frequently came to sit evening vigils. New Orleanians were accustomed to keeping company with people on their deathbeds as cholera and yellow fever raged during the terrible summers. Death always seemed nearby yet could still strike unexpectedly.

Mosquitoes bred in the stagnant, waste-filled water of canals, in muddy ruts in the streets, in the washtubs of indolent tenants, under damp houses, and inside the wet clusters of banana trees. These pests passed the ailments of equine fever, meningitis, and yellow fever from one species to another— the symptoms: delirium, seizures, and black vomit. No one knew that insects were carrying these diseases.

Carts wheeled the dead from their large houses in the American district across town. Enslaved women handed over the bodies of masters to enslaved men, who took them away. In the downtown areas, where people took care of their own, large families wept.

François's family and friends filled his bedroom. Old men with their hats in their hands wore wan, sympathetic smiles as they looked at the dying man. Young men stared sternly ahead to cover their fear of death, as if it were not already contagious. As was customary, they all took turns feeding him lukewarm soup with a silver spoon.

At the end of his days, François's sixty-seven-year-old body laid slack against the pillows. He could hardly hold up his head. Ludger may have stayed at his father's side after the last family member came into Francois's bedroom on the night of his death. Finally at peace, his last moments were as fixed as a tableau. Ludger went downstairs and exited the door of the house on Union and crossed Good Children Street on the way home.

*It is all over! . . . He lived as a man of honor and died as
a martyr. May the two years of cruel suffering that he has
borne with calm and resignation earn him a place near
to the Most High in the eternal tabernacle! . . . Those are
the hopes of his widow, children, and his relatives, for the
tranquility of his soul.*

—*L'Abeille de la Nouvelle-Orléans*, 1845

ON JANUARY 14, 1845, an homage to François appeared in *L'Abeille*,
the French edition of the *New Orleans Bee* newspaper. The obituary was
signed, "A Friend."

At François's death, the community would have embraced Ludger. The
friends of the deceased carried the casket out to the street after Mass and
loaded it onto a wagon. The extended family lined up behind the coffin
and walked to the graveyard, gathering participants along the way.

François Boguille was interred in St. Louis Cemetery No. 2 in a brick
crypt, built like a small shrine above the ground. The workmen had laid
walls in a long rectangle to shelter the coffin. The walls were two rows
of bricks deep and as tall as a man stood. Atop the walls was a flat roof.
Afterward, the bricks were plastered over and whitewashed. The crypt
resembled a miniature two-story house without interior walls. The upper
level held François's coffin. His remains would be cleared out and put

into the lower space when the next person died and took over the upper slab. Before sliding the coffin into the crypt, the priest and the mourners prayed the rosary. During Boguille's time, music was reserved for the indoor services, although someone might also sing a hymn or recite a poem by the tomb. After a few more words of prayer for the repose of François Boguille's soul, the mourners left his gravesite, and the workmen came again to plaster over the front of the tomb. On the front, like an address, was painted "Famille Boguille."

Ludger's house would have filled with people shortly after his father's burial. An extended network of mourners would have brought food to his home. Meals and company would have flowed in for days, and his loneliness would have been more pronounced after the visitors left. His future appeared unclear, his sadness slow to abate. And still, he had not seen the worst.

*And furthermore said E. Faille ... opposes the said account
& tableau as follows.*

*That there are other immovable property besides the one on
which this app[ellant] has a special mortgage & among the
other a slave.*

—Louisiana Supreme Court,
Ludger Boguille v. E. Faille, 1846

$\mathcal{A}$S THE ELDEST MALE, Ludger emerged as the patriarch of the household—watching the bills, supervising his children, and making sure the family operated smoothly. He administered his father's will, directing the inventory of money, land, and furniture. Neither his mother nor his three teenaged siblings challenged Ludger's account. They took for granted that as François Boguille began to fade two years before his death, he had transferred five empty lots of his property to Ludger, making him a relatively rich man.

After François's death, Ludger carefully recorded his father's debts— funeral expenses of $75, including a hundred cards to announce the services, then $8 to the funeral directors, $20 for the filings associated with the death, $10.50 for medicine, $400 for two doctors, $350 for a lawyer, and $100 to inventory the property and furniture. He gave himself $82.50 to administrate his father's estate. The process of dividing the estate, called succession in Louisiana, went before the probate court judge for the usual sign-off to close the accounts.

Ludger returned to his routine after he had handled all the bills for the family. Still, the house seemed empty without François's presence and the visits of his old friends. Suffering the isolation of the firstborn, Ludger may have listened for his father's voice and sometimes turned his head, believing he heard a cough.

Then one day, Ludger could have picked up the newspaper and—amid the advertisements for stores selling boots, fabrics, steel writing pens, and piano lessons—seen the listings of properties for sale in a city auction. The sheriff frequently seized property that was abandoned, in arrears for taxes, or claimed in suits filed by creditors. Boguille would have been shocked to see the listing for his father's property on Union Street. Ludger quickly slipped on a stiff white cotton shirt and cravat, pulled his sleeves through his black coat, and went to a lawyer. He got an injunction on May 21, 1845, to stop the sale. Ludger put down a $500 bond and was given a day for his case to be heard in court. He would forfeit the money and the property if he lost. The process server went in person to the home of Elizabeth Faille—a free woman of color who brought the property to the sheriff's attention for auction—and to her lawyer's office with summonses. Faille countersued Boguille fifty dollars for the cost of her lawyer and contended that he had no right to interfere.

The property did not go to auction. Instead, on June 2, 1845, the case was scheduled to come before Judge A. M. Buchanan. His First District Court was the jurisdiction of many old, French-speaking families. Faille told the judge that François Boguille had borrowed money from her to buy a piece of property and that when he died, she should have been paid. She wanted the Boguille family's property sold to satisfy the debt. She also demanded reimbursement for all the costs associated with Ludger's stopping the sale. Faille claimed that François had signed a document with her to purchase the property, and she produced it as evidence. Despite his wealth, François was not literate enough to sign his name. The court saw, perhaps to Ludger's embarrassment, that his father had written an X.

Faille won with damages, and Ludger's injunction was dissolved on December 5, 1845.

Ludger asked for a new trial. He wanted to defend his father's estate but also his reputation as executor. While people of color could not become lawyers, they could sue one another. Ludger said he did not cheat Faille and that the court's action was "contrary to law and evidence." She had brought him to the wrong court, the First District, while the succession was still under review in the probate court. Boguille added that the sheriff who had gone to seize the property was never brought to the stand in the trial. Boguille also claimed he did not owe damages for stopping the sale, according to Louisiana laws. He made his request on December 12, and it was refused the next day.

Still, Ludger did not give up. Following the state processes, he petitioned the First District judge for a hearing in a higher court, the Louisiana Supreme Court. Judge Buchanan approved his request on December 23, 1845, when Ludger put up a higher bond—$1,200—to cover costs if he lost again.

Faille also challenged Ludger's accounting of his father's succession in probate court. She introduced new evidence. She accused Ludger of cheating her and suggested that he had lied to everyone involved in the estate because he had not properly made the accounting. There was more valuable property involved that he hadn't mentioned. The property's name was Denise.

Ludger knew that an enslaved woman could sell for about $550 in New Orleans, approximately the same cost as a house. An enslaved woman named Denise had lived in his father's home at the time of his death. Ludger could have sold her to pay the bills, but he did not inventory her. She was considered *immovable property*, the term used by the clerks who entered the names of the buyers, the sellers, and, occasionally, the people for sale in the city's record books. Faille was not mistaken.

But in response, Ludger still insisted he had not cheated Faille by ignoring the enslaved woman as an asset. The reason she did not go into the accounting, he said, was that Denise did not belong to his father but to his mother. The same laws of succession that would require Denise to be inventoried if she had belonged to his father could protect her if she had belonged to his mother before marriage. Suzanne Boguille did not have to include anything or anyone she alone had owned in the community property inventory at her husband's death. She could keep her personal wealth or give it away if she wanted to. But there was a problem. Ludger had lied.

Not about his mother's character. She did own enslaved people. At the time of the Haitian Revolution, Suzanne Butel came to New Orleans with Marie Noel, whom she sold to Bernard Marigny in 1813.

If Butel had any misgivings about enslaving others, she did not change her behavior. In her hometown of Jérémie, free women of color ran businesses. They self-employed as contract housekeepers and seamstresses. In New Orleans, they cooked and sold food to stevedores at the port, sometimes by using a small army of enslaved hawkers with items like hot calas, breakfast cakes made of rice. Some owners took in laundry and used enslaved laundresses to do the wash and deliver it to soldiers and others who couldn't or wouldn't do it themselves. Butel acquired at least eight people—washerwomen and housekeepers—who were all under thirty years of age. According to law, they were too young to be free. Once one of them, Collinette, came of age, Butel legally emancipated her. In the meantime, Butel prospered.

By the time François died there were no other enslaved people besides Denise in the Boguille home. Where the others went and whether they were still enslaved was never brought up in Ludger's case before the Supreme Court. This was not unusual, though. The lives of the enslaved were unseen and often went unrecorded.

Hundreds of thousands of people changed hands in New Orleans through notarized sales and public auctions. But not everyone followed these legal routes. The free colored community frequently picked and chose among the regulations, deciding which ones were worth following. Ludger was not the only deceptive person.

One of Ludger's neighbors, Martial Dupart, was the son of a man who had purchased and lived with an enslaved woman as early as 1788. Their cohabitation was against the law, yet they had three children and baptized them in the St. Louis Cathedral before he freed the family in 1793 out of "much love and affection." Fearing God more than the law, many owners sent their enslaved children to be baptized as the Catholic Church required—although their last names rarely appeared in the cathedral records. Another man, Auguste Metoyer, one of the largest landowners among colored planters in Louisiana and the son of an African woman, may have freed a number of enslaved people without ever alerting authorities. He simply did a census of his plantation and undercounted the people. In 1840, he had twenty-two houses for the enslaved but counted only forty-one people living there, including only four children—"all babies at the breast." Typically, there would have been about four people in every house. So he circumvented slave designations for perhaps nearly fifty residents.

Legal emancipations took place in Ludger's community, too. A benevolent society called Dieu Nous Protégé—God Protects Us—began to purchase enslaved workers in 1844 with the intention of setting them free.

Ludger's friend Pierre Crocker was only twenty-two years old in 1825 when he emancipated thirty-five-year-old Marie Eglé, a woman owned by his free colored grandmother Isabel Beauregard. The enslaved woman had lived most of her life in Beauregard's home on Camp Street. Crocker told Judge James Pitot that Marie "always had an honest conduct without having run away and without having committed any robbery or having been guilty of any criminal misdemeanor." Before the age of eight, Marie had lived with Sister Charles Maurin, a nun. In 1837 Crocker freed an enslaved person he owned named Justine, a thirty-year-old mulatto woman for whom he had followed the legal procedure of petitioning the court for emancipation, then waiting until the parish sheriff circulated a notice in the newspapers to see if anyone objected to her freedom. No one did, and Justine was liberated.

People who wanted to free enslaved people they held in bondage had not always needed the government's approval. Laws grew stricter as whites became uneasy with the growing free Black population and as the enslaved gained value. An 1807 rule allowed emancipation through a deceased person's will. An 1823 law permitted enslaved individuals to contract for their freedom. But by 1830, the law required anyone who wanted to free an enslaved person to post a $1,000 bond. If the newly liberated husband, wife, child, or friend did not leave the state within a month, the former owner would lose the bond money. In the years since the rule had been enacted, however, Orleans Parish had not forced any emancipated person to leave. Still, if Denise was living in the Boguille family's home and Ludger wanted to keep her, he may have felt that as the family patriarch, it was his choice to make, and not up to Faille or the fickle legal system. At least, that's what his next actions suggested.

Ludger called a number of witnesses who swore that the enslaved woman did not belong to his father, so Faille had not been cheated. His first witness was a white Haitian refugee who said he knew Suzanne Butel in 1793 and said she owned a woman named Denise whom she brought to New Orleans. "She was bought at St. Iago when she was only ten years old, it is the same slave now in court," he said. Denise sat across from the judge as the witness pointed her out.

During cross-examination, however, the prosecutor suggested that the woman who appeared in the court was not necessarily Denise. Was the witness sure about the identity? The answer was no.

Then another witness, speaking on Ludger Boguille's behalf, said that she knew "the slave Denise" and had hired her for five years before Suzanne's marriage to François. That would have been 1815, proving that Denise was not part of François's estate.

But when Suzanne's 1820 marriage contract was introduced as evidence, it showed that the notary recorded six people among Butel's assets: L'espoir, Choisi, Desirée, Dauphine, François, and Sophia. There was no Denise. Apparently, Ludger and his witnesses had not told the truth.

The reason that so many people were willing to perjure themselves is unclear. Perhaps Ludger disputed Faille's account for the sake of maintaining his family's fortune, since Denise had a monetary value. Or maybe he fought to keep her rather than dispose of her as an asset, sending her into the household of a stranger to meet a worse fate. His attempt to hold on to Denise may have been the first evidence of his newfound compassion. Maybe he was grateful for the enslaved woman who had painstakingly cleaned his sick father's torn, oozing flesh, washed away his fetid waste, and turned him in the bed several times a day during his years of illness.

Whatever the reason, Ludger lied in his testimony, and his friends corroborated his story.

Their respect for the law paled in comparison to their loyalty to one another and, possibly, to the enslaved Denise. They waited to find out whether the courts felt the same way.

We find our hearts full of the ardor necessary to conquer all the obstacles that chain our efforts.

—Pierre Crocker, first president of the Economie, 1836

IF BOGUILLE WALKED FROM the courthouse to the property on Good Children and Union, he may have doubted the wisdom of keeping his mother's enslaved woman. The judge's decision might cost him a small fortune and a home. He stepped over muddy gutters and onto an occasional wooden walkway as he advanced toward the Faubourg Marigny. He passed a sprawling construction site for the new United States Mint. Nearby were the slave pens belonging to the merchants who sold people to the highest bidder.

At the edge of the old city near dark Esplanade Street, high walls enclosed the side yards of nondescript buildings, but they could not contain the foul smells from the corrals where humans stood. The slave pens were like small prisons—unadorned houses with interior locked cells where people slept at night and daytime exercise yards that were crowded and noisy. Boguille could hear the rabble of voices: a woman's shriek to call her child nearer, one man's shout at another, scattered weeping. Conspicuously, there were no cries from children. But they were there. They were too exhausted to say a word.

Ships now brought more of the enslaved from the lower Atlantic states to supply the plantations with laborers. The pens operated as holding cells for the auction houses and brokers. The daily papers were full of advertisements. On January 2, 1846, in one column alone were three advertisements from Beard, Calhoun & Co., at No. 8 Banks' Arcade: "Slaves—Slaves—Slaves. . . . A gang of likely SLAVES, comprising House Servants and Field Hands," "South Carolina Slaves. . . . 47 SLAVES, direct from South Carolina, comprising field hands, blacksmiths, carpenters, house men, women, girls and boys," and "at PRIVATE SALE . . . a COOPER . . . A SEAMSTRESS . . . A SLATER. . . . sold with full guaranty in every respect." Below them was an announcement by Rapides Parish Judge and ex-officio auctioneer J. N. T. Richardson for the sale of a plantation and "one hundred and twelve valuable SLAVES . . . amongst whom are several valuable Mechanics.'"

In the newspapers, Boguille could read the names of thousands of people engaged in the booming enterprise of selling men, women, and children. Among them was the typical large landowner called a gentleman planter, with several echelons of workers between him and the soil. He had an overseer whom he sent to the fields to handle his enslaved laborers rather than speak with them himself. His wife was privileged enough to have youngsters born into slavery who laundered her clothes and watched her children. As house "mistress," she administrated the kitchen while Black women cooked.

The gentleman planters used opportunities to make great profits in the cotton and sugar businesses, and they dressed to show their achievements. They wore five-dollar hats, silk cravats, cashmere trousers, and French linen shirts, while the lower classes of farmers and overseers wore rough nankeen cotton imported from China.

The planters had no more concern for the breakup of enslaved families than horse traders. They squeezed people with their hands, poked them with sticks like livestock, and salaciously appraised women's anatomy for their ability to breed. The buyers had no thought of an enslaved person's past or future beyond his commercial value: was a man's sadness a passing melancholy or a general malaise that would prove troublesome when he labored in the fields? They calculated whether the set of his jaw indicated that his spirit could not be broken enough to take orders. Slavery was a business, and the workers were just part of the equipment.

Crude men at heart, newly minted gentlemen were made from fops and cads. They flew past Boguille in shiny, crowded carriages, and when they stopped on their errands at the shops and offices of tradesmen, they spoke to the colored shoemakers, tailors, and builders without respect.

Like port cities along all of the coasts serving the slave trade, New Orleans offered a panorama of injustice. Boguille had to stop himself for a moment and ask on his journey whether he was moving away from these men by keeping Denise—or toward them.

Boguille's mother had sold others to establish herself. She had owned nine enslaved people in total at various times. She had freed one woman and sold two while the others disappeared from public records, including his childhood companion, the enslaved Dauphine's son François. Butel had complete control over their lives like any other master. Was she kinder or more benevolent to her "property" than the planters were? Did it matter under the laws of the courts or of God?

Some within the free colored community believed all descendants of Africans should be allowed education and intellectual development, among them Boguille's friends, the authors of a volume of poetry titled *Les Cenelles*. They lived in the urban, Creole section of the city, on the same property as the people they owned, usually just a few feet from their living quarters. Some of the free and enslaved people were related.

The family of Joseph Charles Dupart, who hosted the first Economie meeting, shared a surname with any number of people with different ethnicities and legal statuses. Esthere Dupart, born in Africa, was free by 1852 and living with Martial Dupart and his son.

And the phenomenon was age-old. In 1775, a man named Pierre Joseph Delille *père, dit* Dupart, one of the earliest settlers with that surname, wrote his last will and testament and acknowledged his "*cinco hijos lehitimos y naturals*"—five legitimate and natural children. He had fathered some of

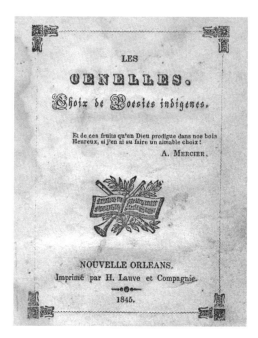

Les Cenelles: choix de poésies
indigènes title page; 1845;
THNOC, 87-632-RL

the children by his wife and some by a woman of color. Delille Dupart did not tell the notary to identify in his will which or how many of his heirs were "natural"—the term for free colored children—so his colored offspring received a large inheritance.

Boguille knew that at least two of the city's mayors cohabited with free women of color. Augustin Macarty was mayor when Boguille's parents married in 1820, and Denis Prieur served twenty years later. Everyone knew. The laws in the 1808 Louisiana Civil Code under the section "Distinctions of Persons" and others in the section "Of Husband and Wife" regulated social behavior among the enslaved, whites, and free people of color. And the rules remained in place after the code was revised in 1825. They said marriage or "concubinage" relationships between whites and people of other races were illegal. But the law had no effect on these white men, and their disregard may have benefited their half-white children.

Could justice evolve out of such unequal power relationships? Boguille had to wonder. Or did it spring only from kindness? And in which camp was he?

As he walked, Boguille could see people for sale on many of the city's sidewalks. Anyone could. To show their worthiness as servants, enslaved men stood against a wall wearing top hats and formal uniforms. The clothes would be returned to the broker's armoires once the sale was made. Others walked chain-gang style from the pens to the auction houses. In the forlorn gaggles of men, women, and older children, none dared to smile: such a dangerous act might get them noticed and purchased.

Boguille saw economics in action every day on the levee, where riverboats and coastal packet ships unloaded their enslaved passengers. He could have viewed more than one hundred people arrive at the port of New Orleans in January 1839 on a brig called the *Isaac Franklin*. The ship bore the name of a co-owner of Franklin and Armfield, once the largest firm in the United States trading people. On this trip, they boarded the ship in Norfolk, Virginia, and it snaked down the Eastern Seaboard, around the Florida peninsula, and through the Gulf of Mexico before coming upriver to the auction houses. The tallest passengers were Anthony Hargrove and Frank Perry, both 6 feet 2 inches. Three-year-old Margaret Taylor stood just 24 inches tall. Hanah Dandridge was the oldest at thirty-six, and the two youngest were Justina Henderson and Amanda Blair, both one year old. The Taylor family consisted only of youngsters aged three to fifteen. Dandridge traveled with her children, aged ten, eight, and three. The two Fry sisters were only two years apart, and the Dickinson brothers even closer in age.

The individuals' names might change once they reached New Orleans, depending on their owners' whims, so the ship's manifest contained identifiers that would stick—their colors. Unlike the slavery practiced in Greece, Rome, or Africa, the American system's most distinctive feature was the ability to identify enslaved laborers by sight. They would always be owned—or thought to be owned—because they were yellow, brown, black, light brown, and dark brown in a nation not of pinks or tans or ivories but whites.

Would their purchasers ever know them as well as Boguille knew Denise? Somewhere in the Upper South, the disappearance of an enslaved person had broken a loved one's heart. Someone yearned to search for a child, husband, wife, father, or mother but could not. They had been taken away. Boguille was a logical man. He knew that he was no different from the human profiteers if he did not consider the feelings of the enslaved, if his motivation was purely commercial—to buy, breed, and sell people like so many dogs in a litter. He had watched over Denise after his father's death, kept her on to work in his own house, and perjured himself to retain her. He took the chance of losing his home and $500, and now $1,200, if the probate court went against him and the Supreme Court concurred. Why did he risk so much? Was it his own arrogance, wealth, or principles that made him bold? Would these questions even apply if he were not a free man of color? If he were white, would slave ownership simply be another of life's advantages?

Cash flowed into New Orleans from both benevolent and conscience-less enslavers, who acquired the people they owned through kidnappings and rapes, and who used the whip to force their people to work faster and cheaper. Certainly the shippers, shopkeepers, bankers, and restaurateurs did not put abolitionist virtues over commerce. Neither did the insurers, hotel workers, cabdrivers, and builders. Everyone knew that their luxury and status depended heavily on the people who had none.

Slavery expanded the new, market-driven, and profitable American economic system. It was available to everyone—except the enslaved, who stayed at the bottom. The Catholic Church owned enslaved people, the government used enslaved laborers, entrepreneurs sent them to run errands, and housewives ordered them to clean. Most enslavers told themselves they were helping the poor "savages" in their midst—repeating the assertion so often that some firmly believed it was true.

Boguille, on the other hand, was neither naive nor willfully ignorant. He knew that any man who purchased another person stepped on him with a heavy boot in order to climb. All the humanitarian excuses for keeping an enslaved person in New Orleans, even his family's, could be dismantled by looking at the finances of a household, a business, or the quickly expanding city—the pearl of the United States, growing fatter with the assistance of unpaid labor.

As for the territories of the heart under this legal system, Boguille, an intellectual versed in ancient history, knew that human nature did not change. The same people who would cheat a customer would swindle their enslaved laborers. The same people who were cruel to their family members were horrific to the people they owned. In this way, the color of the owner hardly mattered. Men of all colors beat their wives, their children, and the enslaved. Women of all colors lashed out at the young enslaved girls who served them. Men of all colors would buy a light-skinned colored girl, whom the slave merchants called a "fancy," to use in bed. Masters of all colors forced themselves on women they purchased, fancy or not, and raped them.

Boguille's friends had come to court and lied so that he could retain Denise, and it was all wrong—the lying, the secrets, the selling, the laws. But lying was all he could do. Or perhaps it was all he chose to do at this time.

FOR OVER A YEAR, Boguille's life had proceeded with the normalcy of the privileged while the processing of all the testimony and filings dragged on. The sheriff had gone to seize the property twice, but the court stopped him each time as Ludger sought injunctions and rehearings filed with the courts' clerks. Each time, his costs for the suit escalated.

Finally, the probate court did its job. In April 1846, the court said that Ludger had to amend his accounting of his father's estate for it to be homologated—basically put to rest. After this point, Ludger would find out in the Supreme Court whether the property would be sold to pay Faille.

Supreme Court Associate Justice George Rogers King read pages of painstakingly handwritten testimony from Faille, the Boguille family, François's friend Adolphe Boyer, doctors, creditors, and many lawyers. They brought pounds of papers in English and, in the French language of the court, *livres* of notes. It had cost Ludger a small fortune to pay lawyers and clerks. But he planned to win the case.

On May 26, 1846, the Supreme Court decided. It, too, sided with Faille. She could seize and sell Boguille's property to pay the debt owed her. Judge King sidestepped the decision of whether Denise was included in the inventory of the succession. The accounting of the estate, he said, had no impact on Faille's mortgage for François's land. The auction would take place, and Ludger couldn't stop it.

Boguille applied for a rehearing, writing to "the Honorable George Eustis, Chief Justice and the Judges of the Supreme Court" to attempt to stop the sheriff again because the previous decision, besides being "contrary to law," would lead to the "gravest consequences" for the heirs. Ahead was another battle involving filing fees, clerks to look for additional legal precedents, and a search for new witnesses. Boguille must have sat for many hours considering how to convince the lawyers to represent him with any bits of evidence he could bring up at the new trial.

Boguille was thirty-four years old and head of his large extended family, but he had risked their house and Denise by taking a position that he could not support. Had he been too cavalier in the inventory of his father's estate? Did he feel too safe making the judgments about what to include and what to ignore? Should he have consulted more people rather than making the decisions independently?

But his family and his wife had backed his decision, as the succession papers showed. Andrénette had gone along, even though the case must have terrified her. What if they lost their home from the costs of the suits, or from the lies? Their young children's lives might be upended. Where would they go?

The humid days heaved past while Boguille waited for the rehearing. He sat in the house that he, Andrénette, and the children shared on Ursulines Street, between Burgundy and Rampart Streets in the old city. Some nights, he may have distractedly pondered the case while the children played at his feet. He consulted frequently with his lawyer. Boguille may have listened for a knock at the cypress door of his house—a messenger with new information.

Finally, the day came for the court's decision. Would it accept his petition and allow him to bring in new arguments?

On June 26, 1846, the Supreme Court said no to the rehearing, and soon the newspaper advertised an auction of the property. On July 31, 1846, at noon, the 60-by-120-foot lot at the corner of Union and Good Children Streets would be sold under the rotunda of the St. Louis Hotel. It was the same place where the auctioneers sold people.

But Denise was not part of the sale. She disappeared from the court records into her previous anonymity. So did Ludger's mother, who presumably kept Denise, since the Supreme Court focused singly on the injunction against the sale of François's property.

Boguille had to live with the court's decision, which included the loss of his father's land and so much money. But Andrénette couldn't. On June 29, three days after the final Supreme Court ruling, she unexpectedly died.

Boguille Finds Support in the Economie Brotherhood

1840s–1857

*Considering all the advantages and the benefits that are
repaid to a group of men joined together in society, in order
to put into practice good morals to mitigate and relieve
human suffering, we have committed ourselves to persevere
and to put all our efforts into instituting a society upon a
solid and strong foundation.*

—Economie Minutes, 1836

THE CORONER RECORDED no cause of death for Ludger's wife in
his report. Her death certificate said nothing, either. Ludger must have
wondered whether her loss was his fault because of the stress consuming
them all. He became a man with a broken heart and too much responsibility. He was a single father with four minor children, a younger sister and
brother, and a widowed mother. He had spent too much money pursuing
a fruitless case.

In his solitude, he turned to the Société d'Economie et d'Assistance
Mutuelle, a benevolent society of many older free men of color. The
members had supported him for a long time. Some knew his father from
Saint Domingue or from fighting side by side in the battles for Haiti or
New Orleans. Adolphe Boyer had testified on Ludger's behalf, telling the
courts about visits to François during his long illness. Boyer lived in the
family's neighborhood and was one of the Economie's founders.

Boyer was likely the representative who walked into a Sunday meeting of the Economie and brought Ludger Boguille's name forward for membership. The actual date of the application disappeared with the minute books from 1842 to 1857. But a membership book suggested that the letter arrived in 1852.

On the appointed day, Ludger's sponsor would have entered through a narrow wooden door in a small house that the Economistes had purchased for their meetings in the Faubourg Tremé. He hung up his coat on one of the wall pegs, walked past the two soft armchairs, and checked himself in the mirror before entering the second room, where men gathered. Candelabra illuminated a large wooden meeting table surrounded by two dozen seats. Men lifted their heads in greeting.

They were contractors, international brokers, clothing store owners, shoemakers, and clerks. By 1846 they had been meeting for a decade. The men had first joined together in the home of Joseph Charles Dupart on January 24, 1836, not far from Boguille's childhood home. Dupart had an oversized room, once part of a corner grocery store. Thick wooden shutters with black iron straps covered the windows and doors. The building was as impenetrable as a castle and as intimate as a courtyard. It corralled the damp, the dark, and the whispers of visitors. Their meetings were necessarily secret because of the white community's fears of insurrection.

The American government suspected that free colored men would encourage enslaved people to revolt. While none of the Economie men moved to lead an armed revolution, all of them likely broke one law or another. Mostly they ignored the ones that they felt didn't make sense, such as one Louisiana statute that said they should not "presume to conceive themselves equal to the white . . . , and never speak or answer to them but with respect, under the penalty of imprisonment." Some founding Economistes like Firmin Perrault and Manuel Moreau served in the First Battalion in the Battle of New Orleans, while François Carlon had fought alongside Charles Joseph Savary *fils* in the Second Battalion. Etienne Cordeviolle traveled to Europe and Mexico frequently on business. The Dupart family name had been known in New Orleans since the city's founding in 1718, and all of the Economistes were literate property owners. They probably thought of most American whites as their inferiors.

The Economistes' first meeting place—Dupart's house—was originally built for Charles Laveaux, a free colored immigrant from Saint Domingue who had died only a year previously. He was the father of a woman named Marie whose reputation was growing as the queen of Vodou. The Economistes never mentioned her name in their minutes, although they had written glowingly about her father, as Boguille would soon find out. They knew much that they never made public.

The Dupart house sat at a location in the Faubourg Marigny that described the founders' lives at the intersection of cultures, eras, and languages. It was a propitious place with a memorable name, the corner of *Grands hommes* and *Histoire*. Translated for the English speakers who were frequently lost when they arrived in this labyrinth of a neighborhood, the intersection was Great Men and History.

The names that are mentioned below, numbering 15, are inscribed on a list annexed to this record that describes our intention and our desire to live together in a society. It will be conserved with care in our archives, as being the original title-page of this social body, and to conserve for Posterity the way that this institution was formed.

—Economie Minutes, 1836

ADOLPHE BOYER DREW A five-pointed star as the first initial of his first name when the members signed a declaration in 1836 promising loyalty to one another. They chose to meet at Joseph Charles Dupart's house because he offered it, but they probably also believed that the location on Great Men suited them. The record of the inaugural meeting appeared in their first journal—a long, marble-faced book of more than 370 pages. The text of the minutes appeared as a graceful waltz of black ink across the sea-foam-colored leaves.

The minutes did not mention that the society formed soon after the publication of David Walker's *Appeal to the Colored Citizens of the United States* to join together and rise up for their rights, nor did they mention Nat Turner's 1831 slave rebellion, which imitated the Haitian Revolution in its fierce, scorched-earth tactics—an end to slavery or the death of everyone in charge. They included no information about the Texas-Mexican war, which in 1836 removed territory from a country where slavery did not exist and created the Republic of Texas, where slavery was law. The founders of the Economie kept their opinions of current events to themselves.

And they held the secrets of their New Orleans families—their health, businesses, finances, loves, and outrages—like the chain of a ship wrapped tightly around its mooring. One circle connected to another. One crimp set everything on edge. One pull, and everything moved. Their relatives and friends linked them to people in Cuba, Saint Domingue, Europe, and South America. The men were well versed in the developments of the world and welcomed in many places. But they were outcasts in their home state.

Louisiana decided it no longer wanted colored stakeholders. A law passed in January 1836 denied colored investors access to shares in Louisiana banks. The flourishing Citizens' Bank refused to acknowledge the investment belonging to François Boisdoré, who had bought $20,000 worth of stock when the bank incorporated in 1833. The bank also wouldn't let him dispose of his shares.

Boisdoré took his case to the First District Court, where the bank's lawyer argued that "when the faith of the State was pledged for the capital of said Bank it was expressly provided that no person or persons not being a *free white citizen* . . . and domicil[ed] in the State of Louisiana should be either directly or indirectly owner of any part of the capital Stock of the company." In fact, the legislature had not made this decision until January 30, 1836. Boisdoré showed evidence that the bank had taken his funds and admitted him as a charter member three years earlier. The district court agreed with him. Then Citizens' Bank appealed to the Louisiana Supreme Court and lost again on June 6, 1838. The bank had to keep Boisdoré as a shareholder and pay his court costs.

The news of Boisdoré's victory moved throughout the free colored community. His win probably helped Boguille feel empowered to appeal his case with Faille.

But Boguille had lost. The Economistes knew that he needed help. Their society shared his language, culture, and friends. Moreover, they were shrewd, wise, and financially secure. In their secret meeting place, Boyer would have introduced new business—a letter from the young son of his old friend François. It was a formal request for admission, written in Ludger Boguille's wide, ornate script full of optimism.

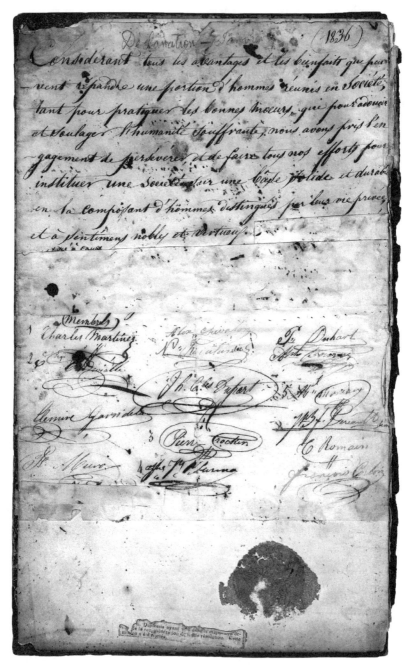

Declaration of the founding of the Société d'Economie, with members' signatures; 1836; *courtesy of Fatima Shaik*

Wherever civilization carries its lights, we see men
bringing themselves together for the purpose of mutual aid
and to hold out against vice and seductions which are able
to beset them in the world; hence imbued by the impor-
tance of their association, they act with restraint and with
the compelling necessity to admit among themselves only
virtuous men to share their efforts in the new course that
they are about to pursue.

—Pierre Crocker, Economie president, 1836

WHEN LUDGER'S NAME CAME up for consideration, the Economie members voted to appoint a committee of three men to look into
his finances and lifestyle. The Economie's investigation team took the
letter that gave his name and address, now 92 Good Children, along with
his word that he was in good health and reliable. Then each committee
member asked people in the free colored community what they knew
about his past.

He still owned property in the Faubourg Marigny that his father had
given him, but there was debate about whether he could receive the property owned by Andrénette Lamy. Their marriage in the church was not
validated in any civil ceremony or document, and her death certificate used
legal jargon to justify this contradiction. It said that she "was married to
Ludger Boguille, her surviving consort." Because of the structure of French
laws that remained in Louisiana, Boguille had to go to court again to be

named the "tutor" of his own minor children, so he would have the legal
right to continue to raise them.

The Economie committees were quick to reject a petitioner whose
family had a bad reputation, who did not keep his word, or who was too
free with his money. They had made an exception once for a man they
admired whose wife did not live up to their standards, adding that "if the
candidate is elected, he will have to take an oath of respect and loyalty to
our rules!"

They depended upon one another for dues, which paid for their medical
and burial expenses as well as their banquets. The Economie also wanted
men who would come to meetings on time and willingly dig deep into
their pockets for charity, such as providing aid to the blind, widows,
and orphans.

The Economie members brought their collections of cash to the Dames
de la Charité, the nuns who worked with the poor and infirm. Or the men
sent a brother with an envelope of donations to knock on the door of a
friend who had an ill child. Sometimes they sent money to people who
were in desperate financial situations—neighbors devastated by a flood
or caring for an elderly parent or disabled relative. They rejected some
people who wrote asking for money, however. The Economistes referred
to one petitioner as "an immoral man" and "a player" because he went to
the gambling houses to beg for support. The brothers decided to put his
letter aside "indefinitely." The society looked for colored members whom
they called *gentilshommes*. The word meant "gentlemen" and implied a
level of trustworthiness and sophistication.

A week after investigating Boguille, the committee decided that he fit
the Economie's requirements. He spoke French without the use of common
phrases such as asking for the bread loaf's *teton*—"titty"—to dip in his
black coffee. He was not quick to throw his money at the daily horse races
or craps games. He was not fool enough to ask another man to duel with
single-ball pistols under the oaks outside the city. In public, Boguille carried
himself with a calm dispassion. Typically, he walked with a cane and wore
a hat. At a time when fine fabric was precious and expensive because of
the labor it entailed, he owned exquisitely fitted trousers and a topcoat to
match. His Economie brothers Cordeviolle and Lacroix owned the most

Receipt from Cordeviolle and Lacroix clothing store; *courtesy of Louisiana Division / City Archives, New Orleans Public Library*

fashionable clothing store in the city. No doubt, Boguille's shirt was the finest white linen, taut and laundered. He had often attended the philharmonic, arriving in a carriage with his wife on his arm, though he had been absent since her death. He was now the sole support of his four children.

The Economistes put his name to a vote. Each of the members dropped his ballot into the urn at the front of the room. Boguille earned more white balls than black ones. Boyer was told to bring his friend to the next meeting.

On August 1, 1852, Boguille stood outside the meeting, which started at seven o'clock, and waited for the deputies of the society to bring him to the podium, where the president of the society stood. The members wore sashes across their chests and ribbons pinned to their jackets indicating their positions and seniority in the organization. They gave one another the secret signal—which they never wrote into the minutes. When one of the members suggested creating a "*signe mystérieux*" at an early meeting, the secretary put down his pen so that no outsider seeing the journals could read the discussion. The gesture passed only from man to man.

One of the deputies of the Economie opened the door to the meeting room, allowing the new member to enter, along with the three men from the investigation committee. They marched him to face the president. He questioned Ludger about articles of the Economie's constitution: did he know the roles of the president, vice president, treasurer, and secretary? Did he know the names of the various committees? Would he agree to pay dues, to participate in their functions, and to respect their procedures for speaking in turn?

At one initiation, the president told a postulant, "Know in advance, that after you take your vow, you will be on an equal footing with the founder of the society himself. But this equality will not mean that you will be able to exceed the limits of decency, of courtesy. Never forget that, whatever your manner be of understanding a matter, you must discuss it with élan, with reason—not with anger and bad language—so that fraternity, union, and concord be always protected by you when others harm them. . . . Know once and for all that we are all avid to learn. We all like to hear a discussion. We like to hear from one side and the other in what way our laws should be interpreted, and we also like to get good advice. . . . The respect you will show to the constitution and to the rules will arm you against all spirit of partisanship."

Boguille took his vows, and the president accepted him in the name of the society, then gave him a traditional blessing. The words he used for one new member were, "Divine Providence, bless our new Brother . . . , grant that among the good feelings that inspire him, the Society glory in having him. Divine Providence, may your benediction spread over this new Brother. . . . May mutual respect, brotherhood, and union hold us together beyond the grave. Brother, you have our hearts and our esteem. May God come to your aid."

Boguille submitted his initiation fee to the treasurer. It was set at twenty-five dollars in the first years of the society—about a month's salary for a teamster or militiaman. Not many men in America of any race had that much cash in their breast pockets.

He received a certificate of membership, which the men in the society called their *diplôme,* a scroll of parchment showing his name and the signatures of the officers of the society. Each of the brothers in the organization approached him to give him the "official accolade"—a bear hug. With that, Ludger became Brother Boguille in their arms.

SOCIETE D'ECONOMIE

ET D'ASSISTANCE MUTUELLE.

Fondée le 1er Mars 1836.   Incorporée le 12 Aout 1850.

CONCORDE

FRATERNITÉ   BIENFAISANCE

DIPLOME

A TOUS! SALUT ET FRATERNITÉ.

Nous, soussignés, au nom de la Société d'Economie et d'Assistance Mutuelle, certifions que _____

a été admis comme membre, conformément aux lois de la susdite Société,

le _____ 18____

En foi de quoi nous avons apposé le sceau de la susdite Société pour garantir l'authenticité de ce Diplome.

Donné sous notre signature, à la

Nouvelle-Orléans, le _____ 18____

_____
PRÉSIDENT.

_____
SECRÉTAIRE.

Société d'Economie membership certificate; *courtesy of Fatima Shaik*

◈

*Gentlemen, the committee of purchases has the honor to
inform you that it has acquired a lot of books, 25 volumes
at 43 cents-3/4 per volume which comes to $10=94c....
Among these volumes, most decrepit and oddments, we find
an Atlas, a precious and indispensable Atlas.*

—Economie Minutes, 1837

IN THE ECONOMISTES, Ludger Boguille gained a community of
like-minded men—thinking men. The society had an entire library. Some
of the books were kept inside an armoire: *Histoire générale de la marine,*
which gave a narrative of pirates, privateers, and slave traders; *Cours de
mathématiques,* a textbook for sailors; and two volumes of the *Procès des
ministres de Charles X,* which provided a lesson on the second French
revolution through its description of the debates and discussions about
treason in the trials of Charles X's ministers. One night a member walked
in with *Précis d'histoire des temps modernes,* a book explaining the creation
of the modern French democracy, so the men could prepare themselves to
be full citizens—if not in Louisiana, then abroad.

Boguille would see his life mirrored in the pages of human development.
The book *Pétion et Haïti* recounted that as Europeans went to the West
Indies and mixed with the natives and enslaved Africans, "the mulatto
seems to have come into the world as if to bind Africa to Europe—the

black man to the white man." But the Haitian author, Joseph Saint-Rémy, added that whites were insensitive to their colored children, as was the case for Pétion, whose white father refused to acknowledge him. The leader of the mulatto faction in the revolution, Pétion rose to be the first president of the Black republic. Boguille saw a reflection of his own political history in the book. It named soldiers from the island who aided the American Revolution—André Rigaud, Jean-Baptiste Chavannes, and Jean-Baptiste Belley—and said, "It is thus that the colored population of Saint Domingue went to the American continent to battle for the liberation of a people, who nevertheless kept no account of its generous devotion, and who, the danger over, cruelly forgot that African blood mingled with their own to bring forth that liberty which they deny to our race."

Boguille had to consider whether the consequences of the American Revolution had repeated themselves when his father and compatriots from Saint Domingue helped win the Battle of New Orleans but never received full citizenship rights in the state they helped to create.

The Economie library also held two world maps and the *Atlas de la géographie ancienne, de moyen âge, et moderne*, with charts of the globe. He could sit quietly and study New Orleans relative to the world's other great cities. He saw celebrated ports such as Le Havre, Liverpool, Veracruz, and Calcutta—the economic crossroads of his time. He saw tangible proof of the progress created by the intersections of cultures. Commercial success gave rise to intellectual ferment.

His brothers in the Economie also mentored him, modeling enlightened ways of life. They spoke and read multiple languages and traveled around the world to visit their foreign relatives and conduct business. Etienne Cordeviolle, whose father was from Genoa, knew that city well. He sometimes lived in Paris, as did François Lacroix. Other members traveled to Mexico and Haiti.

Boguille may have noticed that the measurements on the maps also showed great discrepancies caused by prejudice. On one map a yard wide, the continent of Europe bulged at the center, with France, England, Italy, and Spain stretching the length of Boguille's forearm, while Africa could be covered by the palm of his hand. On some maps, the continents were nestled together like a puzzle, making sense of man's earliest patterns of migration, as explained in the Bible. On other maps, the continents were isolated by worlds of water, and Africa was as distant as stars in the cosmic darkness. The maps before him were informed as much by the sympathies of the mapmaker as by celestial calculations. A good map displayed the distance from one place to another as well as the difficulty of the journey, the legends describing deep water, jagged coastlines, and treacherous seas. Boguille noticed that some atlases, which demonstrated little recognition of countries beyond Europe, suggested extra boundaries for a man like himself.

Travelers who embarked from Louisiana on trips across the Gulf had to be wary of natural hazards and disasters. Some maps showed sandbars where ships could get stuck for days until the tide rose high enough to free them. Some accompanying drawings indicated that tropical storms might ravage travelers at sea until there was no clear demarcation between sky and water. The usual dangers were aging ships that retched their contents into the water and windstorms that shredded the sails. But colored travelers who arrived safely in Mexico, Haiti, and other islands in the West Indies could quietly meld into a population of brown faces. Some of these people were illustrated along the edges of an atlas's pages.

Perhaps other subtleties were also true. Would drawings in the margins of maps showing pale southern inhabitants attended by enslaved Black people indicate that voyages in America might be a problem for a man of color?

A dark-skinned man on a long journey could be perceived as a cook or a crewman. The son of Haitian president Jean-Pierre Boyer, who reportedly stopped briefly in New Orleans in 1839, traveled in steerage to get to New York. No one would take meals with him or speak to him, despite his fluency in five languages. Finally, after leaving the port of New York, an Englishman conversed with him. The Americans never did. Only in Europe were his education and wealth of any use to him.

No maps, atlases, globes, or books advertised such treatment of citizens. Or did they?

The presence or absence of a colored person on the page might be due to an illustrator's imagination, but it also could be a subtle suggestion of prejudice. As Boguille read the maps, they tried to roll inward, as if to retain their secrets and boundaries. To study them, he needed to hold down the edges.

Boguille Teaches His Own

1840–1857

Education ... would become equally dangerous to the
master and the slave. ... It would not only unfit him for his
station in life, and prepare him for insurrection, but would
be found wholly impracticable in the performance of the
duties of a laborer.

—*The South Vindicated from the Treason and Fanaticism*
of the Northern Abolitionists, 1836

THE ECONOMIE LIBRARY WAS an appropriate venue for Boguille's
study about his place in the world. He was a schoolteacher for many years.

Beginning in 1840, Boguille ran his own private academy at 37 Great
Men Street, between History and Bagatelle Streets. It stood a few doors
from the home of Joseph Charles Dupart, on the same block as Joseph
Sauvinet, a broker who reportedly received goods from the pirate Laffite
brothers. The school enrolled forty children, girls and boys—twenty under
ten years of age and the rest between the ages of ten and twenty-three.
Boguille watched over a total of fifty people, including staff.

The Economie's library included *Les annales de la vertu, ou histoire
universelle, iconographique et littéraire*, a book to educate young writers
and artists, along with textbooks and encyclopedias.

Boguille took pedagogical advice from one of his favorite authors.
Fénelon wrote, "As soon as children arrive at a more mature period, or

their reason becomes unfolded, we must be careful that all our words have a tendency to make them love truth, and detest artifice and hypocrisy. We ought never to be guilty of any deception or falsehood to appease them, or to persuade them to comply with our wishes: if we are, we instruct them in cunning and artifice; and this they never forget.—Reason and good sense must be our instruments of regulation."

Boguille was the consummate mentor. He was a poet—a quiet man who secretly wished for the unwavering attention of a crowd. He had this attention in his rooms full of pupils. In the morning, in front of the classroom, he could recite the classic children's verses that he loved:

When Fortune threatens dar'st thou not oppose,
To stem the Tide, and Face the Cloud of Woes?
Be not dismay'd, yet better Days may come,
And you yet see the long expected Home.
Think on *Ulysses*, toss'd by Winds and Seas,
Who bears Misfortunes greater far than these.

Fénelon's epic, *The Adventures of Telemachus*, allowed Boguille's students to see that their challenges in the South were universal to mankind. The book was a challenge to the French monarch's divine right to rule. Following that thought to its logical conclusion, Boguille could say that Telemachus supported the equality of all men.

Boguille typically stood at the front of the room and occasionally paced between the long desks that several students shared. He used the Socratic method, giving them information, then asking them to think about the definition of a word, and afterward pushing them to create an application for themselves. He taught that virtue, besides being a question of morality and purity, was an act of social conscience. He questioned whether they saw this value in their own times. He could ask them to repeat one of his favorite sayings, "Vice alone is low; virtue holds rank; the greatest man is he who is most just."

Boguille believed fully that education—and not the conditions of birth—would slowly allow poor children to advance.

ONE DAY, THE FREE FATHER of an enslaved boy asked Boguille to teach his son. The boy was as light-skinned as others in the classroom, so Boguille sat him among the pupils. But one by one the other parents removed their children from the school. Reading was strictly prohibited for enslaved people. The parents feared the possible legal consequences of ignoring the infraction, but their concerns went beyond that. They didn't want their children being taught in the same room as an enslaved boy. It was an indignity to them.

After their prejudices became clear, Boguille must have keenly felt the difference between his values and those of the families who paid for their children's lessons. Their biases were not only a matter of color. They cared about class distinctions.

Boguille could not afford to close his school—a real possibility with so many empty seats—but he refused to deny the enslaved boy an education. The boy was taken out of the school, and Boguille went to his house to give him private lessons.

In the classroom, Boguille typically began his school days by calling his students to order, listing their names, and then lining them up alphabetically. This way he avoided giving certain students the privilege of sitting at the front of the class because of the size of their parents' donations, their appearances, or their outspokenness. The alphabetical roll call was a small demonstration of life's randomness—a lesson about equality that Boguille could reinforce every day.

I bequeath and order that my land at the corner of Grand Hommes and Union Streets be dedicated and used in perpetuity for the establishment of a free school for colored orphans of the Faubourg Marigny. . . . Also, I declare that said lands and buildings shall never be sold under any pretext whatsoever.

—Last Will and Testament of Madame Marie Couvent, 1832

IN 1848, A SCHOOL opened one block from Boguille's. Its mission was to teach children who had no parents to pay tuition. He saw them on his daily walks—sleeping outdoors in the narrow gaps between houses, begging passersby outside stores, and fighting to port luggage at the docks for a few pennies. Some children whose mothers had died of yellow fever, cholera, or another sickness were left to wander the streets. They ran around the city in rags. They traveled in packs, unless someone took pity on them. If they were unlucky, a slave trader grabbed them and made up a story about how he had purchased them upriver, and they were sold at auction.

Boguille kept teaching at 37 Great Men Street and added a job at the nearby school, becoming one of the first five teachers at the Institution catholique pour l'instruction des orphelins dans l'indigence (Catholic Institution for the Instruction of Indigent Orphans). The school was the first in the United States to provide education at no cost to poor colored children. It also enrolled female students, as Fénelon had advocated in his text *The Education of Girls*, and as Boguille did.

The new school opened when a group of free men of color saw an opportunity in an 1847 Louisiana law that was intended to encourage industry. The legislature wanted to increase the state's economic activity, so lawmakers passed an act allowing groups of men to incorporate "for any literary, scientific, religious or charitable purpose."

Economiste François Lacroix founded the school with a group that included three other members of the society and Boguille's in-law Barthélemy Rey. The men quickly met in the office of the notary Octave de Armas and wrote up a prospectus. Land for a school had been donated in the will of Marie Couvent, a native of Guinea who was once enslaved. She had amassed a small fortune in property and married Bernard Couvent, an enslaved man who lived as a free man for the rest of his life. When the widow Couvent had died in 1837 at the age of eighty, she was financially comfortable and respected by her community. The school's first principal was Félicie Coulon, a free woman of color who also was born into slavery. According to people who knew her, she was "exceedingly intelligent, highly respected, [and] a devout Catholic." In 1847, two months after the school's incorporation, she married André Cailloux, another formerly enslaved person. Admired in the community of color, Cailloux was educated, cultured, athletic, and undoubtedly dark-skinned. William Wells Brown later wrote that Cailloux "prided himself on being the blackest man in the Crescent City."

The principal following Félicie Coulon Cailloux was Armand Lanusse, appointed in 1852. Rodolphe Desdunes would later write that "he made no distinctions among his students based on the color of their skin." Lanusse was a very light-skinned man, and he often walked arm in arm with Louis Lainez, "whose skin color left no doubt about his parentage," Desdunes added.

Boguille joined a distinguished faculty with other Economie members: Nelson Fouché taught mathematics, and Samuel Snaër, a composer, taught music. Basile Crocker, the older brother of the Economie's first president, taught math and brought his students to his fencing salon, where he trained the children of the upper class. The training included lessons in grace, honor, and self-defense—ideas lifted from the romantic novelists, taking root in the Louisiana swamplands.

Boguille taught French. His classroom did not resemble the Victorian-era boys' school with haughty men pacing across the front of the room. It was not the one-room schoolhouse of the West. It did not have a dirt floor for ciphering. But it did have something in common with all of those settings: Boguille's colored boys and girls were privileged to learn in the late 1840s, when only about 15 percent of the entire world was literate.

At the head of the room, Boguille must have appeared to his students as a slightly manic, stoop-shouldered intellectual whose wide eyes squinted at books due to his farsightedness, or creased frequently because of his kindness, and sometimes watered uncontrollably because of his full heart. His hair, dark and thick, rose above his head like a foxtail fern, jubilant in the humidity, unless pruned back. If Boguille's lectures in French resembled his writing, they were so rhythmically paced that they were musical. He was an emotional person with intense feelings about education, so his voice wavered and pitched, dropped a few registers when he wanted to be stern and, like that of all skilled teachers, varied in resonance from a boom to a whisper when he wanted to get his pupils' attention.

In the Couvent School—the name everyone used—the free colored children with parents sat next to their orphaned classmates. They learned the same lessons. Their teachers held them to the same standards. The parents paid no more than fifty cents a month, including textbook fees. The orphans received everything free.

The Economie gave dances to fund the school and collected more money from members every year on November 1, the Feast of All Saints. The schoolchildren also did their part. On the feast day, when New Orleanians throughout the city went to the cemeteries to lay flowers on relatives' tombs, the orphans stood at the cemetery gates next to a basket for donations. They also paid a respectful visit to the grave of Marie Couvent in St. Louis Cemetery No. 2. When Boguille accompanied them, he must have walked over a few rows to the crypt of the Famille Boguille, where he had buried his first love, Andrénette Lamy, and his father, François.

With his own school, Ludger found his calling. At the Couvent School, he found friends. In the Economie, he would find brothers who aspired to intellectual and social freedom in a nation founded on equality.

I am happy to inform you that on the main question I am heartily of your opinion. Slavery is right. It is of Divine appointment. It is neither an evil [n]or a wrong. It is a blessing, rightly used, to the white man; it is salvation & paradise to the Negro. . . .

You remark that the colour of the African always runs back to its original hue. Do you think it capable of satisfactory proof that the wooly headed-flatnosed-thick-lipped-flat-footed Negro may be produced from a Mulatto?

—Rev. C. K. Marshall, Vicksburg, to
Dr. Samuel A. Cartwright, New Orleans, 1854

IN 1848 WHILE BOGUILLE taught at the Couvent School as well as his own, the decorated physician Samuel A. Cartwright, a native of Fairfax, Virginia, brought his traveling bags to New Orleans. He took an office in the medical department at the University of Louisiana. His colleagues came to pay their respects—stopping by to say hello, introducing him to friends, and inviting him into their intellectual circles. Harvard University and other major institutions had recognized Cartwright for his scientific discoveries. He came to Louisiana to do research. His subjects were enslaved people on plantations. At first, he came to study the way that they could avoid diseases. Then he realized that his research could aid enslavers who wanted to get the most work from their laborers.

Cartwright led the way in moving southern medicine from observation to experimentation. He wrote essays on the "Pathology and Treatment of Cholera" addressed to "planters and heads of families." This courtesy and loyalty to the planter class cemented Cartwright's reputation in his adopted home state. Local physicians supported his new theory that southern doctors alone understood the best ways to treat the "diseases and peculiarities of the Negro race." Later critics would call his theories "states-rights medicine" because they helped create the white supremacist identity that justified secession.

Soon the Medical Society of Louisiana gave Cartwright the chair of a most important committee: his job was to report on Negro illnesses and cures. At the University of Louisiana—later incorporated into Tulane University—Cartwright was appointed Professor of Diseases of the Negro, the only such appointment in the United States.

He worked at the plantations through the late 1840s and into the 1850s, when he coined a term for a new type of illness. Drapetomania, from the Greek word for "runaway," he claimed was a condition that made enslaved laborers try to leave the plantation. It could be prevented by noticing the signs of another sickness he reportedly discovered and called "Dysaesthesia Aethiopis, or Hebetude of the Mind," a type of dull-witted laziness. The cure was highly effective and fit naturally within his new paradigm: the condition could be treated by whipping, he said. "A remarkable ethnological peculiarity of the prognathous race is, that any deserved punishment, inflicted on them with a switch, cowhide or whip, puts them into a good humor with themselves and the executioner of the punishment," Cartwright said in a lecture to the New Orleans Academy of Sciences in 1857. "Subordination of the inferior race to the superior is a normal, and not a forced condition," he added.

Cartwright believed his theories also applied to free people of color. He asserted that whites were superior and the most civilized people on earth. The biggest problem with free Negroes was that they had no masters to give them direction. Social and political equality was abnormal, he said, "whether educated or not. Neither Negroes nor mulattoes know how to use power when given to them."

His work attracted devotees as late as the 1940s, when a writer in the *New Orleans Medical and Surgical Journal* noted that while some of Cartwright's "conclusions were incorrect," his work showed "unusual earnestness, sincerity, ingenuity and originality."

The Economie men were not among his admirers.

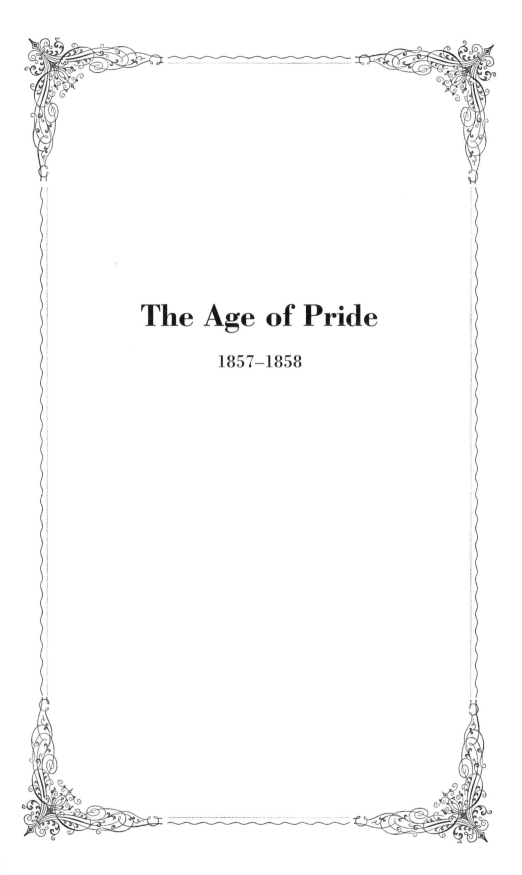

The Age of Pride

1857–1858

Boguille Takes His Place in the Economie Leadership

1857

Société d'Economie et d'Assistance Mutuelle
March 2, 1857
21st Anniversary

Conforming to article 19 of the rules, the meeting was
opened. The roll call demonstrated that 45 members were
present. The reading of the minutes of the last meeting was
made and adopted after several slight corrections. . . . All
the brothers are in good standing, tranquil, joyous, and
happy for the president's inaugural ceremony. . . . This
exchange of courtesy and politesse proves that these brothers
are clever and urbane.

—Ludger Boguille, Secretary

THE ECONOMIE ELECTED BOGUILLE secretary in 1857, and he proved to be the most meticulous and expressive chronicler of the society's meetings. On the society's twenty-first anniversary, he noted the members' comportment. They followed the rules—raising their hands to be recognized, standing when the president called on them, and putting their dues and their extra donations into the treasurer's hands with little complaint. He was proud of the Economistes' generosity. They gave to the poor, the victims of floods, and the religious orders. Their first ball, in January 1841, had supported the Sisters of Charity. They rented the Washington Ballroom, hired musicians for $50, and spent $531 on food, tickets, decorations, and more. They recorded a profit of $369, a significant sum for the average Louisiana worker in the early 1840s.

The Economie's ball was such a success that at the next meeting, one member proposed that the society build its own ballroom above its small meeting hall on Ursulines Street. He envisioned a camelback structure, doubling the floor space by framing an additional room over the back of the building. A committee reported the estimated amount needed for construction: $2,758.15, almost double the cost of the original building. The members complained that this was the price without furniture, "which is indispensable."

More than a decade passed before they took on the construction of a ballroom. They accomplished it by erecting a grand new hall across the street. Member William Belley, a friend of the society's first president, Pierre Crocker, drew up the plans. It would hold not only a large, private meeting hall with a raised platform for officers, but also a public ball-room with a tongue-in-groove floor, and a seventy-foot-long theater for concerts. Musicians would accompany plays from a balcony. Its railing would be smooth and polished with balusters of turned wood, soundly crafted to last into the next century. Special guests would sit in the box seats in the first loge.

The design also showed a ladies' dressing parlor that overlooked the yard. On the opposite wall of the parlor, large double doors led to the ballroom, so a beautiful woman could make a grand entrance.

Belley's plans specified only fine materials. The walls would have wain-scoting four feet high, with smooth, cool white plaster rising to the ceiling. The kitchen building had walls eight inches thick made of bricks over-laid with white plaster. An apartment upstairs would accommodate the *gardienne*, the female caretaker of the hall who also sold gumbo, pâté, and liquor before and after the meetings.

Two columns flanked the large, double-door main entrance. Above the columns were copper cornices, and on the front of the building gold lettering spelled out the name of the association alongside an inscription of one of its symbols, a beehive. To the members of Masonic societies, plentiful in the city, it stood for industry and protection of friends and family. The Economistes borrowed both visual metaphors. They conceived of themselves as being part of both cultures, while actually belonging to neither. They followed French ideals of elegance, sophistication, and justice. They borrowed secret rituals, philanthropy, and brotherhood from the Masons. But the Economie operated independently of the lodge system.

The Economistes were the elites of the ten thousand free people of color in New Orleans, who in 1857 owned real estate valued at $15 million and had a literacy rate of approximately 65 percent. New Orleans was one of the few places in the United States where a man like Boguille could make a living and socialize among his peers. Even in New York, he would find only one in fifty-five colored men with a similar education. The rest were workers and servants. In New Orleans, however, one in every eleven free men of color was a professional such as a business owner, teacher, or clerk. New York was home to no lithographers, masons, architects, bookbinders, brick makers, cabinetmakers, capitalists, or engineers of color. In New Orleans, they were Boguille's friends. They were models of Black freedom in an ocean of oppression.

THEIR ELITE POSITIONS WERE hard won. Men like Boguille knew that their ancestry came from a line of radical freedom fighters that stretched back to the Battle of New Orleans and before that to Haiti. The Economistes wrapped a portrait of Alexandre Pétion to carry from their old hall into the new one. The revolutionary and first president of the Haitian republic was pictured in a military officer's uniform trimmed in gold braid, with a sash running from his shoulder to his hip, where his saber hung. His face was the color of polished cypress, his mouth full and shapely below dark-rimmed brown eyes. Pétion could have been a member of the current Economie community.

When the society had received the painting of Pétion in 1838, well before Boguille was a member, the minutes recorded a note from merchant Pierre Antoine Jonau "offering to the society as a gift, a portrait of fire— Alexandre Pétion—a portrait of a man whose memory is so venerable to his countrymen." All of them knew the story of Pétion, the cast-off, dark-skinned son of a white father whose success came largely through his own efforts and those of his community.

During a ceremony for the hanging of the portrait, then-president Henry Chevarre addressed the members. A veteran of the Battle of New Orleans, Chevarre told the members, "Always observe with veneration the painting of this great man who only caused tears to fall at his death. In imitation of his virtues, we likewise unite to demonstrate our indissoluble ties."

Alexandre Sabès Pétion; between 1807 and 1818; *courtesy of John Carter Brown Library, Brown University*

For the Economistes, the portrait reinforced their importance. The revolutions in France, Haiti, and America showed that a new era of equality was moving around the world. Their hall in the heart of the Tremé neighborhood in New Orleans was the culmination of social and material progress.

As the warmer summer evenings approached, Boguille watched the sun tint the frame of the new Economie hall, shading it from peach to red to purple. At night, the building's skeleton was black-black against the blue-black of the sky. After meetings, Boguille was able to pick his way home by the little globes of light from oil lamps in the neighborhood windows.

Yes, brother Economistes; here it is, a striking circumstance before us manifesting our love, our devotion, and our great willpower for the Society. . . . Never forget that it is with the practice of noble sentiments and the love of duty that the basic virtues are acquired. Then, the monument and the disciples of its cult are uniformly invigorated. . . . Who would not envy this honor, which each Economiste will secure with the gift of his pledge?

—Pierre Crocker's plea, recorded by Ludger Boguille, 1857

LUDGER TOOK CAREFUL NOTES on the night of April 15, 1857. The president told the members that the building fund was short almost $2,000. Brother Pierre Crocker, a spokesman for the finance committee, pleaded with the members to make up the shortfall. Over the course of twenty-one years, the membership had grown substantially from its original fifteen men. Boguille called the roll aloud, as the Economie rules required: forty-three members were present, and four more arrived late. The society had eighty-five members total, including seven living in France, Haiti, and Mexico.

Crocker's tone may have sounded particularly desperate because of the large difference between the costs of building and the available funds. Joseph Jean Pierre Lanna, a member of the building committee, put two dollars on the table to encourage the members to open their purses. A few followed. But Boguille noted that it was not enough.

Lanna told the members, "The society has contracted debts, they must be paid, and here is the big question!!! . . . There is no money, and how shall we manage?" The elder Economiste continued, "It is necessary to impose a few sacrifices on ourselves for a mother one loves, for a society which is admired by everyone—Well, well! These sacrifices for me, one who smokes a lot, I will smoke less or I will smoke cigars of a lesser value. You who eat a lot and like good dishes, eat as much but garnish your table less. Finally, you who are passionate about handsome clothes, diminish your wardrobe a bit, and we will be able to pay the debts of our society and see her conserve her reputation despite her detractors. Economistes, brace yourselves! I am more obdurate than you, but I will set the example, and you, Brothers, imitate the lessons."

One member stepped up to cover the immediate costs of the new building. François Boisdoré *fils*, who used the French suffix rather than "Jr." to distinguish himself from his father, promised to loan the entire sum over eighteen months. Boisdoré's father had won his suit to keep his shares in the Citizens' Bank some two decades earlier, and the family remained wealthy.

With enough funds, several members worked to finish the building in the following weeks. They were master carpenters and plasterers who carried the history of mortars in their hands. The clay used on the pyramids, the lime and sand paste of the Romans, the gypsum deposit at Montmartre, all were part of their legacy. They recited and repeated the possible combinations of ingredients to one another at leisure. They handed samples from palm to palm on their jobs to feel the consistencies. They whispered stories of shame, such as having left a fingerprint or a bubble on a wall. They bonded around this work that traversed countries, generations, and classes so that a clerk also knew the way to repair the interior corners of his house, and a businessman could erase a crack in the ceiling. The Economie men, while being the elite of the free colored community, still considered themselves brother-laborers. The president once encouraged the members to uphold the standards of a "well-bred carpenter, polite and courteous."

The Economie tradesmen worked to finish the interior of the hall as precisely as they did their homes. They laid out the boards, framed the walls, raised them, and plumbed them with the roof and the floor. They ran narrow horizontal strips of pine lath from stud to stud, then plastered it with three coats of fine, sand-like cement. Finally, they took a silk stocking and ran it across the wall with their hands to feel whether it would snag. The finish had to be smooth, like a woman's skin. Sometimes they added a medallion to the center of a ceiling, or rosettes and cornices to the room's corners. Some of their homes would stand for generations as examples of the master tradesmen's handiwork.

The Economie's building plan called for mahogany stairs placed just inside the entrance to the building, leading to the theater loges. A strong staircase represented the pinnacle of achievement in carpentry. A master could make the treads invisibly rest on the risers, then form a balustrade that followed the sweep of the stairs. Tiny holes were drilled by hand, and the wood was pegged together so that there were no squeaks when a person rose step by step. The pieces of wood became one again, as they had been in the tree.

The carefully crafted interior of the hall reflected the members' pride. As the South denigrated free men of color, they clung to a discerning image of themselves. Boguille often wrote the word *vertu* into the minutes. To have virtue in his era meant to give oneself to others. It meant fulfilling one's civic duty to care for the poor, to pay one's fair share to support the community, and to maintain one's family.

The members believed that a man who possessed virtue was the glue that held society together. The Economistes also felt that as members of a large and powerful group representing free people of color in the American South, they could affect global perceptions with their actions.

A later president told the members, "Let us prove to Europe, which has its eyes fixed on us, let us be persuaded of a very real fact—which is—that the philanthropists in this first part of the world are examining us so that they may form an opinion about us. In contemplation, they ask themselves if we really deserve the denigrating position that we occupy."

That night in July, Brother Lanna addressed the group in more perceptible terms, saying, "The achievement of our new building will not only give glory and honor to the brother-Economistes but to our class in general."

⚜

*One great cause of the declension of the free people of
color . . . arises doubtless from their greater indifference as
a class to virtuous moral restraint, attributable, in part,
to the fact of the entire free colored population coming not
very remotely from a state of slavery where but little respect
was paid to parental rights, . . . and perhaps in part to a
condition or estate which tends to depress those ambitious
aspirations which are not barren of effect in the promo-
tion of virtue. That a race forcibly transported to a state of
slavery here, from a country without history, literature, or
laws, whose people remain in barbarism, should not have
been able to attain to an equality in morals with their
intellectual superiors is not surprising.*

—*Population of the United States in 1860, Compiled from the
Original Returns of the Eighth Census*

CRITICISMS OF FREE PEOPLE of color were growing across the
nation, but in August 1857 the president of the Economie focused on their
promising future: "Gentlemen, the Société d'Economie et d'Assistance
Mutuelle, understand, is not only the arbiter of the destiny of those who
are involved now, but she is the arbiter of the destiny of our descendants.
Our pride in conserving her, to perpetuate her, must be immense. What
is it that we need, you are perhaps asking yourself?"

He answered, "You know what it is—your demeanor."

The Economistes believed that their behavior would protect them from
hate-mongering and fake science being spread throughout the South. In
1851 Samuel Cartwright—the doctor who had posited that the disease of
drapetomania induced enslaved people to run away from their owners—
was spreading the news of another affliction that he theorized affected free
Negroes. In one of the principal magazines read by planters and decision
makers in the South, *De Bow's Review*, Cartwright wrote:

Dysæsthesia Æthiopis is a disease peculiar to negroes, affecting both mind and body. . . . There is a partial insensibility of the skin, and so great a hebetude of the intellectual faculties, as to be like a person half asleep, that is with difficulty aroused and kept awake. . . . It is much more prevalent among free negroes living in clusters by themselves, than among slaves on our plantations, and attacks only such slaves as live like free negroes in regard to diet, drinks, exercise, etc. It is not my purpose to treat of the complaint as it prevails among free negroes, nearly all of whom are more or less afflicted with it, that have not got some white person to direct and to take care of them. To narrate its symptoms and effects among them would be to write a history of the ruins and dilapidation of Hayti, and every spot of earth they have ever had uncontrolled possession over for any length of time.

The widely circulated *De Bow's Review* called itself a southern journal of "Industrial Resources, Statistics, Etc., Devoted to Commerce, Agriculture, Manufactures, Internal Improvements, Education, Political Economy, General Literature, Etc.," and bore the name of a professor at the University of Louisiana, James Dunwoody Brownson De Bow, who taught in the school's department of business. In 1858 *De Bow's* published an essay, "The Model Negro Empire," which took advantage of the financial disarray after the Haitian revolution to criticize the country's current leader, Emperor Faustin Soulouque, and used him to generalize about free people of African descent. Soulouque was "cruel and superstitious, so ignorant that he is unable to write his name, and, although possessing a certain degree of shrewdness or cunning, devoid of genius or ability. One cannot fail of being forcibly reminded by him of his countrymen, the barbarian chiefs of Africa." *De Bow's* went on to discuss government bribery and favoritism, and promiscuity and superstition among the island's inhabitants, painting the nation with a wide and unsympathetic brush. "From the time of the revolution . . . the inhabitants of the Haytien empire seem to have receded with rapid strides toward barbarism and anarchy."

The *De Bow's* article made no equal accounting of the barbarism before the revolution by colonists. Nor did the article measure the effects of

Haiti's postrevolutionary status—embargos and nonrecognition by the United States, the battles of colonial powers among themselves that disrupted West Indian trade, or the debt of 150 million francs and the 50 percent discount on commercial goods that France extracted under the threat of a blockade to make the new republic pay for the loss of potential profits. Haiti also endured natural disasters like an 1843 earthquake that brought the country to its knees.

Instead, the author seized the opportunity to place the cause of the island's disruptions on the ancestry of its inhabitants: "Such is the present condition of the island of St. Domingo, or Hayti—a sad commentary upon the capacity of the negro race for progressive civilization."

Proslavery advocates began to dominate the conversation about the island, insisting that the brutality of the revolution was a result of Black people's inherent viciousness. They pointed to Haiti as evidence that slavery must be maintained.

Some northern abolitionists concurred about Haiti's intrinsic afflictions, as a way to explain to themselves the reason for the island's history of violence while still arguing in favor of the need for Black emancipation in the United States. Even Harriet Beecher Stowe in *Uncle Tom's Cabin* included a character who wished to emigrate, but not to Haiti: "The desire and yearning of my soul is for an African *nationality*. I want a people that shall have a tangible, separate existence of its own; and where am I to look for it? Not in Hayti; for in Hayti they had nothing to start with. A stream cannot rise above its fountain. The race that formed the character of the Haytiens was a worn-out, effeminate one; and, of course, the subject race will be centuries in rising to anything." His answer was to go far away from the United States, to Liberia.

Soulouque's murderous policies, the commentary in *De Bow's*, and the pictures being painted of Haitians in periodicals across the United States were painful to the children of Saint Domingue immigrants, who—like Boguille's father—had envisioned a revolution that would produce equality. That goal now seemed far from realization in Haiti, but still possible in America.

"Freedom to Africa"; by Hammatt Billings; from *Uncle Tom's Cabin*; 1853;
THNOC, 85-363-RL

RESTRICTIVE LAWS INCREASED THROUGHOUT the 1850s in New
Orleans and around the state. The goal was clear—to remove free Blacks
from their livelihoods, from their social standing, and from Louisiana, all
while aiding the system of plantation slavery.

Cartwright had claimed in 1851 that "*the negro is not a white man painted
black*" but "a different being, of a different nature; and affected in directly
opposite directions from the white man by the things called liberty and
slavery."

Cartwright wrote an open letter to Daniel Webster, the US secretary
of state, which was published in *De Bow's Review* and excerpted in the
Concordia Intelligencer newspaper of Vidalia, Louisiana, emphasizing that a
Negro was "a slave by Nature." He added, "Thirty-three years of observation
and experience in the treatment of diseases in the cotton and sugar region,
have enabled me to generalize facts, and to discover the important truth,
not less important in a political than in a medical point of view, that . . .
Nature has ordained that the negro shall serve the white man, and the
white man shall take care of the negro."

And the federal government abetted the enslavers. In 1850 Congress passed the Fugitive Slave Act, which said the enslaved who escaped to a free state could be returned in chains to a slave state. Besides valuing property over humanity, the law was greatly misused. Some free men were kidnapped, brought to the South, and suffered the same fate as the enslaved had for generations. Among them was Solomon Northup, who was lured from his home in New York with the promise of work in Washington, DC, where he was drugged, kidnapped, and shipped to Louisiana. Sold at a New Orleans auction, he labored for twelve years on a plantation before being rescued.

In New Orleans, European immigrants replaced free colored men as hotel staff, cabdrivers, and river pilots. Soon, laws would bar them from owning coffeehouses or stores that sold liquor. In 1855 the Louisiana legislature approved Act No. 308, governing the treatment and rights of enslaved and free people. Its one hundred sections included restrictions on travel and the right to carry weapons, among other measures.

Additional laws required free Blacks to prove their status and to keep papers in their pockets at all times showing they were not enslaved. It was the legislature's attempt to bring free men like the Economistes one step nearer to the status of the enslaved, who had to show permission notes from their masters to any white person who asked whenever they went out on the streets.

Now, when Boguille left his home, he folded thick sheets of records and put them awkwardly in his vest pocket. He had the proof of his freedom in his parents' marriage contract, any number of papers addressed to him from his Supreme Court suits, and the births and baptisms of his children. Without this proof, the police could take him to jail and impose a fine or even a prison sentence.

THE ECONOMIE INCREASINGLY OCCUPIED a strange no-man's-land in the fight that was brewing between the slave and free states. Emotions flamed higher with the ongoing battles in the Kansas Territory. Both sides fought violently to sway the voters toward creating a free or slave state. In May 1856 advocates for slavery, including a sheriff, looted and burned the free-state stronghold of Lawrence, Kansas, and killed one man. The response was swift. John Brown, a northern abolitionist, led a raid on a proslavery area in nearby Pottawatomie a few days later and murdered five settlers. Brown had grown weary of lip service to emancipation and decided that violence was the solution. In 1859 he led a failed attack on an army arsenal in Harpers Ferry, Virginia, focusing the nation's attention on the slavery question.

The battles in Kansas rekindled white fears in Louisiana, spurred by the vilification of Haiti and its people. The island's bloodshed remained a vivid image in the minds of Americans. The belief persisted among southerners that instigators such as the Haitian revolutionaries would enrage enslaved people, leading them to slit the throats of whites. "The St. Domingo negro has never taken a place among civilized nations; he has only relapsed into barbarism," the author of *The Relation between the Races at the South* wrote in 1861.

In January 1857 Louisiana governor Robert Wickliffe had asked the legislature for a resolution to remove free Negroes from the state because "their association and example has a most pernicious effect on our slave population." He characterized free people of color as "a source of great evil."

The local newspapers reported similar resolutions across the nation. From Oregon to Missouri to Maryland, politicians proposed laws that would bar free Negroes from entering or remaining in their states.

These fears took a toll on free people of color in New Orleans. Hostilities had deepened with the competition for employment between free Blacks and immigrants. The Irish streamed through the port of New Orleans, fleeing the famine of the 1840s. Germans joined them in droves after political revolutions in the same decade. By 1850 immigrants made up more than 40 percent of the city's population. For every enslaved person Boguille passed on the street, there were three people born abroad.

When the foreign poor began to compete for jobs with free Blacks, race added fuel to the fire. Skin color, hair texture, and "scientific" distinctions were cited as evidence that the white newcomers were more deserving of work. And now, with their economic instability exploited by white elites, poor European immigrants embraced a racialized sense of American identity, including the notion that social mobility was possible for them but not for people of African descent.

In the taverns, barely literate whites read the daily newspapers aloud to illiterate others. The message: that a free Black was dangerous. An article in the *Daily Picayune* said that any emancipated person should be required to leave Louisiana or face reenslavement: "The community has a right to protect itself. If the debauchery, drunkenness, insolence, violence, or tampering with slaves by free blacks, producing insubordination or discontent among them, endangers the public, there can be no doubt of the right or the propriety of placing the offenders under the restraints of masters, or ridding the State of their presence." While noting that some free people of color owned property and followed the law, the paper added, "Unfortunately this is not, however, the character of all. The rising generation are gradually falling into the vices and corruptions by which the more degraded of the white race are characterized. The evil from the commingling of our slaves and free blacks is one of the future."

Boguille saw the newspapers increasingly refer to the Black population in derogatory terms. Over his morning coffee, he read about "free nigger-dom" in the *Daily Picayune*. When his Economie brothers leaned back in their chairs, arranged outside their barbershops and tailoring businesses, they saw themselves ridiculed in the papers as "genmen of color," or "culled persons." A feature story in the *Daily True Delta* told the story of young brides in New York who were deceived by tan-skinned men passing for foreign gentlemen: "A lot of Creoles, and Spaniards, and Cubans, visit our seaboard cities each year, who represent themselves to be men of rank." The paper explained that the groom's father would frequently turn out to be a "woolly head" and his mother would have a "burnt umber complexion, and the amiable style of grin which made so expressive the features of Barnum's baboon."

Now more than ever, the Economistes felt the pressure to rise above the vulgar hordes.

Slander is terribly cruel, and it unhappily has too many echoes.

—Economie Minutes, 1857

HE ECONOMIE MEN WERE not perfect. Boguille had been a widower for five years when he developed an intimate relationship with Marie Françoise Filliette. She was married, with children, and living with a husband who may have been ill. The lovers were not matched in social class, but the people of New Orleans were known for crossing status boundaries at food markets, shops, and other gathering places. They may have met through her work as a washerwoman.

Filliette had an especially difficult job in the years when the cost of fine fabrics made clothes an investment. Laundresses were integral to the process of preservation. They carefully cleaned clothes by hand in tubs, scrubbing the fabric against ribbed washboards with soap. The work required a delicate balance between removing spots and rubbing so hard that the garment tore. The women loaded the clothes into rinse tubs of boiling water. Then, after removing them to cool, they wrung out every article separately. Their muscles knotted under the skin of their arms like wrestlers'.

Maybe Boguille admired Filliette's strength. Or maybe he was afraid of death. Etienne Ludger was gone. So was Andrénette. His younger brother Jean Guillaume lingered in illness before dying in March 1852 at the age of twenty-five. Either by choice or accident, Boguille and Filliette had created a new life. Their daughter arrived on June 5, 1852.

Boguille's usual symbolic naming of children may betray some misgiving. Therese Antoinette bore a name that evoked two tragic figures: Marie Antoinette, the queen of France, and her daughter Marie-Thérèse. The queen was rumored to have said after first seeing her newborn, "Poor little girl, you are not what was desired, but you are no less dear to me on that account." Marie Antoinette referred to her daughter's gender. Boguille was, perhaps, reflecting on the circumstances of Therese Antoinette's birth. His daughter was born out of wedlock to a married woman with whom he was having an affair. The melodramatic Boguille may have named the girl based on his feelings at the time of her birth, like those who knowingly call a child Tristan, meaning sadness, or Dolores, for Our Lady of Sorrows. Or maybe, with Antoinette, Boguille was recalling his dead wife Andrénette. Despite the child's legal name, Filliette called her Angela, a name with more optimistic and heavenly allusions.

Boguille had another reason to regret the affair. By 1849 he had met a woman with whom he had more in common. Mary Ann Taff was an English teacher who had come from New York to work in the free colored community. They may have connected through their love of literature. Mary Ann and Ludger would both have known Swift's *Gulliver's Travels*, in which a man is taken to regions where the people are too small, too greedy, or too evil for him to stay. Perhaps they laughed at the running metaphors in Swift's attack on English aristocrats. Mary Ann would have explained to Ludger that in literature, she saw echoes of the fates of the common man. Ludger would have listened to her accounts and agreed, at least partly because of the messenger's charms.

Mary Ann was not even thirty when he met her. Like the women of her day, she wore a dress with a wide skirt and a lacy, decorative neckline. Ludger could imagine the soft indentation of her clavicle and the rise of her shoulders. Her chest swelled over her tight-corseted waist when she laughed. She was ten years his junior.

Row of Passebon's cottages on Esplanade Avenue; 1844; by Louis Surgi; *courtesy of Hon. Chelsey Richard Napoleon, Clerk of Civil District Court, Parish of Orleans*

By 1851 Mary Ann was teaching at Ludger's school while he was also teaching at the Couvent School, less than a block away. Perhaps they took their breaks together and discussed their laziest pupils, shaking their heads.

Independent and literate, Mary Ann was Ludger's soul mate. But she was also white. They could not marry, according to the law. So they began to live together.

He and Mary Ann were in the same home when the federal census takers came around in 1849, but they did not use the same surname. They were raising Ludger and Andrénette's children, Suzette, Fénelon, Florian, and Jean Hortaire. They also took into their home two minor children, Alida and Zephir Canonge, whose relatives may have been from Saint Domingue.

Mary Ann and Ludger were listed as teachers with the same last name, Boguille, in the 1851 city directory. They stayed at the address 265–267 Esplanade Street from 1852 until 1856.

Their first child together, born in 1857, was named Pierre Butel, for Ludger's mother. The next, two years later, was Jean Horace, named for the Roman poet. In 1861 the family moved down the street to a single house.

The location of the new Boguille home at 198 Esplanade Street was important for many reasons. Having been generously widened, the street offered prestige. The arms of protective shade trees lined the pedestrian passageway and afforded an aura of romance. The house placed Boguille in a more bucolic setting, which he loved, close to white crape myrtles, fat banana tree clusters, and wildflowers of every description. Most important, his home sat next to a new development of cottages built expressly for free people by Pierre Passebon, which were advertised on a poster with a color illustration showing dark-skinned children playing freely and Black militiamen marching in formation nearby. Three women with different skin tones lingered in a doorway, at a window, and on a sidewalk. Two were visibly shaded to show their Negro blood. One was as white as Boguille's new wife, Mary Ann. The illustration showed that their family was welcome.

The Boguilles carried furniture, clothes, books, and everything else into a house that sat urbanely against a brick sidewalk on a block with gaslights at the corner. Their new home was a long, narrow, detached house with a large yard for the children.

With so many youngsters to tutor at home, Boguille would have brought them the same lessons he imparted daily at school—French and philosophy, and history with ethics. He also would have carried home some of the daily papers in French and English, so that the children could learn both languages. As they read the news, much of it negative information about people like them, his students would have seen the world that they were facing.

His real problem was how to prepare the youth—his own and the other children at school—to be as knowledgeable as possible yet equally humble, and to read deeply and critically. They could not, however, believe the descriptions of themselves, which took any one of their flaws, magnified it, and attached it to race.

This was one reason that Boguille, with his house full of children and legions of free colored students, put his faith in the Economie. The society hoped to become "the arbiter of the destiny of those who are part of it and the arbiter of the destiny of our great nephews."

The new family home was exactly two streets from the Economie's hall. From then until nearly the end of his life, Boguille never moved any farther from the society's headquarters.

*Do not offer fodder to our oppressors who say in their
legislation that we are of a race too inferior and incapable
of doing anything that tends to the good.*

—Economie president Pierre Casanave, 1857

IN 1857 THE AMERICAN Colonization Society prepared a twenty-three-page pamphlet for the Louisiana state legislature to encourage free Blacks to leave America for Liberia, purportedly for their own benefit.

The increased pressure on free people of color to get out of the South or face more restrictions affected the Economie members. The minutes of their meetings conveyed their anxieties. When the construction of the society's hall was behind schedule in 1857, the members began to threaten the contractor—and fellow Economie brother—William Belley with nonpayment. Boguille wrote into the minutes that some men in the society said they wanted to charge Belley five dollars for every day he was late, while he complained that he did not have enough funds to finish the job.

Former society president Pierre Crocker felt empathy for the contractor: "I am forced to say that whatever we have been preaching, I do not see brotherhood in the people of the building committee."

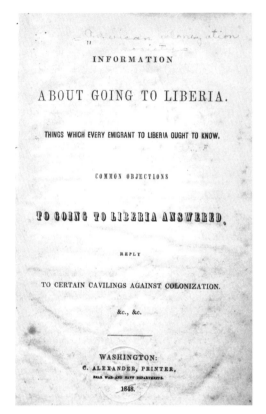

Information about Going to Liberia: Things Which Every Emigrant to Liberia Ought to Know; by American Colonization Society; 1848; *courtesy of Library of Congress, Rare Book and Special Collections Division, Joseph Meredith Toner Collection*

Secretary Boguille wrote that another Economie member "showed wisdom" in his reply: "Lanna rises and gravely says that the society had contracted Belley, within the family." He sought a compromise between the society and one of its brothers.

Crocker agreed with Lanna's interpretation of their situation and complimented himself on his explanation of the problem, "I have fifty-six years in my head, and I know what I'm saying."

Boguille noted with a wry editorial commentary on Crocker's judgement that the cool-headed Lanna had some doubt about the "wisdom of the petitioners," but Lanna nevertheless convinced the Economistes to give Belley $1,000 in installments of $400 and $600 to finish the hall.

Tempers flared again at a meeting three months later, during a disagreement about a prospective member. Boguille wrote meticulous notes about the society's desire to admit a poor but honorable young man into its ranks.

Lanna said about carpenter Philippe Duclos-Lange, "My brothers, if ever man is as he should be, it is Mr. Duclos-Lange. . . . I have good recollections of both his friendship and his good behavior! Yes, the acceptance of such a man as an Economiste can only consolidate our association!"

The minutes noted, however, that Duclos-Lange was not accepted for membership because of a rumor about his character that Boguille didn't record. The Economie brothers were more skittish now than ever about the way they were perceived by the outside world.

Brother François Porée, a former soldier in the Battle of New Orleans, was outraged: "What is this, my brothers? You cannot recommend the petitioner! My God! Lord! A young man who has attained his majority barely six months ago, who has done nothing wrong in the springtime of his life, who has been neither assassin nor thief! Eh! You cannot recommend him? . . . Ah! I don't understand anything anymore! . . . Fraternity doesn't exist anymore!"

Boguille noted that "Brother Porée, so pained, in sitting down, fainted as with an apoplectic attack."

Porée brought up Duclos-Lange's name again six weeks later, and Lanna pleaded the young man's case. "He has no children, but he protects orphans, shelters them under his roof, and gives them all the help possible. But does this humanitarian action attract the attention of the Economistes? Not at all! The philanthropic life of Duclos is enough, more than enough to plead the case of one who does good without ostentation, but by devotion and inclination.

"It is not long ago that we rejected the request of this worthy and excellent man who desires to be an Economiste—not only to bear the title, but to contribute, enrich, and participate in the beautiful and fraternal association we have founded!! See what flagrant injustice! . . . Economistes! Brother Porée asks an electoral reconsideration! I beg of you, my brothers, this time show yourselves more conciliatory, more the friends of order, more philanthropist. In a word, do for him what others have done for you!"

Duclos-Lange was rejected again.

Lanna complained, "When you push away an honest man from your bosom, you bring on yourselves the blame of all men of means, and you cause all the Economistes to be passed under severe examination, for people tell each other, 'They are rejecting petitioners who are a lot better than certain members!' These words do not come from me; it is the expression of common people—the *vulgaire*. Well, well! My brothers, you are bringing on the Société d'Economie, which is already not too loved, as many enemies as you have hairs on your head!!" Boguille wrote that so many members agreed with Lanna's description that he could not continue talking because of "the frenetic applause, the scandalous noise, the shouts, the tintinnabulation—all that creates a symphony that the deafest would suffer from."

In the week after that meeting, François Porée's relative and fellow member Médard Porée saw one of Duclos-Lange's detractors on the street and swung his cane, hitting member Joseph Colastin Rousseau in the face. The cane made a bruise. At the next meeting, the Economie president forced the men to stand and discuss the argument. The victim gave Médard a lecture about brotherhood:

> It is a vulgar spirit if . . . we were unhappy or unfortunate enough to call extreme passions to our aid and then to let ourselves be dominated by anger, that passion so violent that annuls everything that is good and moral in our humble organization. . . . Therefore, my dear brother Médard Porée, you who are brave, you who have a reputation for being boisterous and chivalrous, which is well deserved . . . you must not have any fear of being accused of cowardice, in giving yourself over to what I am about to propose: I strongly blame you for getting carried away against me last Saturday, and without wishing to repeat the injurious and vexing remarks that you threw in your exasperation against all those who were not like you, on the election. . . . I am before you, my cheek still bruised from . . . your Malacca cane. I stand before you, . . . presenting to you the olive branch of peace in one hand and the cypress in the other, that emblem that symbolizes our fraternity. . . . Come, give me your hand, everything has been said between us, and the public—which by your fault has witnessed the events—instead of rubbing its hands together in glee, will learn to the contrary that if the Economistes call themselves brothers, it is not to devour each other, but truly to be real brothers!

Porée stood and listened. Boguille recorded in the minutes that the perpetrator then responded contritely and with great emotion, "No, it is not my hand I wish to give you. It is in my arms that I must receive you, for I admit that I was wrong!" The men gave each other a hug with such fervor that Boguille wrote, "Two hearts formed but one."

In a move demonstrating both the triumph of violence and the need for reconciliation, the members voted the same night to accept Duclos-Lange into the society.

The brothers experienced more stress on March 14, 1857, when the *New Orleans Bee* reported the United States Supreme Court's decision in the Dred Scott case. Scott, an enslaved man who had lived with his master for a time in a free state, attempted to sue his owner to avoid being returned to bondage. The decision of the court, delivered by Chief Justice Roger B. Taney, rejected the idea that an enslaved person could be freed merely by residing north of the Mason-Dixon Line. He asserted that because Scott was enslaved, he had no rights. Taney's opinion reached further, however, saying that the federal government protected citizens' rights, but, as the *Bee* reported, "Negroes, whether slaves or free—that is, men of the African race—are not citizens of the United States by the Constitution." The article concluded that the court's opinion "will exert the most powerful and salutary influence throughout the United States." The news appeared in the French edition of the paper two days after it was reported in the English edition.

For years, society members had picked up the newspapers and read daily about new assaults against their community. Over their black coffee and hot calas breakfasts, they saw their kinsmen and neighbors ridiculed, but they tried to stay strong. The older members put their hands on the younger men's shoulders, looked them in the eyes, and encouraged them to keep their opinions private. Walk away from arguments, they advised one another on the streets. In the coffeehouses, they lectured their brothers to remain virtuous, lest their actions validate any of the damaging caricatures of their community. The younger men promised that they would not curse in response to public slurs. They would not allow their tempers to call attention to their opinions.

But seeing the article in their native language, the Economie men would have lowered their newspapers and examined their businesses, customers, and friends walking on the streets of the city they loved. They looked at their surroundings with bitter resignation. Neither hard work nor hope was enough in this nation.

Ad for a pamphlet containing the Dred Scott Supreme Court decision and Dr. Samuel A. Cartwright's essay "Natural History of the Prognathous Race of Mankind"; from *Harper's Weekly*, July 23, 1859; *THNOC, 79-55-L*

*The men who framed [the Declaration of Independence]
were great men—high in literary acquirements—high
in their sense of honor. . . . They perfectly understood the
meaning of the language they used, and how it would be
understood by others; and they knew that it would not in
any part of the civilized world be supposed to embrace the
Negro race, which, by common consent, had been excluded
from civilized Governments and the family of nations,
and doomed to slavery . . . . The unhappy black race were
separated from the white by indelible marks, and laws long
before established, and were never thought of or spoken of
except as property.*

—Supreme Court of the United States,
Dred Scott v. Sandford, March 1857

BOGUILLE HAD BEEN METICULOUSLY taking the Economie minutes as usual during a March 1857 meeting, noting the installation of officers, the naming of new committees, the collection of late dues and fees, when he inserted the charged phrase *police durant la séance*—police during the session.

On either side Boguille drew horizontal lines like dashes to frame the phrase without further explanation. After that, the minutes resume as usual, with preparations for the next meeting, reports from the contractor, more business, and the adjournment. Again, at the next meeting, Boguille noted, *police durant les travaux*—police during the proceedings—knowing that no outsider could be sure what the ambiguous phrase meant. Idiomatically, the phrases could mean that policies or insurance payments were being entered into the ledger, as an accounting of funds sometimes followed. But in a literal translation, the phrases could mean that the Economie was being monitored, and the police had entered the room.

"Police durant la séance," noted in Economie minutes, March 6, 1857; *courtesy of Fatima Shaik*

Additionally, on some occasions, Boguille signified that immediately after the moment he injected the phrases into the minutes, some members—anywhere from a few men to a half dozen—got up and asked for permission to leave. For more than twenty years, the minutes had noted only those present, absent, or late. Now Boguille noted the early departures, without further comment, which was his own way of saying something important. He must have hoped that the people who mattered—his own Economie brothers and their posterity—would understand his encryptions and realize that the members were under surveillance.

Boguille began to put these ambiguous phrases into the minutes only a month after police broke up a meeting of Masons and jailed a group of free men of color and enslaved men for gathering illegally. As punishment, the freemen needed to pay a fine of twenty-five dollars each, and a judge ordered the enslaved men to be beaten.

The writer Rodolphe Desdunes was a boy in the free colored community of New Orleans during those years. He explained decades later in *Our People and Our History* that at that time, "any free black man who possessed wealth and the respect of his peers was the sure target of arrest, ill treatment, and imprisonment, according to the caprice of the most depraved police officers or of denunciation by the most despicable residents of the city."

As a witness to this era when police and whites terrorized the community, Boguille struggled to conceal his passionate views about liberty, for his own safety and that of his brothers. Boguille's notes expressed the Economistes' condition in code. The minutes were written with great clarity and detail when Boguille wanted posterity to know about their actions.

The humiliations seemed to mount every day.

IN THE SOCIETY'S MINUTES every week, Boguille noted the names of members who lived and traveled abroad: Etienne Cordeviolle, Pierre Antoine Jonau, A. Montfort, Medélice Thomas, and François Lacroix were in France, Haiti, and Mexico, where they walked the avenues with confidence and carried on business without restrictions. They returned to New Orleans after a few months or years. Most important, they returned with books for the Economie library—treatises on history, philosophy, language, and law. The travelers' stories and books brought the local members into a wider world.

On March 20, 1857, Alfred Noel and Joseph Abélard gave each other the fraternal accolade, the Economie's symbol of friendship, in front of the membership. A few days later, Noel boarded a ship for Mexico.

In May 1857 Brother Prosper Avril, who had been living in Mexico, returned briefly to New Orleans. His arrival defied the new Louisiana law that said no person of color who left the state could return. Stealthily, Avril disembarked and went to his house. The night he entered the hall, the men stood and applauded. Avril saluted the members and told them about his life in Veracruz—a life to which he soon would return. How could they fail to consider their own expatriation?

By June 1857 Brother Mortimer Débergue was in Mexico. So was Brother Eugène Chessé. He had met "an unfortunate Mexican named José Sanchez y Perez." Boguille had read a letter aloud in the hall in which Chessé asked the men to show their generosity to Perez. The members passed the plate and collected eight dollars. Several brothers, having no money with them, asked if they might have until the next meeting before the money was given to Perez, so they could assist with the charitable work. They sent $12.50 in total, finding in another country the brotherhood that they didn't find in the United States.

Despite the founders' devotion to New Orleans and the new hall under construction, the men of the Economie sought escape.

Brother Fouché presents a portrait of President Comonfort, sent by his son L. Nelson Fouché to the Société d'Economie as a precious gift of his love, of his esteem, and of his friendship.

—Economie Minutes, 1857

ℒOUIS NELSON FOUCHÉ, son of Nelson Fouché, departed from the harbor of New Orleans, which saw ships from all parts of the world. Men carried heavy Parisian furniture down the gangplanks, carted away trunks of Chinese silks, and hoisted bales of cotton from the wooden docks to the schooners bound for English factories. Sailors mopped the decks, afterward sloshing buckets of water down the sides of the vessels and into the river.

Nearby, in the market, people from every nation thronged the fruit and vegetable stands. Using French dialects from Europe and Haiti, women haggled over food prices. Germans pushed carts. Mexicans, South Americans, and Spaniards strolled under the breezeway. Choctaw from across Lake Pontchartrain displayed baskets for sale on the warm sidewalks. Women of all colors promenaded near the St. Louis Cathedral after Mass. Their dresses were bouffant at the hips and tight in the waist. They held the arms of men in top hats. Free people of color from Louisiana threaded through the crowd like everyone else, with seeming equality—but without the rights of any white person standing next to them.

Fouché would have watched the familiar scene until a horn wailed to indicate time of departure. He approached the steamer, ascended the gangplank, and stood against the aft railing. Then the ship, like a lumbering elephant, turned, pushing against the river's swells. Its pilot found the deep channel of the Mississippi River. The vessel picked up speed and was off.

The trip to Veracruz took just over three days by steamer, but Fouché's mission for his brother Economistes would lay the groundwork for generations of expatriates.

THE FOUCHÉS WERE WELL suited, by occupation, to create a settlement. The son was an architect, and Nelson Fouché was a builder who had designed and constructed many homes. He drew plans for Creole cottages that his friends could build. The men required no more than a day to put up the crossbeams and frame the rooms. They could lath and plaster the walls in about two more days, but then the finishing job took weeks of cigars, drinks, and long conversations. Their camaraderie was the most important form of support for the homeowner.

The men of the Economie community were so close that if some considered moving to Mexico, most all would go, so they could maintain the brotherhood they had created over the past twenty years. A life like the one they enjoyed in New Orleans could be built in Veracruz, with one important exception: there was no slavery.

Louis Nelson Fouché and other young men like him began to distinguish themselves from their fathers on the issue of slavery. The first generation of Economistes felt that they could own people as long as they were fair to the families and manumitted them at will. The second generation did not want to participate.

By midcentury, because of the 1808 ban on importing Africans, most enslaved people were born in the United States. It was only their bad luck to be born with the status of slave instead of free, as Louis was. They were sold from owner to owner and taken from state to state, torn from their relatives without any regard for their attachments.

Some people in New Orleans tried to protect enslaved families—most often, their own relatives. While they made up 7 percent of the New Orleans population, free people of color filed half of the petitions in the courts to free enslaved individuals. Economie member Doresmond Crocker went to court in 1848 to rescue four of his nephews who should have been freed in 1836, five years after their owner's death, yet were still in the hands of his executor. Crocker was able to locate three of the young men, but the fourth had been kidnapped by a new master and shipped upriver, never to be found.

If the enslaved went to Mexico with their enslavers, however, they would be emancipated from an unjust system. The task fell to Louis to travel to Mexico and create a home for them all.

That was the plan. It stayed out of the Economie minutes for a long time.

IT WENT UNWRITTEN, PERHAPS, because Louis Nelson Fouché had entered a tumultuous Mexican republic.

After Mexico abolished slavery in 1829, its government cracked down on American enslavers in the Mexican province of Texas. Americans such as Jim Bowie, a slasher and brawler so brutal that a sharp-edged knife was named for him, joined the Texas War Party and fought the Mexican general Antonio López de Santa Anna when he tried to oust the intruders. Bowie did bloody work—shooting cannons and muskets at Mexicans on horseback as they stormed American fortifications. Neither laws nor violence stopped him. Bowie took an oath of allegiance to Mexico when he first entered the country, then returned to the United States when it was profitable. He grew up on a plantation and engaged in illegal slave trading as a youth, and to American enslavers who wanted to expand into Mexican territory, Bowie was a hero.

Santa Anna was Bowie's moral equivalent. Born in Veracruz, he first fought against Mexican independence from Spain and then for it. He became president by defeating the previous dictator with the help of General Ignacio Comonfort. Santa Anna then proved himself to be dictator, double-dealer, and gambler. Comonfort was disgusted and overthrew the man he had once regarded as a hero.

When Comonfort became president of the Republic of Mexico in 1856, he declared all citizens equal under the law. This meant, among other changes, that members of the powerful Catholic clergy had to sell their unoccupied houses and land so that poor people could have a share of the wealth.

The Proprietors of the Hacienda of the Brotherhood of St. Peter had told Fouché that if he brought one hundred colored families to Mexico over the next two years, they would give him 2,500 acres in Veracruz to cultivate and raise cattle. Unlike Americans, Mexicans appeared to welcome African descendants.

Boguille may have imagined that the Economistes would leave New Orleans the way the Israelites left Egypt, with all their worldly belongings. Wagons would haul their thick-hewn wooden boxes, reused barrels, and leather-covered steamer trunks to the dock. Instead of crossing the desert, the Economistes would cross the flat, blue Gulf of Mexico. They would stand on board the ship taking them to Veracruz and watch the United States vanish.

ON THE NIGHT OF JULY 8, 1857, Boguille watched his brother Economistes file into the building. Their relief was apparent when they entered the foyer. They undid their ties and opened their shirt collars and proceeded into the large meeting room.

After the president called the meeting to order, Boguille read aloud the membership roll and the previous minutes. Then Louis Nelson Fouché's father stepped up to the podium. He faced the eighty-two members seated in wooden chairs. Boguille could feel the excitement in the room. The members stared attentively at the podium. It was yellow fever season, midsummer, but they had gathered despite the fear of increased contagion in public places.

The hall was steamy, even with open windows. The new building was under construction, and the smell of cypress sawdust filled the air. The men had raised money by giving parties, had drawn down their personal savings accounts, and had even skimped on expenses for their children to pay the increased dues for construction. They had brought their hammers and

Ignacio Comonfort; *courtesy of Library of Congress, Prints and Photographs Division*

spent their off days doing finishing work. Their daughters sewed curtains. The men had met on the same block on Ursulines Street for twenty-one years, but they would abandon the new hall and all of this if they could arrange to emigrate together. They had become like a family, so Fouché's news mattered. The floor trembled slightly as he took the podium.

Fouché spoke excitedly: "My son, an Economiste for eight months, is working hard to found a colony in Mexico, which must be—better said—which will be our *patrie*." The men broke into applause for their new fatherland.

Then Fouché unveiled a gift for the Economie's president. It was a portrait of Comonfort, the president of Mexico, who was working on the agreement with Fouché's son.

In the dim light, the men studied the picture. Comonfort was tan, with a receding hairline and a soft widow's peak. His thick mustache almost met the whiskers on his jaw and dark beard on his chin. Above his round cheeks were dark, melancholy eyes. In sum, Comonfort looked like many of the Economy brothers. And Comonfort wanted them.

All of the Economistes could go to Veracruz and raise their families. In the agreement being worked out, Article 5 said, "The colonists, being foreign nationals, will be considered Mexican citizens." They would attain more rights as a result of young Fouché's brief visit than they had after more than a century in Louisiana: in Mexico they would be able to vote and hold public office.

Economie president Pierre Casanave then addressed the members, saying, "My brothers, I ask that Brother Fouché transmits for us our thanks to Monsieur, his son, for his magnificent present that he has given us by sending the portrait of this great man Comonfort. Our admiration for this great liberator must be the same as the one we have for the immortal Pétion! And God willing, for the Mexican nation, and for us, who seek a homeland."

Lanna then took the floor: "Long ago when we were in the old hall, I spilled tears when I learned that we were moving. We also had in our old hall the immortal Pétion, the father of our nation, like Washington. They upheld the principles of liberty, patriotism, good works, universal democracy. My brothers, it is in this society that one finds these admirable qualities that I have just named."

Assured that they could escape the oppression of Louisiana and still remain together, men left the Economie hall that night with lighter steps. At home, they cuddled with their wives in bed and told them the good news. At the breakfast table the next morning, they described the picture of Comonfort to their children. They worked for weeks with smiles on their faces, despite the atmosphere of insults all around them.

Soon a local publishing house printed copies of the contract between the president of Mexico and Louis Nelson Fouché, and it was distributed among the members. At night they read the booklets by candlelight, putting the contracts safely away before they climbed into bed. They could not sleep as their minds danced with images of boarding a ship that would take them, their children, and their grandchildren into the future.

Let us prove, say I to the entire world, that we do not deserve to be diminished by this senseless prejudice that seeks to demoralize us.

—Pierre Casanave, Economie president, 1858

OME OF THE ECONOMIE men did not adapt well to the idea of leaving or to the difficulties of the era. The summer of 1857 had witnessed arguments over new members, the demeanor of the brothers, and the strength of both their building and their bonds.

Pierre Crocker came to the meeting of July 1 in an agitated state. He may have been drinking. His reckless abandon showed when he challenged Pierre Casanave, the society's president, who had fined a member one *piastre* for having talked incessantly in an earlier gathering. Casanave responded by asking Boguille to read out loud the articles in the society's constitution that gave him the authority to levy the fine. After Boguille read the applicable parts, he patted himself on the back in an addendum: "The reading of these articles . . . has done well for the assembly."

Boguille noted in his beautiful script that Crocker was hostile: "I don't see that you should have any articles read. Really . . . you have the gavel, and . . . must strike those who disobey.'"

Boguille might have exhibited more sympathy if he had known that Crocker was as upset with himself as he was with his Economie brothers. In meetings, Crocker asked for money to build the hall, but in his private life, he was borrowing funds he could not pay back. As chair of the finance committee, he was ashamed of his own conduct. It was also incomprehensible that he could be so fallible. He had been the first president of the society, and he ran a brokerage at 65 Exchange Place, the Wall Street of New Orleans.

The street had been cut through the center of the block between two major thoroughfares so that people could carry cash safely between the banks and the St. Louis Hotel rotunda—the site of auctions of everything from household goods to real estate to enslaved human beings. Exchange Alley, as local people called the street, operated at a fever pitch. Crocker's commercial neighbors included attorneys, teachers, real estate agents, printers, and booksellers. One business in the alley that called itself a "loan office" operated like a pawnbroker, advertising "Money—Money—Money" in exchange for watches, diamonds, silverware, pistols, and guns.

Commerce bustled throughout the city. One newspaper printed an advertising supplement that offered "Agricultural Implements"—barrel-making machines, straw cutters, corn mills, engines and boilers, drills and pumps. A lumberyard sold white pine, cypress, and juniper, plus boards cut for flooring and shelving. Trade in luxury goods increased because of the desire for the grander lifestyles of planters and others who profited from the slave-based economy. Specialized emporiums sold songbirds to enliven a household. Liquor stores imported fine brandy, whiskey, and champagne for well-heeled customers. There was "antephelic milk" to remove wrinkles, and a "Medicine Warehouse" that offered hair dyes, pills, cosmetics, ointments, oils, soaps, and creams. New York importers Bruff, Brother, and Seaver sold oval-eye cotton hoes, axes, cane knives, scythes, and guns made in England, Germany, and France. Crocker worked in the center of this whirlwind. He should have known better.

At the real estate exchange on Saturdays, there were at least fifteen auctioneers, pointing to the watercolor posters of houses displayed on walls and, as a newspaper reported, calling out "the bids in a rapid pace, their voices pitched to the highest key and often using several of the most popular modern languages as the occasion may seem to require—all talking at once like firemen at a conflagration." Crocker had recently brokered the sale of a house for $1,880, and he had a long history in real estate. In the 1830s he had handled eleven real estate transactions, including the Economie's acquisition of its first meeting hall.

On the issue of an insignificant parliamentary procedure on the night of July 1, however, Crocker continued to argue. He spoke louder, Boguille wrote, "with more heat and screams at the top of his voice." The president begged him to be quiet.

"No," Crocker said. "I am asking for the right to speak."

The president said, "It is impossible to give you that right."

Boguille wrote in the minutes, "Fined $2."

Crocker began shouting at the president and the vice president. If only he had told them that his trouble was personal.

Boguille wrote, "Ah, ah, ah . . . The noise and the confusion are so loud that the secretary is obliged to drop his plume and scream, 'It's a real *tohu-bohu*!'"

Confusion abounded. Crocker picked up his hat and began to leave the meeting. The president fined him five dollars and said there should be a rule in the constitution that could put him out of the society.

"Fine me $50," Crocker said. Boguille wrote, "He pronounces the word F . . . . . , of which the secretary is taking away five letters of that nice word." Perhaps Crocker blurted out his insult in English, but he probably used the French term *foutre*.

The members returned Crocker's curse, but Boguille tried to maintain some semblance of decorum. He wrote that the members, "indignant about this lack of propriety and disarray, start[ed] to make extreme propositions at Crocker." Then Crocker walked out the door.

"For twenty-one years and four months," Boguille added as an editorial, "this society has occupied this hall, and it is painful that today, the last day that we are meeting here, one of the founders be so lacking in respect by deranging the order of the deliberations. This scandalous scene is happily at an end, and the end of the meeting is more tranquil. Pray to heaven that this is never going to happen again!!!"

With relief, the vice president moved to a new subject. He asked the members to meet punctually at eight o'clock on the following Sunday morning to carry the furniture and books of the society into the new hall across the street.

After the tension in the hall, some members became anxious over the impending move. Boguille wrote as the final entry of that night's minutes, "There is some discussion about the strength of the building, which is assured."

IN THE DAYS THAT followed his outburst at the meeting, the members of the Economie received a letter of apology from Crocker. Boguille read it aloud at the next week's gathering:

> To the president and members of the Société d'Economie et d'Assistance Mutuelle:
>
> My brothers, please believe that I have lacked the dignity of the society in a moment of anger. I pray, my brothers, that you excuse me. Please believe that I will always be with you, for the success and prosperity of the society.
>
> I am, with respect, your devoted brother, Pierre Crocker.

One member made a resolution, seconded by another, to take the letter as an honorable amendment. The president planned to respond to Crocker in front of the assembly the next time he came to the hall.

They moved on to the next order of business: an estimate for installing gas lighting in the new hall. The building was finally finished, and with its ballroom, theater, and meeting rooms, it created a landmark in New Orleans. Thousands of people of every class and race would fill it for more than a century.

At the end of the meeting, the president asked all the members to toast "our first meeting in the new locale."

ON JULY 9, CROCKER was found dead, an apparent suicide.

A few Economistes were heartbroken. But many were furious at

Crocker's behavior. They had heard rumors that he had written a letter that, if made public, might damage their reputations.

Economie president Pierre Casanave, who was a mortician, handled the situation quietly. There was no death certificate. The whereabouts of the letter remained a mystery. The Economie minutes did not mention the way that Crocker died, and Boguille did not write any personal asides.

The Economistes met at St. Augustine Church for Crocker's funeral at five o'clock on July 10, the day after he was found. Most of the men came in mourning clothes. But not all of them dressed appropriately. Some even appeared as if they were attending a party, as a way to disrespect the dead man. They had heard more rumors.

As a brotherhood, the members were required to accompany the body to the grave. But not all who attended remained respectful and quiet. The groundskeeper draped the door of the Economie's hall with black fabric, and the society wrote Crocker's name on a funerary column with those of other deceased members. Still, Secretary Boguille recorded a dispute about whether the drape and the name should be taken down when Crocker's letter—no longer rumored, but real—was printed on the front page of a newspaper a few days after his funeral.

*The essence of fraternity, that which constitutes it above all,
is respect, which we must give ourselves. It is our dignity as
men, as husbands, as heads of families. . . . We need dignity
and to know how to risk everything, sacrifice everything
for the conservation of our honor as men, as spouses, and as
members of the Société d'Economie . . . so that shame will
never be on our side. We have our motto: All is lost without
honor.*

—Pierre Casanave, Economie president, 1857

ON AMERICAN INDEPENDENCE DAY 1857, the *Daily Picayune*
reported the conviction of an enslaved man who had put "his felonious
feet in two pairs of shoes" at a store, and the release of a woman who had
killed "her Negro boy." On the same day, Crocker wrote a desperate letter
of confession. His words revealed a series of tragic events that, over the
next few days, touched everyone in the Economie.

Trapped between the ideals of America, which appealed to him but
excluded him, and the romantic French culture that was quickly dissipating
in Louisiana, Crocker was unable to cope with his double life.

His words appeared on the front page of the French edition of *L'Abeille*
on July 14. Crocker, a married man with several children, addressed an
open letter to his mistress, Héloïse Glapion.

He wrote, "A great misfortune came to strike me Friday at approximately
ten o'clock. I had just received a sum of 1,700 *piastres*." A free carpenter

would need to work sixty hours a week for two and one-half years to earn such a sum.

Crocker had absentmindedly left the cash in a desk drawer, he said. Then he chatted with a friend who dropped by his office, and they went out for a drink. He forgot about the money until he paid a visit at another friend's house.

Crocker rushed back to his office, but the $1,700 was not there. "I said to myself—I am lost. A stranger must have come into the office. There is nothing to be done. I was obliged to give the two men who had come to get their money the sum of 190 *piastres*, which I luckily had."

Whether driven by the tense atmosphere around him or human frailty, Pierre Crocker had wallowed in regret over his terrible mistake. The money had disappeared from his safekeeping—he who had insisted on oaths and integrity from others, who all his life had yearned for respect, the first president of the Economie. He knew he would never be trusted again. The only solution to his shame, Crocker believed, was to kill himself.

Only one person seemed to love him unconditionally: the woman to whom he wrote.

The letter began "My dear Eucarice"—he called her by a pet name. Her real name was Marie Héloïse Euchariste Glapion. She was the daughter of Marie Laveau and Christophe Glapion, a soldier in the Battle of New Orleans, and was a granddaughter of Charles Laveaux, who built the house at Great Men and History Streets where the Economie had held its first meeting. She had been Crocker's confidant for the past fourteen years.

Crocker's wife, Rose, was pregnant six times in the first eight years of their marriage, and the local midwife Marie Laveau may have come around then, or perhaps he had asked her advice with the difficult childbirths. Laveau was a prominent figure in the Creole community. She had a reputation as a woman with strong prayers, both as a Catholic and as a Vodou practitioner. She was legendary also for arranging liaisons. Perhaps in Crocker's time of despair, after four of his children had died in infancy—Rose, Marie Elizabeth, Henriette, and Mathilde—Marie introduced him to her healthy, sixteen-year-old daughter. Or perhaps he pursued the teenager to indulge his lust and feed his ego, which had become bloated with wealth.

Crocker perhaps was moved by some more mysterious reason involving potions and spirits and séances, in which Marie and Héloïse were well versed. Perhaps he acted out of all of these reasons.

Héloïse Glapion's first son by Crocker was born on February 28, 1844, when she was seventeen. Crocker's wife had an infant about a year old at that time. Crocker named both boys Joseph, with E as their middle initial.

The two J. E. Crockers could have swapped identities, shared inheritance, and participated in other sleights of hand used to circumvent the laws against illegitimate children. The Dupart families employed such tricks during the nineteenth century, with free and enslaved branches using the same names—Martial, Marcel, Joseph, and Charles.

Pierre Crocker had proudly given Héloïse's son an additional measure of acknowledgment with a name nearly identical to that of his legitimate half-brother. Crocker was not ashamed of his affair with Héloïse. He loved her.

But Joseph Ernest and Joseph Eugene died as infants within two weeks of each other in the spring of 1845, leaving their father doubly distressed.

BY THE TIME CROCKER died in 1857, he and Héloïse had three more offspring. His message to "Eucarice" in the newspaper was both tender and disgraceful. He wrote that after discovering the money had disappeared, "I thought of you and my poor children, whom I wanted to kiss again one more time, since I had to separate myself from them and from you and the whole family! Do not forget me, I beg you. Defend me if it is in your power; as for me, I will pray for you."

At the end of the letter, he signed his full name, Pierre Crocker.

THE PRIVACY OF THE FREE colored community was exploded in those few lines, exposing all of their faults. Crocker's words highlighted their drinking and socializing to excess, their unmarried relationships, their illegitimate births, and their mishandling of wealth. These were the types of criticisms that often appeared in print about them. Although they may have been no different than other men in their position, the white press so magnified the faults of free people of color that the Economistes felt certain that Crocker's death would damage the society's reputation.

The day after the letter appeared in *L'Abeille*, at the Economie's July 15 meeting, Boguille transcribed the response of Eugene Meilleur, a member who knew that not only the newspaper's readers but also the town gossips would spread the news of the scandal: "My God. By tomorrow, the whole public will know."

One member was so upset that he thought Crocker had been libeled. He wanted an investigation into whether the letter was a forgery.

Brother Lanna disagreed, saying,

> My heart is so sad and my spirit so shocked about a fact so deplorable that I hardly dare speak! Yes, my brothers! It is very sad for me; for one who has lived so long with Brother Crocker that I cannot in this circumstance praise him, but, God forgive me, if I raise my voice—do not increase his anguish!!!
>
> That which sorrows and outrages me is the publication of a letter written by his hand! A letter that . . . he should not have written, a letter that expresses all the feelings that outrage sacred ties: conjugal love, paternal love! Oh! My brothers, if I speak so, it is much less for the unfortunate deceased, but it is for a few Economistes who sometimes forget their duty as husband and father. May the example of unfortunate Crocker and his sad end be ever present in their memories, so that they come to better matrimonial sentiments.
>
> Oh! Economistes, I stop on this sad topic, for if I had to go on, I would have too much to say; let us throw a thick veil on this sad and scandalous affair.

They did. And Ludger Boguille, who wrote every word documenting the Crocker tragedy, must have considered his own failings—including the child born from his lust, even though he gave this daughter his last name. Still, he must have realized that Crocker's letter had acknowledged his children in a way that was much more public than Boguille's trip to the notary. Crocker had not given his children his last name, but he had publicly declared his love for them and their mother. Crocker may have caused a scandal, but he had been true to his feelings.

Boguille closed the journal on the life of Pierre Crocker—founder, mentor, and friend. He then carried the ledger to the Economie's armoire, which held all of the society's important documents, and locked the book away.

Boguille Takes the High Road

1857–1858

All the get-togethers must be composed of people who are exempt from reproach for their conduct and their morals.

—New rules of the Economie, 1857

AFTER PIERRE CROCKER'S DEATH, the Economie minutes never again mentioned him or Mexico, although both were certainly in the members' hearts and on their minds. Now Boguille wrote in the journals with even more purpose, and he continued to inscribe every page with decorative flourishes. On the first page of a new volume, he filigreed an emblem for the Economie in red, blue, and brown. He gave each meeting a table of contents. There were no splotches of ink or unattractive spaces. His mistakes of penmanship were transformed into designs, etchings of diamond shapes and dancing paisleys made with fluid sweeps of his pen. Some resembled the lacework of a cast-iron balcony.

Boguille had always written with precision for his own satisfaction. Now, with his artistry, he also meant to show that the Economistes were worthy and sophisticated men, despite their failings and in the face of increasing external criticism. At a meeting on the night of October 19, 1857, however, there was some discussion regarding whether Boguille should make them appear even more genteel than they actually were.

"Brother François Porée observes that the minutes have been heavily edited, but one should take out those unseemly words that have found their way into the records." Boguille copied this exchange into the minutes with his nose close to the paper because he was beginning to have problems with his vision.

"Brother Rousseau shares the opinion of his colleague F. Porée and says that one should take out the words 'thereof' and others that disfigure the official report."

Boguille did not take criticisms of his prose lightly.

Brother Porée explained that on the contrary, he was not thinking of style but of words like "spy" or "thief" that the members had unceremoniously called each other lately in the heat of anger. They should erase these types of words, he moved.

Brother Meilleur seconded the motion. "These words, dirty and rude, do not honor the society and would be ugliness in the official report."

Boguille wrote quickly as the conversation continued. "Brother Lanna differs with the two who gave their opinion. He maintains judicially that all the words spoken in a meeting, as well as the facts, if the Secretary is efficient enough in rectitude, he must relate them, for the bulletin minutes are the mirror that reflects everything that takes place during the debates.

"'Here, my Brothers,' says Lanna, 'is an example of what I propose; a brother who would have behaved contrary to the rules, and after his death, his name being inscribed on the funerary column, the son who would also be an Economiste and who would see the name of his father, remembering that his conduct was not conforming to the rules, would make every effort not to fall into the same faults as him. Consequently,' says Brother Lanna, 'I uphold the official report such as it is.'"

Justified, Boguille wrote deliberately, "The minutes are thus acclaimed without any objections."

The books continued to resemble beautifully illustrated novels. Meetings were always presented as a narrative with a beginning, middle, and end. Sometimes, rather than summarize, Boguille recorded members' disagreements with precise dialogue and a dramatic climax. The end of

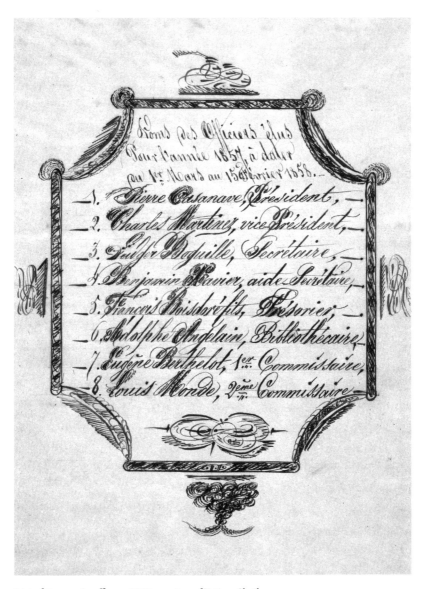

List of Economie officers; 1857; *courtesy of Fatima Shaik*

a page became an embroidery pattern of flourishes that surrounded the term *Ajourné* or *Copie certifiée*. He lined the margins with swirls resembling tornadoes and windswept hearts. He drew the anchor of hope on an opening page in one journal and on another the beehive symbol of the society.

ON DECEMBER 1, 1857, the members gathered in the large downstairs room in the hall, talking excitedly as they waited for the president to pound the gavel at the podium, announcing the beginning of their meeting. They were readying themselves for the new building's inauguration.

After everyone sat down and President Casanave began to speak, Boguille took a place at his side and opened the minute book. He saw the men in the audience with their dark mustaches and crisp white shirts, most of them arriving in the hall after freshening up at home following a day at work. Boguille listed the preparations for inauguration day in the minutes as the president spoke: four members were needed to watch the doors, three members to greet invitees, three members for the refreshment bar. François Boisdoré *fils*, an excellent speaker who had lent the funds needed to complete the building, was named the orator of the day. Boguille wrote a letter on behalf of the Economie to Adolphe Liautaud, asking him to bring together some musicians to "execute a few morsels for the occasion." Liautaud was the former head of the recently disbanded Philharmonic Society, a group of one hundred mostly amateur classical musicians from the free colored community, some of whom would later find praise abroad. Among them was Sidney Lambert, soon to be decorated for his piano compositions by the king of Portugal.

Boguille recorded a deliberation: should important guests be invited by personal letters and others, less prominent, by printed cards? Some of the special guests hailed from foreign countries. Some members agreed that letters were time-consuming but conveyed the appropriate tone. Others wondered whether the society should represent itself as egalitarian and inclusive. The members decided without taking a vote. The overwhelming opinion was that all the guests should get the same treatment—a printed invitation accompanied by a personal, handwritten letter. The solution was genteel and equitable.

Boguille saw the anticipation in the members' faces as they waited for December 20 and "*la grande fête de l'inauguration.*"

AT A MEETING ON the Sunday before the party, Boguille noted the chair's instructions to the membership: "The president urges them to be steadfast in the zeal and courtesy demanded, so that no one could say that the Economistes are novices in the art of hospitality, as well as civilized and gallant manners."

The president turned toward the men alongside him on the dais: "We—officers—and you, brothers, and 1st and 2nd commissioners who are grand masters of ceremonies, be polite, affable, welcome the guests with great consideration.

"Regarding our enemies, even supposing that we had any, if the assassin of our mother will come to present himself to us, we must receive him with all politeness that could be desired, and not to see in him anything more than a guest of the society."

Then President Casanave directed his remarks to a few specific members of the audience, saying, "Those among us who can't hold their liquor, do not allow yourself to be too carried away by enthusiasm, for then our shame shall be general, and we will appear as a bunch of drunkards. Let us observe ourselves. Let us be temperate, mostly before and during our ceremony."

The muscular and the stout, the bashful and the stoop-shouldered, with occupations such as shoemaker, tailor, and schoolteacher, and other working men would have nodded at one another, agreeing with the president about the nuances of comportment.

Then Brother Lanna came to the dais and announced that a priest from St. Augustine Church was going to perform a blessing of the hall. "This inaugural ceremony will not only be a celebration but a solemnity, powerful and sacramental," he said. Lanna encouraged the men to reflect deeply: "Be attentive, faithful onlookers at the moment when the minister, clothed in his sacerdotal robe, will bless the spot designated for our meetings."

Lanna then described the appropriate way to genuflect for this christening of the new hall, "May our knees bend, and may we, withdrawing deeply into ourselves, also observe this baptismal benediction, which will be for us all the token of a holy and fraternal alliance."

Everyone nodded in accord.

The president returned to the podium and said to the members, "Let us swear it in the name of fraternity, of unity, and of the great day, December 20, 1857."

Some men may have bowed their heads while others closed their eyes and made a brief prayer of the president's words.

At the bottom of the page, Boguille sketched exuberant circles and whirlwinds surrounding the words that conveyed his agreement, "*Copie attestée.*"

Come to the hall at a good hour to put up the decoration ribbons.

—Economie Minutes, 1857

O N THE DAY OF THE inauguration, the Economie men unveiled the society's banner at the front of the building. Then they opened the doors with a flourish. The priest from St. Augustine Church blessed the entry, saying, "Let us love one another so that ambition and hatred will vanish from our bosoms, and may love and fraternity remain always alive in our hearts."

The members, families, and guests went inside, while their neighbors in the small wooden houses on either side of Ursulines Street watched. Nothing occurred in this community without their chorus of comments. Sidewalk observers surveyed the decorative parade as it passed into the hall and critiqued the flowing skirts of the ladies, with asides about the changed manners of the gentlemen in their formal dress instead of their usual shoemakers' aprons and paint-splashed clothes.

Inside, Adolphe Liautaud directed the orchestra. Economie member Charles Martinez took his seat in the string section. The enslaved people who lived in the narrow rooms above the neighborhood's outdoor kitchen buildings, the European immigrants who served in the restaurants and mansions, and the free colored Mexicans, South Americans, Native Americans, and others who lived in the small, wood-frame houses nearby could have lingered outside to hear the music that wafted through the glass of the Economie's windows, shut to keep out the December chill. The neighbors may have sat at their hearths and softly hummed along with the waltzes, marches, and mazurkas. From that day until more than a century later, people in the Tremé community would associate significant moments in their lives with the Economie's musical repertoire.

Resolution to show gratitude: the Société votes its thanks to Monsieur A. Liautaud and the members of his orchestra as well as Monsieurs Sidney Lambert and Georges Davis, for the philanthropic token that they have manifested at our ceremony to inaugurate our meeting hall.

—Economie Minutes, 1857

O̶N NEW YEAR'S DAY AT noon, just over a week after the inauguration, the men felt good about themselves. Boguille met with the other members for a celebratory milk punch. A drink like eggnog, spiked with rum, brandy, and nutmeg, it was also considered good for a hangover. As the men drained the sweet, white liquid from their cups, they took time to consider their limitless hopes. The hall was a glittering community center. Downstairs was a restaurant and bar as well as a café where their female caretaker sold chocolate and the Economie men sold caramels and water. The bartenders, housekeepers, porter, and hat checker had all been put on salary and were ready to staff dances, dinners, and concerts. The members' success called for a few more rounds of drinks before they went home.

At four o'clock on New Year's Day 1858, the first public party began—for children. For an entrance fee of twenty-five cents, young people could waltz under the supervision of parents. Some adults, however, could not resist the quadrille. And some of the neighborhood's prostitutes who had watched from the street during the day of the inauguration now put on their best clothes, brought their children, and slipped in among the local gentry. They, too, broke with decorum when they jumped onto the dance floor, coaxing the adult male guests to dance with them.

Boguille noted in the week's minutes that the fathers of the Economie quickly put up a sign announcing that adults could not dance with each other during events that were for children only.

The members made other rules: their get-togethers had to be composed of free colored people. Attendees would be singled out if they introduced or accompanied "a commonplace person, who is reputedly recently emancipated or dubious." The caretakers would bounce the offenders from the hall, "and if it is an Economie member, he will be identified and judged by the society as a troublemaker to the order and the good reputation of the society." The rules added that weapons needed to be checked at the door.

The Economie installed gaslights in the hall. The block sparkled and beckoned people to come at night, just to walk in front of the white picket fence. When the dusty street was suddenly illuminated, a bright future seemed at hand for the whole community.

On January 2, the Economie held its first grand society ball for the public. Elegantly dressed men arrived in top hats and cutaway jackets, tall, stiff collars, and white ties. They rode in carriages to the front of the building and walked with their chests high to escort the ladies to the generous double doors. The ladies' skirts, shiny and voluminous, swished across the threshold of the building and swayed with each step, slowly falling still as the women waited in the foyer to be announced.

Each member brought with him a minimum of four guests at two dollars each. The members worked the party by minding the floor for appropriate behavior and keeping the room spotless, and paid a reduced rate of fifty cents for entrance. The cash box of the Economie began to swell.

After the inaugural ball, the society sent $54.74 to local disabled men, women, and children as well as to several others who were in need, such as women with dependents. The dances gave the society deeper pockets to continue its benevolent mission, helping members and the community. It extended this generosity at a time when the price of an opera ticket was

$1.80 for a good seat, pills to ease rheumatism and coughs were 35 cents a box, and the cost of an interstate ticket on the New Orleans, Jackson and Great Northern Railroad was three cents per mile.

THE SOCIETY'S ANNIVERSARY CELEBRATION brought a festive atmosphere to the hall. On March 21, 1858, the Economie held its private annual banquet, with eighty-three members in the crowded theater. The surviving founders spoke. Boguille squinted at the pages before him, quickly copying the texts of the speeches that expressed their optimism.

President Casanave said, "Brothers, Economistes: twenty-two years ago today several men, of which we have the good fortune of counting three among ourselves, . . . worthy founders of our association, . . . devoted to the well-being of their unfortunate compatriots, bonded together, overcoming the difficulties so that today still we have a sacred organization, the first foundations of this society of Charity, Fraternity, Union, Concord, and Truth!"

Then the first commissioner of the Economie escorted one of the founders, musician Charles Martinez, to the podium. Boguille copied his speech word for word:

Brother Economistes, Glory to God, salutations and venerations to the first of March 1836, which cemented with good will and charity our initial declaration to found this Association!!

I will read to you an extract that I made from a book:

"On the one hand, there is love; on the other, there is hate; here it's intrigue; there it's ambition. Ambition is the trial of Tantalus. The more you drink from this cup, the less your thirst will be slaked. . . .

"Love is a beautiful dream, the aspiration of the known to the unknown, the divine ray ravished by Prometheus. God created the world only because He needed to love."

This is the sincere desire of my heart: that each Economiste share with blessings and love, the unblemished manhood and admiration of our association that we celebrate today the twenty-second anniversary, and under the inspiration of the first of March, 1836, let us repeat our motto: Union, Fraternity, and Charity.

"THIS ANNIVERSARY SPEECH WAS greatly applauded," wrote Boguille.

Joseph Jean Pierre Lanna, another founder, spoke next: "Gratitude, my brothers, is one of the most beautiful virtues, not only in regard to the one who does us good, but it must be accorded to the zeal and devotion of an officer who fulfills his mission worthily; it is for this reason that I collected voluntary contributions from a great number of Economistes whom I was able to see, and I pray those whom I was not able to see to excuse me, for I wanted without any more delay to present an homage to our worthy secretary!!"

Boguille stopped writing briefly when he heard this announcement, but not without adding a few exclamation points.

Lanna walked toward Boguille, saying, "Yes, my brothers, you know as I do that the job of the secretary is one of the most important and difficult jobs, and when someone has done it well, shouldn't we reward the person who deserves it?"

Boguille wrote furiously into his first draft notebook as Lanna came closer: "Brother Lanna comes down from his place and approaches the secretary. He says to him, 'Brother Boguille, deign to receive this pair of

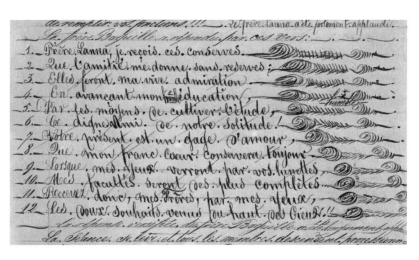

Boguille's handwritten copy of the poem he recited when presented with new glasses; from Economie minutes, March 21, 1858; *courtesy of Fatima Shaik*

*conserves** as a feeble token of friendship that the members feel for you as a brother and as a secretary. May these glasses lighten your vision and give you, as in the past, an easy way to fulfill your function.'"

Boguille replied with a spontaneous poem, which he later copied into the minutes:

Brother Lanna, I receive these conserves
that friendship gives me without reserve.
They will bring me lively admiration
while advancing my humble education
by these means to cultivate study
Worthy friend of mine only,
your present is a token of love.
that my open heart will conserve
when my eyes see through your glasses
and my faculties will be the most complete.
Receive therefore, my brothers, through my eyes
sweet wishes that come from On High.

Boguille later recopied his notes and added into the journal's minutes, "The versified response of Brother Boguille was long applauded."

Relaxed and laughing, the Economistes ended the meeting and went to a large room in another part of the hall with tables set and centerpieces of flowers. Their banquet awaited. Boguille wrote, "The members set themselves to the task to solemnize our twenty-second anniversary next to a table richly garnished with dishes and the most exquisite wines." Toast after toast followed. President Casanave raised a glass to March 1, 1836, and the founding fathers of the Economie.

Vice President Martinez raised a glass and saluted the president: "May God conserve him and grant him long years, as much for himself and his family as for the society."

---

* A French term for glasses that were thought to preserve one's eyesight by slightly magnifying objects.

Boguille followed: "To the eighty-three members who make up our society, forming a single, indivisible heart, now and always!!"

He also reported that "several other toasts, not any less beautiful, were made by various brothers. Several brothers drew attention to themselves by couplets that they sang, principally the brothers L. Angelain and Populus Jr. Brother Forstall read a very beautiful speech composed in verse and in prose. He was wildly applauded. Brother Boguille recited several couplets composed about the officers. These couplets were favorably greeted and applauded."

Lanna made a "short and beautiful speech . . . in praise" of the hall's caretaker and the serving staff. The members took up a collection for them "that came to 10 *piastres* and 25 cents," Boguille wrote.

On the night of the anniversary celebration, after a motion to adjourn, the feast ended, and President Casanave brought one of the table centerpieces to his wife "to show our fraternal affection for her," Boguille wrote.

The Further Erosion of Rights

1858

The color of the slave is the badge of his condition; and does much to make him regard it as his destiny. Even manumission cannot materially change his lot—cannot give him the privileges of the whites—lift him to the rank of a freeman, or wipe away the color which separates him from the mass of our people, and dooms him to inevitable and perpetual inferiority.

—*The South Vindicated from the Treason and Fanaticism of Northern Abolitionists*, 1836

ON THE NIGHT OF March 26, 1858, Boguille sat at his writing table near the flickering gaslight on the wall and carefully noted the names of each man who came through the door of the Economie's large meeting room. There were the founders—the tender-hearted Joseph Jean Pierre Lanna and the loquacious Charles Martinez. The wealthy clothier François Lacroix was in attendance. The former soldiers who had fought in the Battle of New Orleans sat with the boisterous François Porée. Joseph Daniel Warburg was a new member. A marble cutter, he was the younger brother of the well-known sculptor Eugène Warburg. The Jamaican-born architect Nelson Fouché arrived and exchanged greetings with the men around him—shoemakers, carpenters, cigar rollers, and tailors.

During the initiation of another Economie brother that evening, President Casanave, instead of following the usual procedure of reading the rules and regulations to the candidate, began by asking him an existential question. It was not just for the candidate. Casanave wanted to inspire all of the men:

> Have you ever asked yourself, sometimes in your thoughts, what we need to do to get you out of this state of abjection and sickness that outrages nature as well as reason? Without a doubt, you have asked yourself this question more than once. And you have answered each time. We really must quiet all the emotions in our hearts that might make us forget our dignity. We need to understand once and for all that speaking materially, we are men as intellectually gifted as those who believe themselves to be our superiors, with all the faculties that characterize the perfect creature.

A new science had taken hold. Academics in the South like Samuel Cartwright had conducted research and promoted theories that Blacks were inferior. Another "expert" was Professor Josiah Clark Nott. A year earlier, he had come to the University of Louisiana in New Orleans on the strength of his reputation—he had established the Mobile Medical Society in Alabama and a surgical clinic—and through the efforts of his brother Dr. Gustavus Adolphus Nott, who was already part of the university's teaching staff.

Josiah Nott's theories of white superiority were consistent with the writings of Cartwright and De Bow but went even further to claim that the children of intermarriage were doomed. Mulattos, he claimed, had the shortest lifespan and would eventually become extinct. He relished his role as a spokesman for the South, writing to a friend in 1850, "My great aim has been to get the world quarrelling about niggerology and I have at last succeeded, and I think I shall sit on the fence now and enjoy the fight." Like Cartwright, he said that the natural order was for whites to control Blacks in slavery.

Casanave above all was qualified to speak about the equality of men. Besides being an intellectual, he was a mortician.

He had seen the naked bodies of eminent citizens, undifferentiated in death. Their last wastes mottled their bodies. Bruises rose where they had tumbled to the ground. He stitched their cuts and patched each corpse with theatrical makeup to return it to a semblance of its previous glory. Sometimes he gave his clients an appearance of dignity that they had never possessed. He polished their skins with strong soap, stuffed the rotting cavities of their bodies, and wrapped them in silk clothes and elegant cravats. The mourners would see in his handiwork the true nature of the departed—strength where Casanave plumped a chest, kindness where he arranged a smile, and devotion where he folded the hands gently in prayer.

It was all artifice.

Casanave lived without illusions. He knew that all men were born innocent, lived constantly making mistakes, and then died, unprepared. He buried white men and Black men, their children, wives, and mistresses. He made no distinctions of color or class, and he expected that the Creator did the same.

"Man is free," Casanave once told an initiate. "The Creator gave him liberty." But Boguille knew that, in practice, equality did not extend to any of them. He could not stop in any coffeehouse that caught his eye. He could not sit where he wanted at the opera, nor could he travel freely. Most white men in New Orleans would not even shake his hand. They did not touch colored people. Neither Casanave nor Boguille nor any other man in the room had the legal rights of even the poorest white southerner.

Boguille had walked carefully to the Economie's hall that night. He carried his body loosely and not especially erect so that he could move through the streets inconspicuously. He stepped confidently, but not arrogantly enough to attract stares. He must have lectured his young male students in the same way that all American parents have lectured their dark-skinned children for centuries—to temper their wide, rangy gaits so their arms would not swing out too powerfully from their sides, to move slowly and self-consciously. They needed to be aware of the hazards in their surroundings. Boguille was no exception.

Casanave pointed out the illogic of racism to the Economistes, saying, "This African blood that runs in our veins! There it is, our only Crime! . . . Brothers who have been oppressed unjustly, let us preach to our compatriots that they must follow the path to fraternity and come out of the isolation that our oppressors applaud, for they would like to see us forever disunited, tearing each other apart and having only hatred in our hearts for each other."

He encouraged the new member to work together with his Economie brothers for justice: "Let us all be imbued with the noble feelings that shape all civilized people; let us be vigilant to the cries of our miserable ones."

Boguille scribbled quickly to capture Casanave's words. "By our union, our concord, and our sympathy, let us be convinced that our oppressors will be confounded. May their persecution not make us lose our balance. As the rocks beaten by the waves of the ocean, let us remain steadfast with courage and dignity so that ignorance does not intimidate us. . . . Who can harm us if we enfold ourselves in the arms of Fraternity? Let us have patriotism, and like the Girondins, we will cause our executioners one day to weep from shame and rage." All the members knew the Girondin heroes from the French Revolution. They had stood with the French people against the monarchy while maintaining the structure of civil government. This was the position that Casanave wanted for the Economie and its members. They should lead in the issues concerning free people of color and the enslaved.

On that night, like all others, the members left the hall and walked into the heart of a dark city. In New Orleans at that time, some 15,000 people were held in slavery.

The condition of the negro would be greatly improved by his transfer from the barbarism and brutality of African life, to the civilization of America. An emigration to the soil of Louisiana . . . or of any of our Southern States, would not only be a relief but a positive blessing. It would be to them as the passing out of night to day. It would literally be a transition from the most abject servitude, intellectual darkness, and moral degradation, to a condition of assured protection and comparative freedom; to a condition of labor, it is true, but one on which is ever shed the benign rays of the Christian religion. . . . They may indenture themselves for a further time, if it should be for no longer a period than would be necessary to realize a sufficient amount of means to enable them to return to their native country, or to Liberia.

—*New Orleans Bee*, 1858

In the same month as the elaborate Economie dinner and Casanave's lectures to embolden the members, the *New Orleans Bee* reported that the state had decided to transport 2,500 Africans to Louisiana. They would supposedly come as free men—by their own choice—but everyone in the Economie's community knew that this was a new tactic to enslave people. The "free men" would somehow be tricked into staying as unpaid labor.

The justification for the plan was clearly false because no area in the United States wanted more free people of color, especially not Louisiana. As the *New York Times* stated in a report about the project, "In every Southern State the free blacks are the most dangerous and most dreaded portion of the population; and the policy of the whole South has always been to get rid of them as rapidly as possible."

American profits encouraged slavery, not emancipation. In 1857 four million enslaved people fueled the nation's prosperity. The cost of feeding an enslaved laborer on a cotton plantation in Louisiana was about $7.50 per year, or just over 2 cents a day, far below the value of the goods produced. The return on an enslaved person was anywhere between 11 percent in 1849 on a farm with more than one hundred enslaved people to 7 percent in 1859 on a farm with nine or fewer workers in areas along the Mississippi River and in Louisiana. Each person picked approximately three bales of cotton weighing four hundred pounds per year, while the price of cotton was nine and a half cents a pound.

To preserve slavery, whites attempted to dismantle the mobility, reputations, and rights of free people of color. Simultaneously, the Economie members struggled to maintain their status. They wanted to remain insular enough to preserve their advantages yet open enough to enforce the organization's commitment to equity.

One night, the members had to examine their own prejudices against a man who had an English last name and who was not born from one of their ancient Louisiana families. The Battle of New Orleans veteran François Porée spoke up, "I've known him for about twenty-three or twenty-four years as a man of honor, full of probity, intelligence, and dignity. I know that there is among us a strong presumption against the said Charles Butler who people say is a *Mulâtre Américain*. I would beg you to set that aside and all to vote for him, my brothers, for he is worthy of the honor of finding himself with us and among us." Porée intimated that some brothers were not fond of the descendants of whites, especially English-speakers. The prejudice extended further to the first-generation offspring of an Anglo-American white and an enslaved person. The biased members, however, were in the minority. The Economie took in Butler that night, but not without a long deliberation and two black balls cast among the forty-three.

Still, Casanave saw that the smugness some members exhibited could infect the society.

In May 1858 he initiated another new member by telling the assembly, "Let us beat down egoism, which is the cause of the distancing of the one from the other. . . . We know our oppressors clap hands and are fortified in their opinions that we are incapable of anything good, we are born to be their slaves, that the passion of degradation is insinuated in our hearts." He suspected that some of them did not agree with him. They were being swayed by public opinion, which ridiculed the enslaved and denigrated poor people of color. They had adopted elitist attitudes, not just pride in their own successes.

Because of their new hall, the society was more visible than ever. People wrote daily asking to join the organization, often for the wrong reasons. Some men hoped to use the association to climb the social ladder. The Economie members employed one another to build homes, teach their children, and run their companies. They brought each other the finest goods from their trips abroad—bolts of linen from Cambrai, France, rolls of Chinese silks from Paris, and cases of French and Italian wines.

Boguille saw the collective wealth of the Economie every time he walked into the hall. The building sparkled with chandeliers and gaslights. The members served excellent food at their banquets and parties. Even the minute books told the story of the Economie's prosperity. One journal had the English word "Record" embossed in gold on its leather spine. The marbled endpapers had a zigzag pattern of gold, cerulean blue, olive green, and yellow. The pattern was replicated on the edges of the closed book. It was precious and an obvious reflection of privilege. Some of the members may have come to share in the belief, popular in the scientific community and increasingly widespread beyond, that superior and inferior people existed. Casanave's view of the world was quite different.

He asked one initiate, "What are the sentiments that have animated you in taking the pen to write a letter to us to be a member of the Société d'Economie et d'Assistance Mutuelle? Is it the fraternity pure, simple, and sane that was expressed in your letter? Then, without a doubt you will be a good member!—because what does fraternity demand? It wants nothing but good, Union, justice, and impartiality. . . . If it is only the title Economiste that you solicit, that you look for, that you want, you will not prove to be a good member. You would let yourself be influenced by passion, intrigue, partisan spirit, indifference, and would earn the distaste of the members who sacrifice themselves for the good of the society in general. Because a society composed of enemy brothers will not be strong for long."

Casanave told all of the members to stand, and he began to pray, "As
we are able to resist, Great God, these bad sentiments with which some
wish to control the others, this egotism that misleads us, that deprives us,
it is to you therefore that we elevate our hearts, our feelings, and our ideas.
We beseech you to prevent us from being blinded by our heinous passions,
and do not permit us to get carried away by intrigue and hopelessness but
deliver us from the biggest and worst insanity that is capable of destroying
our society—the false love of self and senseless hubris. God of Mercy, watch
over our parents, our spouses, and our brother Economistes, who without
doubt contemplate your greatness in a better world. God of Clemency,
enlighten our oppressors to our position and bless our new brother."

The members chanted "Union, Concord, and Equality," then gave acco-
lades all around.

The notes for this May 10, 1858, meeting were the most detailed of
Boguille's tenure. Then, before the members adjourned, he resigned his
position as secretary.

IN 1858 THE LOUISIANA artist Marie Adrien Persac painted idyllic scenes
of the city in a blue- and brown-toned palette reminiscent of John James
Audubon's colored engravings of birds. Persac imagined an aerial view of
the Mississippi River's landscape—sailing ships on the glistening water,
three chatting gentlemen in three-quarter-length jackets and wide-brimmed
hats, and hundreds of bales of cotton sitting on the golden wharf like
white dominoes in the dust. Another of Persac's watercolors, this one
of a plantation, shows thirty men, women, and children cutting thirty
rows of cane while an overseer watches from his perch on a white horse.
Plantation scenes like this caused Louisiana historian Charles Gayarré
to call the locally recognized inventor of sugar refining "the savior—the
savior of Louisiana." The man happened to be Etienne de Boré, Gayarré's
grandfather.

A worker's view focuses closer to earth. For the enslaved, each day was
eighteen or more hours of bending from the waist, grabbing a hard shaft
of cane low to the ground with one hand and swinging a machete with the
other, then pitching the cane behind their backs so that younger workers
could pick up the stalks and make stacks. Cane, thick like bamboo but

Port and City of New Orleans; 1858 or 1859; by Marie Adrien Persac; *THNOC, acquisition made possible by the Clarisse Claiborne Grima Fund, 1988.9*

more sinewy, required the strength of a person's back, shoulders, forearms and fingers to hit thousands of stalks thousands of times. The people who cut cane could not lose rhythm, ask for water, or complain. If they did talk about their miseries, it was in a whisper. They did not dare proclaim their resentments. Is it any wonder that when Boguille's sympathies became seditious, he fell silent?

He did not record any significant quake in the Economie's history. The minutes simply note that Boguille and, a few weeks later, the outspoken president Casanave submitted letters of resignation. There were no explanations in the minutes.

Clearly, a secret discussion was taking place off the page. Anyone with his ear to the ground knew what had happened.

THE FACT IS THAT the Economie leadership had been deeply committed to their plan to emigrate from the United States a year earlier. And while they remained hopeful for many months, the plan eventually failed. Boguille and Casanave may have felt responsible.

The timeline of this personal and political disaster began when the man who had assured the Economistes that they would have a new home,

Mexican president Comonfort, had been driven out of office in January 1858 after only seven months. The *New York Times* reported that "he was the only man of political eminence in Mexico who had at heart the liberty of his country. He was earnest and honest in his desire to promote wholesome reforms." Yet Comonfort was too "weak" and "irresolute" to control military factions in the country. He was overthrown and escaped to the United States.

He came to New Orleans, arriving by steamship on February 10, 1858. He must have been in contact with his friends in the Economie, as men from the society had been traveling back and forth for years. Comonfort's presence undoubtedly animated the organization politically. Two weeks after Mexico's deposed president arrived in the city, Casanave was more vocal and transparent in the minutes about liberty than any Economie leader had been before or would be afterward. His opening remarks to the members at their banquet of March 21, 1858, included the statement, "Remember that we have brothers in foreign climes and that, God willing, one day we will find ourselves at their sides on this fraternal table as we are sure that we will rejoin those who have already departed us for Eternity." Casanave's increasingly bold statements about justice and equality lasted from March to July.

By August 1858 Comonfort had been in New Orleans for six months. But then something happened—perhaps a rift between the Economie and their visitor. Or maybe the men realized that without Comonfort in power, they could not migrate. The August 1 Economie meeting had no quorum.

On August 9, 1858, the evening roll call found Ludger Boguille in the meeting, although not acting as secretary. Casanave was not there. Only thirty-seven members attended. Another forty-five were absent, including eleven who were out of the parish and five in other countries. Yellow fever was raging in New Orleans. It would claim more than 4,800 people in 1858.

The minutes that night recorded, "Brother Frilot announced that he was sick." The rest of the page was left blank.

NOTHING WAS WRITTEN IN the journals again until years later. It was not because of the members' inactivity—probably just the opposite.

Comonfort left New Orleans in August for Lynchburg, Virginia. The only news about him appeared in the *New York Times*. It said he had taken a train from the South and was ridiculed for his officious behavior. He sat down to eat at a hotel restaurant before the ladies arrived at the table. In addition, the other passengers thought he looked laughable wearing his cap with a "gold band."

In New Orleans, the sentiments of the Economie members went unrecorded. But Comonfort's presence in New Orleans must have given the members reasons to feel hope—either of leaving the United States or of obtaining the equality that Casanave described. Then, when Comonfort left, they became disheartened. The Economistes folded up their maps of Mexico and put them into their cabinets, slumped in the entryways of their barbershops and shoe repair businesses, explained to their children and grandchildren the reasons they would not be climbing aboard a steamship anytime soon. Or maybe they didn't.

The complete silence in the Economie journals perhaps indicated the depth of their disappointment. The reality they faced lay between the lines of the Economie journals and in the pages of the national newspapers. The *New York Times* wrote,

> That the people of the United States will, in process of time, extend their control over Mexico, is as certain as any future event can be. It is easy to carp at this tendency to empire, but quite impossible to check it. If the Mexican Republic had a population like our own, the case would be different. We do not look for the annexation of Canada, for the reason that the people of the British Provinces possess all the requisites for national respectability and progress. But to suppose that a few millions of Indians, Negroes and enervate Creoles are forever to hold exclusive occupancy of a territory rich in all mineral and vegetable productions, and two-thirds the size of our own, is no less absurd than the theory of those who claimed a century ago that the red man should never give way to the advance of European civilization.

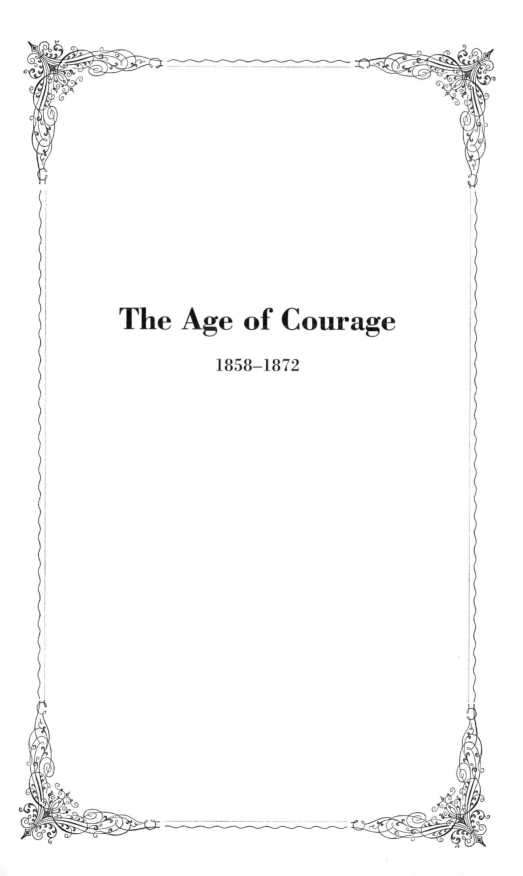

The Age of Courage

1858–1872

From the Militia to the Meeting

1858–1863

*In spite of this unforeseen dismemberment and this state
of abeyance, the experiences made us conscious of all the
advantages that can arise from an institution in which
the principal goals will be to help one another and to
teach one another while holding out a protective hand to
suffering humanity.*

—Economie Minutes, first page, January 1836

FTER THE AUGUST 9, 1858, meeting, many life-changing events
occurred for Boguille and the Economistes, but none of them were
recorded in the Economie journals until March 1, 1864, when the society's
minutes resumed on the next page. During that strange blank period, the
society was invisible yet active, gaining twenty new members.

About a month after Boguille's resignation in May 1858, his nephew
Henry L. Rey began writing the minutes of another group that had just
begun meeting on Sunday nights in a downstairs room of the Economie's
hall. Rey had joined a nineteenth-century religious movement called Spiritualism. Adherents believed that they could communicate with the dead.
Spiritualists were all over the United States in those years and included
Horace Greeley, editor of the *New York Tribune*. Their ranks would come
to include President Abraham Lincoln's wife, Mary Todd Lincoln.

Rey called his Spiritualist community the Cercle Harmonique, a reference to the unifying bonds of friendship. Several Economie members

Illustration from Cercle Harmonique register; *courtesy of René Grandjean Collection, Earl K. Long Library, University of New Orleans*

attended the séances, including Pierre Crocker—as a ghost. He admitted to his suicide as the result of his weakness and proclaimed, "Death is the awakening!" But other more militant voices entered the Cercle Harmonique journals, such as St. Vincent de Paul, a Catholic cleric of the seventeenth century who dedicated himself to the poor. Also appearing were political figures like abolitionist John Brown.

In the context of the free colored community, with its deep Haitian roots, Spiritualism also intersected with that revolution's values. "Throw away the thoughts of / the Whitegod who thirsts / for our tears, listen to / freedom that speaks to our hearts," said Boukman Dutty—some spelled his name "Bookman" because he taught people to read—a Vodou priest whose ceremony in Bois Caïman had sparked the beginnings of the rebellions in Saint Domingue.

Rey wrote in the Spiritualists' registers, "Each man in his sphere wants to dominate and yet he admits that God has created us all equal."

The group's journals gave voice not only to the dead, whom the mediums believed that they conjured, but also to the growing radical feelings of the Economie community.

AS THE SOUTH MOVED to secede from the Union, Louisiana was the sixth state to join the Confederacy, on January 26, 1861. Men from fourteen to seventy years old knocked on the doors of enlistment centers to give their names. If Boguille strolled past a group of volunteers near his corner, he couldn't help but hear their excited voices proclaiming that they would defend the city from the coming Northern invaders. They stood close together and shouted into one another's faces, echoing the sentiments in the newspapers. A *Daily Picayune* headline described an uprising against President Lincoln's troops in Baltimore as a "Baptism of Blood." A letter on the front page of the *Picayune* spoke for local recruits: "If . . . our independence from Black Republican misrule can only be gained through war, let it come, say our patriots." The paper called Lincoln's party "Black Republicans" as an insult to the color of the people in bondage and the government's antislavery support.

New white militias formed every day. On April 21, 1861, the newspaper reported the recent creation of the Mounted Guards of Jefferson, the Orleans Home Light Guard, the Confederate Guards, and the new Cavalry, Artillery, and Navy of the Confederacy. The same day an article invited whites to meet at the Merchants' and Auctioneers' Exchange "to devise means of ridding the city of all suspicious characters and sympathizers with the Black Republican horde."

The names of committee members appeared the next day in the newspapers. The *Daily Picayune* called them "our oldest and most influential merchants and citizens." The committee's goal was to remove "the persons scattered in our midst who are believed to sympathize with our enemies," and the speaker assured the assembly that "the officers in authority are with us and will exercise eagerly all powers necessary to free the city" from Black Republicans. A cheer went up for Jefferson Davis, president of the Confederacy, before the citizens' meeting ended. Another article revealed that people were already moved to action. With the headline "Arrest under the Charge of Black Republicanism," the story said that a local dentist was charged by a fellow citizen for having "uttered treasonable language in the Fourth District, saying, for instance, that Lincoln is a second Jackson." The dentist was brought to jail and arraigned by the city's recorder but not released, the paper said, because "treason is a capital offense."

About half of the whites that Boguille encountered now had been born or had arrived in New Orleans within the previous decade, and for every six people he came across, only one was Black. The city's population was very different than it had been during the first three decades of Boguille's life. Most of the residents he saw in his youth were people of color. Until 1840 they made up more than one-half of New Orleanians.

The newcomers had little interest in social equity. Boguille saw their eyes widen with envy when he left the bank with a purse stuffed with cash, paid the full fare for just a short trip on the streetcar, or dusted off his suit coat when he descended from the car and walked into a fine private home.

Boguille understood the newcomers' perspectives: they might wonder why he needed more rights if he—unlike they—had a full stomach. Why should they worry if Blacks were beaten for insolence, when the immigrants had received similar treatment in Europe? And why should they spend their resources educating Negroes when they themselves could hardly read and write?

Just under 20 percent of free adult men owned any enslaved people, and even fewer—barely more than one-tenth of one percent—owned more than one hundred enslaved people. Still, many immigrants and other white Louisianians found common interests with large planters. Their livelihoods supported the plantations by providing shipping, selling luxury goods, and importing wine, for example, and would be affected by the end of slavery.

The secessionists also considered the effect on the labor market if they had to compete for wages with formerly enslaved workers. Many freemen, skilled and unskilled, might be employed quicker and more cheaply. These practical concerns fueled political passions.

Boguille must have conferred with his most knowledgeable brothers in the Economie—Casanave, Lanna, and Nelson Fouché—about the volatile environment. These leaders knew the history of Mexico and the tactics that achieved victory. Both Santa Anna and Jim Bowie had first joined a revolution, then overthrown its leaders. Boguille may have spoken with Louis Nelson Fouché, who knew Comonfort, the man who beat Santa Anna. Boguille certainly would have discussed the situation with Armand Lanusse and Félicie Cailloux, his colleagues at the Couvent School. They wanted to take action.

On April 22, 1861, a large group of whites met who were moved to action by their hate of Black Republicans. Meanwhile, a number of free people of color gathered at the corner of Great Men and Union Streets in the Couvent School to organize themselves "to repel any enemy who may invade the soil of Louisiana." The *Daily Picayune* noted that nearly 2,000 people attended the latter meeting and about 1,500 signed up to "offer their services to the municipal authorities, in case of an invasion by the enemy; and if allowed to form themselves in military companies, they take the engagement to take arms at a moment's notice for the defense of their native soil, and fight, 'shoulder by shoulder,' with the citizens as their fathers did in 1814." Several Economie members joined a standing committee at this meeting—Joseph Jean Pierre Lanna, François Tervalon Sr., and Joseph Lavigne.

Were these free men, so recently engaged in plans to emigrate to Mexico, now committed to the ideals of the Confederacy? The Economie journals had gone silent, but the members made a great public show of their loyalty. They weren't the first African descendants to hold one idea privately while publicly seeming to cooperate with the powers around them. The enslaved did this every day.

On May 12, 1861, Governor Thomas Overton Moore created a militia regiment of free people of color, intended to protect New Orleans in case of a Union attack, called the First Louisiana Native Guards, Louisiana Militia, Confederate States of America.

Approximately one month later, Boguille and his nephew Henry L. Rey began to form units. On June 11, 1861, they met with at least twenty-five men, including Economie members François Boisdoré *fils*, Lucien Capla, Eugène Rapp, Joseph Abélard, François Porée, and Benjamin Xavier.

Boguille organized a company of seventy-six men, calling them the Young Creole Native Guards. His second lieutenant, Zephir Canonge, was one of the children Boguille had raised. Now a twenty-one-year-old shoemaker, Canonge was a boy of ten when he first entered the Boguille home.

Both Boguille and Henry L. Rey were captains in the Confederate militia. Rey organized a company of a hundred men named the Economy Native Guards, composed of many society members. They were among the more than 340 men in units headed by Economie brothers. More than half of the eligible free men of color in New Orleans volunteered.

Were they men who feared being enslaved themselves, slave owners whose economic interests or skin tones gave them more affinity with the planter class, men who sought the respect of New Orleans whites, or Blacks simply loyal to the Confederacy? Those were the reasons that white newspaper reporters gave for the enlistment of free people of color. The *Daily Picayune* editorialized in its news column, "What will the Northerners have to say to this?" The questions lingered. Later writers, looking into the rearview mirror of history, hypothesized about Black loyalties.

Among 1,500 men, all of these reasons would have been represented. Frightened, wealthy, and color-prejudiced Negro men joined the Confederacy. So did men whose families had lived for generations in Louisiana and owned land that might become battlefields, who understood the folly of being defenseless in a place where guns and murder were commonplace, who were already men in their own right, and who knew strategies for survival. In a city at the mouth of a river, the phrase "any port in a storm" was not only a metaphor but a reality.

On an individual level, however, Boguille knew the history of the Haitian Revolution, which had involved his father and his friends. They had changed sides as the conflict evolved, making alliances with the French, the Spanish, the enslaved, and the island-born free people to achieve liberation in any way possible. Boguille was an intimate of veterans of the Battle of New Orleans, such as Economistes Manuel Muro, François and Joseph Porée, Henry Chevarre, François Tervalon, and Engle Bart, as well as others who were members of the society or of the Société des Vétérans de 1814–15, who used the hall as their headquarters. These elders were definitely strategic partners.

They would have told the younger men stories of shrewd midnight negotiations, liquored-up arguments over land, friends turned traitors, and cowards carrying weapons alongside them. They knew about slicing the limbs of their enemies, blood pouring from an ally's wounds, and seeing friends die at their feet. Boguille considered all of this before he signed on.

He must have also thought about his family. His son Jean Horace, only two years old, was named after the Roman poet whose father had been enslaved. Pierre Butel, named after Boguille's dead mother's family, was just three.

Boguille certainly didn't join the Confederacy because he hated northerners. His partner in literature and in life was his white, New York–born wife. His love for her would not have predisposed him to sympathize with the increasingly rabid secessionists. Also under Boguille's roof was his son Florian, who, like his father, taught Negro students at a time when southerners disdained education for Blacks. Proslavery advocates said education would lead the enslaved to rebellion. But Boguille had taught an enslaved boy, first in his school and then privately. Ludger's parents had held people in bondage, but he had never sold anyone from their family or his. According to the 1860 census, living with Ludger, Mary Ann, their children, and Zephir Canonge was a dark-skinned adult named Henry, a man with no last name and the only person identified as Black in a neighborhood of people whose race was recorded as mulatto—or left blank, to indicate that they were white. Henry, a 45-year-old laborer, may have begun life enslaved but was free and living in Boguille's house, possibly as a sleight of hand to free the man without going to court. Or Henry's presence could have indicated Boguille's benevolence or bargaining—an exchange of work for housing. In any case, the Boguille family, with its variety of colors and origins, showed an openness that would not have sat well with the white supremacists.

Boguille may have worn the appropriate angry facial expressions in public conversations and may even have been spouting a Confederate slogan on the day he signed the paper to volunteer. At the same time, he may have been praying that none of the rebels would look too closely at his living situation to test his devotion to the Confederacy's values.

Boguille didn't need to trust the Confederates to join. He trusted himself to take care of his family, protect his property, and act with integrity, as he had taught his students to do for more than twenty years. He also trusted his Economie brothers, whom he debated and consoled, hugged and quoted in the journals. These men were not naïve about the treatment of colored warriors in the South.

They knew there was little choice. They could either join the Confederacy or be recruited into it. Boguille and the others concluded that there were two groups of Americans preparing to battle on the streets of New Orleans: the one they knew and the one they didn't. Given this situation, the free men of color wanted to protect their own community.

By August 3, 1861, the Congress of the Confederate States had passed "An Act Respecting Alien Enemies." The Southern government reserved the right to arrest and remove any male of fourteen years or older, including native-born United States citizens, who adhered to the laws of the United States in the case of a war. By then, however, the Louisiana free men of color had legitimized their right to remain as militiamen. They also could openly carry weapons in their own defense, just like the white men in their vicinity.

On November 22, 1861, the *Daily True Delta* reported that all white men in New Orleans between the ages of eighteen and forty-five were called into militia service to defend the city. The following week, they were required to assemble and be counted in a "grand review." The members of the First Division's three brigades of white men were instructed to form their columns along major streets throughout the city. Finally, the report added that "regiments of Native Guards and other organizations of free colored men" should gather at the end of all the white brigades, around Tonti Street in the Seventh Ward.

Boguille's decision was sound for his situation. In the words of one soldier, "If we had not volunteered, they would have forced us into the ranks."

By joining the Louisiana Native Guards, Boguille made history, becoming one of the first Black officers in the North or South. The Civil War lasted until 1865. Boguille was a Confederate for only a few months.

*The Native Guards have seen the whole rebel army
fleeing shamefully, leaving their women and children—
to the mercy of the victors, who happily protected them
magnanimously.*

—Henry L. Rey, quoted in the *New York Times*,
November 5, 1862

NEW ORLEANS WAS THE largest city in the South, with the biggest slave market, and its port controlled access to the Gulf and the upriver states, so the Union attacked it early. General Benjamin F. Butler's forces occupied New Orleans on May 1, 1862. The white Confederates abandoned the city, leaving the Native Guards behind.

A group of officers took their regiment's weapons and hid them. Most of their rifles and pistols had been passed down in Economie families for decades, kept since the Battle of New Orleans, purchased in the thriving weapons market near Exchange Place and while visiting Europe, or bought from free men of color who forged them, like Adolphe Duhart, a gunsmith from Cuba. Having arms in a city at war was a high priority. Two of the hiding places were Boguille's favorite locations—the Couvent School and the Economie's hall.

Boguille must have been aware of the plan. He had been at the school for more than fifteen years by then, and he had attended all the meetings that discussed the construction of the Economie's hall.

During the summer after the city fell, five Economie members—Boguille's nephews Henry L. Rey and his brother, Octave, plus Edgar Davis and Eugène Rapp, with Charles Sauvinet acting as translator—went to speak to General Butler. They came to give up their weapons, submitting fully to the Union occupation of the city. Their fates during this period were yet to be determined. In a large room, the thirty-year-old Rey sat near the balding general. The Northerner was overweight and no doubt sweating under his uniform in the August heat. Butler looked at Rey as he spoke in French and then at Sauvinet as he translated. Rey convinced Butler that the free men of color had joined the Confederates to take care of their families and that they couldn't have done any differently. Now they had an army of free men ready to fight. Butler invited them to join the Union forces in an August 22 proclamation:

> Now, therefore, the Commanding General, believing that a large portion of this militia force of the State of Louisiana are willing to take service in the volunteer forces of the United States, and be enrolled and organized to "defend their homes from ruthless invaders;" to protect their wives and children and kindred from wrongs and outrage; to shield their property from being seized by bad men; and to defend the flag of their native country, as their fathers did under Jackson at Chalmette . . . it is ordered that all the members of the "Native Guards" aforesaid, and all other free colored citizens . . . who shall enlist in the volunteer service of the United States, shall be duly organized by the appointment of proper officers, and accepted, paid, equipped, armed and rationed as are other volunteer troops of the United States.

On September 27, 1862, the First Regiment of the Union Native Guards was mustered with some 1,000 soldiers. But only about 11 percent of them were free men. Most of the men in the regiment had departed from their enslavers.

Captain Louis Antoine
Snaer, Company B,
Seventy-Third US
Colored Infantry;
between 1863 and
1865; *courtesy of Glen C.
Cangelosi, MD*

Octave Rey's enrollment
card, US Company E,
Sixth Louisiana Infantry
(Colored); *courtesy of
National Archives and
Records Administration*

The colored troops who did not enlist in the Union army, however, did not necessarily favor the Confederacy. If any did, "the number was too few to give rise to any serious reproaches," according to Rodolphe Desdunes, in *Our People and Our History*. Just fifteen men of African descent could be counted among the 65,000 soldiers in the Louisiana Confederate army. The Second Regiment of the Union Native Guards was mustered on October 12, 1862, and the Third Regiment on November 24.

Boguille, almost fifty years old, decided not to join.

A NUMBER OF ECONOMISTES became officers in the Union regiment of the Native Guards. Charles Butler, Edgar Davis, Alcide Lewis, Eugène Rapp, Louis A. Snaer, William Belley, François Tervalon, Charles Sauvinet, and Boguille's nephews Henry and Octave Rey were society members in 1862 or would be in years to come.

A *New York Times* reporter went to visit the First Regiment of the Union Native Guards when it was stationed at the Louisiana racetrack in October 1862 and wrote that "several were, to all superficial appearance, white men, fairly formed, and soldierly in appearance; one of the Captains was evidently of unmixed African blood." He went on to liken the "diversity of color among the men and officers" to that of "the Mexican soldiers I saw in Mexico." The comment was unintentionally ironic. The Economie men had planned to become Mexican citizens to escape racism. Although they decided to remain Americans, the nation's biggest newspaper, loyal to the Union, focused on their color.

When the regiment paraded down Esplanade and Canal Streets on October 27, 1862, "their line of march was marked by crowds of enthusiastic friends, who cheered them lustily as they moved on, gaily singing patriotic songs," the *Times* reported. The journalist thought he saw a white man among the soldiers, but the man was Edgar Davis, who would soon join the Economie. "This officer, Capt. E. Davis, of Company A, was a fine looking young man, (not unlike Gen. McClellan in mold of features,) with light blue eyes, ruddy complexion, soft silky hair, and a splendid moustache of a sandy color nearly approaching red," the correspondent wrote. "I would have defied the most consummate expert in niggerology, by the aid of the

Capt. Charles Beaumont, Co. D.   1st Lieut. J. D. Lewis, Co. A.   2d Lieut. J. L. Montieu, Co. A.   Capt. E. Davis, Co. A.
        1st Lieut. V. Lavigne, Co. D.

OUR COLORED TROOPS—THE LINE OFFICERS OF THE FIRST LOUISIANA NATIVE GUARDS—SKETCHED BY OUR SPECIAL ARTIST.

Economie member Captain Edgar Davis (far right) with other officers of the First Louisiana Native Guards; from *Harper's Weekly*, February 28, 1863; *THNOC, 1974.25.9.7*

most powerful microscope, to discover the one drop of African blood in that man's veins; still there it was upon the record against him." Henry L. Rey was also light skinned, as the newspaper later reported, but he would not have found any compliment in seeing his name in the paper with a reference to "niggerology."

Inside the Economie's hall, the brotherhood included François Lacroix, once described as having a "white complexion," and Etienne Cordeviolle, who a neighbor said was "coppery" colored with "crispy" hair. Brown-skinned Alexandre Pétion's picture hung near a pale George Washington with pink cheeks and alongside tan, bearded Ignacio Comonfort. Boguille had entered long dialogues about ideas and values, character and integrity into the society's minutes. Imperfect men, they argued about morality, criminality, terms of respect, and attitudes, but never skin tones. If any member felt superior about his color, such prejudice wasn't a quality that the Economistes admired. Never was skin color lauded in the minutes, while so many other qualities were. Rey took on the hypocrisy of New

Orleans whites in an open letter to the radical newspaper published by free people of color, *L'Union*. Writing from Camp Strong in Gentilly, he complained that many whites who called themselves Creoles referred to his regiment derisively as "Natifs." But being called Natives did not make him ashamed, he added, because most of the "nègres" in the First Regiment of Native Guards were whiter than half of the whites in the Garde d'Orléans.

"Know that we have no prejudices; we receive the world in our camp," he said.

But hardly anyone took him at his word. Outsiders preferred to apply the easy narrative of colorism and the vocabulary of race to the free men whenever possible.

Capt. Cailloux, of the First Louisiana, a man so black that he actually prided himself upon his blackness, died the death of a hero, leading on his men in the thickest of the fight.

—*New York Times*, June 13, 1863

A YEAR AFTER OCCUPATION, the Civil War outside of New Orleans was bloody and real. Boguille's friend André Cailloux had fallen in a terrible battle at Port Hudson, Louisiana. The site was one of the last Mississippi River strongholds of the Confederate Army, and the First and Third Regiments of the Louisiana Native Guards joined the Union attack. The June 13, 1863, *New York Times* reported on the Black troops: "On going into action they were 1,080 strong, and formed into four lines. . . . When ordered to charge up to the works, they did so with the skill and nerve of old veterans, (black people, be it remembered, who had never been in action before,) but the fire from the rebel guns was so terrible upon the unprotected masses, that the first few shots mowed them down like grass, and so continued. . . . When, by a flag of truce, our forces in other directions were permitted to reclaim their dead, the benefit, through some neglect, was not extended to these black regiments. The deeds of heroism performed by these colored men were such as the proudest white men might emulate. Their colors are torn to pieces by shot, and literally bespattered by blood and brains."

On the morning of July 29, 1863, Boguille dressed to march in Cailloux's funeral procession. He left through his front door, which faced northeast. The pink dawn served as inspiration on most mornings, but today he was distraught. Boguille knew Cailloux well. He was the husband of Félicie Cailloux, the first principal of the Couvent School. Boguille may have seen André Cailloux waiting for his wife after school meetings. They both attended the many fundraisers held in the Economie's hall for Couvent students. They both rallied their families for parties, student recitals, and dramatic readings. They both petitioned their neighbors for donations for orphans, and they stood near each other at political gatherings.

Boguille could picture Cailloux—so honorable and committed—rushing into the Confederate line of fire. Then he imagined the man riddled with bullets, shot down near the American flag. And the indignity that his body lay for days as the battle raged, and then longer as the white soldiers—both Union and Confederate—were taken away first! More than a month passed before Cailloux's remains came home to New Orleans.

Around the corner at the Economie's hall, Boguille met his society brothers. The men planned to go together to the hall of a society called Les Amis de l'Ordre, the Friends of Order, where Cailloux's body lay under an American flag. One of the Economie members was a pallbearer.

As Boguille turned the corner, he could see people lingering in the street, waiting to join the funeral procession. The men greeted him with solemn, downcast shakes of their heads. Death was in the air. On the sidewalks and porch steps women gathered in groups and talked quietly. They would walk together to Claiborne Street to wait for the hearse.

Colored New Orleans was a small town. They all knew Cailloux in the neighborhoods. He had been born into bondage downriver, and the woman who held him, Aimée Duvernay Lartet, manumitted him when he was almost twenty years old. After working for a while as a cigar maker, he purchased his mother. The colored women of New Orleans respected Cailloux as one of their sons.

Boguille saw women going to the procession leading a rainbow of children who clung to their skirts. Some women carried miniature versions of the Union Stars and Stripes flag in their hands. Others had it pinned to their dresses. They wiped damp white handkerchiefs across the backs of their necks to keep themselves cool in the August heat. Occasionally they removed the handkerchiefs from their necks to dry their tears or to wave the cloths back and forth. The gesture did not signal surrender; it was meant to call the spirits from Africa, as was usual in ceremonies in West Africa, Haiti, and New Orleans—the route of the slave trade.

Cailloux was a member of Les Amis de l'Ordre. Its hall stood about a mile from the Economie and, like it, provided burial and medical assistance to its members. To get there, Boguille and the Economistes needed to walk from the Faubourg Tremé to the back of the Faubourg Marigny, through the areas that held most of the free people of color in New Orleans.

They passed the small houses of working people who went unnoticed to outsiders but were well known within their community. Boguille recognized many of the residents who stood on their porches to watch almost a hundred men from the Economie pass. The neighbors went to the main corner of the funeral route—St. Bernard Avenue and Claiborne Street—to see the entire funeral cortege. Thirty-six societies marched besides the Economie. They included the United Brethren, Arts and Mechanics' Association, Free Friends, Perseverance Society, Star of the Cross, the Children of Moses, and God Protects Us, known in Boguille's circles as Dieu Nous Protégé, a group that had been purchasing and freeing the enslaved for more than two decades. Cailloux's was the largest funeral procession in New Orleans during the Civil War. The second largest was for a rebel captain, evidence of the divided city.

The head of the Catholic archdiocese—sympathetic to the Confederate cause—had warned the priest at St. Rose of Lima Church not to say Mass for Cailloux. The church promised to excommunicate Father Claude Pascal Maistre. Nevertheless, Father Maistre went to the hall and said Mass. During the eulogy he called for everyone gathered to imitate Cailloux's bravery and to stand for "justice, freedom and good government." He added that Cailloux died an enviable death because he had given himself for his country.

Funeral of the Late Captain Cailloux, First Louisiana Volunteers (Colored); from *Harper's Weekly*, August 29, 1863; *THNOC, 1974.25.6.559*

Maistre's words resonated in the minds of the free colored community as a reminder of the 1848 Revolution in France. The Black Parisian author Alexandre Dumas *père* had written the lyrics for "Les Girondins: Mourir pour la patrie" ("The Girondins: To Die for One's Country"). The song proclaimed, "To fall for our country is a privilege high. The noblest of deaths is in battle, for freedom, to die." The revolutionaries in Paris sang the song in the streets.

Men carried Cailloux's casket to the horse-drawn hearse provided by the Economie's president, Pierre Casanave. The hearse was a four-wheeled wagon with black ironwork corners holding in glass panes so that the flag-covered casket was visible. The driver wore a top hat. The *New York Times* described the scene:

> Immense crowds of colored people had by this time gathered around the building, and the streets leading thereto were rendered almost impassible. Two companies of the Sixth Louisiana (colored) regiment, from their camp on the Company Canal, were there to act as an escort, and Esplanade street, for more than a mile, was lined with colored societies, both male and female, in open order, waiting for the hearse to pass through.

After a short pause, a sudden silence fell upon the crowd, the band commenced playing a dirge, and the body was brought from the hall on the shoulders of eight soldiers, escorted by six members of the society and six colored Captains, who acted as pall-bearers. The corpse was conveyed to the hearse through a crowd composed of both white and black people, and in silence profound as death itself. Not a sound was heard save the mournful music of the band, and not a head in all that vast multitude but was uncovered.

L'Union said that Cailloux was "loved and respected by all who knew him." Boguille certainly remembered the man in the same way as the newspaper reporter did. The reporter praised Cailloux's "gallant bearing, his gentlemanly deportment, his amiable disposition and his capacities as a soldier—having received a very good education."

But the *New York World* reported:

A Defunct Darkey Canonized

Among the "American citizens of African descent" that occupied those "prominent positions" in the assault upon Port Hudson, May 27, was a *well-known "bull-nigger" of New-Orleans, named Cailloux.* He was one of those much-praised native guards that had the choice between the batteries of their foes in front and the bayonets of their friends in the rear. Cailloux fell. His carcass lay rotting on the ground, exposed to sun and rain for forty-one days, from the date of the assault to the capitulation of Port Hudson. . . . For weeks past scarcely a wench in the city has appeared in the streets without a crape rosette in memory of "Saint Cailloux."

This version of the story did not resonate with the followers of Cailloux. They believed that he had martyred himself for them.

If the love of the fatherland had no echo in our hearts,
would we hesitate to defend the cause of humanity? Has
the Black Code left our memory? Will it still be possible to
restore the reign of whip, handcuffs, and yoke?

—Edouard Tinchant, June 30, 1863

TWO WEEKS AFTER THE death of Cailloux, Economie brothers Fouché, Lanna, Chessé, and Boguille had called a mass meeting of Black men. The invitation went by word of mouth to the Economie brothers where they gathered in their dry goods stores, in their boot making and tailoring shops, and conversed over the fences of neighbors. Other representatives who were not Economie members also spread the news to their friends in activists' circles at coffeehouses or in the homes of intimates.

One goal of the organizers was to purchase an American flag to hang outside the door of the Economie's hall in memory of the fallen soldiers at Port Hudson. More importantly, the Economistes intended to catalyze the free men of color to achieve their full rights as citizens.

The meeting took place in French, with the exception of one speaker, and was reported by the Black, French-language newspaper, *L'Union*. It was the only paper to cover the gathering, and the article included an apology for its abridged account. *L'Union* led the summary with its editor, Paul

Trévigne, telling the audience about resolutions proposed by "la Ligue Nationale Loyale, Unité Africaine" (the National Loyal League, African Unit). The group encouraged people of color to celebrate the Fourth of July as a display of patriotism and a statement on their inclusion into the Union. The league's second resolution urged men to join local Union militias, and when Trévigne reminded the audience of Cailloux's sacrifice, the Economie's hall rang with applause.

Edouard Tinchant spoke next. A New Orleanian and descendant of a Senegalese woman who had immigrated from Jérémie like Boguille's mother, Tinchant frequently spoke against hierarchies in color and social status. He rallied the crowd that night to demand equal rights for all men by asking a question in the call-and-response manner of his African roots: "Citizens, The world is watching us. . . . Will we believe as our enemies do that our race should be enslaved?"

The audience responded, "*Non. Non.*"

"If it is true that the most precious gift to man is honor, let us save this inheritance for our children, and let them know, if we die, that their fathers preferred death to shame and infamy."

The men in the room did not wish to be known only as victims of American slavery or live in its shadows. They enthusiastically applauded Tinchant.

Economiste Lanna encouraged the assembly to sign a petition advocating for their right to vote. One of the most compelling requests for suffrage in the United States by literate, Black property owners began in a French-language gathering. The environment might have seemed strange, except that the roadmap for citizen revolutions had been handed down from France to Haiti to the Economie's hall.

Lanna's suggestion was implemented a few months later in a gathering that took place mostly in English of "six or seven hundred people," the *New York Times* correspondent in New Orleans wrote. The night of November 5, 1863, marked "unquestionably one of the most important and significant meetings which have ever taken place in this city."

ON THAT FIRST THURSDAY in November, around sunset, the caretaker of the Economie's hall mounted its front steps, unlocked the double doors, and braced them open. The crisp air was giving way to a damp chill. By evening members would crowd into the large meeting room, and the mass of bodies would create heat. The men would peel away coats and vests. They were accustomed to the extreme changes in autumn temperatures in New Orleans. This year, the volatile weather both indoors and outdoors reflected the mercurial political atmosphere.

As the sun went down, the caretaker lit the gaslights. The room filled quickly. Men took all the seats and stood along the walls. Ludger Boguille had yearned for this meeting. The Economie was hosting its largest public gathering yet to discuss securing the right to vote. The veterans of the Battle of New Orleans attended, as did men from the present generation of fighters. Among them were François Boisdoré *fils*, who had recently left the Native Guards, in which he had served as a private. His military service and upbringing showed in his confident bearing.

Once everyone assembled in the hall, Josiah Fisk came to the podium. He was a white Presbyterian minister and ardent Unionist from Texas who for many years had been at odds with the Confederate authorities. The Economie men and the others listened politely when Fisk said that Lincoln had freed the enslaved in the rebellious states, and that was enough. The free men of color in Louisiana should be patient.

Boguille may have wanted to say something. If free people waited until whites decided to believe in racial equality, they might wait for another century. Boisdoré's grandfather François Dubuisson was white, and his grandmother Adelaide Boisdoré was a free woman of color who had to buy her freedom and that of her children over many years. Boguille may have felt the heat rising from Boisdoré *fils* as he considered the speaker's logic.

A *New-Orleans Times* reporter, observing the complexions of the club members, remarked that the hall "contained more white American blood than African." The audience simply matched the composition of the free people in New Orleans. Seventy percent of the light-colored, mixed-raced people in the city were free, as were 20 percent of the dark-skinned people. The families and friends of the Economie included Jews, Germans, Frenchmen, Mexicans, Italians, and people from West Africa.

Outsiders always focused on the light skin shades of the Economie members to show the extent of their equality to whites, but a rational man like Boguille knew that color was an illogical argument. The goal of the free people of color was not to achieve whiteness, only an equal condition of liberty. Pétion, the Economie's hero and Haiti's first president, had written into the nation's constitution that all Haitian citizens should be called Blacks. It was his way of rejecting the past and combating the colonial preoccupation with skin tones and status. The arbitrary nature of race was not lost on the men in the room that evening when Fisk concluded there was no chance the free men of color would gain equality in the near future, as there was a "vast amount of prejudice to remove before the question of franchise could be considered."

Boisdoré then raised his hand, stood, and took the floor. He said, "I am not a speaker and never before addressed an audience. It is only the impulse of the occasion that has induced me to attempt to speak to you at this time." He exaggerated his lack of experience. He had spoken before the men of the Economie in that very room.

As soon as he stood and began his response, the audience applauded. They knew him very well. He was a prominent second-generation free man of color. Twenty years earlier, his father had sued the Citizens' Bank and won. The younger Boisdoré consistently attended the debates among members of the society. His brothers had trained him for just this moment. A shiver of excitement passed through the crowd.

Boisdoré sensed their confidence and must have spoken loudly, because *L'Union* was able to write a three-column article with the text of his speech, and, because he spoke in English, the *New-Orleans Times* quoted him word for word: "When our fathers fought in 1815 they were told that they should be compensated; we have waited already a long time for it. I agree with the gentleman fully as far as regards slavery, but not on the main point. We have waited long enough; we have never been slaves." His voice resonated against the smooth plaster walls.

Boisdoré's remarks rang true to the audience. The veterans who met regularly as a group in the hall would now have glanced at one another, murmured, and nodded in agreement. The crowd held its breath as Boisdoré continued.

"When the Federals came to New Orleans would any others than us give them a drink of water without poison in it? We were actuated by no motives but patriotism. In the love of our country we have fought its battles. If the United States has the right to arm us, it certainly has the right to allow us the rights of suffrage."

Then he applied the logic that he heard daily in the conversations among the educated free men of color: "True, where slavery exists there can be no equality, but there is no slavery in Louisiana now. The laws of the State of Louisiana are dead. Louisiana is a Territory not a State. This is told us every day in the Courts. If the Government has the right to set aside these laws in one way, it can set them aside in another."

He went on, "The gentleman says that . . . we can do nothing, on account of the prejudices against us. Well let them sneer and let them kick. If we cannot succeed with the authorities here, we will go to a higher power. We will go to President Lincoln, and then we shall know who we are dealing with."

A few men may have laughed out loud at the boldness of this idea, while others went wide-eyed as they imagined Boisdoré walking into the president's office.

"We have always been told by persons, who come here with a vast amount of patriotism, no doubt, that we must postpone, but I must urge that we have already postponed long enough. When men come here from Ireland or Germany they are not treated like puppies. After they have been here a certain length of time, they are admitted to all the rights of freemen. Go to the registration office and see the crosses there of Irishmen and Germans, who cannot write their names. There are no such men here."

Boisdoré meant Boguille, Rey, Lanna, and hundreds of others seated in the room. He addressed the audience, "You can all at least read and write, and can appreciate the right of suffrage. Gentlemen say that we should wait till we have a free State Government. We offer them our assistance to establish a free State Government, and will they refuse it?"

The hall filled with applause. Some men stood and shouted. They didn't see any democracy in a new Louisiana government that didn't reflect the will of all its citizens.

The *New-Orleans Times* reporter presented Boisdoré's remarks, with their stirring concluding questions, "as a specimen of the eloquence of the colored citizens of New Orleans."

L'Union wrote, "The assembly, composed of the elite of our population, was full of enthusiasm and the decorum observed would have done honor to any other public assembly held by well-educated men."

Boguille may have read the paper every day looking for Lincoln's response to Boisdoré's offer. Would men of color participate in the formation of the new state?

If the United States has the right to arm us, it certainly has the right to allow us the rights of suffrage.

—Economie member François Boisdoré *fils*, 1863

DESPITE THE ENTHUSIASM IN the Economie's hall in November, François Boisdoré's appeal did not have the intended effect. President Lincoln endorsed a kind of reconstruction that did not take Black men into account. Lincoln's so-called Ten Percent Plan was established in December 1863 and allowed any secessionist state to rejoin the Union if 10 percent of prewar voters pledged loyalty to the United States. The states had to elect a new government, draft a new constitution, and agree to abolish slavery, but the plan levied no other penalties against the vast majority of Confederates.

Enough white men in Louisiana pledged loyalty to the United States to hold elections, and Michael Hahn assumed the governorship in March 1864. But despite the installation of a state government sympathetic to the Union, the white electorate did not favor extending suffrage to Blacks.

Undaunted, free men of color continued to gather signatures on a petition they would personally deliver to the president. Economistes Tervalon,

Arnold Bertonneau;
*courtesy of Thomas F.
Bertonneau*

Chevarre, and Moreau, as Battle of New Orleans veterans, were at the top
of the list. Thomas Durant endorsed it, too. He was a radical white lawyer
and a leader in the Union Association of New Orleans, which included
northern transplants to the city (like Durant) and local professionals and
businessmen who had remained loyal to the United States during secession.
Durant had encouraged the free men of color to request suffrage only for
property owners.

On March 4, 1864, the meeting with Lincoln took place. The free
colored community sent the cofounder of the daily French-language, Black
newspaper, Jean Baptiste Roudanez, to Washington along with Arnold
Bertonneau, who had first joined the Confederates, and then the Union,

as an officer. The men took the petition to the president with signatures from more than one thousand men of color, all property owners. They told Lincoln that they deserved the vote because of their loyalty to the United States. Their fathers had fought in the Battle of New Orleans, at least four of the men who had signed the petition were Union soldiers, and one was once an officer for Napoleon. The men appealed to Lincoln's sense of morality: men such as themselves should be citizens and voters. Didn't he agree?

Lincoln responded coolly. He accepted the signatures without making any commitments. The *New York Times* reported that "having the restoration of the Union paramount to all other questions, [Lincoln] would do nothing that would hinder that consummation, or omit anything that would accomplish it." The article added that the president "did nothing in matters of this kind upon moral grounds, but solely upon political necessities."

Possibly moved by the delegation, however, Lincoln suggested that Louisiana in its constitutional convention could give the vote to free men of color. He wrote privately to the new governor, Michael Hahn, on March 13, 1864:

My dear Sir:

I congratulate you on having fixed your name in history as the first free-state Governor of Louisiana. Now you are about to have a Convention which, among other things, will probably define the elective franchise. I barely suggest for your private consideration, whether some of the colored people may not be let in—as, for instance, the very intelligent, and especially those who have fought gallantly in our ranks. They would probably help, in some trying time to come, to keep the jewel of liberty within the family of freedom. But this is only a suggestion, not to the public, but to you alone.

Yours truly

A. Lincoln.

Whether Hahn was sympathetic or held back by his legislature, the free men of color did not receive suffrage. But they did not lose hope.

THE ECONOMIE'S TWENTY-EIGHTH ANNIVERSARY celebration took place in its hall on March 1864. The banquet was the first recorded in the minutes since they ended suddenly in 1858. The members installed the orator François Boisdoré *fils* as the society's president. The seventy-two men present included veterans of two United States wars, businessmen and traders, teachers and builders. They met in the hall now, just as their families had gathered in one another's homes for generations. But the war had brought changes.

Their proximity to northerners had altered their language. Many men no longer called their new president Boisdoré by the term *le fauteuil*, a word that literally meant "armchair" but figuratively signified the head of the meeting. Now they called him the *cherman*, meaning "chairman," but spelled the way it sounded to them. The French word *cher* means "dear," so they probably considered that, too, as a good way to distinguish the person who led their organization.

Their new Americanisms did not change the Economistes' anniversary traditions. They regaled themselves at the annual banquets with ham, bread, cheese, and cake. The men drank bottles of wine, sang to one another, recited poetry, and made toasts before presentations of flowers, fraternal hugs, and farewells.

Boguille Steps Forward

1864–1866

Slavery . . . can never again exist in Louisiana, but with slavery abolished must vanish every [v]estige of oppression: the colored man must be allowed to vote, the doors of the public schools must be open to their children so they may study together.

—Arnold Bertonneau, at a dinner with
William Lloyd Garrison, Frederick Douglass,
and the governor of Massachusetts, 1864

ONE OF THE MEMBERS of the Union Association who remained loyal to the United States government during the secession of Louisiana was William Henry Hire. He was a physician, had been named secretary to the board of health, and served as head surgeon of several military hospitals under General Butler and the subsequent commander of Union forces in Louisiana, Major General Nathaniel P. Banks. When the federal government occupied New Orleans, it opened Negro public schools, called Freedmen's Schools. The term "freedmen" distinguished the newly emancipated from the people of color who had not been bound by slavery before the war. Hire wrote to the superintendent of schools to recommend two people for jobs:

April 5, 1864

Sir

Permit me to introduce to your notice my friends Mr. and Mrs.
Boguille, who are old and experienced teachers of this city.

I sincerely trust that you will give them the consideration they deserve.
They are particularly well qualified to teach among a Creole population
whose mother tongue is French, as I have found from experience that
the knowledge of both languages is very desirable.

I shall have much pleasure in waiting on your Board.

Your obedt. servt. Wm. H. Hire, M.D.

By May, Mary Ann was head of the Douglass School for Negroes. The
Republican inspector who came to see her at the Roman Street site wrote
at the end of that month, "Mrs. Boguille began alone . . . with 20 pupils. At
present, she has 44 pupils." A year later, she had 78 students in her class.

Women of all races began teaching in the New Orleans schools, with
class sizes ranging from 13 to 182 students. Some were New Englanders,
members of abolitionist organizations or Christian missionary societies
whose moral convictions moved them to help newly freed Blacks.

Newspapers across the South satirized them as "Yankee school-marms."
A letter to the *New York Times* from a correspondent in Georgia was
reprinted in other papers throughout the nation, describing the typical
volunteer from Maine as having a "ruddy complexion, solid square-built
form, and one or two curls hanging down from her light brown hair."
The writer satirized teachers from Massachusetts as "little, natty girls with
looped up skirts, and fashionable outfit[s]" and claimed that whichever
northern state they came from, they were "the bitterest most uncompro-
mising Radicals imaginable."

Critics expressed horror about single white women entering the Negro
schools. White southerners shunned these women for empowering students
with lectures on their rights, saying that the teachers were making John
Brown into a martyr and a saint. These objections echoed the pamphlets
written for enslavers in the 1830s, which claimed that education for a Black
person "unfit him for his station in life"—in other words, made a man into
a less willing slave.

The Misses Cooke's School Room, Freedman's Bureau, Richmond, Va.; by James E. Taylor; from *Frank Leslie's Illustrated Newspaper*, November 17, 1866; *courtesy of Library of Congress, Prints and Photographs Division*

One disparaging article datelined New Orleans epitomized these arguments:

> We know that they come here simply to make the negro discontented, unwilling to labor, and teach him to expect to be supported in idleness. . . . They do not try to improve the intellectual and moral nature of the negro. . . . It is strange to see young unmarried women leaving home and friends and undertaking a long journey alone without any protection, or else the rather questionable protection of some young officer. . . . The most we can do for them so long as they do not seek to ruin the race that have been placed in our charge, by seeking to instill into their minds impossible, foolish, and evil principles, is to let them magnificently alone. We allow them to live with and enjoy entirely the society of those whom they desire to benefit.

That was all right with Mary Ann. She had come to New Orleans almost a decade before the Civil War and had met her soul mate.

THE RECONSTRUCTION GOVERNMENT HAD opened public schools for white children, too, but students learned different lessons there. At one, the teachers instructed their charges to draw the rebel flag in their textbooks.

Outside of the city, violence and harassment were continual threats. Some Black children were stoned for going to school. Marauders threw rocks through the windows of Black schools during classes. One rural school was vandalized every night for eight months.

Still, Boguille saw progress. Before the Civil War, the law prevented the enslaved from being taught to read or write, and free people of color had to pay for private schooling for their children. By March 1864 the city had eight public schools for colored students, with twenty-five teachers.

In April of that year Arnold Bertonneau, who had met with President Lincoln, went to a dinner in Boston with the abolitionist William Lloyd Garrison, the orator Frederick Douglass, and Governor John Albion Andrew of Massachusetts (who had raised funds for John Brown's legal representation). The dignitaries sat on the dais while Bertonneau spoke to the audience about education in Louisiana. He noted that many free people of color in New Orleans were property owners who paid real estate taxes. None of their money went to support their schools. He wanted the state to pay for the education of all the children—Blacks and whites—in integrated settings. The audience applauded this radical idea.

The agitation for Black education started a slow burn in Louisiana that grew in intensity among people of color and their supporters. But school integration was too radical for many whites.

Major General Banks, General Butler's replacement as administrator of federal Reconstruction, issued an order to add more Black schools rather than integrate. The proposal was to tax the people of Louisiana for the creation and maintenance of both school systems.

Louisiana's constitutional convention of 1864 tried to ignore the order by tabling it for two months, then refused it. "I never will be so dishonest as to cast my vote in such a manner that I will tax a white man for the education of a negro," one delegate said. "No, sir! I never will disgrace myself by such a vote."

A compromise solution of separate educational systems for different races, funded through separate taxes for each, then came up for debate. The conversation turned to who would be admitted to white schools—because it was not at all clear who was a Negro. There were so many light-skinned Blacks in Louisiana, the delegates feared that nonwhite students would sneak in.

One delegate urged the members to create a definition of whiteness, saying, "I simply offer this resolution, because I know that if an assessor goes to many families and assesses them as colored people, he will be liable to have the top of his head shot off. . . . We must define it and have it understood whether a fourth, seven-eighths or any other proportionable intermixture, is to cause a man to be considered as white or black. Now is the time to settle the question."

Another delegate suggested that anyone who claimed to be white could be admitted into a white school. But the original proponent of the measure said that he knew a man "with a fair and rosy complexion" and "as good French blood as Napoleon." This man could seemingly change races, the delegate added, with a change in climate—becoming tan or pale, depending on his exposure to the sun.

The resolution for a definition of color also did not pass.

Later the state auditor—Dr. A. P. Dostie, a strong advocate for equal schools—wrote a letter that was read to the convention. He asked the delegates not to insert words such as "color," "black," and "white" into the education portion of the constitution because they were inappropriate. And, in a political move, he warned them that he had heard that many delegates would reject the entire constitution if words indicating color were included, slowing down the process of drafting laws for the state. The constitutional convention adopted a plan for public education without any requirements for the separation of races or a definition of whiteness. The result was that all children in Louisiana had equal access.

The victory thrilled Boguille. Now he could envision a future without prejudice for his students. And he could tell them that fairness won out because it was the best choice. Equality was extended to Black children, just like everyone else.

When Boguille opened the door of his classrooms, he inhaled the aroma of his vocation. It was a smell that truly satisfied only someone who spent many days bent over an inkwell. The acrid scent of the ink, the mist of chalk dust, the earthen residue of slate, and the sour humidity of anxious children hung in the air. Boguille was in his element. His wife had a classroom, and his son Florian had another. At fifty-two years old, Boguille had brought together his childhood dreams.

We want labor, education, and progress.

—Economie president François Boisdoré *fils*, 1865

THE EMANCIPATION PROCLAMATION, WHICH took effect January 1, 1863, applied only to people enslaved in Confederate territory. New Orleans was under Union control by that time, so the enslaved experienced no freedom, simply irony. New Orleanians moved one step closer to emancipation in April 1864, after the Thirteenth Amendment passed the Senate. Boguille, who had been working with freedmen since New Orleans fell to the Union, could imagine victory.

Some Economie men saw no benefit for themselves. They had argued for voting rights and full citizenship, and they had lost. But Economie brother Lanna encouraged the other members to recognize progress.

At the May 16, 1864, meeting, Lanna told the others, "My brothers, the era of the regime of liberty governs our country."

Lanna continued, "When one says that we never have won, one deludes oneself, because if slavery is abolished, the Code noir is also, and that is good." From the earliest days of the Louisiana colony, people of color had been restricted—first by the Code noir, imposed by the French in 1724 and maintained by the Spanish, and then by other so-called Black Codes imposed under American rule. From Lanna's perspective, the free men of color and the enslaved had a common enemy in the restrictive laws.

Eugene Meilleur raised his hand and volunteered to organize a celebratory dinner at the Economie's hall. The society advertised in the Black-owned *New Orleans Tribune* that "A Grand Ratification Dinner Will Be Held on Thursday, September 29, 1864." Tickets cost fifty cents and could be purchased at four coffeehouses, including one run by the boisterous Economie member Médard Porée. The price was much less than the entrance fees for special events that the Economie had sold before the Civil War. Admission to its first ball in 1841 had cost two dollars, more than a day's pay for a carpenter. By 1864 a ticket cost one-quarter of a day's pay. Fewer dollars were circulating among the members now. They also wanted the banquet to be open to as many people as possible.

But Boguille couldn't wait for the Economie's September dinner. He took on the role of grand marshal for a coalition of citizens from across the city. He called together five local ministers and their congregations, twelve representatives from four neighborhood districts, the Masonic orders, and a number of the city's benevolent societies to plan a public celebration that would take place on June 11. *L'Union* published frequent advertisements for meetings to organize the event at the Republican Exchange, a building at 3 Levee Street, next to the federal customhouse. Participants were told to contact Boguille and his deputies, among them Economistes Louis Lainez, A. Populus, and Eugene Meilleur.

When the day arrived, people came to Congo Square by the thousands. Despite the heat, they wore their best clothes—women and girls carrying parasols, men in dress coats—and hundreds of military veterans arrived in uniform. Children from the colored schools traveled in groups, and so did many societies carrying banners and American flags and accompanied by field bands. They came from every direction to the large area bordering Rampart Street and across from the old city, under the oak trees, where a platform was set up for the occasion. They started filling the streets at nine o'clock in the morning, and by eleven the program began.

On the platform adorned with small flags and decorative plants were more than a dozen veterans of the Battle of New Orleans. A reporter said they were "as strong and hearty as the day when they showed their devotion to the glorious Stars and Stripes." In the shade nearby were a number of female schoolteachers from the colored schools.

Mayor Stephen Hoyt attended, as did Governor Hahn, who said he "had not come there to take any active part in the proceedings, but merely as a looker on; he was highly pleased with the propriety, order and zeal."

François Boisdoré *fils* addressed the crowd in French to frequent applause. Then the Fifteenth Battery Light Artillery of Massachusetts, stationed in New Orleans, fired a one-hundred-gun salute. The governor ordered the fire department to ring the bells in the fire alarm boxes throughout the city one hundred times. Afterward, the celebrants proceeded out of Congo Square with bands playing and banners flying. The colored soldiers marched across town in a line, as did the veterans of the Battle of New Orleans, the public school children, and the societies—including the Economie and the Artisans, Boguille's old friends—and the moderate and radical branches of Republican clubs.

One part of the event perhaps moved Boguille's heart most of all: the children sang patriotic songs, and a man who had formerly been enslaved came up to the podium. He was the Reverend Stephen Walter Rogers. He had been free only twelve years, but long before the Civil War he had secretly been a schoolteacher. His master's young son gave Rogers a spelling book one day and told him that he might be killed if he were found with it. Rogers carefully hid the book and learned every word. Then he began teaching others on the plantation in the middle of the night. He took students only from among the other workers who could keep a secret. The school operated from ten at night until two in the morning, while the whites were asleep. The students met in a carriage house and learned by candlelight. They made the candles themselves, and they plugged cracks in the wall with rags and moss so that no light would leak out to the yard. About forty people usually attended nightly.

For a while, Rogers had only a few books. Five students at one time read from each speller. Then a Jewish merchant passing through town sold him more books. The school disbanded after a year. During that time, all but five of his students had been sold to other masters.

Rogers slowly revealed his literacy after he came with his master to New Orleans. Rather than punishment, he received approval because his ability made him a more valuable worker for renting out. Among other jobs, he began to run errands for banks and steamboats.

While he was still enslaved, Rogers had written and published a book about his public and clandestine activities. In 1852 his master died, and Rogers wrote a letter to a magazine revealing his work. His letter said, "You will see by this little book, which I published in the year 1850, while I was a slave and superintendent of a Sunday-school of nearly three hundred scholars, which I gathered in one of our colored churches, that our colored Sunday-schools were in operation before the war. This book was a daring piece of my own; and you may safely say that you have seen a book published by a slave before the war, and at that time it was quite a curiosity, and a secret to the friends of freedom." After being freed, Rogers had stayed on in Louisiana as the leader of his own church.

For some of the men in the Economie and across New Orleans, social status was still a great distinction. It was more of a practical separation to Ludger Boguille: some people had resources, while others had needs. He was ready to serve.

The day of the meeting of this Convention has inaugurated a new era. It was the first political move ever made by the colored people of the State acting, in a body. . . . It was a great spectacle, and one which will be remembered for generations to come. . . . The speakers whom we have seen rising to prominence in this Convention will be the champions of their race.

—*New Orleans Tribune*, January 15, 1865

FREDERICK DOUGLASS CONVENED AN assembly of men seeking equal rights and the vote for Blacks on October 4, 1864, in Syracuse, New York. On January 9, 1865, Boguille attended a similar convention in New Orleans.

The *New Orleans Tribune* wrote about the men attending the Louisiana State Colored Convention, "seated side by side the rich and the poor, the literate and educated man, and the country laborer, hardly released from bondage, distinguished only by the natural gifts of the mind. There, the rich landowner, the opulent tradesman, seconded motions offered by humble mechanics and freedmen. Ministers of the gospel, officers and soldiers of the US army, men who handle the sword or the pen, merchants and clerks,—all the classes of society were represented, and united in a common thought: the actual liberation from social and political bondage."

Some Economistes attending the Louisiana convention were members who had returned from abroad—Etienne Cordeviolle from Paris and

Eugène Chessé from Mexico. Local attendees were Henry Chevarre, who had been a soldier in the Battle of New Orleans, and François Boisdoré *fils*, a veteran and the son of a veteran. An editorial in the *Tribune* praised several Economie members: "Speakers in the French Language must not be forgotten. Messrs. J. Curiel and L. Boguille, well known to our Creole population, have temporarily occupied the chair; Mr. E. Chesse was firm, and took a manly stand in defense of his opinions; Mr. C. Martinez could not possess a better knowledge of parliamentary rules, had he been for ten years a Congressman at Washington."

Other city luminaries included Father Maistre, the Catholic priest who had officiated at the funeral of André Cailloux, Battle of New Orleans drummer Jordan Noble, and Native Guards Capt. James H. Ingraham, who had attended the 1864 gathering in Syracuse. Ingraham was the president of the Louisiana convention. He had resigned from the Union Army, as had many other colored Louisiana volunteers when they discovered that the white troops and officers were as cruel and prejudiced as some of the Confederates.

Boguille became a vice president of the convention and chaired the French-language portions of the meeting. The agenda focused on education, labor, and a topic that would remain a struggle from one generation of civil rights activists to the next: integration of public transportation. By 1865 Negro soldiers could ride on the streetcars, but their family members and other colored citizens were excluded. Integration of public transportation was a radical idea, not even accepted in the North. As early as 1862, a correspondent for the *New York Times* wrote about New Orleans streetcars, "I should say that the city cars here, as in New-York, have certain ones appropriated to colored people. These specialties are designated by a star. Recently, a formal decision of the Court here . . . rendered these distinctions nugatory, and in New-Orleans respectable black men and white men, if they behave themselves, ride together."

This editorial style openly demonstrated prejudice in a description of the Emancipation Proclamation celebration in Congo Square as "a procession, composed of all shades, from ebony to lemon color" that "presented a grotesque appearance enough—the women, some with their gaily-colored handkerchiefs, twisted fancifully around their heads, and others aping the latest styles of Olymp and Sophie. The men, especially the Marshals of the day, evidently felt their importance."

The event and his participation certainly were important to grand marshal Boguille. After emancipation, he advocated a progressive, integrated society that was radical even to northerners. As the *New York Times* correspondent said about New Orleans's move toward integrated streetcars, "We hope this fact will not cause a commotion on the Sixth-avenue Railway of Gotham, nor make the mules that draw those vehicles along bray with indignation."

But the mule-headed perspective of some whites did not slow the convention delegates who, by the end of the five-day meeting, agreed to petition the railroad about the segregated streetcars. The delegates also formed a state Equal Rights League based on the principles from the Douglass-led convention in Syracuse:

> 1st. We declare that all men are born free and equal; that no man or government has the right to annul, repeal, abrogate, contravene, or render inoperative, this fundamental principle, except it be for crime; therefore we demand the immediate and unconditional abolition of slavery.
>
> 2d. That, as natives of American soil, we claim the right to remain upon it: and that any attempt to deport, remove, expatriate, or colonize us to any other land, or to mass us here against our will, is unjust; for here were we born, for this country our fathers and our brothers have fought, and here we hope to remain in the full enjoyment of enfranchised manhood, and its dignities.
>
> 3d. That, as citizens of the Republic, we claim the rights of other citizens. We claim that we are, by right, entitled to respect; that due attention should be given to our needs; that proper rewards should be given for our services, and that the immunities and privileges of all other citizens and defenders of the nation's honor should be conceded to us. We claim the right to be heard in the halls of Congress; and we claim our fair share of the public domain, whether acquired by purchase, treaty, confiscation, or military conquest.

4th. That, emerging as we are from the long night of gloom and sorrow, we are entitled to, and claim, the sympathy and aid of the entire Christian world; and we invoke the considerate aid of mankind in this crisis of our history, and in this hour of sacrifice, suffering, and trial."

The Louisiana convention also promoted moral, educational, and economic development with a plan for representatives to go throughout the state "to inquire [into] the condition of our race, and to register complaints." They proposed a Bureau of Industry to gather information about freedmen in rural areas and facilitate their "coming and going freely" and "to take care for the sick and disabled." The *Tribune*, reporting on the convention, suggested that all the colored people of New Orleans should support the Equal Rights League, which was determined to secure the vote for Black men.

Boguille spoke on the second evening of the Louisiana convention. The setting could not have been more suitable: the School of Liberty, the American Missionary Association's showpiece that now educated five hundred students. Just over a year later, it enrolled eight hundred, and the cover of *Harper's Weekly* featured a drawing of the school, the largest educational institution for freed people in the nation. The site of Boguille's talk also made a statement about Reconstruction. The building had once housed the Medical College of the University of Louisiana, the site where white supremacists Cartwright and Nott had worked.

Before taking the stage, Boguille no doubt thought of his favorite author, François Fénelon, who had described the responsibilities of an orator to his audience: "He must infuse into their minds the love of moderation, frugality, a generous concern for the public good, and an inviolable regard to the laws and constitution: and the orator's zeal for all these must appear in his conduct, as well as in his discourses."

However, contrary to the *Tribune's* prediction that the names of these leaders of the race would be remembered for generations, Boguille's speech that night was not even reported. The paper published only a short paragraph in its French edition that said Boguille recited a bit of verse. It was enthusiastically applauded.

THE "ABRAHAM LINCOLN SCHOOL" FOR FREEDMEN, NEW ORLEANS, LOUISIANA.—[PHOTOGRAPHED BY LILIENTHAL, NEW ORLEANS.]

The "Abraham Lincoln School" for Freedmen, New Orleans, Louisiana; by Theodore Lilienthal; from *Harper's Weekly*, April 21, 1866; *THNOC, gift of Harold Schilke and Boyd Cruise, 1953.82*

*It is, unfortunately, a policy of the planters to ill-treat and
miserably pay the freedmen, in order to discourage them
from working, and to be able to say afterward that "the
negro is lazy and will not work unless compelled by the
whip and the whole machinery of slavery."*

—*New Orleans Tribune*, on the
Freedmen's Aid Association, July 11, 1865

BOGUILLE HAD JOINED THE privately sponsored New Orleans
Freedmen's Aid Association as one of its twelve directors while also working
as a teacher for the government-run Bureau of Refugees, Freedmen, and
Abandoned Lands, commonly known as the Freedmen's Bureau. The Freedmen's Aid Association was a local relief organization that cooperated with
the federal Freedmen's Bureau but differed sometimes in its approach
toward the newly emancipated. The Freedmen's Aid Association, a more
radical group than the bureau, believed that laborers should have more
control over their working conditions. The *New Orleans Tribune* pointed
out that the association "should be better known than it seems to be by
our fellow-citizens."

The similarity of names and goals could have led to confusion. New
Orleans, like other cities around the United States, was home to both
private aid associations and the Freedmen's Bureau, and both sought to

find help for the four million people suddenly released from bondage. In addition, the tasks of Reconstruction, like the aftermath of a hurricane, could have overwhelmed many people in the free colored community, concerned with their own well-being.

The harsh reality of emancipation was that the people who had been shipped, sold, and controlled in the most minute ways on the plantation were now responsible for managing all aspects of their lives themselves. They needed to find employment and shelter. Their apparel was rudimentary. A square-cut, straight-seamed cotton dress or pair of pants might be the only clothes a freed person owned. Having footwear was not always possible. Most had only the clothes on their backs. Many had acquired only specialized agricultural skills. Few had received general education, except the small measure of learning gained either surreptitiously or through the newly organized schools after the passage of the Thirteenth Amendment only months earlier. They needed help on all fronts.

The United States had acquired and parceled out former plantations for the use of the newly freed men and women. But the workers did not always have the tools or the seeds to farm. The Freedmen's Aid Association tried to provide implements to the freed people. "They are now cultivating these portions of the soil of the State, in squads of men, women and children, varying in number from fifteen to one hundred, and sometimes even more. . . . They necessarily need the aid and co-operation of their friends to raise their crops. Their immediate wants are seeds to plant, instruments to break up the soil, animals for ploughing, and a moderate supply of pork," the association said in the May 5, 1865, *New Orleans Tribune*. The group sent out identical notices to sympathetic organizations, announcing its formation and soliciting money to support the farmers. Their appeal was reprinted in the British *Anti-Slavery Reporter*.

In June 1865, when the New Orleans office of the Freedmen's Bureau opened, it offered sample forms for some former plantation owners and laborers to enter into contracts for planting and harvesting. Frequently, the parties to the contracts were former masters and their formerly enslaved workers. Together, they negotiated the terms of salary and lengths of employment. The paper contracts were made out in triplicate and approved

Glimpses at the Freedmen's Bureau—Issuing Rations to the Old and Sick; by James E. Taylor; from *Frank Leslie's Illustrated Newspaper*, September 22, 1866; *courtesy of Library of Congress, Prints and Photographs Division*

by the local parish agent for the bureau. The employer kept a copy, and the other copies were sent to the government agency in New Orleans and to the federal office in Washington, DC. The laborer had a representative in the agency but kept no documentation himself. Parish agents and plantation owners were often friends. The association saw the possibilities for abuse.

Some employers then complained of subpar work, but the Freedmen's Aid Association countered this was a result of poor labor conditions. The association's approach to labor was to encourage the newly emancipated people to lease land and work for themselves, not their former owners, or instead of accepting the Freedmen's Bureau's annual contracts, they should negotiate contracts for shorter periods with "regular weekly cash payments of their wages."

One evening a week, Boguille went to the office at 49 Union Street, between Carondelet and Baronne Streets on the American side of town, to attend the Freedmen's Aid Association's meetings. He was no longer focused only on the concerns of his family or social class. If helping the poor and giving them justice was a radical act, he was well on his way to becoming a revolutionary. Like so many people who advocated for local, invisible communities, Boguille and the other activists made small steps that didn't echo in the halls of power but resounded on parched Louisiana ground. On July 9, Boguille reported that he had received six dollars from the Sisters of Charity to be put toward freedmen's relief. The organization also had gotten assistance from local benevolent societies and supporters abroad. A "handsome sum of money" came from donors in the rural parish of Terrebonne, the *New Orleans Tribune* reported. It added that the association had purchased mules, hoes, and food for people on three plantations run by "free workers." By November 1865 the association had helped fourteen farms run by "independent laborers"—in all, "about seven hundred men, women, and children."

"It has been shown that when acting under the stimulus of fair profits, accruing from their labor, they were as industrious as any other class of men—perhaps more," a *New Orleans Tribune* reporter wrote. Boguille hoped to see the fruit of his postwar efforts.

The Freedmen's Bureau, too, had a major success on the former plantation of Pierre A. Rost. The bureau had confiscated the land, and the newly freed workers raised crops there and sewed clothes. The bureau operated a small office on the second floor of the big house. Off the wide porch with a vista of the nearby yard and distant fields, the bureau's local administrator worked at a small roll-top desk. He inscribed the names of the formerly enslaved people who worked the land into his record books, along with their medical needs and their daily production. The bureau required laborers to work ten-hour days in the summer and nine-hour days in the winter. The workers negotiated their wages or a share of the crop as a salary. They also paid for their living expenses. Five percent of a laborer's earnings was deducted to fund freedmen's schools. The bureau would turn a profit of $14,150 in 1866.

The Rost plantation could have been a model for the other farms in Louisiana, but critics said that the bureau's system of paying the freedmen for labor, while also taking their money to pay for their food and housing, was fiscally unsound. Too much money was spent on relief for the formerly enslaved people in some places, more than the freedmen's wages would bring for their upkeep. And there was corruption among bureau officials. Some of them, along with former plantation owners, tricked freedmen into debt so that their living costs exceeded their earnings.

The Freedmen's Aid Association also complained that planters could hold wages and have laborers arrested and forced back to their farms if they felt the work was unfinished. The stern tone of a Freedmen's Bureau announcement published in the *New Orleans Times* in October 1865 strongly suggested that freedmen could not count on much more support from the bureau:

> To the Freedmen of Louisiana
>
> The Government has made you free. . . . Slavery has passed away, and you are now placed on trial. It is for you to prove that you are able to take care of yourselves, and that you deserved to be made free. In the abrupt change brought about by the sudden passing away of slavery, you required some assistance—some power that would take care of you for the time, and that would properly direct you in a new path of life. . . . But you must not mistake the objects of this Department. It is not the intention of the officers of this Bureau to nurse and pamper you, to feed and clothe you, or to give you any privileges that other persons do not enjoy. . . .
>
> If you do not work of your own accord, or if the law can not compel you to work, then you must leave the country, and the good opportunities that you now have of gaining a living and making yourselves independent, will be given to more deserving persons. I advise you all to return to your old plantations, where you have been kindly treated, for there you are known and there you can get better wages. . . .
>
> All has been done for you that you can expect. . . . *No land will be given to you.* Already a large quantity of the land that was held by this Bureau has been returned to its owners, and even had it not been returned, it would not have been given to you or divided amongst you.

The letter was signed by J. S. Fullerton, Assistant Commissioner of the Bureau.

Just over three months had passed since the bureau opened its New Orleans office. Boguille could not understand the government's lack of patience, given the upheaval on plantations and the newly freed people's need for education, health care, housing, and work. The *New Orleans Tribune* was blunt about the collusion between the government and planters: "Compulsion is nothing short of disguised slavery."

Pierre Rost, whose plantation supported the most successful of the Freedmen's Bureau's efforts in Louisiana, returned in December 1865 to New Orleans from Europe, where he had served as a Confederate ambassador to Spain during the war. Within a few months, he was pardoned by President Andrew Johnson for his seditious activities. The bureau compensated Rost by paying $15,000 to rent his land and $90,000 for other costs associated with workers' housing, food, and crop production. Shortly afterwards, the government returned Rost's plantation to him.

God damn them, I am going to kill every negro in New Orleans.

—Overheard by Pierre Crocker Jr., 1866

LUDGER BOGUILLE WAS ACTIVE on many fronts as he and the Economistes pushed forward to attain justice. He and society member Charles Martinez were members of the local executive board of the National Equal Rights League. In February 1865 they asked white Republican Thomas Durant to speak at a mass meeting of the league in the Economie's hall. As an advocate for Black suffrage, Durant had previously addressed the Economie community, invoking the name of Toussaint Louverture, to encourage the men to pressure Congress for their rights of suffrage. His rhetoric converged neatly with the Economistes' vision of their roles in the revolutionary movements for equality.

By June, Durant took the lead in forming a new organization called the Friends of Universal Suffrage, made up primarily of local whites who supported the Union cause and who were in favor of Black equality. They set up an office in the same building as the headquarters of the Freedmen's

Aid Association. Several Economistes who also belonged to the Equal Rights League joined the Friends of Universal Suffrage. In addition to Boguille, they included Henry L. Rey, who served as assistant recording secretary to its Central Executive Committee, and Colored Convention delegates Martinez and Eugène Chessé. The Friends of Universal Suffrage began working that summer to register Black voters.

Boguille was one of the commissioners on the organization's board of elections, which encouraged freedmen to sign up voluntarily, even though the state had not yet given Blacks suffrage. He welcomed men from the former free colored community and the newly emancipated into the wide double doors of the Economie's hall. Sitting at the wooden table he had occupied as the society's secretary, he took the names of people who could not read and entered them onto an increasingly long list for the Second District. Registration also took place at the Couvent School and six other sites around the city.

On September 25, the Friends of Universal Suffrage met in the Economie's hall for a convention to nominate state representatives, just as they would have if Blacks had secured the right to vote. Boguille was a delegate. A preface to the convention proceedings explained their desire to obtain the vote for all of the people in the state, no matter their color or social status.

An unnamed clerk copied the statement on rag paper, then brought it down to the office of the *New Orleans Tribune* to be set into type and printed in a chapbook. It circulated throughout the city with this introduction: "This pamphlet will be a useful manual in the hands of the unenfranchised, and will exhibit to the people and their representatives that four and a half millions of true and law-abiding citizens will not remain deprived of their rights and privileges of citizenship."

The booklet suggested that freedmen who could read should explain the pamphlet to others who could not. It encouraged colored men to push for the vote so they would "not only enjoy the blessings of Freedom, but [would] also have a majority."

There were two important factions at the convention, both advocating for the Black vote. The radicals were led by Durant and the Friends of

PROCEEDINGS OF THE CONVENTION

OF THE

REPUBLICAN PARTY

OF LOUISIANA,

HELD AT ECONOMY HALL, NEW ORLEANS, SEPTEMBER 25, 1865,

AND OF THE

CENTRAL EXECUTIVE COMMITTEE

OF THE

FRIENDS OF UNIVERSAL SUFFRAGE

OF LOUISIANA

NOW,

"THE CENTRAL EXECUTIVE COMMITTEE OF THE REPUBLICAN
PARTY OF LOUISIANA."

NEW ORLEANS,
PRINTED AT THE NEW ORLEANS TRIBUNE OFFICE, NO. 21 CONTI STREET.
1865.

Title page of *Proceedings of the Convention of the Republican Party of Louisiana, Held at Economy Hall*; 1865; THNOC, 76-1451-RL

Universal Suffrage, while a more moderate group called itself the National Union Republican Club. At the convention, they decided to join forces and designate themselves the Republican Party of Louisiana.

The politically expedient merger didn't sit well with either camp. The more radical men, like Boguille and advocates at the *New Orleans Tribune*, didn't trust the moderates, led by Henry Clay Warmoth, a former Union officer who had previously opposed emancipation but now said he wanted Black suffrage. Still, the two sides came together in the belief that the federal government was the only legitimate authority in Louisiana, not the state government or the constitution created by white former rebels. The Republicans wanted the US Congress to return Louisiana from statehood to a Union-held territory, and they appointed Warmoth as their territorial delegate to Washington.

Since the Friends of Universal Suffrage had already registered Black voters, it called on them to participate in a voluntary election during the November 1865 governor's race. The vote did not count but was held to demonstrate the potential power of Black citizens. The group tallied 15,605 Black votes, equivalent to approximately 79 percent of the Republican electorate—men who could have been counted but were not allowed to vote because of their race.

Eligible white men cast 28,000 votes in the November elections, and conservative planter James Madison Wells, who had been serving as lieutenant governor, gained the governor's seat. He did not support Black suffrage and was more interested in aligning with former white rebels, Democrats, and conservative Unionists. Wells appointed them to government jobs and ejected his opponents. Statewide elections held the same month also returned Democrats to local offices. The conservatives then went about reinstating the Black Codes.

With the results of the Friends of Universal Suffrage's voluntary election in hand, the Warmoth Republicans were incensed at the loss to the Democrats and supported a plan to revise the 1864 Louisiana constitution, since it was created by a government they considered illegitimate. The radical Durant faction of the Republicans opposed this tactic, believing that it would simply incite a backlash from conservative voters and not create any lasting change. The radicals wanted to wait for the federal government to take action, which would require more time and political savvy. Republican moderates decided to go ahead with their plan to reconvene a convention that would replace the 1864 constitution. They scheduled a meeting at the Mechanics' Institute, a workingmen's club, on July 30, 1866.

Some of the Durant followers went to the convention in solidarity, hopeful that even if they did not agree with the plan, it still might work. Other radicals and many Economie men stayed home. Boguille, a member of the radical Durant faction, was one of the first and boldest advocates for Black suffrage and justice when he joined with the founders of the Equal Rights League. Perhaps the French Revolution's motto of "liberty, equality, fraternity" resonated with Boguille at this moment in history. He had to attend the convention to see what was going to happen.

Boguille left home on the morning of July 30, walking over sidewalks strewn with the golden undersides of magnolia leaves and beneath conclaves of oak trees knotted together by Spanish moss. He passed brown-skinned vendors, workingmen who were pink and sweating under the midsummer sun, people of all colors chatting, while others turned away or gave side-long looks. The people of New Orleans were enmeshed by their bitter history and a recent war. Activists like Boguille searched for the best ways to proceed in a world of political choices that promised to change all of their lives.

Besides Boguille, a few Economistes made their way to the convention that morning. Lucien Capla, the son of a Battle of New Orleans veteran, brought his child, Arnold, with him to see the political process firsthand. Members Sylvester Edward Planchard and Demosthenes Charles Azaretto came to make up their minds about the best way to advance politically. Second-generation Economistes Pierre Crocker Jr. and Victor Lacroix, sons of founding members, also attended.

The Mechanics' Institute was just off Canal Street, a 170-foot-wide avenue that separated the traditionally Creole and American sections of the city. The conventioneers passed out flyers and buttonholed men on the sidewalk, insisting that Wells had won because Blacks could not vote. Boguille crossed four lanes of traffic, weaving between horse carts and the streetcars going in both directions, to reach the building. As he approached, he saw a crowd of police officers. He recognized a few of them. Oddly, they were in civilian clothes. One who knew Boguille asked why he was attending the conference.

To "see what was going on," Boguille replied.

The policeman said drolly that nothing that day would be interesting.

Reaching the hall, Boguille stepped quickly through the entrance and foyer and went into the auditorium. As he waited in his seat for the conference to begin, a man came to the podium and announced that the morning speeches had been postponed, so Boguille went outside and stood on the sidewalk.

That's when he saw Victor Lacroix, wearing his well-tailored vest and gold watch chain. The Mechanics' Institute convention wasn't the first time he and Boguille had the opportunity to attend the same events. In the past year, the Economie's hall had hosted a production of *Uncle Tom's Cabin* in March, and a concert to benefit the orphans of freedmen in April. Lacroix seemed to have similar political views, and Ludger may have wanted to talk to him about his impressions of the July convention. But they saw each other at the Mechanics' Institute only briefly that day, and that was their last meeting.

WHILE BOGUILLE WAITED ON the sidewalk for the meeting to begin, he saw a band and some marchers carrying the American flag coming up the street. Ever since the funeral of André Cailloux, the colored community had taken pride in carrying the Union banner. It symbolized not only that the United States government had legitimately won the war over the Confederates, but that all people of color, including the previously enslaved, had federally secured equal rights. Boguille then watched, horrified, as hundreds of policemen descended on the marchers, shooting at them and hitting them with clubs. Some of the police rushed toward the Mechanics' Institute.

Boguille ran back up the steps and into the building. Behind a brick portico were several tall, arched windows through which he could look down on the street. He heard shots.

"I saw a colored man killed," Boguille later told a committee of three US Congressmen investigating the scene. The members had come to New Orleans after hearing news that the police and their allies had murdered citizens. The northern public was incensed by the slow process of Reconstruction in the South and the ascendancy of local and state governments hostile to the Union. The testimony of eyewitnesses like Boguille increased their outrage.

"The firing was going on in every direction—through the windows, through the doors, and into the back part of the Institute," Boguille testified. "The chaplain having been one of the first wounded . . . he took a white handkerchief, tied it to a long staff, and addressed the people inside the Institute, advising them to surrender, and saying we should not be injured any more. He went as far as the door and was met by a crowd of policemen, 40 or 50 in number, who immediately commenced firing, and there he was shot—about two paces from the door."

Lucien Capla of the Economie and his son Arnold were standing inside the door of the building. Capla "saw policemen firing, and shooting the

The Riot in New
Orleans—Murder of
the Rev. Mr. Horton
in the Vestibule of the
Mechanics' Institute;
by Theodore Russell
Davis; from Harper's
Weekly, August 25,
1866; THNOC,
1974.25.9.307

Black people; they were shooting poor laboring men, men with their tin
buckets in their hands, and even old men walking with sticks." Capla said,
"Although they prayed, 'For God's sake, don't shoot us!'" the police shot
them anyway and then "tramped upon them, and mashed their heads with
their boots, and shot them after they were down."

"I was at the door of the Mechanics' Institute," Capla said. "I saw
policemen kill the people in this way, and I began to get uneasy when
they began to fire upon the Institute, for the balls were coming in every
way through the windows."

He witnessed the destruction resulting from the siege and the innocence
of the men who had gathered for the meeting. One of the convention's
speakers said, "Keep quiet; we have here the emblem of the United States,
and we will be protected by that emblem; they cannot fire upon us." The
man waved the flag as the shooters entered the meeting room.

Capla continued, "They came in and fired upon us although he took up
the flag of the United States, it was not respected, for they continued to
fire. Then those who were inside took out white handkerchiefs and waved

them; but these they did not respect, but still fired upon us, and I saw the people fall like flies." He and Boguille were trapped.

In his testimony, Boguille told of his escape: "We seized some chairs and tried to defend ourselves, and succeeded in repulsing those who fired the volleys. . . . I received one wound in the left arm and another in the knee, and several blows which did not injure me much."

Then Boguille rushed out of the building. "In going down the steps I was constantly struck over the head with butts of pistols and blows from sticks," he reported.

Boguille survived because as he was trying to push his way out of the building, the crowd grabbed the man running out ahead of him. "They immediately rushed upon him and massacred him, and commenced hurrahing for Jefferson Davis. I escaped in that rush," he said.

Capla grabbed his son and ran out the door while being shot at by police. He later explained, "If I was not killed quite, it was because God did not want me to be killed; but my son was separated from me, and left on the banquette for dead. . . . He has lost one eye, his right eye, where he was shot with a bullet." Abandoned on the sidewalk, Arnold, not yet nine years old, had four bullet wounds in his head. He also was stabbed three times.

The elder Capla was thrown into jail and, he said, "miserably maltreated; my head was broken and my leg injured, and I was shot in the side, but it was by a spent ball. The wound became black a few days afterwards. I was badly treated in the calaboose."

Capla was one of the Native Guards who had welcomed the Union occupation of New Orleans. He had not only served in the army, but in the space of twenty-four hours, he had raised a company of colored men to fight for the Union. The Confederates were malicious to him because he spoke out against them before the war. They had appropriated his shoemaking business to use as a recruiting station, he explained to the congressional committee. "I probably did not sell a pair of shoes in this city for six months, and all for my opinions," he said.

Economiste Sylvester Edward Planchard, another member of the Native Guards, stayed in the hall as the police fired near the building. He testified that a friend with him said, "Do not go out; they will kill you." But

Planchard finally decided to leave, saying, "We will all be murdered if we stay here."

After Planchard stepped outside and went down the steps, he saw "three or four black men shot dead." He got away from the crowd and was walking slowly down a street when he heard the cry, "Kill him! Kill him!" He began to run and realized that the police were among the people chasing him. Though they fired at him fifteen to twenty times, he was not hit. A woman saw Planchard escaping and told him to hide in her house, but the crowd saw him go into her door. They ran to her house and said, "You have somebody in here; we want to kill the damned son of a bitch, the dammed nigger, the dammed rascal."

The attackers pulled Planchard from the residence and demanded, "Are you a member of the convention; are you armed?"

Planchard responded, "No."

The policemen said they were going to kill him. One of the men put a pistol to his head, pointing it directly in his face.

Planchard heard somebody say, "Don't shoot," and the gunman put away his weapon. An anonymous voice of conscience saved Planchard's life.

Instead, he was taken to the police station and robbed of his valuables. Planchard told the congressional select committee, "I asked them what they took me for; I had committed no crime. I said to them, I am a citizen born here. The only answer they gave me was, 'Shut up, you damned rascal; shut up, you damned nigger; shut up, you damned son of a bitch.' After they had searched my person, and taken away all the things upon me, they said, 'Put him inside among his nigger friends.' They then put me inside, where there were about thirty men; some wounded, some dying and weltering in their blood, on the floor."

Demosthenes Azaretto, another Economie member, testified that he also tried to escape from the hall: "One-third of the way down stairs I received a lick on the head which stunned me. . . . From there I was taken by two policemen, with a pistol in each hand, to the station, but I was released after giving bonds for $2,000; they made me pay $1 for the bond."

Pierre Crocker Jr., the son and namesake of the first Economie president, told his story to a panel of military officers who investigated the crimes just two weeks after they happened: "I was up in the hall, when the gentleman

THE RIOT IN NEW ORLEANS—MURDERING NEGROES IN THE REAR OF MECHANICS' INSTITUTE.
[SKETCHED BY THEODORE R. DAVIS.]

The Riot in New Orleans—Murdering Negroes in the Rear of Mechanics' Institute; by Theodore Russell Davis; from Harper's Weekly, August 25, 1866; THNOC, 1979.200 i

says, 'surrender;' I lay down myself and done the best I could, with the gentlemen there, when I saw them taking white gentlemen out of the hall. I staid until they took the last gentleman out; he was a white gentleman."

Crocker said the only people left in the hall were colored. He gave himself up, saying, "Gentlemen, here's me—do what you please with me." The policeman called Crocker a "damned son of a bitch." He pointed his pistol at Crocker's head and shot him twice with musket balls.

Then Crocker got up and ran: "I was running so fast I fell down. When I rose again and started to run again one ran a dirk in my side, and the dirk hung through so I could not pull it out, and I could hear them say they intended to shoot me." When they shot him again, the ball pierced his eye and exited through the top of his head.

Crocker continued, "While I was lying there some one said, 'God damn them, I am going to kill every negro in New Orleans. God damn their making laws;' and some one took my watch from me. . . . I laid there in the street two hours looking in the sun. I thought the sun would burn me up. I knew nothing about anybody. I do not know the people but I know the place."

THE RIOT IN NEW ORLEANS—CARRYING OFF THE DEAD AND WOUNDED—INHUMAN CONDUCT OF THE POLICE.

The Riot in New Orleans—Carrying Off the Dead and Wounded—Inhuman Conduct of the Police; by Theodore Russell Davis; from *Harper's Weekly*, August 25, 1866; *THNOC, 1979.200 iv*

Crocker heard men talking as they stood above him.

"God damn him, I think he's not dead yet."

"God damn it, he is dead; don't you see all his brains are out?"

"I think I saw him wink; he is not dead."

"O, God damn it, he's dead as hell, only the sun makes him wink."

"God damn it, let him be: he's dead all over."

Crocker said he was then thrown in a wagon with dead bodies. "They flung a man in first, and then flung me in after him. I went down in the cart, and my heels up and my head down, and they brought in more men and flung them in on top, and carried us down to the work-house. At a kind of office a man said, 'God damn you, what are you bringing so many dead negroes here in the workhouse for?' When they took out those that were dead, they carried the rest of us to the hospital. Then they pulled out those men that were on top, not quite dead. I was away down, my head down and my heels up. I pulled my heels up on the side of the cart so they might see I was not dead. They pulled me out, and put me down there. Then I was put into another cart and taken to the hospital." The hospital that received the injured men was run by the Sisters of Charity.

On July 30, 1866, eyewitnesses said, there was so much shooting that the entrance to the Mechanics' Institute was slippery with blood.

VICTOR LACROIX MAY HAVE heard the band coming, and then the shots and the confusion. He may have seen the gunfire pumping into the hall, heard the alarm that brought the police and firemen, and encountered the mob, which witnesses estimated at two hundred to seven hundred people. He may have seen men falling all around him and may have hoped that the American flag would provide refuge. He may have waved a white handkerchief, as some men did. Lacroix's handkerchief would have been made of the finest French linen, and if any of the thugs who stormed the hall noticed it, his wealth would have made them even angrier.

Boguille said Lacroix "was a young man of very wealthy family, and had his watch-chain and a great deal of money on him at the time. . . . His body was found, but his watch-chain and the large amount of money he had with him have never been seen."

THE ECONOMIE DID NOT meet from July to September 1866. At the September 1 gathering, President Boisdoré entered only a brief mention of the murders at the Mechanics' Institute into the minutes: "My brothers, you all know, as I do, the causes that have prevented the meetings since the 1st of August. I want to speak of the massacre of the 30th of July." But no conversation about the massacre was recorded. The minutes only picked up with a mention of dues and delinquencies for missed meetings.

Only a few Economie members had gone to the convention because they believed violence was possible—which was exactly what transpired.

Boguille felt betrayed. The president had ignored their petition. The battle was now on the streets of New Orleans, not the plains of Port Hudson. Where was the patriotism of the Economie members?

In the meeting room that night, bearing battle scars, was Pierre Crocker Jr., who had almost died. Lucien Capla, beaten and brought to jail, was absent. His son Arnold suffered at home.

One night in 1869, though, Victor Lacroix came back to the Economie's hall—as a ghost addressing the Cercle Harmonique.

He told the men to keep fighting. "Patience, because your recompense is on its way," the spirit said. "You will be paid for your suffering."

Boguille, the Radical

1866–1871

*I then tried to withdraw to go home, to bandage my
wounds. When grasping the street car, as I was attempting
to get into one, I was fired upon again. One of the shots
passed close to my head. At the moment I was stunned
in trying to get into the car. . . . I was constantly on the
alert[,] expecting to be attacked, my neighborhood being
surrounded with copperheads. General Baird furnished
me a guard to protect me, for the reason that I am the
teacher of a republican school. . . . I am still in the same
school-house and still carrying on my school. I have a large
number of republican scholars, and this displeases the
people of the neighborhood in which the school is situated.*

—Ludger Boguille, congressional testimony,
January 1, 1867

THE VIOLENCE OF THE Mechanics' Institute massacre left some residents of New Orleans mute, unbalanced, and fearful. They stood over the coffins of family members or sat nearby, at a loss for words. Some witnesses had felt warm blood spurt from the bodies of their friends onto their clothes. When their injured neighbors fell lifeless, the observers ran screaming. Some who had participated in the march now trembled in their quiet houses, jumped at the crack of a driver's whip, and felt their hearts skip if a vase tumbled from a shelf.

But other men emerged stronger. Boguille became more vocal, political, and impatient. He had lost too many friends. He had slid on their blood as it streamed across the Mechanics' Institute floor. He couldn't get the scene out of his mind.

On the street and in coffeehouses, Boguille may have tried to repeat his story. Perhaps many Economistes had been wise to stay away from the meeting at the Mechanics' Institute, given the violent outcome. But what was the use of wisdom, moderation, and manners when others had no conscience? Even the white flag of surrender and the flag of the United States didn't matter. So why should his society brothers wait patiently, hoping that their refined manner of dress and comportment would eventually lead their oppressors to recognize their equality? The truth was that their enemies wanted them dead.

He began to work harder for suffrage along with white Northerners, whom the rebels hated and cursed on the streets. The Southerners called them "carpetbaggers" whether they had good or bad intentions. Local white men who supported Black suffrage were termed "scalawags." Durant, the leader of the Friends of Universal Suffrage and the white radical with whom Boguille and many others from the colored Equal Rights League had joined, ran from the conflict. He disappeared the afternoon of the Mechanics' Institute massacre. Durant later told the congressional committee that he had feared for his life, so he took a carriage and then a steamer out of New Orleans and went to Washington, DC. He never came back.

BOGUILLE, BY CONTRAST, BECAME even more committed to equality for Blacks after almost losing his life. He had experienced a horrible day of violence. But he saw the youngest victims of injustice subject to brutality their entire lives. Thousands of children, newly released from slavery, needed help. Many were orphans. They made their way slowly, like specters, into the Freedmen's Bureau.

He stared into the ashen faces of boys and girls coming into the offices. They appeared exhausted and broken. Their hair had turned rust-colored from malnutrition. He wondered how he could help all who arrived: nine-year-old Hannah Johnson; Emma Landry, fifteen; Sam Kevis, six; Odele Davis, ten; Mary Ann Smith, three; the five Bertell children, ages four to fourteen. During the week between Christmas Eve and New Year's Eve, the bureau processed eighty-two orphans.

How many more children ran barefoot in the streets of New Orleans, and how many more unfortunates were in the rural parishes? The children were lost during their flight from slavery on the plantations or had been separated from their parents earlier and watched over by other enslaved families. Maybe some of their parents had been enslaved in the city—laborers now with their lunches in tin pails, working in the vicinity of the Mechanics' Institute. Maybe they were among the people shot and thrown in the river, never to be retrieved, much less identified. Maybe the parents roamed the streets, lost and hungry themselves, looking for work, and did not want their children to live as wanderers, too. Maybe the parents had lost their minds from the burdens of living. Maybe the parents lived now in other decimated southern cities.

In any case, the children came in like ghosts of children—pale, dusty, and quiet, except for a rustle of rags as they dragged their bodies along with their fading spirits: James Brooks, Samuel Smith, and Mary Rosseau, all four years old; the Johnsons: Lewis, eight, and Joseph, four, carrying two-year-old Noah.

While the men of his class debated the values of politics and representation, Boguille saw rooms full of children: Billy Dunton, fourteen, and John Fox, ten. George, eleven; Susan, twelve; Edward and Emma, fourteen; Cecelia, five; Harry and Zeno, seven; and Maurice, ten—all Greens.

The sheer insanity of the situation weighed on Boguille. Rather than help the children pursue education, the former rebels continued to harass their teachers. One educator at a colored freedmen's school tried to hold an exhibition so his students could demonstrate their achievements. The police told him that he needed a fifteen-dollar permit from city hall. White schools obtained such permits for free. The teacher argued with the officials and secured a permit without paying. On his way home one night a few weeks later, he was stabbed with a "dirk knife, the blow being accompanied with savage curses."

Boguille may have searched his logical mind for historical precedents: the Romans had enslaved the Greeks; the Egyptians had chained the Hebrews. How did those oppressed people get away, and how did they advance? What did they carry with them? Only their faith and their Book.

He looked at these innocents. He saw sadness and hunger. How could he teach children who were numb with loss? How could he convince them that slavery and the war were moments in ancient history, when these hardships had lasted the children's entire lives?

Politicians could fight their battles, arguing over the precise wording and punctuation of bills—and he knew, as the most meticulous secretary of the Economie, that words had great repercussions. But the children he saw now needed even more than laws. They needed radical kindness.

"What is the state of feeling of the colored people, as a class, towards our government?"

"Intensely loyal."

"Have they intelligence enough to understand the relations which they sustain to the government, and which the government sustained to them in giving them their freedom?"

"[. . .] There is not a colored man who does not understand what he owes to the government of the United States. There is not one but would do everything for the government. I presume the black man here in Louisiana could wield the ballot as well as the musket."

—Charles Sauvinet, congressional testimony,
December 22, 1866

FEDERAL OFFICIALS KNEW Charles Sauvinet as one of the first men of color to approach the Union Army when it arrived in New Orleans. He had served as a translator, speaking to General Butler in English and to Henry L. Rey in French when they met, negotiating between the worlds of Creole New Orleans and the Northerner. Sauvinet, along with the other Black former Confederate militia members, had enlisted in the Union Army. He became the quartermaster of the Second Regiment of the Native Guards, serving on Ship Island in the Gulf of Mexico, about sixty miles east of New Orleans. In the regiment were companies A through K. Of the eighty-nine men in Company E, eighty-eight were from Sauvinet's native city.

Newspapers around the United States covered the 1866 tragedy in New Orleans because the bloodshed had focused the attention of Americans in a visceral way on one of the most important issues the nation faced

The New Orleans Riot—
The Military Commission
Examining Witnesses; by
Theodore Russell Davis;
from *Harper's Weekly,*
September 1, 1866;
THNOC, 1974.25.9.198

THE NEW ORLEANS RIOT—THE MILITARY COMMISSION EXAMISING WITNESSES.—[Sketched by Theodore R. Davis.]

after the Civil War—voting rights for Blacks. Now working for the Freed-men's Bureau, Sauvinet came to testify before the visiting congressional select committee investigating the massacre at the Mechanics' Institute. When he approached his chair in the chambers, some of the members may have wondered whether he was a Black man. He was quite European in appearance. Perhaps that gave him a bit more credibility with some of the investigators. They asked him questions that probed beyond typical eyewitness accounts.

"What is the state of feeling existing in New Orleans and in Louisiana towards the government of the United States on the part of those engaged in the rebellion?" one of the Congressmen asked.

Sauvinet answered, "Sir, they are just as much rebel today, and just as inimical to the government of the United States, as they ever were."

"Would it be safe, so far as safety depends upon the loyalty of the electors, to entrust the government of one of the States of the United States to those people who are now electors here?" the Congressman asked about the former rebels who were registered to vote.

"No, sir; . . . if things are to remain as they are, with the same kind of electors, it would not be safe at all."

The committee chairman asked how the whites showed their distrust in the government.

"By words, by cross looks, as though they were trying to cow down parties," Sauvinet explained. "I have been in the street cars when a gentleman began to curse and damn the Yankees: he had fought against them four years, and God damn them, he would kill several others before he got through."

After Sauvinet's testimony and the horrible eyewitness accounts of others went into the public record, the nation felt great sympathy for the men who had been treated so brutally for attempting to discuss suffrage. Newspapers described violent incidents that people in other cities couldn't imagine. Until they read the detailed accounts, readers may not have even believed that prejudice could produce such brutality. Outrage swept the country. *Harper's Weekly*, the *New York Times*, and other national periodicals reported that men such as Sauvinet were former Union soldiers with education, goodwill, and patriotism, and deserved the vote. People around the United States pressured Congress for a solution.

The change came after the national elections in 1866, when voters installed a two-thirds Republican majority in both houses. The newly elected officials enforced Reconstruction under strict military control. The Fourteenth Amendment, giving Blacks the vote, had passed in June 1866, but it had not been ratified by the whites who made up the electorate. When the majority approved, justice moved quickly.

Soon, suffrage came to Black men.

LIKE CIVIL RIGHTS VOLUNTEERS a century later, an army of people came south to register voters. In shacks behind the big houses, formerly enslaved men talked about their new power as citizens. In churches, grocery stores, and fruit and vegetable stands along the Mississippi River, and anywhere else Black people gathered, there were questions about the ballot. People who could read coached those who could not, teaching them to sign their names and write their addresses.

The Central Executive Committee of the Louisiana Republican Party— now called the Radical Republicans after having aligned with that party on

Electioneering at the South; by William Ludlow Sheppard; from *Harper's Weekly*, July 26, 1868; *THNOC, gift of Harold Schilke and Boyd Cruise, 1959.159.40*

the national scene—continued to meet at the Economie's hall. The *New Orleans Tribune* called the location "the cradle of the equal rights party in Louisiana" because it had hosted the Friends of Universal Suffrage and "nearly all the representative men of the disenfranchised population."

Radical Republican ward clubs met at private homes, colored churches, and halls, even at a ballroom and beer garden. In every part of the city, activists gathered to organize and discuss the vote. The Sixth Ward club had 116 members and met on Tuesday nights in the Economie's hall.

On May 25, 1867, they joined like-minded men—laborers, intellectuals, and politicians—from throughout the city for the Radical Republicans' torchlight procession and rally in Lafayette Square "to carry dismay in the ranks of our hidden and over-political enemies, and at the same time draw into the folds of the party those that might be wavering." Another goal of the march was to "publicly and openly express their gratitude to the loyal Congress of the United States for the passage of the immortal 'Reconstruction Bill,' that so eminent, just and effective law which guarantees to all men their privileges and immunities, and which will conduct Louisiana and the whole country to a stage of prosperity never before known." Octave Rey was the parade's grand marshal. Fifteen thousand men marched, carrying Chinese lanterns. Drums rumbled. Fifes trilled. And several bands trumpeted rhythmic "patriotic tunes," including one group named the Louisiana Brass Band, led by T. A. Martin and Adolphe Liautaud, the maestro of the Société Philharmonique. He had brought together the musicians for the inauguration of the Economie's hall. Among the officers of the Radical Republican Party who marched were at least eight Economistes, including Henry L. Rey, Charles Martinez, and François Lacroix, who had lost his son in the Mechanics' Institute massacre. For Lacroix, the march perhaps gave him some hope that Victor's life was sacrificed for justice.

In September 1867 the *New York Times* reported, "Taking the census of 1860 as a basis, and making allowances for changes wrought by the war, it was estimated that Louisiana contained at present 47,000 whites and 23,000 blacks over twenty-one years of age. This was the estimate made previous to registration. But the returns [from recent elections] show that only 44,723 whites have registered, while 82,867 blacks have registered. This is a falling off in the anticipated white vote of about 2,000, and an increase in the anticipated black vote of nearly 60,000. This fact has been a disagreeable surprise to the late rebels and their friends, and it far exceeds the highest hopes of the most sanguine Republicans. The latter predicted a few weeks ago that the negroes would have a majority of 37,000 in Louisiana; and the majority actually exceeds 38,000. Add to this a white vote of about 20,000 Republicans, and there will be a majority of about 75,000 in Louisiana for reconstruction."

Let those men who were with us in the hour of peril be first to receive their recompense. We remember those who advocated equal rights one year or even two years ago; we remember those who were at the Mechanics' Institute, standing with the oppressed, and contending with them for the cause of justice. Their names are not and will not be forgotten. We remember those who previous to that sad event, assembled with their brethren, without distinction of race or color, at the Convention at Economy Hall, and sat with them in the Central Committee. All of them have good and genuine claims upon our gratitude. They were our friends at the time that we were in need of support. . . . At this moment the law of suffrage is an accomplished fact, and the power is now with us and in our votes.

—*New Orleans Tribune*, May 8, 1867

LUDGER BOGUILLE RAN FOR the office of Second District alderman in April 1868 with a campaign typical of its time. His friends rallied new supporters with enthusiasm or pleading. And the candidate hired boys to stand on the backs of moving wagons and shout his name to passersby. If his campaigners handed out printed broadsides in grocery stores and on corners, they were careful to give them to men who looked literate and promised to read them aloud to others, not simply use the paper to practice their own handwriting.

Political life was exhilarating but dangerous. In October a group of former rebels prowled the streets all over the city to intimidate voters in advance of the November elections. Democratic party marches morphed speedily into mobs. On the night of October 26, 1868, gangs ransacked a colored teacher's house and school at 300 Common Street and destroyed a colored church on Dryades Street between First and Second Streets.

At the corner of Claiborne Avenue and St. Ann Street in Tremé, they chopped their way into the cigar store of Armand Belot, a brother of the state legislator Octave Belot, and destroyed the contents of both the shop and the Belots' attached home.

Then they moved to destroy the Economie's hall. The rebels had been waiting for a reason to ambush the building. As early as 1863, the members had hung an American flag on a pole mounted on the front of the hall, making it a prominent target. Finally, the gangs acted. The October 28, 1868, issue of the *New Orleans Republican* displayed the story on the front page:

More Mob Violence.
Economy Hall Sacked.
Furniture and Fixtures Destroyed.
Registration Books Scattered.

Last night at half-past ten o'clock a mob of disorderly white men broke into Economy Hall, and completely demolished the mirrors, windows, chairs, banners, benches and other articles of furniture. The damage resulting from the visit will amount to at least five hundred dollars.

The registration books were partially destroyed.

Mr. Gaillardet, the guardian of the hall, was absent at the time of the visit, as he had received information that such an occurrence was in contemplation.

In fact, the damage was at least $1,800—equivalent to six years' pay for a laborer on a Louisiana sugar plantation.

But the white mobs' attempts to suppress voters did not work. Octave Belot served as a representative to the state legislature for several years. Still, a Democratic newspaper continued to refer to him as "Hon. Octave Belot . . . a *cafe-au-lait*-colored nigger."

Boguille became a New Orleans alderman.

OTHER MEN FROM THE Economie gained government offices as a result of their activities in the Radical Republican Party or efforts to bring new voters to the polls. Henry L. Rey won a seat in the Louisiana House of

Representatives. He served from 1868 to 1870. Henry's brother, Octave, was appointed as captain in the Metropolitan Police—an integrated, federal force—a position he held for almost a decade.

As the ranks of Black voters became visible, politicians throughout the state considered the new environment. They huddled together in the dark hallways of cavernous limestone government buildings. They leaned forward over shiny hardwood tables and discussed the potential of the new, reconstructed state. They debated the role of citizens who could not read and considered whether the newly enfranchised would make informed decisions or be led by the loudest voice.

The political parties and small clubs that backed them now imagined the possibilities. Everyone had his own picture. Some men thought about long lines of voters and ways to accommodate them. Others considered the burgeoning power of the new electorate, mostly uninformed and self-motivated. A few men wondered about ways to get rich by manipulating these people. The sheer number of new citizens and their political affili-ations seemed limitless.

The future was also complicated.

The coalition of Radical Republicans fractured at the nominating convention for governor in 1868.

The more dedicated faction of radicals—men such as *New Orleans Tribune* publisher Jean Baptiste Roudanez—had supported black suffrage and equal rights since the formation of the party. One of them, Joseph S. Soudé, nominated Francis Ernest Dumas. He was a rich man of color who had inherited an estate that included many enslaved people. But because of the conditions on manumission before the Civil War—among them, putting up thousands of dollars in bonds and requiring the freedmen to leave Louisiana—Dumas kept them. Then he joined the Native Guards with his formerly enslaved workers. At the time he was quoted as saying, "I only wish to spend what I have, and fight as long as I can, if only my boy may stand in the street equal to a white boy when the war is over."

But a majority of the Republican convention delegates supported the candidacy of Illinois native Henry Clay Warmoth, who had been in New Orleans only five years. In 1868 he was twenty-six years old, outspoken, and passionate. His handlebar mustache was barely controlled, and his

Francis Ernest Dumas; 1863;
courtesy of C. P. Weaver and
LSU Press

hair sported two cowlicks on either side of his center part. A member
of the moderate faction of the Republicans, Warmoth had witnessed the
Mechanics' Institute massacre. He told the investigating committee of
Congressmen that he had gone to the hall in the morning but left during
the adjournment to visit a house on Canal Street. While he stood on
the building's gallery, he saw policemen murder two defenseless men.
He explained to the committee that he did not trust the former rebels
to respect the United States government, and he supported the vote for
Blacks. Still, Warmoth was an outsider. His youth and political inexperience
made him a questionable candidate in the eyes of the more established
and integrated faction of Republicans. The Warmoth bloc included more
whites who had only recently become Black advocates. Many of the original
radicals feared that Warmoth was a carpetbagger, a northerner who had
come to the South only to exploit its opportunities after the Civil War.
Still, he received two votes more than Dumas.

Warmoth took Oscar Dunn as his running mate. A tradesman who
had formerly been enslaved, Dunn could secure the trust of the freedmen
and former free colored community. He moved in the social circles of the
Economie community alongside his friend Pierre Casanave. Boguille knew
Dunn from the Freedmen's Bureau. He was a former Native Guard as well

and could represent visually that the era of Black prosperity was imminent: Dunn was brown-skinned and rotund. Ultimately, the compromise was successful. The ticket won. Warmoth became governor, and Dunn was sworn in as America's first Black lieutenant governor on June 13, 1868.

The *Tribune* faction of Republicans felt cheated. They had been the earliest and most vocal radicals, and now they were outmaneuvered politically at the convention. They left the party. Their punishment was swift. Once the official organ of the Republicans, the newspaper lost its affiliation and financial support and was replaced by the *New Orleans Republican*, in which Warmoth had a 23 percent interest.

Boguille may have been disappointed at first, having been one of the allies of the *Tribune* from the beginning. But he was now a sophisticated participant in a coalition of advocates and, apparently, a genial member of several communities. He had managed to join the Confederate militia and support the Union Army without reenlisting. He had resigned from the Economie before the war but lived around the corner and worked there all of the time for meetings with the Société des Vétérans de 1814–15, various Republican clubs, and possibly the Spiritualists, who mention his deceased family members' visits in their séance registers. Boguille was a radical in a most organic way—not just by his political affiliations but by his actions and personal history from Haiti. He was present at the major events of the era that brought together advocates for equality, and he promoted literacy, culture, and an integrated community in a way that most of America had never seen.

Oscar J. Dunn; between 1868 and 1871; by Currier and Ives; *The L. Kemper and Leila Moore Williams Founders Collection at THNOC, 1949.24*

Prejudice! does not the very word imply an absurdity? . . .
Yet a day will come when, by the logical march of that
progress which has already given us steam-power and the
telegraph, all the nations will be fused into one brother-
hood, and harmony reigning upon this earth, war will
become an impossibility. A long time will yet elapse, we
know, before the annihilation of the tyrants and oppres-
sors will usher in that happy epoch for humanity; but the
oppressed of all nationalities, the thinkers, and those who
believe in the constant progress of man have faith in this
idea which seems utopian to skeptics.

Yes, we have faith in progress.

—*New Orleans Tribune,* August 18, 1864

THE YEAR 1868 WITNESSED Louisiana's leadership in American civil rights. The new state legislature created the most progressive constitution in the South. Article I affirmed, "All men are created free and equal," and meant Black men as well as white. Article II specified that "all persons, without regard to race, color, or previous condition, born or naturalized in the United States . . . and residents of this State for one year, are citizens of this State." This meant that enslaved people who had filled the ships docked in the port of New Orleans, who had been jammed into its auction stalls and sold to work every humiliating job on the plantation, now had the same rights as their former masters.

The state had at least 210 Black officeholders during Reconstruction, with almost one-quarter of them from New Orleans. About 20 percent of the New Orleans contingent were Economie members.

Winning elections was the most visible part of the struggle for Reconstruction in Louisiana. Less apparent was the community-based army of everyday collaborators working with Boguille to help formerly enslaved people.

The former free men of color and Economie members tried to provide stability for the thousands of freedmen, women, and children leaving the countryside and flooding New Orleans. Boguille's colleague Charles Sauvinet had joined the New Orleans branch of the Freedman's Savings Bank eight months after it opened in January 1866. Poor workers and their supporters became depositors.

Sauvinet rose from a position as a clerk at the bank to its director by 1867. Economie members were among the first to invest. Joseph Jean Pierre Lanna, who had announced at an 1865 meeting, "The society, which has at all times taken the initiative in all meritorious questions, should be represented in the effort to aid some newly freed people," took up a collection of twenty dollars. He still called dollars *piastres*. Sauvinet understood the language and sentiment.

Meanwhile, Boguille collected funds through the Sisters of Charity. Soon many societies followed, taking the money they collected and putting it in the Freedman's Bank. Among the depositors were the Lutheran Benevolent Society, the Sixth Street Relief Society, the Society of Saint John the Baptist, the Beneficial Benevolent Society, and Fraternité No. 20 Masonic Lodge.

In October 1867 Sauvinet had reported to the *New Orleans Tribune* that in one month, deposits totaled more than $1,300, people withdrew almost $5,000, and the bank had $50,000 on reserve. The Freedman's Bank had a network of local branches across the United States that in total held almost $2 million.

Individual Economie members also opened accounts. Lucien Capla, who had been injured in the Mechanics' Institute massacre, entrusted the bank with his savings. So did Henry and Octave Rey, and even a woman with the suggestive name of Heloise Laveau—which combined the surname of the Vodou practitioner Marie Laveau and the given name of her daughter Héloïse Glapion. Jordan Noble, musician and drummer in the Battle of

Extract from the Reconstructed Constitution of the State of Louisiana; 1868;
THNOC, 1979.183

New Orleans, who had the admiration of Black and white citizens, made
a deposit, as did Paul Trévigne, the editor of the *New Orleans Tribune*.

Sauvinet confidently opened an account for his seven-year-old son,
Charles Silas Sauvinet Jr. The deposit form included questions about age,
occupation, relatives, and "complexion." The clerk said that Sauvinet's
boy had a "white" skin tone and went to school. Sauvinet later deposited
a $600 check.

On the night of the Economie's thirty-third anniversary, March 1,
1869, the members held a banquet and celebrated their political victories.

Henry L. Rey toasted the society and reminded the members of the American flag that had been torn from the pole in front of their building: "To our beautiful banner missing and stolen by our mercenary enemies, yet to be replaced by our rights."

"To the memory of John Brown," one of the brothers said, toasting the abolitionist.

Rey, ever the Spiritualist, added, "To the memory of our deceased brothers, that they defend us on high."

RECONSTRUCTION WAS SUCCEEDING WITH prayers and work—in the fields, banks, societies, schools, and every place where injustice remained in New Orleans. Charles Sauvinet became the civil sheriff of Orleans Parish in 1870. Soon after, equal justice was tested in the courts.

On January 20, 1871, Sauvinet stopped into a coffeehouse owned by J. A. Walker in the old city on Royal Street. He asked for a drink. The owner refused him. Although Walker had seen Sauvinet on several previous occasions, the issue of access had become political. Walker said he did not serve colored people.

Sauvinet asked again. He was told again that he would not get a drink, no matter that the law had changed. Then the owner asked Sauvinet to leave.

Sauvinet sued Walker.

The *Daily Picayune* reported, "under the constitution and laws of the State he had the right with others, irrespective of class or color, of access to said establishment, and to be supplied with such refreshments as he might call for. He alleges that he has always enjoyed the esteem and friendship of his fellow-citizens: that he has several times been chosen to fill offices of great trust, profit and honor."

In the Eighth District Court, Sauvinet won the largest monetary award for damages in a civil rights case in America. The court granted him $1,000, equivalent to more than a year's wages for a bricklayer.

Boguille and the Economistes
Move toward Social Equity

1871–1872

THE ECONOMIE JOURNALS DO not reveal why Ludger Boguille left his position as secretary and then disappeared from the society's rolls. He never lived far away or disconnected himself politically from the members. He stayed attached to them emotionally, too, as the minutes of March 1, 1871, attest. That is the night that he came back into the brotherhood.

Less than two months after the Sauvinet incident, Ludger stood at the front of the meeting room and recited the constitution as if he were a new initiate. Then his nephew Henry L. Rey reinstalled him with the following words: "Your arrival among us doubles our hope in the future, augmenting the fraternal charms of the society."

Boguille took the floor to deliver his new poem, written for the occasion: "An Ode to the Week of His Return to His Family." After beginning his recitation, Boguille stopped and apologized. He couldn't remember it. Boguille was fifty-nine at the time. He said, "One gets older and his faculties diminish." He pulled out a folded sheet of paper and read the poem.

The current secretary, Pierre A. Duhart, wrote, "This ode impressed the society by its composition and by the warmth of its truth, from the applause heard and the thanks given to brother Boguille. A pain lifted, the members arranged themselves at a table, otherwise scrumptiously decorated—but for a hint of frill—with charming modesty, a perfect taste and an admirable culinary art, that satisfied the eyes and the mouth with pleasure frank and fraternal among companions. The Committee of Arrangements merits praise for the prodigious work of its brothers."

The men sang and gave brief, sincere toasts to one another. One brother recited a "morsel of English poetry with a strong intonation," and the secretary added, "A gaiety, happy and pure, reigned among the brothers. They were in true harmony. It was certainly a reunion of the family."

At the next installation of Economie officers in March 1872, Boguille became secretary again. He demonstrated his enthusiasm for the society with his love of metaphor. He had once titled the Economie's meetings with their literal French translation—"séances." Now he called them "réunions," using a term expressing the spirit of community that he felt.

A people is no less a member of the human race, which is society as a whole, than a family is a member of a particular nation. Each individual owes incomparably more to the human race, which is the great fatherland, than to the particular country into which he was born.

—François Fénelon, 1718

THE ERA OF RECONCILIATION in the Economie reflected New Orleans's embrace of its diversity. A population that had been integrated since the city's beginning finally exercised its rights and gained legal—if not common—acceptance. *L'Union*, the *Tribune*, and the *Weekly Louisianian* newspapers reported about the ways that the community of Blacks and mixed-race people lived. They built and traded just like their white counterparts. They went to "amusements" such as music recitals, concerts, and plays, and they sponsored philanthropic benefits—from dances to magic acts—many held in the Economie's hall. A French opera company was booked for two performances. In the spirit of openness that had long existed in the Economie but was now also recognized in the public sphere, the French singers were accompanied by amateurs from the Economie community and on the piano by Basile Barès, the composer who had formerly been enslaved.

A multiplicity of human natures, appearances, and origins had long existed in private. When families gathered—especially those who lived near the Economie's hall—their members were often of different nationalities and various hues. They joined one another after Mass to eat, play the piano, tell stories, and watch children run through the yards.

By the 1870s the state had more than 56,000 "mulattos," the term the census used for people of mixed race. Mulattos had made up 10 percent of the Negroes in the slaveholding states in 1850 and 12 percent in 1860, an increase of about 170,000 people. The 1860 census counted more than a half million mixed-race people in the South. In New Orleans, the Scorsa family consisted of a mother and five children, all mulatto, and a father from Italy. The Rodriguez family included a father who was a fisherman, born in Spain, and his mulatto wife and daughter. There were entire families of mulattos as well as those that were a mix of individuals marked in the census as *W* or left blank, meaning white, or marked *B*, meaning Black—designations based entirely on the enumerator's eye, because he had no knowledge of his subjects' ancestries.

The Duparts, the family that hosted the first Economie meeting, had many branches. An 1870 Dupart home in the Seventh Ward held three people, all born in Mexico, whose neighbors in the nine nearby houses included residents from Italy, Prussia, France, and Haiti, as well as the states of New York, Florida, Texas, and South Carolina.

In these multigenerational, multinational, and often multilingual settings, there was food to prepare—gumbo and roasts in the winter. Clothes needed to be mended. Doctors and herbalists made house calls, as someone always took sick among large extended families. Daily life in New Orleans, as reflected in the newspapers, entailed gossip, theater, music, horse racing, shipping, building, selling, and more.

As early as 1866, the *New Orleans Tribune* had noted in an article titled "Miscegenation" that "it is only natural that people of the same race join amorously," but if some people married outside their race, "there is no law to forbid their unions." But the white *Tri-Weekly Advocate* of Baton Rouge stated a stronger editorial opinion: "Negro equality means miscegenation and miscegenation means social and political damnation."

By the 1870s the Economistes led the way in the quest for social equality. The society embraced the members of its community with "African blood," as Casanave once described them. The Economie also accepted a variety of people into its hall to join together for justice and friendship. And Boguille, an activist in politics and a leader in education, now saw his work bear fruit.

AFTER ATTENDING THE ECONOMIE'S mass gatherings, people throughout New Orleans wanted to come to its parties. However, some members feared that opening the doors to the public on holidays could wreck the building and damage the Economistes' genteel reputation.

At a January 1872 meeting, Jules Déjean, a member of the balls committee and an accountant, asked to rent the hall for a celebration and dancing on Mardi Gras day, the bacchanal before the fasting season of Lent. Some of the other brothers thought this was a bad idea, saying that it would "kill the hall." Déjean countered that the Economie's hall was always empty on Mardi Gras, and he had visited the hall of a new benevolent society called the Francs Amis, which was open to the public on that day. The partygoers were reputable and well-behaved, Déjean said. Similar people could come to the Economie, especially younger revelers. Brother Benjamin Xavier agreed: "It is unfortunate that the youth of today seek license and they believe that the Economie is too rigid. They prefer places where there is more liberty." Déjean said, "This hall was destined to be used. Use it, then!"

The final decision, as written into the minutes, was that the hall could be rented for public parties, but not on Mardi Gras, which was reserved only for the Economie's official functions. The most telling statement in the evolution of the society, however, was the opinion noted in the report from the balls committee several months later. The members decided to permit a Sunday concert, which was not allowed in the early years of the hall. The rules needed to be amended, in the words of one member, "to change this Aristocracy and to rent the Hall to those of Congregations or to all honest persons." The society did adjust its rules, and in that instance signaled a move beyond its French, Catholic roots to accommodate other, different cultural traditions.

In 1872 Déjean ran for president and won. He modeled acceptance of Anglo-Americans and their customs. Rather than use the French term *fils* to indicate that he was named after his father, Déjean used the American suffix "Jr."

On the night of his inauguration, he presided over a banquet of fifty-one members. In typical Economie fashion, the banquet table was decorated with food, including oranges, lemons, and bananas that were consumed for dessert. Following a first course of gumbo, the main course consisted of any number of dishes—dozens of roasted chickens, turkeys, veal roast, red snapper, stew and rice, ham and potato salad. Bread and butter were within reach of every plate, as was alcohol.

Only a couple of months earlier, for a different party, the society had purchased whiskey, brandy, cognac, anisette, champagne, gin, and absinthe. For Déjean's inauguration, the members also drank "the most exquisite wines." The banquets of the Economie were more than a celebration of friendship. The occasions recalled the ban in France before the Revolution of 1848, when members of the middle class were not allowed to hold political rallies. Instead they held a "campaign of banquets" that raised funds and offered a way to criticize the government in a private setting. The Economie brothers had been using the same technique since the society began, and the night of Déjean's inauguration was a celebration of political success. They had won the fight for an integrated and open society. They now expressed themselves openly.

Boguille also returned to his artistic roots. He wrote a song with a couplet for each of the new officers that Brother Angelain sang. Then Boguille recited a speech in verse called "The Fraternal Affections, or the Renovation of the Société d'Economie et d'Assistance Mutuelle."

At a later meeting Boguille dedicated a sextain in tribute to the president:

Déjean, your presidency is so tender.
Receive our kind wishes on your day of splendor!
Jules, always maintain the friendships fraternal
Led by your true model, peace eternal.
We pray to the Almighty that our company
Will be led by His hand into immortality!!!

On the evening of Déjean's inauguration and Boguille's return to the position of secretary after his long time away, he wrote, "It must be said, in praise of the brothers, never have harmony and discourse been better observed than at the thirty-sixth anniversary."

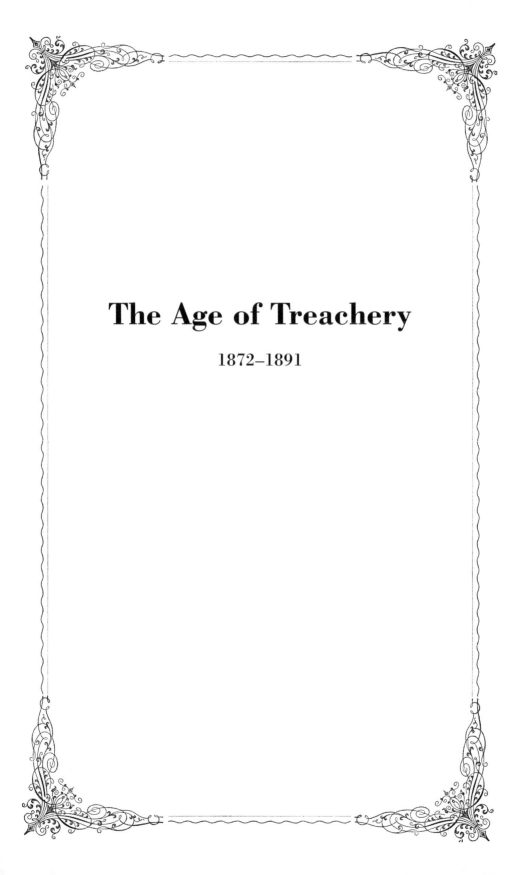

The Age of Treachery

1872–1891

The Former Rebels Push Back

1872–1874

They have managed to invoke the aid of special and severe penal laws violative of the natural and political rights of white men to choose their own companions, to regulate their own property and conduct their own occupations. . . . We have laws and judges who give them judgments of a thousand and five hundred dollars for declining to sell them a glass of soda water or a seat in the dress circle of a theater. And this is the persecuted race!

—"The Oppressed Race," *Daily Picayune*, June 14, 1874

BLACKS NOW HAD THE right to vote and to hold office, and receive equal treatment in public transportation, accommodations, and education. The backlash to progress was violent retaliation. Anonymous white gangs ambushed Blacks all over the state. As early as 1866, a colored school-teacher, George T. Ruby, was taken from his home in Jackson, Louisiana, by thirty men in blackface. He was walked into the woods and pummeled. On Christmas Day, just downriver from New Orleans, a freedman named Washington Rehan put his pistol on a bar, and bartender Santiago Artialla grabbed the gun and shouted at him, "Look out!" as if jokingly warning Washington to duck. He didn't. Artialla shot Rehan at point-blank range and was not punished for the murder. "There were at least 100 colored men murdered and assassinated in a manner and under circumstances repugnant alike to Christian civilization and to the most ordinary dictates of humanity, decency and honor," a rural newspaper editor wrote about autumn 1868 in Bossier Parish.

But the most shocking death was that of Lieutenant Governor Oscar Dunn, a formerly enslaved man who had worked as a carpenter and studied as a musician before the war. He served along with Boguille in the Freedmen's Bureau and with Economie member Sauvinet in the Freedman's Bank. He was put forward as candidate for lieutenant governor by the Republican Convention of 1868, and he won. It was the highest political post a Black man had gained in United States history.

In November 1871 Dunn became ill. He was dead in three days.

Rumors abounded that he was poisoned. Economie member Gardane Casanave, a mortician like his father, was outraged. He wanted to test the body, but others discouraged him from demanding an autopsy because they feared that the results would incite riots. Instead, Dunn's body was brought to New Orleans and transported through the crowded streets in a massive funeral attended by as many as 50,000 people. His casket was taken to St. Louis Cemetery No. 2. Gardane Casanave, in an effort to help Dunn's family, paid for the funeral and placed the body in the Casanave family crypt.

Two days after Dunn's death, the Economie president read a letter to the members from the Cosmopolitan Club, a Black political organization. It invited the society to participate in a grand meeting, in part as a commemoration of the deceased lieutenant governor.

Significantly, the meeting was called at night in Congo Square. It was the place where Africans who didn't share a language and didn't dare speak their thoughts aloud had communicated their ideas and identities through dances and songs during the time of slavery. Their continued use of certain drum rhythms, especially the bamboula, showed bonds that stretched from New Orleans to the West Indies to Senegal and Gambia. When the free colored people could gather in their halls, and the colored gentry could mingle privately in their parlors—the word derived from the French *parler*, "to talk"—the enslaved had no space of their own to communicate, except outdoors. After the war, Congo Square remained an important location for Black citizens to gather for events announced mostly by word of mouth. When politicians and the colored elite of the city met in the square, they demonstrated their sympathy with the freedmen.

"The square was illuminated with lamps, and the stands, three in number, decorated with national flags, banners, etc. In front and along the side were mottoes and inscriptions. Suspended from the centre of the chief stand, between two portraits of the late Lieutenant Governor, was a chair, draped in mourning, with the words, 'The Vacant Chair,' inscribed in silk, secured to it. . . . The evening was cold and windy. All told, there were about fifteen hundred persons within the limits of the square, at 9 o'clock," the *Daily Picayune* reported.

The paper identified the site of Dunn's memorial as Place d'Armes, the city's official name for the location, and added Congo Square in parentheses. It was the traditional name everyone knew. The choice of the square for Dunn's homegoing celebration in the era of Reconstruction was a direct response to his critics. They had complained that he was trying to "Africanize Louisiana."

Madame,

In the name of the Société d'Economie et d'Assistance Mutuelle, I address this letter of condolence on the premature death of your dear spouse, our beloved brother. We must console you, and you must submit to the will of the Supreme Being!!! For us, his brothers, we sincerely regret his death, especially in a manner as sudden as it was natural . . . but, as I told you: We submit to the decrees of Eternal Providence!!!

I end this sad note, Madam, in praying that you believe that the memory of your spouse, our esteemed Brother, will always be in our thoughts, and to perpetuate his name, it is inscribed on the Funeral Column, placed in our meeting room, so that it is venerated and remembered, along with all our brothers who are at peace in the Chapel of Rest!!!

I am, Madame, in sympathy,
Your humble and devoted servant,

—Ludger Boguille, Secretary, New Orleans, April 22, 1872

THE MURDERS BEGAN TO hit closer to home.

One of the newer members of the Economie was Joseph S. Soudé, a secretary of Branch No. 1, Seventh Ward Club, a political organization representing an area where many Economie families had migrated, across Claiborne Street toward Lake Pontchartrain. Boguille knew Soudé's character. He was sincere and optimistic. He worked as a US Custom House officer, inspecting the freight that arrived in the busy port of New Orleans.

Boguille also knew Soudé as an early Radical who had worked hard to secure education and jobs for formerly enslaved people. He sat weekly in the meetings of the Equal Rights League and had been the first man to reach into his personal funds for money to convene a Radical Republican convention in Louisiana in 1867 with an organizing committee composed of whites and Blacks. This was a year after the Mechanics' Institute massacre. Soudé also rented the hall for at least one ball that invited young men and women to attend, dance, and raise money for "liberal and patriotic work."

Soudé spoke about his devotion to equal rights on the night in 1871 when he became a member of the Economie. He said, "Brothers, I thank you for the kind benevolence that you have given me. I have desired to be part of the Society for a long time, and I have undertaken to fight, and always will fight, the disturbing realities with regard to prejudice and the rest, with a free spirit. I will not hesitate. I will not hold back. I come to you without social ambition or political ambition." Soudé added, "I am coming here to put into practice the magnificent preamble of your Society, which moreover I am going to introduce to men here and abroad."

No doubt he was still thinking of Haiti. He was the secretary of the Société des Bienfaisance des Frères-Unis, which had begun to assist free people of color to emigrate from Louisiana to the island approximately a decade earlier. By 1867 its "operations were cut short," but the organization still met in the Economie's hall and had evolved to aid the local poor.

Soudé wanted to expand the reaches of the Economie's association, but he didn't get the opportunity. His job was the cause. He worked on the waterfront, where smuggling, stealing, and violent confrontations were frequent. The nearby streets held brothels and dance halls. Murder was almost commonplace before the Civil War. Afterward, assaults and stabbings continued. The *Daily Picayune* reported on the persistence of dirty, whiskey-filled bars on Gallatin Street near the river. A reporter witnessed a drunken woman threatening to brawl with her male dance companions and being taken outside, laid on the paving stones, and doused with water. The *New Orleans Republican* reported a stabbing at a "whisky resort" over cards.

Similarly, danger was always present along the docks. Soudé, while honored to be an inspector, was also probably a little anxious about his post. The port was disorganized, and after the war, ship traffic had moved upriver to places that ran more smoothly than New Orleans. One reason the port lost business was that the owners, merchants, and stevedores who had supported the Confederacy did not want to work with the multiracial Reconstruction government. Gangs lurked near the harbor.

On April 20, 1872, Soudé got in the way, said the papers, when one gang member tried to shoot another at the pier. An eyewitness reported, "This morning about 6 o'clock I was sitting on the Levee, in company with Mr. Soude. I was reading the paper, when I heard a shot fired. Mr. Soude and myself jumped up, and he attempted to go on the schooner . . . and I moved towards a pile of goods on the wharf. . . . One of the shots struck Mr. Soude in the back. . . . Mr. Soude called me and I went to him."

Soudé died on the way to the hospital. Many people believed his death was the result of being in an unlucky location, where Sicilian gangs were engaged in ongoing territorial wars. The Economistes concluded that Soudé had died an "accidental death." But others suspected a growing conspiracy against men of color in important positions. Among the latter group was Rodolphe Desdunes, the author and activist who wrote about Soudé's death that "at this time, to kill a black man or to kill a Republican regardless of his color was considered a commendable and patriotic thing to do."

All of the members of the Economie went to Soudé's funeral, along with two other benevolent associations and employees of the customhouse. The Italian community took up a collection for his family, perhaps to deflect the rumors of a vendetta between their gangs or because of personal relationships. Many Sicilians had moved into the Tremé neighborhood near the Economie's hall.

On the afternoon of Soudé's funeral, his Economie brothers met at his home. Among them were Lucien Capla, who had been shot in the Mechanics' Institute massacre; Ernest Lacroix, whose brother Victor had been murdered there; and Boguille, who had witnessed the carnage.

Each man wore a black crepe ribbon in the band of his hat. Some stared as the priest blessed Soudé's coffin, and they groaned reflexively as it was lifted onto a horse-drawn carriage. Then the presidents of other benevolent societies and their officers began to march at the head of a long procession. According to tradition, the men walked in straight lines with their chests high and heads raised. Following the organizations was a slow-moving group of relatives and friends of the deceased, bumping against one another and whispering hopeful consolations. At the cemetery, some of the mourners must have felt anger and others disappointment at Soudé's sudden death. They prayed just before the coffin was slid into the tomb.

Boguille wrote in the minutes that the men carried branches of the native Louisiana cypress tree as symbols of their organization. It was the hall's construction material. Cypress was plentiful in the swamps just outside the city. With hunched, sinewy bark and swollen knees coming out of the water, groves of cypress trees sometimes resembled a gathering of old men. The trees grew tall and spread wide branches. Alligators and snakes met near the base of the cypresses, as did egrets and pelicans. When cypress was polished for furniture, it shone like gold. When it was planked, it swelled and made a tight wall. Like the ancient Romans, the Economistes carried cypress branches to the burial as symbols of respect, death, and immortality. Boguille wrote about the Soudé funeral that "the members silently, regretfully, and fraternally put their cypress branches into the grave as their way of saying goodbye."

The Economistes paid the costs of Soudé's burial: $2 for the death certificate and $7.50 for his coffin. But the psychological costs were higher. Although the First District Court set the bail for the two shooters at $10,000 and $5,000, the murderers went unpunished.

Today the society is strong not only for its number and by its resources, but with the attitude it has—progressive. . . .

It inspires confidence, wisdom, thrift, justice, and works for the goals of its founders.

—Jules Déjean, Economie president, 1874

DESPITE THE POLITICAL TROUBLES, the brothers were optimistic. Some may even have found purpose in resisting prejudiced opposition. The Economie's hall thrived. More and more organizations met under its roof, including the St. Barbara Society, named for a martyr venerated by the French, Greeks, Spanish, and men in the military as the saint of fire and lightning. The Société de Cigariers also asked to meet regularly in one of the rooms on a weekday night, at the request of Brother Joseph H. Gomez. The Société des Vétérans de 1814–15 and an organization called the Cavaliers used the hall to give balls. The Workers Society and the organization of Young Friends, or Société des Jeunes Amis—which even English speakers called the Jeunes Amis—assembled during the week. The new organizations and men from around the city filled the hall, where once there had been only Economistes. Many of Boguille's society brothers had passed away. Pierre Casanave, the mortician, died six months after the Mechanics' Institute massacre in 1866. Etienne Cordev*i*olle died in 1868 near Paris in one of his many houses. Joseph Jean Pierre Lanna died the same year in Louisiana, and Charles Martinez died of consumption in 1870.

Joseph Charles Dupart died only a month before the Economie's thirty-sixth anniversary, on February 6, 1872, at home in the Faubourg Marigny, where the men had first held their meetings. The Economie orator François Boisdoré *fils* identified Dupart's body for the death certificate.

Meanwhile, a new generation of colored men joined: Raoul and Doresmond Crocker, from an original Economie family. François Tervalon *fils* followed his father, born in Port-au-Prince, into the Economie. Francisco and Marco Diaz, Joseph Sepero, and Dominique Caderon were born in Cuba. Michel Madison came from Virginia. New member Emile Dussuau was identified as a "Mexique Amérique," and Antonio Luciani's birthplace was Italy. The outreach into other communities and cultures showed in the Economie's financial statements. On St. Joseph's Day, dedicated to the patron saint of the Sicilians, the Economie's ball brought in almost as much money as those held during the Carnival season. The annual dance given on the night of the saint's feast day garnered enough to generate a hefty sum for the nuns, the orphanage, and tuition for colored children at the Couvent School.

In 1872 the committee in charge of the St. Joseph's ball spent $142, including $63 for liquor and $36 for music, but the dance generated $123 at the door and a $120 profit from the sale of food and drinks—almost seven weeks of work for a Louisiana carpenter.

In 1873, the Economie began to attract applicants from a society of men who called themselves Les Amis de l'Équité—the Friends of Equity. They had organized to achieve civil rights. One of these new Economie members, Peter Joseph, was a thirty-year-old captain in the Metropolitan Police, an integrated force, when he went with a white friend to the Academy of Music to hear a performance on March 7, 1874. His friend James Rierdon bought two tickets in a private box, called the Family Circle. When they got to the door of the theater, the ticket taker allowed Rierdon inside but stopped Joseph from entering and threw him out. Joseph sued the theater and took his case through district courts to the Louisiana Supreme Court, where he won two years later.

For the anniversary banquet in 1874, the society purchased more chairs to accommodate the overflow of initiates. Among them was future society president Alfred Jourdain.

"*Mes frères*," began President Déjean, "I am going before you to give you the history of the society in the past twelve months." The Economie had grown to a total of 163 members.

The society printed and purchased one hundred more certificates of membership, and the minutes noted, "Resolved that the new constitution be printed, one part in English and one part in French, as we have members who do not understand French, and this is in the interests of the Society."

The editor of the *New Orleans Tribune* translated and printed the copies of the Economie constitution. The society assessed members twenty-five cents each to defray the costs. Still, the spirit of collaboration did not mean assimilation into Anglo-American culture. Boguille took the minutes in French and noted the members' fee for translation into that language as "25 *sous*." He meant cents.

To overthrow this domination, to relieve the white people of this oppression of ignorance, brutality, vice and semi-barbarism, to give the political and legislative power of the State to men of intelligence, virtue, honesty and capacity, should be the sole object of the political organization which alone can save this State from the Africanization and Barbarization with which it is menaced.

—"The Oppressed Race," *Daily Picayune*, June 14, 1874

THE MILITANT ARM OF the Democratic Party did not succeed in frightening the new freedmen away from the polls in 1872. The Republican William Pitt Kellogg won the governor's seat, but a state election board refused to accept his victory. His Democratic rival, John McEnery, claimed to have won and was inaugurated on January 14, 1873, in New Orleans's Lafayette Square. The same day, Kellogg took the oath of office at the Mechanics' Institute. Then he moved into the governor's office.

About seven weeks later, McEnery's supporters attempted to secure their win with violence. An armed group of two hundred to three hundred men came to the Third District Police Station on Chartres Street opposite Jackson Square and began firing. Economiste Octave Rey was a captain of the Metropolitan Police force at the time. The station police shot back, and reinforcements brought in a twelve-pound cannon. The police got the upper hand against McEnery's militants. About fifty were jailed, and bond was set at $1,000.

The gun battle alarmed the nation. The *New York Times* described the aftermath of the attack:

> The railing of Jackson-square is . . . broken in several places, and here and there the buildings near it are chipped. The trees in the square are fairly riddled with bullets, and the ground is strewn with broken branches. This gives a faint idea of the severity and briskness of the fire. The police hold the street immediately in front of the station. They are armed with Winchester rifles. The station itself is occupied by United States soldiers, who have their guns stacked in the court-yard, with several men guarding them. People are constantly entering the office inquiring for friends and relatives. Permission to see them, however, with one or two exceptional instances, was refused.

On April 13, the McEnery supporters pushed their violent agenda again. This time they refused to allow a Kellogg appointee to take his office in Colfax, Louisiana. When the local Black militia defended the courthouse, the whites began to riot. They set fire to the courthouse with the militia members inside, then murdered and lynched others in the town. As many as 150 lives were lost in one of the worst massacres of the era.

Finally, on September 20, 1873, President Ulysses S. Grant attempted to settle the battles in Louisiana by affirming Kellogg's election as governor with an executive order.

The measure provoked more outrage.

A group calling itself the White League formed. It was an openly vicious sibling organization to the Knights of the White Camellia, which had been intimidating and murdering freedmen in many rural parishes. The White League hung nooses on trees in areas outside of New Orleans to frighten Blacks and their allies away from the polls. Its stated goal was to terrorize voters: "Therefore we enter into and found this league for the protection of our own race against the daily increasing encroachment of the negro, and we are determined to use our best efforts to purge our legislative, judicial, and ministerial offices from such a horde of miscreants as now assume to lord it over us."

THE LOUISIANA MURDERS—GATHERING THE DEAD AND WOUNDED.—[SEE PAGE 396.]

The Louisiana Murders—Gathering the Dead and Wounded [Colfax Massacre]; by Charles Harvey Weigall; from *Harper's Weekly*, May 10, 1873; *THNOC, 1974.25.9.196*

In New Orleans, the former rebels, radical Democrats, high-ranking white citizens, and gangsters united to overthrow the state government. A shipment of arms awaited the White League in the port of New Orleans. But the Metropolitan Police and state militia blocked access to the dock. The White League claimed that its "dearest rights [had] been trampled upon," and it assembled more than 5,000 vigilantes from all walks of society on the morning of September 14, 1874. By afternoon many more followers had joined them, so that about 8,400 people faced off against the police at the foot of Canal Street, intending to overthrow Kellogg's administration. The White League had more than twice as many fighters as the combined 3,600-man Metropolitan Police and state militia.

The armed battle took the lives of twenty-one White League supporters and eleven of their opponents. Captain Octave Rey escaped, but two members of the Economie who fought on the side of the government died.

THE LOUISIANA OUTRAGES—ATTACK UPON THE POLICE IN THE STREETS OF NEW ORLEANS.

The Louisiana Outrages—Attack Upon the Police in the Streets of New Orleans [Battle of Liberty Place]; from *Harper's Weekly*, October 3, 1874; *THNOC, gift of Harold Schilke and Boyd Cruise, 1959.159.21*

Charles Charbonnet; *courtesy of Phil Flott*

The *Daily Picayune* declared a "Citizen's Victory," praised the "honorable and brave men" of the White League, and insisted that no colored citizens had been insulted, mistreated, or killed. Kellogg was reinstated after three days of mob rule. But the rhetoric of the White League insinuated itself into the memory of some New Orleanians and into the city's monuments. In 1882 the outgoing city council renamed the site of the battle Liberty Place, and the city erected an obelisk on the spot in 1891 as an homage to white supremacy. It stood in the middle of Canal Street, the city's central thoroughfare, for more than a century.

ONLY NINE MEMBERS OF the Economie appeared at their meeting the day after the battle. President Déjean announced after the roll call that "in memory of Brother Edouard Simon, killed in the battle of the 14th of September, the meeting is adjourned."

Three days later, Charles Charbonnet, the new secretary of the Economie, sent Simon's widow a letter:

Madame,

We know you are profoundly pained, touched and heartbroken. I myself am writing in the name of the Société d'Economie to send you a few lines, inadequate expressions of our sorrow, and our sympathy, considering the part we have in this misfortune. It has descended on you in a most unforeseen manner.

Certainly, those whom you bewail and rue, in some measure, deserve your tenderness, love, tears, and sympathy.

Still, cry. Cry for a husband justifiably missed. Cry because your tears and your prayers—not to mention our consolations—may little by little bring peace to your heart and will give you the strength and courage necessary to endure without complaint and murmur the cross which the Almighty has given you to bear.

Know, Madame, that you have our sadness, our profound heartache, and actually our sorrow so great that it should be silenced before yours, and we offer you all consideration and respect.

The second Economie casualty, Aristide Rivarde, died three weeks later, on October 6, from injuries sustained in the fighting. The society sent another condolence letter:

> Madame Widow Aristide Rivarde,
> The torments, the despair and grief as deep as it is painful—where the death of your dear and beloved husband has plunged you—has found in our grieving hearts, believe it well, Madame, a doleful echo.

She responded with anger,

> To the President and Members of the Société d'Economie et d'Assistance Mutuelle,
> Sirs, since the death of my husband A. Rivarde, one of your brothers, last week, I have found myself without resources for my four children. My children have eaten everything and cry. They have a right to your benevolence.

In response, the Economie sent her ten dollars in donations, less than a week's pay for a carpenter like her husband.

Madame Rivarde's tone reflected a feeling common among some of the people who had been dedicated to equal rights. They were growing tired. The work was difficult and dangerous. They weren't sure that their political activities would ever improve their lives.

Violence Escalates and Boguille's Health Fades

1874–1877

*You call these measures violence and intimidation. We
think they are justified by the necessities and exigencies of
the situation. We believe that self-preservation warrants the
use of a pistol in the parishes of Louisiana, as it justified the
use of a rifle in the fields of Virginia. . . . From an economic
point of view the negro is valuable to us. Politically you
have made him in the South what the wild Indian is in the
far West, and we propose to stake off a political reservation
for him, and keep him on it.*

—A leading southern Democratic Representative quoted
anonymously in the *New York Times*, April 4, 1879

AFTER THE BATTLES OF 1874, when Boguille walked through the
Economie's doorway for meetings, he would glance up at the names of the
deceased members—Casanave, Dupart, Lanna, and Boisdoré *père*—the
first generation, who died peacefully in old age. The more recent deaths—
Lacroix, Soudé, Rivarde, and Simon—occurred in struggles for justice,
violent confrontations in the New Orleans streets. Not even a decade had
passed since the massacre at the Mechanics' Institute.

The funeral column, where the Economie recorded the members' names,
stood in the *salle d'audience*—literally translated, a courtroom for the
society. The chamber served as the meeting room where the men conducted
initiations and discussed private matters.

"Apprends á vivre et su suras mourir!"—Learn to live and know how to
die! The members had painted that phrase on the column at the time of
the building's construction, but the quote they had chosen for inspiration

now described real choices they were facing every day. On the city streets, men were challenged to stand up for their beliefs. They could be shot for their ideas.

Following the murders of September 1874, the former rebels strutted around the city with weapons close at hand. At the polls, especially in rural areas, where a sea of Black faces once thronged, election days promised slaughter. New Republican voters stayed home.

In the war's immediate aftermath, the former Confederates had tried to convince the freedmen that they were being manipulated by northerner politicians. Allen Thomas, once a brigadier general in the rebellion, spoke to an audience of Blacks at a barbecue in 1868. He reminded them that they had never received the forty acres and a mule that the Republican Party promised them after the war. But if they used their votes to elect Democrats, they could get their own farms. "If you want land, make your money; we will sell you land," Thomas said. "The Government has no land to give you."

The last part of Thomas's argument was intended to frighten the formerly enslaved people into staying on the plantations. "If you go West, the Indians will scalp you; if you go North, you will die of cold, and you have no privileges there. . . . The white man is too sharp for you there. This is your home; we have the lands; you have the labor; there is room here for us all; our interests are one and indivisible."

But the freedmen were not listening. That barbecue took place before the election of 1868, when the Democrats lost miserably, and Louisiana became the most progressive state in the South.

Since that election, the former rebels had terrorized the electorate. General Philip Henry Sheridan, who served in the Fifth Military District during Reconstruction, said that as many as 3,500 people—most of them Black—had been wounded and killed in Louisiana between 1868 and 1875, more than one person a day.

The Economie members had a plan to show that they were not afraid of the violence. In a March 5, 1875, meeting they passed a resolution to parade through the streets en masse for every occasion—from celebrations to funerals. They would dress in a way that showed their unity and commitment to equality: black suits and white vests, shirts and cravats with the Economie's insignia, a blue rose. Furthermore, to show that their solidarity had its roots in marches for suffrage and in the military units that joined the Union during the Civil War, the Economistes would call people to the streets with the sound of a band. The rules additionally required "one American flag for representing the nationality; and one corps of musicians" to march at the head of the procession.

The new president of the Economie had just been sworn into office when the resolution passed to hire a band for each procession. He was Myrtil Piron, whose brother Octave taught music to the children in his family at a young age. At the turn of the twentieth century, Myrtil's nephew Armand Piron would become a famous bandleader, a regular at the Economie's hall, and one of the key players in the creation of jazz.

The Economistes wanted a band to lead their parades, so they would be loud and conspicuous. These ritual processions echoed the ill-fated march to the Mechanics' Institute just before the massacre in 1866. The men in that parade had carried a United States flag at their head, and a small band played and walked behind them.

Piron insisted that all members appear in uniform to march in the celebrations and the funerals of members. When a new brother said at his initiation ceremony that his job didn't permit him to leave at a moment's notice, the president responded angrily. He said that the member should "make his vows or . . . resign." In these difficult times, loyalty was more necessary than ever.

The society paid bands up to twenty dollars for funerals and as much as fifty dollars for other important "solemnities"—marches with other societies, for example.

In 1875 the bands that led these processions were quickly developing a new sound. Some musicians were freedmen who had once entertained white landowners on plantations. Others had received musical education as workers.

During the March 5, 1875, Economie meeting, members debated the way to describe the kind of band they wanted for funerals and marches. It was a heated and very important question, an issue of culture and language in this time of change. They sought a vocabulary for the new style of music and instrumentation that would characterize the sound. It needed a bandleader and was slightly military, but it also exhibited elegance. It was modern. It expressed them—their pride, steadfastness, style, virtue, and optimism.

Someone said, in English, "brass band."

"After a long discussion relative to the words 'Brass Band,' the secretary . . . asked if those words could be given to him in French. A point of order was made that the secretary did not have the right to require these words in French." The secretary may have heard the suggestions *orchestre de cuivres*—copper orchestra—or the word *laiton*, which referred to the alloy used in foundries for locks, plumbing, and doorknobs. The members could not find the appropriate terminology. There was no French phrase for the new music. "The brother E. Alix, seconded by brother H. Boutté, made a motion that the words 'Brass Band' remain. The motion was adopted by 26 against 11." The secretary wrote that their outings required "*un chef de musiciens* (brass band)." While the Economie journals continued to be handwritten in French, the English words describing the music for their marches jumped off the page.

Pay the insurance, just in case there's a fire at the hall.

—Economie Minutes, 1872

IN 1874, THE SAME YEAR that two Economistes died in the street
battle with the White League, the Freedman's Bank closed its doors.
During the bank's nine-year tenure, 70,000 accounts had been opened
nationwide. Deposits totaled more than $57 million from patrons such
as soldiers returning from the Civil War, domestic workers, sharecroppers,
carpenters, and supporters of economic independence for people of color.
Henry L. Rey, the former president of the Economie, had opened his
account a year earlier. According to the bank's records, in the week that Rey
made his deposit, accounts were also opened by a clerk, a washerwoman,
a steamboat worker, and a soldier from Bavaria. Their application cards
identified them by their race or complexions as white, yellow, black, and
"white speckled," respectively.

The bank had thirty-seven branches in the United States, and its charter said it would invest all of its deposits, except funds used for operating

248   HARPER'S WEEKLY.   [March 29, 1879.

WAITING.

A DEBT THAT THE REPUBLICAN PARTY OUGHT TO WIPE OUT.

"Waiting. A Debt That the Republican Party Ought to Wipe Out"; by Thomas Nast; from *Harper's Weekly*, March 29, 1879; *THNOC, 79-55-L* costs and emergencies. But the bank's swift expansion was untenable. Expenses were too high, profits too low, and mismanagement rampant. The Reverend John W. Alvord, an abolitionist who conceived of the bank and became its first president in 1865, had no banking experience. He relied on his board of directors who, in an effort to earn more money, changed the bank's charter in 1870 so that it was able to lend its funds to real estate speculators. It quickly became a cash cow for unscrupulous investors. In addition, a national bank panic in 1873 caused Freedman's depositors to demand their money from its branches. The institution barely survived, and in 1874 it installed Frederick Douglass as president to bolster public confidence. He had high hopes when he saw its new headquarters in Washington, DC. Douglass also believed in its good intentions. He invested $10,000 in the bank. Later, he said that by investing in the bank, he had unknowingly become "married to a corpse." In the nineteenth century there was no federal banking insurance for depositors.

In 1877 the bank's last commissioners held a public auction to sell the headquarters and a few lots on Pennsylvania Avenue in Washington. *Harper's Weekly* satirized the closing in an 1879 cartoon by Thomas Nast, pointing out that years after the bank closed, depositors still waited and hoped to recoup some of their losses. The illustration showed a dark-skinned man in a ragged hat and coat waiting with his hand on the doorknob of a closed entrance near a sign that said, "The First Savings of the Emancipated Slave Embezzled Here, by Men That 'Tried to Do Some Good.'"

In New Orleans, Economiste Charles Sauvinet, head of the local Freedman's Bank branch, was despondent. The people he had fought for in the Civil War and encouraged to invest their life savings would be lucky to get 10 percent of their deposits returned to them from the sale of the bank's physical assets. This bad news only added to the anxieties of the Economie brothers.

Alfred Jourdain, a new member and a Republican activist, was thrown in jail on Election Day 1874, accused by poll watchers of voter fraud—specifically, perjury. The charge could have meant a number of things: perhaps he gave a different address than the one on the rolls, or failed to sign his middle initial, or hesitated when asked to name all of the presidents of the United States since Washington. Those were the ways, in addition to threats and murder, that white Democrats kept Blacks away from the polls in the South.

The story about Jourdain in the *Picayune* newspaper began with the words "The fraudulent voters yesterday came out in force, and though a number were arrested, a still larger proportion doubtless cast their ballots helping to increase the minority of the Republican party in the city." Jourdain and forty-one others, two of them Economie members, were jailed that day, but only until the polls closed. The newspaper called the arrested men "henchmen"—undoubtedly because they were Republican leaders in the district.

In the same roundup of city news reporting the charge of voter fraud by perjury against Jourdain, the *Picayune* congratulated the Conservative Party official in charge of canvassing voters and noted that he received a gold-handled cane from his workers.

Another blow to the Economie men was the theft of the society's good name. In 1870 a group of eighteen investors calling themselves in English "The Economy Mutual Aid Association" had incorporated as an insurance company. The charter members of the "Economy" in 1870 included none of the members of the Société d'Economie et d'Assistance Mutuelle. The act of incorporation was signed before an English-speaking notary and written entirely in English, unlike any of the Economie documents at that time. City School Board treasurer Warren Van Norden bought 225 shares of stock in the company at one hundred dollars each and was by far the largest shareholder. Other investors purchased from one to fifty shares each. Van Norden became the first treasurer of the association, which advertised the purchase of insurance policies for ten to fifteen dollars in the *New Orleans Republican* newspaper while agents traveled around the state to get customers. The group was a moneymaking enterprise and not a philanthropic organization, but the similarity of its name to the Economie confused many people. The Economie's hall was well-known as the site of progressive Republican politics and freedmen's aid. The use of the name Economy Mutual Aid Association appeared to be an attempt to mislead the public.

Two years later, Van Norden, also vice president of the Louisiana Savings Bank and Safe Deposit Company, was implicated in a scheme to bribe a state senator, according to the *Daily Picayune*.

Perhaps the members of the original society had these deceptions in mind when they sent fifty dollars to the mayor's office to aid local victims of an April 1874 flood that inundated land along the Mississippi River, including parts of Orleans Parish. The *Picayune*, which rarely had anything good to say about people of color, wrote on April 25, 1874:

The Economy Society

It is one of the special privileges of this association that its services are frequently employed in behalf of patriotic and benevolent movements. With laudable zeal, the members of the Economy Society have come forward to assuage the present distress of our people caused by the late overflow, and made liberal contributions.

In years gone by, when the crevasses and other calamities afflicted a large number of persons residing along the Mississippi and in other portions of the State, this society promptly devoted its attention to the relief of the poor, and animated by a noble and generous feeling of charity, distributed among them abundant provisions and other necessaries of life.

The Economy Society, which has for several years been established on Ursulines street, in the Second District of this city, and is composed of some of our oldest and most respected citizens, has truly at heart the welfare of New Orleans.

Shortly afterward, the society negotiated with the governor to be recognized by the state. On June 1, 1874, the president of the Economie "announced that the Act of Incorporation of the Society has been signed by the Governor of the State, Mr. William P. H. Kellogg." The members framed the incorporation document and hung it in the hall. The charter listed the names of the 167 members. Boguille must have admired his name, appearing third on the list.

The Economistes had rectified the confusion over their name and reputation, but the next week they noticed a problem with the hall. Insidious drops of rainwater against the building were rotting the fascia under the gutters. A member of the ameliorations committee said the problem was that the society had tried to save money by making the repairs one at a time, spending twice the amount it would have if the work had been completed properly at the beginning.

They argued among themselves, blaming one another for small errors. The political and economic pressures, the threats of violence, and the uncertainty of life for Blacks in Louisiana began to wear away at the Economistes' confidence and power.

⚜

To the respective Assessors of the Parishes of Louisiana:

*It is indispensable to the future honor and prosperity of
Louisiana, and to the supremacy of the Caucasian race in
her councils, that the benefits of a liberal education should
be extended to every white child.*

—Robert M. Lusher,
State Superintendent of Public Education, 1866

ℬOGUILLE HAD BEEN TEACHING for at least thirty-four years by
1874—in his own home, at the Couvent School, and for the Freedmen's
Bureau. His literary guide Fénelon had written, "Of what use are a man's
fine thoughts if they do not advance the public good?" As a teacher, his
lifelong occupation, Boguille put the beloved author's philosophy to work.

He knew that the need for schooling was great. In 1866, in the wake
of the Mechanics' Institute massacre, Economiste Charles Sauvinet had
testified to the US congressional committee that formerly enslaved people
yearned for education: "Old men, to my knowledge, are learning every
day to read and write, and if I were allowed to speak of what I have seen
in my regiment, as soon as they were free of their regular duties, they all
had their books, and you could see them all day long trying to learn. Out
of my regiment I presume there are some 200 men that went in who were
slaves before the war and who came out of the regiment knowing how to
read passably."

But it wasn't easy. In January 1868 Boguille must have felt the tension rise in his body when he read the federal report on schools for freedmen. One lawmaker was quoted as saying that a New Orleans school "of niggers" was "*the climax of absurdities!*" How could anyone reason with that attitude?

And yet the community persevered. Henry L. Rey sent his children to the new integrated schools, as Louisiana's constitution allowed. He enrolled his son Albert at the Fillmore School. The *New Orleans Republican* praised Albert's recitation at a public performance in 1876.

But Black people's success in education meant nothing to those who believed in racial differences. Near the end of 1874, the Economie's most difficult year so far, a group of white boys at the Central High School went on a rampage against students in integrated schools. The *New Orleans Bulletin* wrote that the boys went to the Chestnut Street School, a girls' high school, to eject colored students. The gates were locked, so the boys marched to the school board office to protest. They were told that the law still allowed mixing, and they needed to write a letter of protest.

The next day, boys went to a girls' lower school on Royal Street that was known to enroll children of different races. They told all the colored girls to leave on their own or they would be forced out. More than two dozen departed. Others began to cry.

Then the mob went to a boys' school to "unmix" it but found out that all the boys were Negroes. The schoolboys chased the white gang away. By the time the white boys reached the Keller School, parents from the neighborhood had heard about the trouble and had gone to pick up their children. There was a melee outside. The *New-Orleans Times* reported that "a Negro of fair reputation" fell dead. He was Eugene Duclos-Lange. His unusual surname suggests that he may have been a relative of Philippe, the kind-hearted carpenter who took care of orphans and had gained admission to the Economie in 1857 on his third try.

The *New-Orleans Times* newspaper satirized Duclos-Lange's murder in an article headlined "The Regulators: The Young Men and the Mixed School Question." Mangling the young man's name as "Duclostonge" and "Duclostouque," the newspaper speculated that, "becoming greatly alarmed," the twenty-seven-year-old "ran violently, and in passing the upper end of the Keller Market, he fell in the gutter and instantly expired. It is believed he broke his neck in the fall." A nearby man was arrested in connection with the death. The paper reported in a sarcastic tone that the assailant was simply a grandparent going to pick up a child near the location of the incident who happened to have a stick in his hand: "The arrest, therefore, of old man Bertrand on the charge of killing Duclostouque is wholly unwarranted by the facts."

The *Bulletin* egged on whites to fight integration:

> We know, without urging, that the Caucasian race of this city, will resist, nay will even become aggressive if the attempt is again made to degrade the white pupils of our public schools—schools supported by the white race—to the social equality of the African race.
>
> The white race rule the world—the white race rule America—and the white race will rule Louisiana—and the white race shall rule New Orleans.

The *Daily Picayune* added, "A 'mixed school' is an institution which cannot exist in this or any other community in the United States."

The *New Orleans Times* concurred, reporting that the students at the Upper Girls' High School had no intention of accepting integration, whether it became law or not. The "young ladies," the paper wrote, "stand on their rights as members of the world's ruling race, and the shadowed livery of inferior blood cannot parade its dusky tints with them on the same social platform. All this may be prejudice; but if so, it is a prejudice which has become part of our average white human nature, and to change it requires something stronger than law—a willing popular acquiescence."

The school board temporarily closed all the schools.

Boguille and the newspapers' audience found out later that the White League had prompted the teenaged enforcers to disrupt the schools. When they invaded the buildings, though, they could hardly distinguish the Black students from the white—so they had ejected at least a half dozen white students and overlooked some Blacks. They had tried to toss out one girl because of her dark complexion, only to discover that she was a relative of John McEnery, the would-be governor. Later the White League learned that one of the boys in the mob was actually "colored . . . causing an amount of private and public scandal as to 'race purity,'" the *Weekly Louisianian* reported. If the situation hadn't been so critical, Boguille would have laughed—as many New Orleanians surely did that morning, reading the newspaper aloud to their friends over their thick chicory coffee.

Integration was not a popular idea, even with northerners. In its 1868 state constitution, Louisiana had allowed integration more than a year before Massachusetts senator Charles Sumner proposed a national civil rights bill in 1870. Congress finally passed the bill into law in 1875, eliminating discrimination in all public facilities—except education.

The *New York Times* said, "Mixed schools are plainly far from desirable at present either in Louisiana or in any other of the ex-slave States. . . . Any measure insisting on an admixture of races in the school-room would be destructive of civil order in communities where its enforcement was attempted." The newspaper disparaged the efforts of "the negroes who now and then, actuated more or less by jealousy, and inflamed to anger by the Caucasian's assumption of superiority, try to pass examinations for, or even to enter, white schools."

Some colored parents, the paper suggested, had voted for the White League candidates in the recent city elections in the belief that mixed-race children would be able to enter among the qualified colored few. The *New York Times* advised these "colored persons of mixed blood" that "their only remedy is to encourage moderation, and to do all that they can to obtain in separate schools, school facilities equal with those enjoyed by the whites."

The New Orleans Republican school board persisted, desegregating twenty-one schools, or about one-third of those operating. It even put a Black mathematician, E. J. Edmunds, on the faculty of the white Central High School. Edmunds had trained in Paris at the École polytechnique and graduated fifth in his class. Shortly after his appointment, one of the pupils stopped him outside the school to call him "nothing but 'a nigger.'"

It sometimes happened, if the father were a man of wealth and influence, that the free child of a mixed race was sent to the most fashionable schools in this city, and it was no uncommon thing for them to be sent to the white boarding-schools at the North. . . . In many instances they were educated in the best schools in France. The number of these colored creoles who have received a foreign education can not be exactly stated, but it will not fall much short of two thousand.

—"Education of the Colored People of Louisiana," *Harper's New Monthly Magazine,* 1866

WHEN THE REPORTER Nathan Willey Came from New York to New Orleans in 1866, he interviewed Ludger Boguille for an article in *Harper's New Monthly Magazine* about schooling for Blacks. Willey wrote a compact history of educational opportunities for people of color in New Orleans, including the tutors, private group lessons, and classes held secretly during the antebellum period so that the schoolmasters would not draw the ire of the law. Boguille told Willey that many private schools were opened long before emancipation, including the Couvent School, where Boguille had worked. The article stated, no doubt with Boguille's inside information, that the Freedmen's Bureau still did not have knowledge of fifteen or twenty of the private schools for colored students in operation. They kept themselves outside of the political life swirling around them. Some of the private schools served the elite. Others, like Couvent, reached out to orphans. People of color with financial means also sent their children to Europe, Mexico, or the West Indies for higher education.

Boguille acknowledged to the reporter that he had broken the law when he accepted an enslaved boy as a pupil, prompting parents of some other students to withdraw their children. He mentioned this incident so the reporter would know that not all colored people felt the same about class differences—even within the intimate community of former free people of color.

He had dedicated his life to education, so he schooled the writer from *Harper's*, who would have had little of this information on his own. Boguille revealed the secrets of his community because he believed—along with rational men such as the American Thomas Paine, a friend of the Girondins—that given the same information, all people would come to good, moral decisions.

This mission was apparent in his own teaching—first with his sons and then his scholars. Boguille's son Florian became a headmaster. Zephir Canonge, who had joined their family as a child, worked as a shoemaker when he was twenty years old and took a job as a clerk in the city recorder's office eight years later. Boguille likely encountered many of his students when he walked through the community—boisterous young men who were shy and respectful as he approached, who bowed slightly from the waist as they shook his hand and told him that they now handled the accounts for shops, ran their own businesses, and went abroad for more education. The young women he taught might greet him as well, and announce that they, too, ran small enterprises, worked as tutors, and wrote letters for their families in English and French.

Boguille may have wished that he could remember all of their names, but he couldn't. Perhaps he recognized his former students by the title they used for him—Professor—the deference they showed, and the quickness with which they pushed their children forward for an introduction. These were the manners of educated people. He encountered them everywhere, and he wanted the reporter from *Harper's* to know that.

But these thoughts did not appear in the magazine. Perhaps he didn't boast about his accomplishments, and if he did, the reporter may not have thought that all of Boguille's stories were relevant.

By 1874 Boguille probably would not have remembered the conversation in any case. His memory seemed to flag with the stress of the years following the war. Taking a toll on him were the deaths of his Economie brothers, the pain he felt for the poor widows, and the political winds that altered and destroyed friendships in his community like tornadoes.

Boguille was sixty-two in 1874. His physical strength seemed to wax and wane, as did his mental abilities. If he turned back the pages in the Economie journals, Boguille could see his thoughts and his brothers' affection for him. He could read that he was very happy as secretary again when he rejoined the society. He felt joy as the Economie opened its doors to a wider section of society and worked for equality.

But as violence increased in the city again, Boguille's energy seemed to dissipate. His participation in the Economie was erratic. In March 1875 he became the chairman of the *secours* (relief) committee, overseeing efforts to visit ailing members and take care of their needs. By November he was so ill himself that he missed months of meetings. The swings his health took seemed to match the fluctuating struggles for justice in his home city.

Equality, as applied to human beings, is entirely Utopian. No two are alike; no two are equal. The wise man and the fool, the honest man and the rogue, are as different from each other in mental and moral attributes as the white man and negro are in their physical aspects. Why they were thus created is a question which the Almighty only can answer. . . . It must therefore be evident that there can be no such thing as human equality.

—*New-Orleans Times*, December 18, 1874

THE NEW STATE SUPERINTENDENT of education, Democrat Robert Mills Lusher, began to dismantle integrated schools as soon as he he took office in 1877. His report a year later said, "No such unwise and unnecessary mingling of social relations in public schools is to be found in the constitution of any other American State." Local school boards followed, including the one in New Orleans, which ejected Negroes from schools for whites.

"The injunction recently issued against the School Board . . . forbidding separate schools for white and colored children, was to-day dissolved by Judge Rightor, of the Sixth District Court," the *New York Times* reported on October 24, 1877.

A month later a *Times* editorial echoed the school board's position that "the demand of a few colored demagogues that black children shall be allowed to attend the schools set apart for the whites" was "simply ridiculous. . . . The educational facilities provided for the colored children are quite as good as those enjoyed by the whites. . . . The great mass of the colored people know, and readily acknowledge, . . . they are entirely content with their present opportunities of educating their children, and they have no desire to force them into the white schools."

P. B. S. Pinchback, a free man of color before the Civil War who had taken the lieutenant governor's seat at the death of Oscar Dunn in 1871—and stepped briefly into the governor's office the following year—responded to the editorial in the name of "the colored fathers and mothers and the colored masses, tax-payers, peaceable and law-abiding citizens." He said they stood "against an unauthorized and dangerous abridgement of a sacred right—a right involving the very essence of liberty and equality before the law. . . . The right of our children to attend the public schools is no more unpopular than our right to vote. If we should yield the former in deference to an unreasonable prejudice, why not the latter also?"

Out of nineteen thousand students enrolled in public schools in New Orleans at the start of the academic year in September 1877, three hundred Black children were attending integrated schools. By the following summer the Black students had been removed from schools that white children attended.

During the same period, the federal government abandoned Louisiana, too. An electoral commission was formed to determine the winner of the disputed 1876 presidential contest between Republican candidate Rutherford B. Hayes and Democrat Samuel J. Tilden. In a compromise, Hayes received the presidency in exchange for removing federal troops from three southern states, including Louisiana. The outcome of the 1876 governor's election was similarly challenged, and as part of the national compromise, Republican Stephen B. Packard had to yield the office to Democrat Francis T. Nicholls. The progress of Reconstruction ended not only in schools, but in all areas of life.

At noon on April 24, 1877, federal troops left the statehouse in New Orleans. As he surrendered his claim to the governorship, Packard said to his supporters, "It grieves me beyond expression that the heroic efforts you have made, and the cruel sufferings you have undergone to maintain

THE LOUISIANA RETURNING BOARD—TAKING THE OATH.

Economiste Gardane Casanave (at left, leaning toward seated man) served on the
Louisiana Returning Board, which certified the results of the November election; from
Harper's Weekly, December 9, 1876; *The L. Kemper and Leila Moore Williams Founders
Collection at THNOC, 1958.43.8.*

Republican principles in Louisiana have had this bitter ending. . . . To all
I counsel peace, patience, fortitude, and a firm trust that eventually right
and justice will prevail."

Henry J. Hearsey, the editor of the *Daily States*, one of the most influential newspapers in the South, later bragged about his participation in
the demise of racially equal Republican Louisiana: "We bulldozed the
negroes; we killed the worst of them; we killed carpetbaggers; we patrolled
the roads at midnight; we established in many localities a reign of terror."

Boguille's health took a turn for the worse.

Nil Desperandum: Never Despair

1877–1891

We observe that many of our contemporaries got the word bulldozed into their dispatches and editorials as "bull-dogged." We gave the etymology of the word a few months ago. . . . The brethren were in the habit of administering a bull's dose of several hundred lashes on the bare back. When dealing with those who were hard to convert, active members would call out "give me the whip, and let me give him a bull-dose." . . . And soon bulldoze, bulldozing and bulldozers came to be slang words.

—*New-Orleans Times*, November 16, 1876

The worthless "nigger" should be driven from the South.

—*Weekly Louisianian*, December 20, 1879

OGUILLE'S EYESIGHT CONTINUED TO fade. In a meeting one January night in 1876, secretary pro tem Jules Déjean noted in the journal that brother Boguille "is still sick and getting treatment. He is not able to go out at night." The secretary made the announcement so that Boguille's friends could stop by his house for a visit and cheer him up. The announcement also alerted the *secours* committee. Composed of three men, this committee aided the sick. One of them would go to Boguille's home to collect his medical bills and assess his needs.

In addition to gradually losing his eyesight, Boguille had suffered incalculable losses. His oldest son, Fénelon, died in the early 1870s. Then his beloved wife, Mary Ann, died on January 4, 1875. Her passing took a toll on his heart. He now lived alone with his sons Horace, seventeen, and Pierre Butel, nineteen. They may have walked into his room sometimes only to find Boguille staring out the window or into the armoire where

Mary Ann's clothes had hung. The wood would have carried her musk. The humid days of summer overcame any perfume. A woman might start the day smelling of rose water, but by noon her sweat soaked through to her outer garments. Women hung their dresses out to air on the clotheslines in the back of the house or along the side porch, but the smell never left. Even the cedar armoires retained a salty scent that wafted into the room every time anyone opened the doors. The essence of Mary Ann stayed with Boguille. He was losing his sight, so his memory of her aroma was infinitely more pronounced.

She had not gone easily. She had "softening of the brain," the coroner said. The ailment produced strokes, a creeping paralysis, and talking out of her mind. Mary Ann suffered, and so did her once-vibrant lover, who became frailer after she died. He had been sick for two months by the night the secretary announced his absence.

The society didn't record his diagnosis in the general minutes. Besides blindness, Boguille had sadness, melancholy, and forgetfulness. People in old age suffered all of these.

But the depth of Boguille's forgetfulness and confusion affected his ability to remember words, names, days. It was a harsh penalty for someone who had prided himself on his bilingual vocabulary and his oratory.

Then, sometimes, in an odd twist, his mind came alive.

As if he were still in the meeting room at the Economie's hall, the words of society president Casanave might run through his memory: "Who can harm us if we enfold ourselves in the arms of the fraternity? Let us have patriotism and like the Girondins, we will cause our executioners one day to weep with shame and rage." Boguille then might find himself recalling the Girondins' revolutionary song, written by the French writer of color Alexandre Dumas *père*: "*Mourir pour la patrie*," he hummed—to die for one's country.

Mexico may have appeared to him as clearly as if he had traveled there: the white beaches of the Gulf, the men who met him at the ship. He had never seen Mexico, but the Economie's emissary Louis Nelson Fouché came back to New Orleans and sat with Boguille in meetings. They would have talked about the country that had almost been their homeland.

He may have remembered that a founder, Etienne Cordeviolle, had been married in France to a woman from Cambrai—the historic archdiocese of Boguille's beloved François Fénelon. Cordeviolle lived in Paris until his death in 1868. Boguille mentally might travel to Haiti as Economiste Joseph Colastin Rousseau actually had. His wife was the granddaughter of Major Charles Joseph Savary. Boguille knew the family well.

After months of being bedridden, he felt particularly animated on the night of March 5, 1876. Boguille walked around the corner to the meeting hall for the society's annual banquet. However, when he arrived, he found that the dinner had been held a week earlier. That night, members discussed regular business—typical resolutions for upkeep of the building such as the purchase of a mop head, dusters, and sponge for the janitor, and an allotment to disinfect the women's bathroom and to fix the hall's drainage. Outsiders would have perceived these as meaningless tasks, but Boguille remained at the meeting, seeing a higher purpose to these mundane chores.

The hall had to be maintained and repaired, even cherished, because it was their sanctuary of culture. The society hosted recitals, concerts, dances, school performances, political meetings, and more. The members had welcomed communities and congregations of color to use the hall and had opened the door to visitors and organizations of "honest persons" from all over the world.

As a practical venue, the hall sponsored events to raise funds for families when money was tight. As the birthplace of a community philosophy, the hall welcomed an exchange of ideas and dialogues about values. Generations could perpetuate these legacies.

The construction of the Economie's hall had just finished the year Ludger's son Pierre Butel was born, two days before Christmas 1857. The same month, Ludger Boguille had joined his brothers for milk punch in celebration of the hall's opening.

For decades, Ludger had been closely involved in the building's construction and maintenance. He noted the people who hired the carpenters and paid the taxes, insurance, and gas bills, and the daughters of members who sewed the Economie banner and mosquito nets. He knew the *gardienne*'s salary and had watched the men frame and plaster her apartment in the building. He had recorded in the minutes members' discussions about the chocolate, caramels, and water sold on the premises, the dates of the balls as well as the fees collected, and whether the dances were for adults or children. In the building were a library of two hundred books, a space for theatrical performances, and a luxury restaurant where Economie members and their friends were able to relax and have a drink. Ludger had helped create the organizational structure and institutional values for the society. The sum of his work was a beacon to the community. In 1876, the Economie's hall was an island of civility amid the city's barbarity.

No more despair. . . . Hearts, that have borne with me
Worse buffets! drown to-day in wine your care; To-morrow
we recross the wide, wide sea!

—Horace, *Odes*

OGUILLE WAS NEVER AGAIN well enough to return to an Economie meeting after March 5, 1876. He remained around the corner from the Economie's hall with his sons Horace and Butel. The Economie members continued to convene while Ludger stayed home.

In 1881 the members called an extraordinary meeting after the murder of President James Garfield. He was a strong advocate for equality and only the second American president to be assassinated, after Abraham Lincoln.

Garfield had been a friend of suffrage for men of African descent. In the minutes, new member Alfred Jourdain called him *"notre chef bien ami,"* our greatest friend. The society planned to mourn the president for thirty days by hanging a black banner across the front door of the hall and participating in a citywide memorial march. The roster of participants included government officials and benevolent and labor organizations from across New Orleans, including colored teamsters, screwmen, longshoremen, and cotton-yard workers. Jourdain suggested that the Economie purchase a huge new American flag, eighteen feet long and nine feet wide.

The September 26, 1881, parade was a three-mile-long procession that included thousands of marchers, perhaps the last great expression of liberal unity across the city. The *Picayune*'s report did not mention the Economie, but four hundred men marched behind the benevolent societies L'Avenir and the Young and True Friends, "bearing three neat looking flags." Economiste George D. Geddes marched at the head of the Tenth Division along with three other representatives of the Black community. They followed a brass band. The Economistes hung the American flag outside of the hall to show that their members had fought honorably in the Civil War and gained equality during Reconstruction. They were patriots by bloodshed and were not going to let anyone forget.

The next year, on March 1, the Economie celebrated the forty-sixth anniversary of its 1836 founding. Jourdain was inaugurated as president, and the members purchased ten gallons of Bordeaux, two gallons of whiskey, two sixteen-pound hams, and seventy-five loaves of bread, as well as cheese, eggs, bananas, olive oil, and pound cake. The members and guests feasted and toasted each other until late in the evening.

On March 1, 1883, the society gave an even more extravagant party, installing Octave Rey as president for the third time. As the members had resolved years earlier for all gatherings, a brass band led a parade for the annual event. The members gathered at the hall by 8 a.m. to march on a route designated by a committee. All day, they made toasts to one another and heard speeches by their designated orators, prime among them Alfred Jourdain. They also installed a new state flag in their hall.

Brother Alfred Capla, a second-generation member, was the society's secretary. He told the members that their uniform was required—"*costume de rigueur*." It included a black suit coat and pants, white shirt, black vest, cravat, formal hat, and white gloves.

Once the members lined up in the morning, they marched to Economiste Ernest Alix's house with their chests high and their shoulders back. Characteristically, the men slid their feet in unison, intentionally making a rhythmic scrape across the streets paved with pebbles and broken shells. Only the officers and the grand marshal rode in a carriage above the crowd.

At Alix's residence, Brother Anatole Steel's daughter, Victoria, made a speech congratulating the Economie on its anniversary, and Brother Firmin Diaz responded in the name of the society. Afterward, the band played a waltz while other members, their wives, and invited friends looked on, as did the people in the neighborhood.

Then the band and the members organized again, followed by a ragged line of onlookers and children. They marched to the next venue, the Scottish Rite Masonic Hall, where the officers dedicated the state flag in a ceremony called a "baptism." An Economiste's daughter, Pauline Meilleur, held it on one side while her father, Albert, held the other. After two more speeches, the members took up a collection of about twenty-six dollars for the poor, equivalent to a little more than one and one-half weeks of a carpenter's salary.

They drank punch made by former president Myrtil Piron, and the members and their families went home. A few hours later they reconvened with the band at the home of grand marshal Homer Boutté, where they drank another champagne punch and a bottle of cognac as the president, chairman, and marshal made toasts to the women. Another brother had planned to provide the men with cigars, but he forgot them.

The music took up again, as did toast after toast. The minutes of the day noted that "the president ordered the march, then the grand marshal . . . conducted the march of the Society to the house of the banquet chairman François Tervalon. A magnificent ceremony was presented by the young Demoiselle Tervalon, who made a very flattering discourse in honor of the forty-seventh anniversary of our association. Brother Alfred Jourdain made a discourse very appropriate to the fête." More music played.

"The house, full of Dames and Demoiselles, was open to the members, all partaking of the punches and exquisite liquors. Toast upon toast was made. The society regaled itself with two waltzes," the minutes noted. Some of the men and women returned to Alix's house while others rested and rejoined the entire society at the hall for the evening banquet.

The tables were cleared at eight o'clock, and music began again, continuing until ten thirty. The minutes made no more specific mention of waltzes or orchestra music but noted that the *dames and demoiselles* of the members had a brilliant fête of dancing."

TIMES WERE CHANGING. In October 1885 Economie president Jourdain held a public meeting that drew five hundred people to the hall to hear about preparations for the North, Central and South American Exposition, an economic world's fair scheduled to open in New Orleans the following month. To add to the excitement, the Eagle Brass Band played. William M. Burwell, the secretary of the New Orleans Chamber of Commerce, spoke. He had been a Confederate colonel in Virginia and an editor for *De Bow's Review*, but a feeling of optimism prevailed in the Economie's hall. Members were seeking a remedy to the backlash against Negroes. Burwell was welcomed as a proponent of a new, progressive South.

Advocates of the so-called New South said that the former Confederate states should no longer depend on the agrarian economy but create an industrial revolution just like the North's. After the Civil War, Blacks had sought to escape southern violence and farm work for factory work in distant cities. Louisiana and other states suffered from the loss of their labor. The New South's proponents encouraged Blacks to remain in the South with the promise of better, industrial jobs.

Burwell now worked with the Republican Party to improve business in the state and brought the plan to the Economie's stage. So did S. B. McConnico, an agent for railroad companies in New Orleans and Honduras who was serving as president of the Exposition Board of Management, which administered the world's fair. He encouraged audience members to participate in the fair so that they could gain business partners in South and Central America.

Jourdain and the committee of Economie officers sat on the podium as the speaker suggested that men could have more opportunities for jobs that required skilled labor, and women could work in occupations such as weaving and spinning, cigar rolling, and making jute bags for shipping. Luminaries of the former free colored community attended, including the *Tribune's* editor Paul Trévigne, who spoke in French. The final speaker, a lawyer in the colored community, Louis Martinet, addressed the audience and called for a resolution: first, that the men and women in the

Economie's hall that night would support the exposition; second, that they would invite the president of the United States to New Orleans; and third, that they would call on Frederick Douglass to visit them on January 1, 1886, in celebration of Emancipation Day.

Jourdain glowed in the resounding applause and saw the hundreds of hands raised to approve the resolutions. Another man was just as excited by the prospect of the new cooperation—Ludger's son Pierre Butel. A colleague of Martinet, Butel was embracing his father's legacy.

*Our young friend Butel Boguille, has shown his energy and
popularity since he received his appointment as agent of the
Southern Brewing Company. The officers of the company
have not misplaced their confidence, for if anyone has a host
of friends, Boguille has.*

—*Weekly Pelican*, 1887

ＢUTEL BOGUILLE HAD WORKED with the lawyer Louis Martinet
in 1882 to create a political club to support Chester A. Arthur, the Republican vice president who became president in 1881 after the assassination of James Garfield. The Crescent City Arthur Republican Club supported the president's efforts to do away with the spoils system, which awarded government jobs on the basis of political patronage. In 1883 Arthur signed into law the Pendleton Act, named for the senator who proposed the measure, which required civil service job applicants to pass qualifying exams and banned layoffs for political expediency every time a new party won an election. The federal government remained the hope of the southern Negroes. It was their only chance to get decent work. The former rebels who controlled local government weren't going to hire them.

In May 1887 Butel and Martinet attended a dinner in New Orleans for the US consul to Santo Domingo (now the Dominican Republic), the nation on the eastern side of the island that Haiti shared. A newspaper engraving showed the Negro consul, H. C. C. Astwood. He had a narrow face, close-cut hair, and a handlebar moustache and wore a modest, medium-height collar with a neat, flat tie. Butel met Astwood at Dejoie's Creole Restaurant, where, the newspaper said, "the bounteous meal had been partaken of, washed down by a liberal draught of excellent wine." Former lieutenant governor C. C. Antoine attended the banquet. So did L. J. Joubert, president of the Société des Jeunes Amis benevolent association, and George G. Johnson, who had risen from working as a janitor in the US Treasury Department to a job as a customs inspector. The *Weekly Pelican* newspaper noted the presence of Butel and Zephir Canonge, Ludger's former lieutenant in the Native Guards.

The consul spoke about business opportunities on the island and suggested, "If these enterprises are carried out, in the near future large commercial avenues will be opened up for the young men of our race, and New Orleans ought to be benefitted by these industries. Politics may be a very good thing . . . but to succeed and secure the respect of our opponents, we must force a recognition in the commercial and industrial pursuits of the country. These will bring wealth with economy, and will bring respect." Butel may have reflected on the lives of his father and the other Economistes when he heard Astwood speak. Some of these men had been wealthy and had owned businesses for generations but now received less respect than ever.

The consul continued, "Color will no longer be the barrier to our civil and political rights, but condition will be the all-important factor." Antoine, Martinet, Joubert, Johnson, and a committee of local citizens decided to test this statement.

THE US CONGRESS HAD passed Senator Sumner's civil rights bill in 1875 mandating equality in jury service, transportation, and public venues, but the Supreme Court struck it down in 1883. In Louisiana, many of the rights granted during Reconstruction were still in effect. In 1890, however, the newly elected state officials created the Separate Car Act to segregate white and Black passengers on public transportation.

On September 5, 1891, the Comité des Citoyens—the Citizens' Committee—publically announced its challenge to the return of segregation in Martinet's newspaper, the *Daily Crusader*. The group consisted of local activists of color including Antoine, Joubert, and Johnson, with Martinet as their lawyer. Butel Boguille undoubtedly approved.

Economiste Myrtil Piron was an organizing member of the committee. He brought several letters of information to the Economie, which the secretary did not enter into the minutes except to say that "the question is whether to contribute aid to this committee of citizens to prosecute the said question of separate cars, which the majority of the members already think important."

In an "extraordinary" meeting two weeks later, the Economie's first order of business was to respond to a letter from the Comité des Citoyens about "le Jim Crow car." The Economie members quickly debated whether their constitution allowed them to assess individuals an extra fee for a cause that was not part of the society's mission, and they decided to make an exception. They resolved to impose a charge of twenty-five cents on each member, so the society could give twenty dollars to the committee. The sum was almost equal to one and one-half weeks' wages for a local carpenter.

The Comité des Citoyens began to test the Louisiana transportation law that required people of African descent to sit apart from white customers. On February 24, 1892, the committee sent Daniel Desdunes, the son of activist and writer Rodolphe Desdunes, to board a railroad car reserved for whites and then get arrested. The Louisiana Supreme Court ruled that the state's law did not apply to interstate commerce, however, so the case was thrown out.

The committee rethought its challenge.

The Age of Transformation

1891–1919

An Ode for Boguille

1891–1892

Amis Inséparables
La Concorde
La Modestie
Le Comité des Jeunes Amis
La Renaissance
L'Expérience
La Propagande
La Vigilance
La Candeur
La Réforme
Les Dames d'Harmonie
La Dignité
La Fidélité

—Economie Minutes, 1892

COLORED SOCIETIES FLOURISHED throughout New Orleans after the Civil War to encourage self-sufficiency and to advocate for the men around them who had just been emancipated. Their commitments to philanthropy and justice inspired their names: Dignity, Fidelity, Experience, Reform. They embraced the vision of equality painted for them by the Union. They rented the Economie's hall for monthly meetings and anniversary celebrations. And they issued forth, en masse, on special occasions, none more festive than the annual Fourth of July outings.

The Magnolia Gardens was a favorite destination for these events. The men of the Economie gathered to parade and "pique-nique" at the private park and party venue, wearing their uniforms, including white gloves. Magnolia, orange, and cedar trees proliferated on the eighteen-acre grounds along the Bayou St. John. Amid the foliage were recreation buildings. A large wood-frame structure held a barroom and a musicians' platform above the crowd.

The Magnolia Gardens also held a smaller brick building with a kitchen and dining room, which offered park views from front and rear galleries. In other locations were a ballroom, a stable, and chicken coops. For one holiday excursion on July 5, 1880, the Economie paid $40 to rent the resort and $40 to hire a band. The society purchased twelve gallons of ice cream for $18 and spent $39.40 more for groceries and liquor. A "base ball" game was one of the main events. The society sent out invitations and sold tickets. The day cost the society about $225 and netted $63 in profit—more than two months of a farmworker's salary. The Economistes returned to parade and picnic the following year.

While seemingly frivolous entertainments, these gatherings and excursions were rooted in Black political unity and power. *L'Union* editor Paul Trévigne had addressed the Economie community in French in 1863, introducing the then-radical idea of celebrating the Fourth of July from the National Loyal League of United Africans as a demonstration of equal rights. An increasing number of societies with parades mimicked the march of Black soldiers and suffrage seekers. President Jules Déjean had ushered the Economie into an era of more cultural openness among the French and English-speaking worlds of Black New Orleans in the 1870s. Subsequently, the groups who rented the building showed the comingling of Anglo and French descendants.

The Economie was staying afloat by bringing the extended family of Black New Orleans together through wakes, parties, picnics, and dances. The events employed the community's musicians and cooks, supported its businessmen and laborers, benefited its educators, and took care of its widows and their families. The people became more connected with one another as their celebrations and funerals wove through the city streets. The arms of this family embraced downtown New Orleans and extended across the Mississippi River as well as to parishes below and above the city.

The society, which had presented theater, opera, and classical music to its audiences, now integrated popular entertainment. One form was called minstrel music. It began as Black vernacular tunes sung by the enslaved on plantations, then evolved into theater. Blacks and whites performed sentimental and comic pieces, the latter darkening their faces with burnt cork and parodying the freedmen. White minstrel shows in front of white

LEFT: Armand J. Piron; 1923; by Arthur P. Bedou; *THNOC, partial gift of Priscilla and John Lawrence and Burt L. Barbre, 2009.0228.* RIGHT: "Brown Skin"; 1915; by Clarence Williams and Armand J. Piron; *THNOC, 86-742-RL*

audiences confirmed the stereotypes of Blacks as lazy, foolish, and childlike. By contrast, Black minstrels, before Black listeners, were appreciated for their talents as comics and singers. These audiences understood that the skits were not supposed to represent the race.

Some Black groups that sang plantation-inspired songs became internationally known, including the stately Fisk Jubilee Singers, founded in 1871 and credited with popularizing American spiritual and gospel music.

But minstrelsy was the first way that some Black performers were able to gain national attention. W. C. Handy, a formally trained musician, worked with a minstrel show early in his career before becoming a master of blues compositions. Louisianian Clarence Williams ran away to become a minstrel at age twelve. Less than a decade later, he had started a music publishing company and an important band with Armand Piron, the nephew of former Economie president Myrtil. Williams went on to produce recordings by Louis Armstrong, Sidney Bechet, Bessie Smith, and many other celebrated performers.

On September 1, 1890, the society approved a rental for a minstrel show on its premises.

The events in the hall and on the streets showed the growing reach of the Economistes, and moreover, their efforts to align with the broader Black community of New Orleans.

Alfred Jourdain's installation as Economie president for a second time, on March 1, 1891, was another demonstration of the way that politics and culture merged in the Economie's hall. On that day, several colored societies gathered in the building. Their names were noted in the minutes in French—Le Silence, Les Nouveau Amis Sincères, Les Frères de la Louisiane, Les Amis-Inséparable, and Les Vrais-Amis. The name of another organization combined two languages: "Les Young-men Vidalia." The group from Vidalia, an upriver town, joined the celebration of the Economie brothers, once composed only of French urban elites. Journalists from the colored newspapers the Republican *Pelican Standard* and the radical *Crusader* were present. All of the men walked from the hall's upstairs theater to the downstairs banquet room as the Eagle Brass Band played.

Inside the Economie's hall were joy, music, and dancing. But the festivities and amusements were not enough to insulate the community members from the injustices around them.

I declare that the truth above all others to be worn unsullied and sacred in your hearts, to be surrendered to no force, sold for no price, compromised in no necessity, but cherished and defended as the covenant of your prosperity, and the pledge of peace to your children, is, that the white race must dominate forever in the South, because it is the white race, and superior to that race with which its supremacy is threatened.

—Henry W. Grady, architect of the New South creed, 1888

THE ECONOMIE MEN CONTINUED to meet, strategize, and celebrate with brotherhoods across the city. At the same time, racial propaganda and white terrorism increased throughout the South. The annual count of Negro lynchings rose from 39 in 1883 to 192 in 1891. People were killed without trials for reasons ranging from accusations of rape to miscegenation to nothing at all. They were burned to death, their eyes lit with matches, and hot irons run down their throats while people watched, laughed, and applauded.

In New Orleans, the Sicilians were another suspect group because of their dark skin, their work as plantation laborers, and their vast numbers as recent immigrants. More than seventeen thousand Sicilians were living in Louisiana by 1900.

The Economistes' and the Italian community's fates had long been intertwined. During the pre–Civil War years, traders from Italy moved into the downtown neighborhoods, where they integrated with African women and other women of color to create many of the Economie families. Etienne Cordeviolle's father, Stefano, came from Genoa. So did the grandfather of Demosthenes Azaretto. By the mid-1870s shoemaker Ernest Luciani had joined the Economie community, as did lottery seller Antonio Luciani, possibly an Italian-born relative.

In time, the church of St. Augustine, which interred many Economie members and whose pastor rented the society's hall on occasion, opened its parish to the immigrants from Sicily, perceived as New Orleans's underclass.

In the 1880s the St. Joseph's night dances at the Economie's hall were second in popularity only to Mardi Gras celebrations. The Sicilians' patron saint since the Middle Ages, St. Joseph became revered by Black fathers and workers as well, and they celebrated his feast day.

As these communities of color worked together, they were being similarly villainized in white society.

In 1891 eleven Italian men were lynched at once in New Orleans—the largest number recorded within the city. Their murders occurred after a trial in which they were found innocent of killing the city's police chief. They were acquitted but kept in jail because of threats to their lives and a suspicion that they were tied to Sicilian gangs.

A group of prominent men calling themselves the Committee of Fifty put a notice in the *Daily Picayune*, urging concerned citizens to gather on Canal Street to protest their acquittal. At ten o'clock the next morning a mob of thousands formed on Canal. The *New York Times* described them as "young and old men, black and white, but mostly of the best element." After a series of speakers further inflamed the mob, they marched to the parish prison, where they broke down the doors and lynched the prisoners. Most were shot, their bodies riddled with bullets. Two were hanged, one on a lamppost and the other on a tree. It was the same type of "justice" being practiced regularly on Blacks across the South by organizations such as the Ku Klux Klan. The lynchings were a sign that terrorism had entered New Orleans and the rule of law could be ignored.

Both the trial and the punishments were corrupt.

Rumors abounded that the trial had been fixed. Jurors were hand-picked or "were visited at their homes during the evening or early morning, intercepted while on their way to the Court House, stopped in the corridor of the court," the *New York Times* later reported. "One favorite expression was that 'big money might be made by going on the jury and doing right,'" the paper noted, strongly implying that bribes had been offered. Jurors were "silent from fear or had been seen and cautioned about incriminating anyone, till their tongues were silenced as with the hand of death."

However, the murders of men whom the court had acquitted—even in a suspicious manner—caused the Italian government to get involved, asking the US federal government to investigate the killings.

Local officials had assembled a list of citizens to serve on a grand jury to look into the mob violence. The federal government planned to do the same in case federal laws had been broken. One prospective federal juror was Economie president Alfred Jourdain, who was empaneled on April 11.

He was not prepared.

Jourdain had not felt nervous when he presided—at least twice a month, sometimes more—over the nearly one hundred Economie members who filled the hall for meetings. They planned futures in real estate, education, and trade, and Jourdain felt proud. But the social influence he had once sought now made him tremble.

Just recently, he had shared a podium with leading lights of the New South ideology. This alliance came at a high price: Negroes could collaborate in the economic outreach of the New South as long as they acquiesced to its prejudice.

Did he begin to have doubts as he listened to William Burwell, the former *De Bow's* editor, speak in the Economie's hall? Burwell's language hewed to the lines drawn by Henry W. Grady, the movement's most prominent spokesperson. Grady strategized that "the negro must be led to know and through sympathy to confess that his interests and the interests of the people of the South are identical." But all the while, "the supremacy of the white race of the South must be maintained forever, and the domination of the negro race resisted at all points and at all hazards, because the white race is the superior race. This is the declaration of no new truth; it has abided forever in the marrow of our bones and shall run forever with the blood that feeds Anglo-Saxon hearts."

Jourdain stood at the crossroads of self-interest and principle, and he was afraid. He was not prepared for the responsibility of his high-profile posts—neither as president of the Economie nor as a member of the federal grand jury.

Perhaps people came to him in the night, ready to bribe or frighten him, promising him money or threatening him with death. Perhaps he received pressure from both sides—the Italian mobsters and the police—to fix the federal trial. People knew Jourdain. They saw him lead the Economie parades. His name was in the newspapers when the Economie gave a ball. He worked as a barber in the Vieux Carré, where he crossed paths with the city's leaders.

Jourdain's potential to influence politics or prevent corruption in New Orleans must have consumed his thoughts. But he did not have the courage or the inspiration of Boguille, who had forged alliances with like-minded whites and brotherhood with the radicals in the Economie. Boguille's era was different, and he and his peers cultivated hope of equity, not just survival. Jourdain was contemplating a far less welcoming future.

And he was not the only one. The most optimistic, prosperous, and politically active men of color in New Orleans had become discouraged. They were exhausted from decades of fighting. Their businesses had stalled during the Civil War and faltered even more when the federal government abandoned Reconstruction. As the plantation economy crumbled, Black leaders had become the scapegoats of the South.

The Negro radicals of New Orleans were getting older, and the progressive aspirations of their community began to dissipate. Their descendants shied away from political protest because they had never experienced the agonies of slavery, the dangers of civil war, or the massacres that the Economie men witnessed. The young people imagined that the privileges won during Reconstruction and beyond were permanent, so the rhetoric of the southern conservatives did not horrify them as it did their elders. In fact, a new society called L'Avenir Mutual Aid Association, or the Future Mutual Aid Association, described itself as "representative young colored French-Creoles of the Catholic faith" and banned "professional politicians" from membership.

Rising at the same time on the national scene was a man named Booker T. Washington. Formerly enslaved, he was listening closely to the New South's proponents and looking for a way to use them politically while they used him. For Washington, social equality seemed a lesser concern than the Black masses' need for work so they could feed themselves. Unlike the free colored activists who had considered civil rights a priority, Washington hoped that equality might come someday.

The future looked bleak to the Economistes. They were seeing their life's work dissolve. They became uncontrollably despondent. Charles Sauvinet was one of those men. He had served in the Union army, the Freedman's Bank, and the sheriff's office. A year after the federal troops left the state in 1878, Sauvinet killed himself after watching his sixteen-year-old son's health decline due to a failing heart. They had lived at the corner of Dauphine and Kerlerec Streets. The same intersection was known in previous generations as the juncture of Great Men and History, where the first Economie meeting had taken place.

Samuel Wakefield, whom the *Daily Picayune* classified as a "bright mulatto" due to his light skin color, was another overachiever—former postmaster, tax collector, state senator, and naval officer. He fatally shot himself in the yard of his sister's house in 1883.

Albert Boyer, the son of Pierre Boyer, a friend of Boguille's father, died by his own hand in 1883 with a bullet to the brain.

J. B. Jourdain—possibly a relative of the Economie president—had been among the first Black detectives on the Metropolitan Police force and worked hard to become a Republican state representative in 1874. However, when his term in the legislature was over, the only work he could get was as a drummer for a furniture store. In 1888 he walked to his family tomb and committed suicide with a Colt revolver.

Aristide Mary, former treasurer of the Republican state central committee and a zealous philanthropist for the Couvent School, would shoot himself with a new Smith & Wesson weapon at home in 1893, but only after politely asking his wife and housekeeper to step outside into the yard.

When Alfred Jourdain was called to serve on the federal grand jury, he was just a barber—and perhaps an unwitting lackey for the New South's white men. Like so many similar men at the end of a hopeful century, he began to despair.

Jourdain had been educated abroad in language, history, and philosophy, but now he stood for long periods in his Royal Street shop. He clipped the yellowed and rancid locks of rich patrons, yanked out their rotten teeth, and stuffed clots of boiled rags into their gum abscesses. This was not the life he had anticipated.

A month after the lynchings, Jourdain decided to make a statement about his position in the world. On April 13, 1891, he sat quietly at a table and composed an ominous note. "When life becomes a burden, the sooner we get rid of it the better," he wrote quickly in French on a sheet of rag paper, with beautiful penmanship.

In the letter, he left instructions to pay his debts to the society. The members had taken care of his doctor bills when he was sick, danced alongside him at the masked balls, and celebrated each of his inaugurations with a royal feast. Over the seventeen years since he had joined the society, they had done so much together—taken up a collection for the flood victims of April 1874, mourned their brothers killed by the White League five months later, paraded in the streets for the assassinated President Garfield, and settled the bills of his sick Economie brother Ludger Boguille.

Jourdain asked his friends to give the balance to his daughter Alice at a dance in the Economie's hall scheduled for later that night. He sent the letter to his Economie brother, Joseph Mansion, who received Jourdain's note that afternoon.

Mansion was an undertaker with a successful funeral home. His business always accelerated in New Orleans during the city's heat waves, which prompted rash behaviors like gunfights and stabbings. The city had one of the highest death rates in the nation. Fifteen out of one hundred babies would die before they turned one year old. About 3.5 percent of the colored people and 2.3 percent of the whites would be gone by the end of 1891.

The annual malaria and yellow fever epidemics made many colored morticians rich. In the Economie alone, fortunes blossomed for the Casanave, Geddes, Charbonnet, and Morand families. Typically, Mansion charged sixty dollars for a funeral, which included a coffin with a velour or metallic finish, yards of black crepe fabric to drape the above-ground tomb—called the *maison mortuaire*, or mortuary house—fifty leaflets to announce the death, "a clean and decent hearse," two carriages to travel to the church ceremony and the opening and closing of the tomb, and filing the necessary paperwork in the office of birth and death records. The brass band cost an additional twenty-four dollars, or two dollars each for twelve musicians.

Every man attended every funeral, offering support, as the Economie minutes noted, "through the miseries and the vicissitudes of existence." As a unit, the members marched through the streets, sometimes accompanied by the Eagle Brass Band.

While Jourdain's letter was in transit, he went to his job, had a couple of drinks with his business partner, and left just before four o'clock, after announcing he was tired of living. He stopped at a confectionary store before he headed alone to Congo Square. The clearing in the center of the city was surrounded by sprawling oaks. Africans and their descendants had met there for over a century. People had gathered in Congo Square in 1864 to celebrate the Emancipation Proclamation, led by Ludger Boguille, the grand marshal. Jourdain and many other Economie members had attended political rallies there in the 1870s and 1880s. Jourdain planned to make his last stand in this place. Congo Square would hold his spirit, along with those of the vanished Africans.

He had been not-so-secretly plotting his death. Jourdain had asked another Economie member, Bernard Cohen, a few days previously whether a man who tried to shoot himself and failed would be strong enough to pull the trigger again. Cohen cut him short: "Don't speak that way."

"You fool. I am not going to do that," Jourdain replied, but his mind calculated the strength needed to balance the gun at his temple, the pressure required to squeeze the trigger, and the force of the explosion. He worried about his courage.

The resolve came to Jourdain as he placed a .38-caliber revolver in his pocket before he left his home. The weight of the gun made his plan solid, real, and unchangeable. He strolled the downtown streets with the morbid secret of his impending death and the heady power, finally, of control over his destiny.

Unknown to Jourdain, Mansion had received the suicide note. He ran out of his office and burst through the door to the sidewalk. People on the street told him that Jourdain was headed to the square, as he had mentioned his destination to all of them. They had no reason to suspect his intention. Mansion rushed to reach Jourdain before he ended his life.

Mansion arrived across the street from Congo Square just after Jourdain was nearing a park bench. Mansion could only watch as Jourdain sat, pulled the revolver from his pocket, and put the muzzle to his ear.

A newspaper account said that "pulling the trigger was but the work of an instant . . . a little puff of smoke, followed by a sharp report, told that everything was over."

Mansion ran to Jourdain and pulled him close to his heart. The police came next, then an ambulance. Without ever gaining consciousness after the shot, Jourdain died in Charity Hospital.

Jourdain's suicide note said, "As life is very uncertain, it is perhaps wise to make known one's wishes before it is too late. . . . I desire that my body shall be exposed at the hall of the 'Economy Society.' . . . Bid good-by to my friends."

The two newspapers that covered his suicide rarely wrote about men of color. But that day, the pages of the *Daily Picayune* fascinated and entertained readers with details of the incident. The headline read, "In Congo Square. Alfred Jourdain, the Prosperous Royal Street Barber, Blows Out His Brains with A Revolver." The *Times-Democrat* headline said, "Another Suicide." Both papers claimed that Jourdain's death was the result of a lover's quarrel.

But there was more to the story than the newspapers could possibly know or would ever acknowledge. They gloated now when the city's mighty citizens of color were brought low.

Jourdain came to his decision because his life was interwoven so intimately with the once-confident Economie community, because his heart was breaking over the belittling of his friends despite their great achievements, and because his future was untenable and his death insignificant. He tried, at least, to make himself memorable.

But he wasn't.

He was forgotten, as were his triumphant forebears and patriotic contemporaries. The truth about Negroes like him practically disappeared, except in the records of the Economie.

They lived to be very much loved,
And they died to be mourned.
May the clarity of heaven, be to you, dear brothers!
May you, in your rest, think of us!
On your tender breasts, very estimable brothers,
We will guard, alas, your sincere memories.

—Ludger Boguille, 1871

FOR THE DEATH OF the Sicilians lynched by the New Orleans mob, the Italian government accepted money from the US government. But no reparations came to the families of the approximately 2,528 Negroes lynched between 1882 and 1900 in the South.

Grieving Negro communities quietly memorialized their deaths and any number of lost ancestors. These mourning traditions were hardly known outside the circle of believers. The Economie members honored their brothers every year on All Souls' Day when the men stood together in a circle and held hands "to form a solid chain—mortal and spiritual." They walked together around the funeral column in their hall that displayed the names of their dead. Each mourner read the name of a deceased friend and held a branch of cypress tree in his hand.

At the end of the prayers, one by one the members went to the altar and laid down their cypress branches. Native and strong, the cypress was symbolic of the men. The tree existed in the shadowy Louisiana swamps yet grew muscular and tall. Cypress had an afterlife as the sturdy planks of a Creole cottage, a polished table for family dinners, and a reliable timber for armoires and bed frames.

The minutes noted Jourdain's suicide in just a few oblique sentences. "Messieurs," read the entry, which continued in French, "since our last meeting, we have had the misfortune of losing our good friend President Jourdain, who was for us an admirable member—a devoted friend—a good president. His death, for us, was so grievous."

No description followed of his wake or funeral, possibly because the suicide added shame to their already aggrieved community. But Boguille's meticulous notes in previous decades described the Economie's rituals: on the night of a member's death, the men sat with the body and kept vigil with his widow. In the weeks that followed, they would pay her expenses and those of her children. On the morning of an Economiste's funeral, the members stood in two rows outside of the house while pallbearers carried the coffin to the hearse. The entire society accompanied the body to the grave. They slid the coffin into the crypt. At the end of the funeral, the treasurer of the Economie took out his billfold and put money into the hands of the grave openers. There were no minutes to say whether Jourdain received this treatment.

The Economie president's death marked not only the culmination of one man's grief but the retreat of an entire community. It was soon engulfed in silence.

IN MID-JANUARY 1892 Ludger Boguille lay in bed at his son Pierre Butel's house on North Roman Street and struggled with his memory. He had been losing the names of his friends for years. He misplaced words not only in English, which he hardly used, but also in his native French. The Greek and Latin poetry he had recited to his students for decades had disappeared. But sometimes, perhaps, a poem might burst into his mind with clarity: "He can lowliest change / And loftiest; bring the mighty down / and lift the weak." The hymns of the Roman poet Horace floated up from his subconscious, as did the name of his youngest son.

Jean Horace Boguille had died at the age of twenty-eight in 1887. And Ludger's oldest son, François Fénelon Boguille, had passed away at least twenty years earlier. But time was incomprehensible to Ludger as his mind circled through worlds and generations. Still, even when he was in good health, the concept of death was fluid not just to him but within his community. The Spiritualists had welcomed his son Fénelon as a ghost in a meeting on February 25, 1872. From the afterlife, Fénelon gave the believers guiding principles for their spiritual journey: "sublime charity toward all without exception is the way to universal brotherhood, solidarity among Beings, one God for everyone everywhere, true understanding, and knowledge of His laws of love and peace."

On his own deathbed, Ludger may have tried to remind everyone standing in the small room that Fénelon had returned from the dead. But they couldn't understand him, even if they did believe him. He had lost his ability to communicate. Their wan smiles perhaps increased his frustration.

At one time, they would have listened to his every word as he recited any number of lessons and poems. He performed spontaneous quatrains often in the meetings of his society, the Economie. Yes, perhaps occasionally he recalled that he was a brother of the Société d'Economie et d'Assistance Mutuelle.

While he may not have known their names, men came to sit at his bedside frequently. He heard the English speakers say "the Economy Society." He also heard the French speakers now mixing English with their old dialect. They spoke of "the Economy Hall," including the article before the name, just as they had always referred to "la Salle d'Economie" in their native tongue.

Boguille perhaps remembered that a brother in the society once called the organization "a mother one loves."

But words faded in and out of his mind like the ghosts of thought.

His son Pierre Butel may have spoken to Ludger to ground him in reality as his thoughts floated randomly, and his unfocused gaze wandered around the room. Butel may have reminded his father that they lived together on North Roman Street, not in the Vieux Carré, where his own father, François, had had a shop. The Vieux Carré was the name the new real estate people gave the old quarters to sell the colorless charm, not the rough diversity of a place that had been built by people of all hues from so many nations.

The people around Ludger's bed would have talked about current events, about white people and Negroes. How easily they used these designations, race words that had no rational basis.

"All wars are civil wars, as it is always man against man," François Fénelon had said. Ludger may have thought that Fénelon was a friend, not the author who was his inspiration, or he may have confused him with his deceased son. Ludger may occasionally have remembered himself in front of the classroom. A picture of himself slimmer and younger, holding a thin wooden stick to point to the chalkboard, floated behind his glassy eyes. His dark pants carried the chalk dust of writing and erasures. His narrow shoulders were slightly rounded from reading next to the window by day and close to the oil lamp at night.

Did tears come to Ludger's eyes sometimes if, looking back, he thought he hadn't prepared his students well enough? He had taught them to pursue logic. He had prepared their minds. But he had lived as a rational man in a nation with an irrational measure—race. He had taught his students to use their minds, and prejudice was a disease of the heart.

Still, could he ever have looked into the faces of his students and told them that they would not be judged by their poetry, memory, morals, and values but by their skin colors?

He didn't even have a tangible definition of race to give them. No one did. Not the legislature. Not even the United States census, which had constantly evolved its racial designations, from colored to Black to Negro, and in some years including mulattos, quadroons, and octoroons—all categorized by the eye of the beholder, the census taker. Seventy more years would pass before the government would accept the ethnicities that people used for themselves.

Boguille could hardly accept that color now determined the fates of his family, students, and community. Character did not triumph. This dissonance took a toll on him. The two opposing realities that he knew to be true, but that he could not defend, put him in conflict with his own sensibilities. It was a deep, painful fissure, perhaps increasing his confusion or bringing it on. The doctor diagnosed him with senile dementia—a brain at war with itself.

When Fénelon, his son, had come back as a ghost, he had said through a medium, "The spiritual life is acquired by searching; the spiritual path is that of a good man. Revelations are the fruits of constant research and persistence." The afterlife, Fénelon explained, was like opening a book: "Every step ahead in spiritual knowledge, a new reader discovers a world to explore, a power, and an immense lesson to learn."

Ludger Boguille died on January 18, 1892. His mortal mind emptied, and his soul took flight to study the universe.

Transformation

1892–1917

Henceforth nothing else could be expected other than continuation of this policy by which people were divided into upper and lower class according to their color and origin.

—Rodolphe Desdunes on the Plessy verdict, 1911

LUDGER BOGUILLE'S BURIAL RECEIVED no notice in the newspapers, and his grave went unmarked. He may have been interred in St. Louis Cemetery No. 2 alongside the crypts of the Lacroix, Lanna, Boisdoré, and Rey families. He did not go into the same tomb as his cherished first wife Andrénette Lamy. Maybe Pierre Butel put him to rest in one of the large crypts that the other societies used, those that had taken their inspiration from the Economie and met in its hall. They named themselves for their aspirations, which English and French speakers could understand. They were the societies named l'Equité, Bienfaisance, and Inséparables. Perhaps these men, like the Economistes, were the last generation who believed that they could become brothers with all Americans, despite their diverse ethnic roots. They found out just how far their ideals were from those of the nation.

A member of the Comité des Citoyens and one of the Economie's past presidents, Myrtil Piron, had kept the Economistes abreast of the case for equal public accommodations. After the Daniel Desdunes test case in 1890, the committee had appointed Homer Plessy to challenge the law again. On September 7, 1892, at 4:15 p.m., he boarded a train at Press and Royal Streets in New Orleans and sat in the whites-only car. After the train departed, he admitted that he was a man of color, riding in violation of Act 111 put in place by the 1890 legislature.

Plessy was arrested and brought to the city's jail. The Comité des Citoyens bailed him out immediately and then went to court to argue for integration. The only difference between him and the nearby white men, he argued, was his African ancestry, yet the Constitution had given him the right to equal protection in all things. The case began to make its way slowly through the lower courts, finally reaching the United States Supreme Court.

The danger for Plessy and his supporters was obvious at the time. Prejudice throughout the South was flagrant and violent. In 1890, the year the Louisiana state legislature enacted the Separate Car Act, mobs murdered 171 people, primarily in southern states. There had been 1,200 lynchings in the United States over the ten years before Plessy's attempted challenge— on average, one every three days.

The *Daily Picayune* reported—falsely—that Plessy "refused to ride in the negro car, and tried to force his way into the white car." It also wrote that his lawyer argued, "If a man is but one-sixteenth colored he may claim to be, and to all intents and purposes is, white." Actually, Plessy, whose color was quite light, described himself as "seven-eighths Caucasian and one-eighth African blood." The point Plessy's lawyer wanted to make was that the fractional designations of color were irrational. How could the law say that whites were so different from Blacks? And why, then, would the law say that segregation was right? Plessy was living proof. There was no difference.

But Plessy lost in the US Supreme Court on May 18, 1896. Judge Henry Brown wrote the majority opinion, focusing on the Fourteenth Amendment to the Constitution:

> The object of the amendment was undoubtedly to enforce the absolute
> equality of the two races before the law, but, in the nature of things,

it could not have been intended to abolish distinctions based upon color, or to enforce social, as distinguished from political, equality, or a commingling of the two races upon terms unsatisfactory to either. Laws permitting, and even requiring, their separation, in places where they are liable to be brought into contact, do not necessarily imply the inferiority of either race to the other, and have been generally, if not universally, recognized as within the competency of the state legislatures in the exercise of their police power. The most common instance of this is connected with the establishment of separate schools for white and colored children, which has been held to be a valid exercise of the legislative power even by courts of states where the political rights of the colored race have been longest and most earnestly enforced. . . . The argument . . . assumes . . . that equal rights cannot be secured to the negro except by an enforced commingling of the two races. We cannot accept this proposition.

Justice John Marshall Harlan dissented, saying that the Constitution had already made equality legal. He added, "In my opinion, the judgment this day rendered will, in time, prove to be quite as pernicious as the decision made by this tribunal in the Dred Scott Case." The Dred Scott decision, saying Negroes had no claim to the rights of citizens, was handed down in 1857. That was the year the Economie built its grand hall and filled it with literate men in political meetings, composers and performers in concerts and theater productions, and people of every color who danced at the balls.

The members had been publicly demonstrating that they were inferior to no one for more than a half century, but in the Plessy decision the court sidestepped the issue of equality to say that a person could be equal but still separated from others of a different race by any law a state put into place. With this judgment, legal segregation spread its cancer across the South and, with it, virulent white supremacy ruled.

Before the killing of the three Negro men on Saturday night one could hardly keep a chicken in the yard after nightfall. . . . Since the killing there has not been one chicken stolen in the village. The residents in the immediate neighborhood say that measures taken the other night had some good effect, anyhow.

—*Daily Picayune*, September 21, 1893

[The race issue] has aroused within the breasts of ignorant and vicious negroes the wildest dreams of social and political equality with the white race. . . . The struggle [has] now [become] one for the political supremacy of the intelligent white race.

—*Baton Rouge Advocate*, March 8, 1896

No certainty of death or of torture worse than death can exert any deterring influence upon the negro who commits violence upon women of the white race. He is carried away with a salacious fury that renders him oblivious of every other consideration; he is transformed into a wild beast of the most ferocious type, and he merits extermination as does any other dangerous and venomous creature that carries his ferocious assaults into human homes and haunts. Judicial methods in such crimes are too slow to meet the necessities of such cases.

—*Daily Picayune*, June 22, 1899

ℛODOLPHE DESDUNES WAS A columnist for the *Crusader* newspaper, which took up the civil rights struggle in 1889, nearly two decades after the demise of the *New Orleans Tribune*. The *Crusader* was owned by Louis Martinet, the lawyer with whom Pierre Butel Boguille associated. Looking back on the last years of the nineteenth century in his book *Our People and Our History*, Desdunes wrote that Blacks and whites had been fighting inequality in the courts, newspapers, and streets but began to distance themselves from radical causes during the last years of the nineteenth century: "Seeing that the friends of justice were either dead or indifferent, they believed that the continuation of the *Crusader* would not only be fruitless but decidedly dangerous. Seeing too that the tyranny of their oppressors was limitless, that they were using all of their genius to multiply degrading laws against blacks, our people believed it was better to suffer in silence than to attract attention to their misfortune and weakness."

Less than a month after the Plessy decision, Harvard University awarded an honorary degree to Booker T. Washington. He was quickly becoming the spokesman for the Negro race in the United States, in large part because of a speech he gave on September 18, 1895, approximately seven months before the Supreme Court heard arguments in the Plessy case. Washington's vision of Black life conformed very closely to the agenda of the New South. He addressed the overwhelmingly white attendees of the Cotton States and International Exposition in Atlanta, using flattery to seek their support for the Black masses and humility to accept segregation and prejudice:

> [T]he opportunity here afforded will awaken among us a new era of industrial progress. Ignorant and inexperienced, it is not strange that in the first years of our new life we began at the top instead of at the bottom; that a seat in Congress or the state legislature was more sought than real estate or industrial skill; that the political convention or stump speaking had more attractions than starting a dairy farm or truck garden. . . .
>
> The wisest among my race understand that the agitation of questions of social equality is the extremest folly, and that progress in the enjoyment of all the privileges that will come to us must be the result of severe and constant struggle rather than of artificial forcing. No race that has anything to contribute to the markets of the world is long in any degree ostracized. It is important and right that all privileges of the law be ours, but it is vastly more important that we be prepared for the exercise of these privileges. The opportunity to earn a dollar in a factory just now is worth infinitely more than the opportunity to spend a dollar in an opera-house.

His speech was a clear rebuff to the New Orleans men who used the Constitution and court system to push for equality in restaurants, schools, transportation, and the dress circles of the local theaters during the period of Reconstruction and later, when threats of violence kept Black voters from the polls, and white supremacists rolled back equal rights. Washington's address came to be called "The Atlanta Compromise" and was circulated in newspapers throughout the South and the North. His words alleviated the fears of some whites about racial mixing, assuring them that

Blacks wanted segregation, too. An additional result of Washington's speech was that it led to financial support for agricultural and technical schools in Negro communities. In this area, his strategy worked. Segregation provided education for large numbers of Blacks, while equal rights advocacy had produced little but heartache.

Desdunes later wrote, not about Washington specifically, but about giving up on the quest for equality: "It is more noble and dignified to fight, no matter what, than to show a passive attitude of resignation. Absolute submission augments the oppressor's power and creates doubt about the feelings of the oppressed."

He saw that segregation allowed myths of superior and inferior races to flourish and stereotypes to thrive. Together, this was enough to drive some people crazy—both Blacks and whites.

On Monday night, July 23, 1900, a Black man named Robert Charles was sitting on a doorstep on Dryades Street talking with his nineteen-year-old roommate, Lenard Pierce. They were a few blocks from their home. When two white policemen came to arrest them for being "suspicious," Pierce surrendered to an officer holding a gun in his face. Charles pulled out his own gun, wounding the other policeman. Charles escaped and went into hiding.

In the early morning hours of Tuesday, the police found Charles in his rooming house on Fourth Street. Again, they pulled their guns. But Charles had already slipped home and armed himself with a rifle, which he now used to kill two policemen.

The New Orleans newspapers took up the chase of "the Negro desperado" whose "terrible dexterity with weapons makes him one of the most formidable monsters that has ever been loose upon the community."

The mayor offered a $250 reward for Charles, dead or alive, and the governor promised another $250. Police searched his apartment and found pamphlets about immigration to Liberia. In the inflamed, racist environment, these tracts solidified whites' opinions about his criminality and, by association, that of every Black person in New Orleans.

By Wednesday night white mobs surfaced throughout the city, including one estimated to number about two thousand that gathered at Lee Circle near the statue of the Confederate general Robert E. Lee. From there the men and boys headed up St. Charles Avenue, "and there was no plan except 'to get at the niggers.'" They injured and killed any Black person in sight.

The *Times-Democrat* reported that "in the melee a man was shot down, while just around the corner somebody planted a long knife in the body of a little newsboy for no reason as yet shown. Every now and then a Negro would be flushed somewhere in the outskirts of the crowd and left beaten to a pulp." The mob pulled a man from a streetcar, yelling, "We will get a nigger down here, you bet!" They chased him and, as the *Times-Democrat* described, beat him badly before killing him:

> A vicious kick directed at the Negro's head sent him into the gutter, and for a moment the body sank from view beneath the muddy, slimy water. "Pull him out; don't let him drown," was the cry, and instantly several of the men around the half-drowned Negro bent down and drew the body out. Twisting the body around they drew the head and shoulders up on the street, while from the waist down the Negro's body remained under the water. As soon as the crowd saw that the Negro was still alive they again began to beat and kick him. Every few moments they would stop and striking matches look into the man's face to see if he still lived. To better see if he was dead they would stick lighted matches to his eyes. Finally, believing he was dead they left him and started out to look for other Negroes. Just about this time some one yelled, "He ain't dead," and the men came back and renewed the attack. While the men were beating and pounding the prostrate form with stones and sticks a man in the crowd ran up, and crying, "I'll fix the d— Negro," poked the muzzle of a pistol almost against the body and fired. This shot must have ended the man's life, for he lay like a stone, and realizing that they were wasting energy in further attacks, the men left their victim lying in the street.

They shot and beat Louis Taylor sitting at a French Market soda water stand, then one of the rioters joked, "I understand that he is still alive. If he is, he is a wonder. He was certainly shot enough to be killed." A newspaper reporter saw Taylor later at Charity Hospital: "His clothing was covered with blood, and his face was beaten almost into a pulp. . . . There is hardly a chance that Taylor will recover." By Saturday, he was dead. They pulled the shutters off an old Black woman's house on Rousseau Street after midnight, shot through the glass of her doors, and killed her with a shot to the lung as she was lying in her bed. As volunteers came to her rescue, a crowd of onlookers called them "Nigger lovers."

Baptiste Fileau, seventy-five, was walking to work in the French Market, where he ported baskets of fish and meat to the stalls, when the mob began shooting at him. He ran and encountered other rioters who shot and beat him. They left him where he fell, at the corner of Dauphine and Kerlerec streets, once called Great Men and History.

Police attempted to discourage the crowds in some cases. But there were no arrests. The violent mob disassembled and reassembled in clots through the streets until the wee hours of Friday, beating and maiming people of color.

On Friday, Robert Charles was discovered in an old wooden house on Saratoga Street near Clio Street. Police surrounded him, as did a crowd of about five thousand people, in addition to a "squad of special police, half a hundred regular police, and a company of militia," according to the *Daily Picayune*.

Charles weaved throughout the building, firing a rifle through windows and taking return fire. In the process, he killed four more men, fatally wounded another, and injured nineteen. Finally, to overcome him, the mob smoked him out by setting a mattress on fire. Charles came to a rear door of the house, where he was fatally wounded, as the *Times-Democrat* reported, in a "thrilling climax."

The *Times-Democrat* described the scene: "He struck the floor, and half a dozen men, swarming into the room from the front, riddled the corpse with bullets. . . . A moment later the bleeding body was dragged to the pavement and made the target of a score of pistols. It was shot, kicked and beaten almost out of semblance to humanity."

That same day, riled-up mobs in other parts of town shot "colored" George Ford and Sim Reeves, and murdered two "unknown negro" men. They also set fire to the Thomy Lafon Colored Institute, at the corner of

Sixth and Howard Streets, destroying the school, a longtime Economie beneficiary.

In 1900, after the Robert Charles incident, the insanity of race became normalcy. The threat of violence appeared ever present, and race itself was inalienable and real. A member of the Louisiana state legislature and a supporter of the separate car law told a *Daily Picayune* reporter, "The negroes are not subdued, and are as burly as ever. . . . In Alabama and in Georgia there are many cities where a Jim Crow law is working splendidly. I have been investigating the case in Montgomery and other cities, and they tell me they could not do without separate cars. . . . It is not only the desire to separate the whites and the blacks on the street cars for the comfort it will provide, but also for the moral effect."

The legislator told the reporter, seeking his approval, "The separation of the races is one benefit, but the demonstration of the superiority of the white man over the negro is a greater thing. Don't you know that?"

They had a song out on Robert Charles, like many other songs and like many other . . . bad men that always had some kind of a song and somebody originated it on 'em. But this song was squashed very easily. . . . Due to the fact that it was a trouble breeder and it never did get very far. I used to know the song, but I found it was best for me to forget it. And that I did, in order to go along with the world on the peaceful side.

—Musician Jelly Roll Morton,
interviewed by folklorist Alan Lomax, 1938

THE MINUTES OF THE ECONOMIE in 1896 said nothing about the Plessy decision and, in 1900, were silent about Robert Charles and the midsummer riots. The meetings, which once had been held every few days to at most two weeks apart, now took place on the first of every month.

Businessman Walter Cohen became president in 1896. A man who had quit elementary school to help support his family, Cohen had joined the society in 1883, three years after his brother Edward and a year earlier than his brother Bernard. Walter had substituted briefly for the secretary in 1886, writing the minutes exclusively in English for the first time. When he took notes—always in English—he less frequently referred to the men as "brothers," calling them simply "members."

He did not attend the August 1900 meeting, which was quite unusual for the president. The gathering took place only a few days after the Robert Charles riots, when mobs of white men and boys beat and shot any Black

Walter L. Cohen (front row, fourth from left) and the People's Life Insurance Company staff; *courtesy of Archives Photographs Collection, Xavier University of Louisiana Archives and Special Collections*

people they could lay hands on. The minutes make no reference to any social or political issues raised for the members' consideration.

The hall now hosted many organizations with English names, such as the Phillis Wheatley Club and the Colored Industrial Home and School. They shared the space with long-standing French-language societies like the Francs Amis and La Candeur.

During Cohen's tenure, the finance committee submitted its report in English, and the French-speaking secretary Anatole Steel transcribed it in a mix of two languages: "Rapporté par le comité de finances. That the committee recommend that all member pay their $1 monthly due wether [*sic*] they are sick or well and in case they are sick long enough to draw pension that the one dollar be taken out of their first week pension. . . . Reçu et adopté."

Cohen was still president of the society in 1909 when, at a special meeting, he "took the gavel and gave an explanation of the insurance company" he wanted to establish with an investment from the society, because it would be "a good thing for the race." The members agreed that Cohen, plus the Economie's treasurer, secretary, and finance committee chairman, would sit on the insurance company's board.

In other financial dealings that year, Cohen encouraged the society to buy a property adjacent to the hall, to allow the organization to expand, but he suggested that the purchase take place in the name of a member to avoid taxes. Also in 1909, the Economie needed to break an existing contract for rental of the hall on All Saints' Day, which was against the society's bylaws. To avoid a confrontation with the man who had rented the hall, Cohen used his contacts with the mayor to induce the government office issuing permits to cancel the event's liquor license.

Cohen and lawyer J. Madison Vance operated an eight-hundred-seat sports venue on Bienville Street called the Orleans Athletic Club, a tony location for spectator sports like boxing. Its middle-class members' combined fees made it the one of the wealthiest associations for Black sports fans in the nation. The Orleans Athletic Club rented the Economie's hall for parties during the Carnival season from 1909 to 1914, at first paying $100 for one evening, and later $585 for two evenings. The popularity of the events, swinging with music, brought Negro patrons from throughout the city. On the Orleans Athletic Club's advertisements, "the Economy Hall" appeared in big block letters on posters nailed up on trees around the neighborhood. "A Grand Fancy Dress, Masquerade and Disguise Ball" one 1910 poster read, "25 cents, Music by the Peoples Favorite Imperial Orchestra."

Significantly, in 1909, Booker T. Washington had corresponded with Methodist Episcopal minister Robert Elijah Jones of New Orleans about Cohen's character. Washington had received a request for help from Cohen to secure a federal government job. Jones wrote to Washington, "I know nothing against Mr. Cohen's life and personal habits, except that he drinks and gambles and plays baseball on Sunday. I do not think that he denies this or attempts to conceal it. I do not know that we can say Mr. Cohen is allied with the forces that make for righteousness and moral uplift. While I do not mean to infer that his leadership is negative in this regard, it certainly is not positive. . . . Now, my personal attitude toward Mr. Cohen is this: I greatly admire, along with others, his courage and force as a political leader. . . . He is shrewd and capable."

As a result of his loyalty to the Republican Party and with behind-the-scenes help from Washington, Cohen worked in several federal offices. In

Poster for St. Joseph's Night masquerade ball at Economy Hall; March 19, 1910; *The William Russell Jazz Collection at THNOC, acquisition made possible by the Clarisse Claiborne Grima Fund, 92-48-L.331.941*

Walter L. Cohen on the day of his inauguration as federal controller of customs in New Orleans; 1922; by Arthur P. Bedou; *courtesy of Arthur P. Bedou Photographs Collection, Xavier University of Louisiana Archives and Special Collections*

1922 President Warren G. Harding appointed him federal controller of customs in New Orleans, "one of the most lucrative Federal offices in the South," according to the *New York Times*. The story highlighted Cohen's race as well as his salary. The headline read, "Negro Gets $5,000 Office."

By comparison, the average annual salary for Negro teachers in the state was $467, and only 2,209 were employed to teach more than 130,000 students.

The upper class, composed of professional men, wishing to distinguish themselves, had formed the Société d'Economie, which confined its membership to those Creoles with tendencies toward exclusiveness.

—Rodolphe L. Desdunes, *Our People and Our History*, 1911

IN AN EFFORT TO set the record straight, as W. E. B. Du Bois had done with *The Philadelphia Negro* in 1899, Rodolphe Desdunes's book *Nos hommes et notre histoire* described the participation of the free men of color in the Battle of New Orleans and the Civil War, the migrations to Mexico and Haiti, and the role of men and women in his community throughout the nineteenth century. But he could not get the book published in the United States. In 1911 it appeared in Canada, in French. It was 1973 before Louisiana State University Press made the book available in English as *Our People and Our History*.

Desdunes criticized the Economie in his 1911 book for being elitist, even though he applauded individual members, like president Henry L. Rey and his brother Octave, Joseph Soudé, and several others—and even though he privately wrote at least four letters to the Economie in the mid-1880s, addressing the society in glowing terms.

HIS PUBLIC ASSESSMENT of the group, however, was deeply damaging, considering the breadth of its distribution. The Economie offered no written rebuttal to the French edition of Desdunes's 1911 book. And when the 1973 English edition appeared, most readers accepted his judgement, not knowing any better.

Another twentieth-century assessment came from René Grandjean, a native of France. In the 1920s his father-in-law gave him the journals of séances held by Henry L. Rey's Cercle Harmonique, which took place frequently in the Economie's hall. After reading the books, Grandjean wrote an enthusiastic poem about a generation of early Economistes, "The Flowering—from 1848 to the War," a reference to the date that the Couvent School for orphans opened. This event was a high point in the history of the free Black community because it made top-quality education available to poor Black children—a radical act then and maybe even now. Grandjean wrote:

> It was the duty of those who were still breathing,
> To transmit a precious treasure to the next generation,
> In order to not ignore the work of our fathers
> Which afforded us sweeter and more prosperous times.

> Those who rose in support of Madame Couvent,
> Of this Félicie, a heart so benevolent,
> Their names are always in memory;
> We guard them in our hearts, as well as in history. . . .

> Coming afterwards, Lacroix, and Lanusse, and Boguilles,
> Their service received the support of our families;
> These predecessors had honest companions
> History asks us to repeat their names:

Grandjean's reference to the Boguilles is undoubtedly to Ludger and Mary Ann. Among the other Economie members he names are Lacroix, Crocker, Lavigne, Snaer, Chessé, Populus, and Duhart. The poem continues:

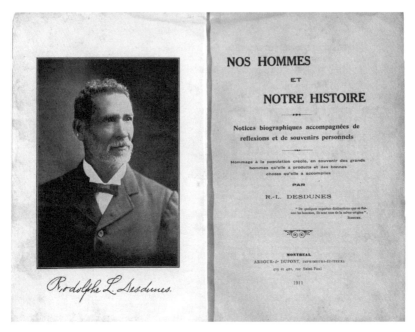

Frontispiece and title page of *Nos hommes et notre histoire*; 1911; by Rodolphe Lucien Desdunes; *THNOC, 69-201-LP.5*

The memory of people with such rare merits
Must remain forever in our records;
History will witness, for him who reads it again,
The name of benefactors who survived their deaths.

Their history, however, is hard to find. So are the life stories of millions of enslaved and free people of color who moved through the port of New Orleans and inhabited its homes.

The lapse is deliberate.

[Members will consist of] white persons of good moral char-
acter, who were in the service of the Southern Confederacy,
and of their white descendants of good moral character, and
also of white persons of good moral character who were not
in such service, but who have been citizens of Louisiana
for more than five years previous to their application for
membership.

—Act of Incorporation and By-Laws
of the Louisiana Historical Association, 1889

BY 1910 LOUISIANA LAW categorized African American people as either negro, griffe, mulatto, quadroon, or octoroon, based on appearances alone. A griffe, for example, was described in the state constitution as "a person too black to be a mulatto and too pale in color to be a negro." The law now said that all were colored—except octoroons. Traditionally defined as a person with one Black great-grandparent, Louisiana's legal code now stated that "an octoroon is not a 'person of the negro or black race' within Act No. 87 or 1908, Sec. 1." Moreover, because interracial marriage was illegal, if a negro was married to an octoroon, they were committing a felony.

Light-skinned men and women with darker spouses now had to hide, move, or face possible prosecution. People who might have been considered octoroons by appearance and who held no prejudices remained silent so as not to bring attention to themselves. Many of them, whose ancestors were members of early mixed families, lived in Tremé and the Seventh Ward. Some descendants moved away, to the West and North, for safety. Others left for better economic opportunities.

The wealth of the Economie members had declined with segregation. The charge per member to support the annual banquet now ranged between 50 cents and "25 *sous* for a souper." The 1913 banquet consisted of a barrel of beer, punch, and sandwiches. Members had very little money for private tutors or education abroad.

The handwriting of the Economie secretaries showed less flourish and precision. No public high school existed in the city for its more than ninety thousand Negroes until 1917. McDonogh 35, named for John McDonogh, a plantation owner who willed money and land to the city for education, was the only public high school for Blacks in New Orleans until 1942, when the Negro population reached almost 150,000.

English had crept into the Economie minutes since the Civil War, with occasional words like "cherman" in 1864 and "brass band" in 1875. One report from the ameliorations committee included a fusion of French and self-taught English expressions in a discussion of repairs that were needed for the hall, such as "the stair-way," "valley gutter," and "dancing room." The minutes remained in French throughout the nineteenth century, however, with only these occasional departures. In a 1912 vote, the members resolved to keep the journals in French. Two years later, though, the records were in English only. It was not good English.

THE ELDERS OF the community were dead or silent because of their devastating losses and the threats of violence at the turn of the century. In addition, a generation of people who had matured after Reconstruction experienced discrimination laws—barring Blacks from jobs and keeping them out of libraries and archives in New Orleans—as common practice. With education and access, they might have discovered the documents and books showing that for five decades before the Civil War, almost half of New Orleans Negroes had not been enslaved. And they might have read that the former free people of color worked hard alongside emancipated people and whites to obtain voting rights and equality for all men, until the end of Reconstruction ushered in a reign of terror. If there had been high school, or simply more access to documents, Blacks growing up in the late nineteenth and early twentieth century might have known that their ancestors had marched in the streets and fought in the courts until they were murdered, outnumbered, and disenfranchised.

Instead, assertions that people of color from New Orleans—called Negroes, coloreds, and, occasionally, Blacks—had an illustrious past could not be proven in any mainstream books or newspapers, all written to reflect white supremacy and a society classed by color, with the darkest person on the lowest rung.

In 1917 the *Times-Picayune* noted the death of 108-year-old Angele Soude, with no accent on her last name. She was the granddaughter of a Congolese royal family, the paper said. The Economistes once knew her as the widow of Joseph Soudé—the Radical Republican leader who collected donations for Haitian migration and New Orleans's poor, and served in the Reconstruction government and in the Freedmen's Bureau.

The *Times-Picayune* mentioned the death of Angele's husband but not his name. His widow made news because she was "one of the finest types of 'quality' mammies of the ante-bellum era," the paper said. It complimented her for working in white households, speaking French, and possessing a wardrobe of "marvelous prints" that she wore "in the . . . style of dress always conserved by the head handkerchief mammy of old." The Black newspapers would never have called her a "mammy." She was likely still stylish among "nos jeunes beautés néo-orléanaises"—our young New Orleanian beauties—who attended a grand ball at Economie Hall, with an orchestra and Cuban conductor, that Joseph Soudé gave in 1865 to fund "patriotic and liberal work," as described in the *New Orleans Tribune*.

"I can't help it if I am pretty," the *Times-Picayune* quoted her saying in response to "the exclamations of Northern folk." The obituary concluded, "Thus has passed the stateliest and comeliest of that dying type, the Louisiana mammy." In 1917 white supremacy even pervaded the realm of compliments. They had to be qualified by a racial status.

Many readers did not even notice any discrepancy between the reality of Black life and its image as viewed through a racist lens. The limitations on education—of whites as well—had deep roots.

The seeds of a southern propaganda movement had been sown early. Before the Civil War, around the same time that Samuel Cartwright advocated whipping the enslaved to cure the "disease" of running away, one of his admirers, the Reverend C. K. Marshall, wrote Cartwright a letter suggesting that enslavers should publish their own textbooks to refute the messages of abolitionists. Marshall called it "the scheme of providing Southern books by Southern authors printed and published by Southern schools and colleges."

The letter explained:

> At present all the slave states are flooded with Yankees' books and teachers. . . . Just look at the humiliating position in which we place ourselves. We whine at the abolitionists at putting Uncle Tom's Cabin into their Sunday schools and coolly place Wayland's Moral Science with its rank hostility to Slavery into our own institutions male and female. So we build up his fortunes and those of the fanatical and mercenary publishers and printers while men of great ability lay away their Manuscripts and cannot afford to put a work of real merit into the pack. Now We Must have Southern Authors and studies. We have them and we must raise up Southern Teachers. We must print and publish our own books and maintain the ancient renown and dignity of the South whose heads and hearts and books and pens have nurtured the world. . . . Young abolition teachers . . . mould the minds of our children and fill their tender minds with impressions, the maturity of which would lead them not to honour—but to despise their father and their mother—and to look upon them as savages—holding human beings in Slavery.

Long after the Civil War but before the Economie journals ever saw the light of day, with their record of events, historians of the late nineteenth and early twentieth centuries—Charles Gayarré, Grace King, Alcée Fortier, and many others—chose to largely ignore the Black people who made up more than one-quarter of the population in their midst, except for the occasional stereotypes. In his Louisiana encyclopedia, Fortier used the words of an unnamed Georgia writer to prove the "peaceful" character of the Negro and the relations between enslavers and the enslaved. He claimed that whites and enslaved people exhibited "personal attachment and mutual confidence." Fortier added, "The same was true of the situation in Louisiana."

The desire to justify their racial hierarchy led these writers to insist that Creoles of color could not properly be called "Creole," denying their common history. To support their conclusions, they quoted one another. Fortier's encyclopedia entry on the term borrowed heavily from an 1885 lecture Gayarré gave on "The Creoles of History and the Creoles of Romance." Gayarré claimed the word *criollo*

> was first invented by the Spaniards to distinguish their children, natives of their conquered colonial possessions, from the original natives whom they found in those newly discovered regions of the earth. *Criollo* was derived from the verb *criar* (create), and used only to designate the Spanish-created natives, who were not to be confounded with the aborigines—with beings of an unknown origin—with the mahogany-tinted small fry of God's creation. Therefore to be a *criollo* was to possess a sort of title of honor—a title which could only be the birthright of the superior white race. This word, by an easy transition becoming *creole*, from the verb *créer*, was adopted by the French for the same purpose—that is, to mean or signify a white human being created in their colonies of Africa and America—a native of European extraction, whose origin was known and whose superior Caucasian blood was never to be assimilated to the baser liquid that ran in the veins of the Indian and African native. This explains why one of that privileged class is proud to this day of calling himself a Creole, and clings to that appellation.

Paraphrasing Gayarré's explanation, Fortier asserted in his own work that *creole*, the French version of the term, "was extended to cover animals and plants, hence such expressions as creole horses, creole chickens, creole figs, etc. Negroes born in tropical countries are also sometimes called creoles, but . . . this is an erroneous use of the term, as the negro's ancestors were not European." He added, "it is neither proper nor just to apply the term creole to any member of the colored race, and the use of the word in that sense is very properly resented by the French and Spanish descendants of Louisiana."

The Louisiana Historical Association, founded in 1889, similarly confined its membership to former white Confederates, their white descendants, and any white who had lived in the state for more than five years. The South came to tell its history in a segregated manner, as if people of different skin colors and ethnicities had never lived side by side, argued complex ideas with one another, fought in the same wars, eaten at the same table, and loved in the same bed.

The history of the Black South, and, in particular, the Economie and the men of its community, remained mostly in the stories they shared orally among themselves. Outsiders hardly believed that educated, cultured, and wealthy men of African descent existed who did not hate their skin colors and those of their brothers.

The stereotypes persisted, even though their legacies were visible throughout the late nineteenth and twentieth centuries. The Economistes and other benevolent associations had joined and supported institutions for Blacks of every hue such as the Sisters of the Holy Family, the Thomy Lafon Boys' and Old Folks' homes, Straight University, Flint-Goodridge Hospital, Southern University, and Corpus Christi Church, as well as organizations like the Ear, Eye, Nose, and Throat Hospital, which promised to accept people of all races.

There was also Economy Hall.

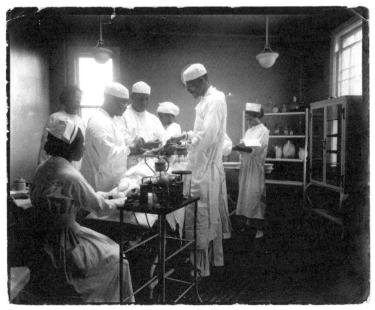

UPPER: Sisters of the Holy Family; by Arthur P. Bedou; *courtesy of Arthur P. Bedou Photographs Collection, Xavier University of Louisiana Archives and Special Collections* LOWER: Dr. Rivers Frederick performing surgery at Flint-Goodridge Hospital; *courtesy of Archives Photographs Collection, Xavier University of Louisiana Archives and Special Collections*

The Carnegie Hall of Jazz

1919

⟨ornament⟩

THE ECONOMIE EVOLVED FROM an elite to an inclusive society, and along the way nurtured a new, radical music called jazz. It took hold in the society's celebrations and convocations. Members and entertainers mingled and were often related. The Eagle Brass Band had been the house band of the society's functions since 1880. In addition, Economie member William J. Nickerson taught any number of musicians, including some of the earliest brass players from the plantations, to read compositions and score them. Myrtil Piron, the society president at the end of the nineteenth century, was from a family of musicians, and his nephew Armand became an orchestra leader whose song "I Wish I Could Shimmy Like My Sister Kate" took off across the nation. The Economie's hall was an incubator for musical innovation and the *gardienne* of its members' joy. They celebrated defiantly in spite of their segregated circumstances.

William J. Nickerson; from *Beacon Lights of the Race*; 1911;
THNOC, 2017.0362

The night before a dance, the band typically stood and played on the porch of the hall to advertise the program with popular tunes such as the comic blues number "Go Along, Mule," or the jaunty "Chicken Reel," which people began to call "Turkey in the Straw." Sometimes the musicians would play other songs suited to the mazurka, polka, or waltz to encourage listeners to come to the party. The socialites who came—married couples and young women with escorts—left by 11:30, and the "sporting class of people" stayed until 4 a.m., or daybreak.

The Economie employed hundreds of community members, relatives, and friends as entertainers. The society rented the hall for parties, recitals, and performances. The Economie charged little or nothing if the event was for a charitable cause. If not, the society received a fee or a percentage of profits.

A generation of musicians now descended from the former free people of color as the doors closed on education and financial opportunities. The first volunteer for the test case of the 1890 Separate Car Act by the Comité des Citoyens, Daniel Desdunes, was a member of the Creole Onward Brass Band. Charles Dupart was a musician who lived at the same corner of Great Men and History in 1891 where his namesake held the first Economie meeting. Posters for balls in 1909 and 1910 name the Peerless and Imperial Orchestras, which included trombone player and Economiste George Filhe and drummer John Vigne, occasionally known as Jean. He was the brother of Economiste Léon Vignes, with the "s" added to the family name when it was written in French, as in the Economie minutes. When Léon died, Walter Cohen was one of his pallbearers.

President Cohen remained at the helm of the Economie for thirty-four years, from 1896 to 1930, the year Ludger Boguille's grandson Raoul Boguille was elected assistant secretary. Raoul was eight months old in 1892, when the family lost two pieces of land because the property taxes of $16.45 were overdue. Perhaps money was tight. Or maybe no one read the fine print in the English-language newspaper. It identified the properties as an area on Union Street bounded by Virtue Street. This was François Boguille's land, kept in the family through Ludger's circuitous efforts. Raoul Boguille was identified as Black in 1900, as white when the census taker came around in 1920, and as Negro in 1930.

For over thirty years, Cohen supported Negro causes that kept the community afloat and fostered the society's ever-expanding reputation as the proprietor of a dance hall. At least one hundred musicians mention Economy Hall in oral histories recorded as late as the 1970s and held in the Hogan Jazz Archive of Tulane University.

In 1958 bassist George "Pops" Foster told jazz historian William Russell, "Economy Hall was high class." Foster was born in 1892 and played in New Orleans for many years. He described the sophistication of the early audiences, saying, "Whatever dance the people dance, you had to have the music to play that dance. . . . You got to play them waltzes. . . . You better play the waltz in the right tempo." Otherwise, the dancers would notice the error and chide the band.

Clarinetist George Lewis—perhaps a descendant of Alcide Lewis, who had volunteered for the Native Guards in the Civil War—recalled that at the Economie's hall, the jazz bands played a special song when the club's members made a regal entrance for their anniversary celebration, marching in two columns. The song was "The Gettysburg March," though the historians who quote Lewis did not name the reason the band played this particular march, other than tradition.

In interview transcripts, musicians often use the words *buffet* and *bonkay* (sometimes spelled *banquay*) to refer to the members' annual dinner. The latter is the French pronunciation of *banquet,* the supper party of the societies, and particularly the grand annual dinner of the Economie from 1836 to the end of its existence, sometime in the 1950s.

Economy Hall's jazz history evolved as legend and myth. Most of the people who wrote about the hall never entered the building and probably knew none of the Economie members. After the Plessy verdict and until the civil rights era—precisely the time when jazz bands drew crowds to the hall—whites could not legally enter any Black establishment. So when the Economie's hall was called "Cheapskate Hall" in the 1967 book *New Orleans Jazz: A Family Album,* by Al Rose and Edmond Souchon, it is unclear whether the authors knew the term was ironic or whether their sources just weren't aware of the history of the Economie's wealth.

A few exceptions allowed whites entry into Black halls during segregation. In 1919 members of the Streckfus family, owners of a Mississippi riverboat company, obtained written permission to attend a dance at the Economie's hall to scout for musicians who might play for excursions. They came on a Monday night. Longshoremen and truck drivers did not work on Mondays, so it was a good night for parties. Bandleader Kid Ory rented out the Economie's hall every Monday. His dance band improvised new rhythms and sounds into familiar written arrangements. The performers infused marches and popular compositions with the syncopation of ragtime, the bent tones and vibrato of blues, and the enthusiasm of spirituals, as European musical traditions gave way to the vernacular of African descendants.

The band played the songs "ragged," as if the musicians were happy drunks marching the street. The horns could also wail as if crying in a funeral procession. Sometimes, at the chorus, the performers hit the down-beat straight, as if they were stepping like soldiers. Other times they made the rhythm swing, reminiscent of beautiful young women waltzing across the Economie's smooth wooden floor.

On this particular Monday night, Ory sat a new trumpet player, Louis Armstrong, on the bandstand with a borrowed cornet to fill in for a regular member, Joe Oliver. The Streckfus family noticed. Armstrong had a solid sound and was soon hired for a regular gig on upriver excursions. When he played on the riverboat, it was the first time he had performed for white audiences. It was also the first time he had left New Orleans.

Around 1919, the noun *party* began to appear in common usage as a verb, perhaps taking its cue from the parties in Economy Hall, as the upbeat rhythms of the modern New Orleans sound entered the mainstream.

People heard the music of New Orleans as it traveled upriver, not only with Armstrong but with so many others, to Memphis, St. Louis, and Chicago. It spread to New York and Los Angeles. The music was written about in books and picked up as a style, and it named the next decade—the Jazz Age.

Few people knew that jazz music had incubated in one of the most important venues for equality in the South, the Economie's hall. They only recognized the democracy of jazz music, a style in which each performer played a different line in conversation with the others. It was as if each instrument told its own story, a personal story, and its individuality made the music better.

The audience heard the rough and spontaneous harmony without understanding that the songs came from the history of slavery and the struggle for suffrage, the irrationality of race prejudice, and the violence of its application. In jazz, someone was always pacing a little off beat or dancing around a note or sliding deliberately in and out of a musical line. Listeners didn't know the path—because sometimes a new route had to be found individually in music and in life. In jazz, musicianship was just part of the sound. A player with formal compositional training didn't necessarily have an advantage over another who had strong improvisational leanings. It seemed that anyone could play jazz, everyone said. The music required training the ear to listen, the hands to avoid the easy, familiar notes. The heart of a jazz musician had to be open to the feelings of others. People sometimes wondered how this music came into being. They knew only that the sound was always alive.

IN 1972 SAXOPHONIST Harold Dejan sat down for an interview with Roger Mitchell, a treasurer during the 1930s for the San Jacinto, another club that owned a dance hall. By the time they recorded their memories, the Economie had been defunct for decades, and the hall had been demolished seven years earlier. The men did not remember anything specific about the organization that had owned Economy Hall, describing it only as "some benevolent to-do." But they extolled the parties. Mitchell said, "I'm telling you, them was some wonderful days."

EPILOGUE

The People Who Stayed

IN 1919, THE YEAR Louis Armstrong left New Orleans, my father
was born. He grew up in Tremé, not far from the Economie's hall, and
attended the only public high school for Blacks in the city. Then he went
to Xavier University of Louisiana, the only Catholic institution of higher
learning for Black people in the United States. His teachers and classmates
were descendants of the city's earliest people of color. He graduated with
a degree in physics in 1941 but could not get a job.

My father began to deliver groceries on a bicycle. For extra cash, he
played saxophone in the many nightclubs of the city. Sometimes he filled
in for Frank Crump, a man my great-aunt helped raise. One night my
father substituted for Frank at a gig with Billie and De De Pierce, a couple
now in the jazz history books. My dad tried to read the sheet music on the
bandstand, but the musicians were playing a different song. The written
composition, De De told him, was only there "for the people." Audience

Piron Band; between 1923 and 1924; *The William Russell Jazz Collection at THNOC, acquisition made possible by the Clarisse Claiborne Grima Fund, 92-48-L.331.1835*

members felt that the music was somehow more legitimate if they could see it on paper. But the musicians knew the score, actually and metaphorically.

I asked my father about the Economie's hall—Economy Hall—which was near his childhood home in the Tremé neighborhood. He didn't remember the interior, only the location, so I asked family friends.

Virgie Demas Robichaux was the seventy-nine-year-old wife of John Robichaux, an eighty-three-year-old drummer, when I spoke to her in 1999. She was the aunt of my grammar school friend, so I respectfully called her "Aunt Virgie." She started going to the Economy Hall when she was about eighteen years old. This was before her marriage in 1939 to John. She described the plain wood building with large interior columns. There was also a bar inside. The room was "decorated with fancy paper" when she attended the carnival balls. She heard bands led by music innovators Harold Dejan, Sidney Desvigne, and Herbert Leary, who employed her future husband. The music she remembered was "sentimental," Mardi Gras music, or second line. The last category had a heavy polyrhythmic beat, a syncopated backbone of sound that dancers could mirror in their shoulders, spines, hips, and knees. Aunt Virgie distinguished the second line music from other songs only by the attitude of the musicians. The same popular compositions could be performed as written or improvised into second line music. "It depends on how you play it," she said.

Over the evening, partygoers danced "the two-step, the one-step waltz, and did the second line at the end of the party," Aunt Virgie told me. She and John lived until 2005. They could have lived longer. They drowned at home in the floodwaters of Hurricane Katrina when the levees failed.

Other elders in my community were Mildred Meilleur Boissiere and Adrienne Woods Blache. Both were daughters of Economistes and married into Economy families. The great-grandfather of Adrienne's husband was Ernest Blache, who joined the society in 1857. Adrienne's father, Numa Woods, was one of the society's last members in 1948. The final document that I have from the Economie is a printed booklet containing its constitution from that year. The society may have lasted until the early 1950s, when it emptied the hall.

In 2003, when I interviewed Mrs. Blache, she was eighty-four years old. She remembered going to many dances where the important bandleader and jazz violinist Armand J. Piron played. He "had the sweetest sound this side of heaven," she recalled. He played "a medley of waltzes, about three or four at a time." At the end of the night he played "Home Sweet Home." The lyrics say, "be it ever so humble, there's no place like home." It was a suggestion for everyone to leave the hall.

Mrs. Blache also recalled listening to Piron on a Mississippi River dock. The SS *President*, a steamboat, offered nightly parties where Blacks were not allowed. Blache's sister-in-law's brother was Elliot Taylor, who sometimes played with the Piron band. One night, Blache's brother took her, her mother, and Elliot's mother to stand as close as possible to the vessel so that they could hear the music.

In 2007 Mrs. Blache's cousin Ernestine Josephine Landry was 103. She told me, "Oh. Yeah! I remember Economy Hall." Her half-sister Anne Regina Joseph, ninety-three, demurred, "That's not one of the halls that we wanted to—that they wanted us to visit."

Ernestine went to waltz and do the Charleston at the hall in spite of the warnings: "It was nice. It was nice, real regular dancing and everything."

Her sister, however, would not elaborate on the reason that the Economy Hall, while nice, was off limits. My guess is that during the years Ernestine went to the hall, Anne was too young and the freedom of the jazz dances was a little too dangerous.

The music of the 1920s was a reflection of the streets, not the music of conservatories, musician and historian Michael White told me. Opportunities were slim for education, and work declined in the agricultural South and the industries it fed. But big money could be made by expressive musicians playing popular music in urban bands. The shift in the culture was palpable, exciting, and unpredictable.

The memories of these elders carried a similar refrain. They improvised their lives while their finances, musical culture, and rules of social relations swung like a pendulum throughout the decades. My interviewees shared a singular desire to contribute their memories to my understanding of history. They wanted me to carry their stories to the next generations. Their kindness and candor increased my commitment to the long quest through government records and handwritten papers.

I read in the Economie's journals that on November 8, 1928, with Walter Cohen's encouragement, the members tried to sell one of the Economie's real estate holdings to pay its bills. A rental property at 1428 Ursulines was next door to the Economie's hall and abutted a property where the New Orleans School Board had recently finished building a school for Black children. The structure was named for Joseph A. Craig, a post-Reconstruction school board appointee. His son Joseph B. Craig was an Economie member. Cohen offered the school board an asking price of $20,000 for 1428 Ursulines, then reduced the price to $16,000. The school board declined and, in 1947, a man named Henry Ellis began paying the property taxes and eventually acquired the building.

On December 28, 1930, Walter Cohen died. Joseph Craig spoke about him at the funeral. The minutes note Cohen's passing with the type of English that was creeping into the journals: "Member Jos. Craig eulogize the memory of our late deceased President Walter L. Cohen and a silence prayer for one minute was held by the Organization."

By 1932 the Economie was in severe financial straits. The minutes note with a diction that was now overformal and awkward, "Whereas

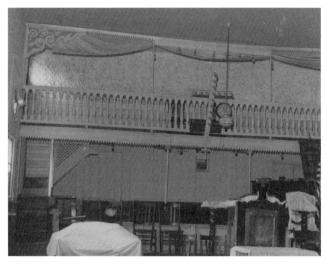

Interior of Economy Hall as St. Mark Missionary Baptist Church;
ca. 1959; *The William Russell Jazz Collection at THNOC, acquisition
made possible by the Clarisse Claiborne Grima Fund, 92-48-L.331.1266*

on account of the depression and hard times, it has become necessary for
the association to curtail some of its expenses and allowance, which are far
exceeding its revenues and if continued will in a very short while deplete its
surplus . . . it is deem proper that the amount allowed to invalid members be
dispensed with and the same be discontinued." At this point, compensation
ended for sick members who could not work, and the society confined their
paid doctors' visits to a maximum of two. Only nineteen members were
present at the July 1, 1932, meeting. The secretary had stopped counting
absences.

The membership dwindled even while the Economie's hall continued
to be the center of its community. The society donated funds to Corpus
Christi Church in 1928 and 1929. Economistes received an invitation
in 1930 to view the laying of a cornerstone, likely for an expansion to
the Corpus Christi School, which I later attended. In 1932 a fundraising
committee from Corpus Christi gave a party at the hall. The same year,
the Sisters of the Holy Family used the hall to raise funds for the Thomy
Lafon Home, where I visited elderly friends.

The following year, the members rented the hall to a Spiritualist
church—a Black religious congregation that drew on Catholic and

Christian rituals and on a belief in communication with the dead. The minutes say about the Economie president—in an unlettered voice that began to characterize the journals' writing—"that a gentleman had call upon him and ask to rent the hall for Spiritual meetings."

Other organizations took the hall for conventions—of morticians and of laundry workers. Mardi Gras and Lundi Gras parties continued, even though the annual Economistes' banquet in 1933 consisted only of sandwiches and soft drinks.

Newspapers provided me with the continuing political history of the Economistes and their building. In 1934 the International Labor Defense organization of Louisiana, an offshoot of the Communist Party, held a meeting to protest the execution of the Scottsboro Boys, young men who were convicted by a biased jury of raping two white women in Scottsboro, Alabama. In 1939 the Workers Alliance of America, created by the Socialist Party of America, met at the Economie's hall to discuss reductions in pay for the employees of the Works Progress Administration and others on low wages. An FBI informant later claimed to have attended meetings of the Communist Party in the Economie's hall and the halls of other benevolent organizations during the 1940s.

In 1945 the Economie sold its hall at 1422 Ursulines Street to Arthur James Alexander, the pastor of the St. Mark Missionary Baptist Church. The site had a special significance to Reverend Alexander. He had played cornet with the Deer Range Plantation band under James Humphrey, the music teacher whose work with instrumentalists on the Magnolia Plantation helped usher in jazz. The parishioners could see where jazz greats Buddy Petit, Kid Rena, and George Lewis had scratched their names into the plaster wall near the bandstand. The jazz players had recognized the importance of Economy Hall to music history. So did the community. St. Mark's owned the structure in the mid-1960s, but a century after the building's construction, local residents still called the place Economy Hall.

In 1964 tornadoes spawned by a hurricane called Hilda tore off the structure's face. And in 1965, Hurricane Betsy delivered the death blow. Jazz historian William Russell wrote about picking through the rubble of Economy Hall with the Reverend Alexander. They both took memorabilia

Economy Hall in ruins after Hurricane Betsy; October 1965; *The William Russell Jazz Collection at THNOC, acquisition made possible by the Clarisse Claiborne Grima Fund, 92-48-L.331.1268*

from the debris. Russell retained a baluster from the mahogany bannister. The hall was torn down eventually, and the property became the play yard of the Craig School.

The demolition of Economy Hall in 1965 went undocumented except by one source, Russell, the jazz fan who took photographs and kept them in his private collection until the end of the twentieth century. I found his images in a folder at the Hogan Jazz Archive that contained notes on the oral histories of jazz musicians who played at the hall.

In the same folder were two photocopied newspaper pictures of a building suspected to be Economy Hall, as a handwritten note in the margin indicated. The images appeared in the *Louisiana Weekly*, the local Black newspaper, which kept track of all the important developments in the Negro community.

The cutlines under the photos actually identified the structure as the neighboring Zion Hill Baptist Church. One showed the building's interior exposed like the open side of a three-story dollhouse, with square rooms and high ceilings. The other showed a man preparing to haul away

Odd Fellows parade outside
Economy Hall; October 13,
1957; *The William Russell
Jazz Collection at THNOC,
acquisition made possible by
the Clarisse Claiborne Grima
Fund, 92-48-L.158*

Reverend Alexander and
William Russell amid the
ruins of Economy Hall after
Hurricane Betsy; October
1965; *The William Russell
Jazz Collection at THNOC,
acquisition made possible by
the Clarisse Claiborne Grima
Fund, 92-48-L.331.1264*

a nearby automobile wrecked by falling debris. When I saw that picture, I got chills. He was Felton Bailey, who owned an auto body shop where my father—and I, as his shadow—spent many free hours.

I knew Mr. Bailey well. He and my father liked to make the rounds of the musical hangouts, to drink and talk. Bailey employed Lee Dorsey, an R&B singer and hit maker who sometimes changed from his coveralls to his showman's suits near the garage. Bailey was an in-law of a member of one of the last families in the Economie, the 1948 vice president, Lambert Boissiere. His son Lambert Jr. had married Bailey's daughter and became a state senator. I had met Lambert Jr. when I was a teenager working in grassroots political campaigns of the civil rights movement to get Black people elected.

The men of the Economie seemed to surround me: Mr. Wilderson gave the books to my father, and Mr. Bailey showed up when I first sought the hall in the jazz archives. I felt that a spirit had called me to this work, moving through my community and my family before residing in the many journals stacked in my parents' home.

But this spirit was not exclusive to my family. It was the soul of New Orleans, and it had a voice—that of bricklayers who joked in musical cadences while they walled a house, elders who gave advice while they stirred the pots, and women who sang old tunes while they hung the wash. Our local musicians captured and carried our feelings. The neighborhood gossips wrapped snippets of histories within their tales. In my childhood, people used the word *conte* as a noun derived from the French verb *raconter*—as in "I have some good *conte* to tell you." It was a story meant to be circulated.

I heard the secrets of my city as I half-slept on the back seat of my father's car while he and Mr. Bailey leaned against the fender and talked, and as I cleaned shrimp and cut okra in the kitchen while the women in the family spoke and cooked. I still remember sitting on my mother's lap while she sang Creole songs to me and told me to remember them. I trusted that this was important, these moments with no written equivalents. This was history lived and felt.

I SOUGHT TO CALL out this spirit from the Economie journals. My charge was to integrate lives with events and documents with ghosts.

On the inside cover of the first journal, fifteen men of African descent embellished their signatures with filigree scripts. Their steady hands crafted large initials with distinctive swirls, intended to identify the authors, despite universal punishments across the South for enslaved Blacks who wrote and for free Blacks who thought too much of themselves. But in January 1836, the members committed to a "Déclaration." It expressed their desire to create a powerful organization, so the world would know about them—their successes, failures, and most of all, their realities.

I looked carefully at the signatures. I tried to decipher the men's feelings—their sensations when they flourished the quill, the pressure they used to place the tip of the pen against the coarse paper stock. There was meaning in these inscriptions, rivulets of dark ink indented into the soft rag paper flowing from worlds of experience.

These men took pride in their given names and claimed both Africa and Europe as their ancestral homes. They sought to live out their own destinies and aid their brothers to do the same.

Their journals communicated power, ambition, loyalty, and optimism. And yet, their stories had advanced and receded from American society and international attention with the winds of commerce and social awareness.

I was privileged to write this book as an accounting of their work, the assembled whole that needed to be told in their voices. It contains their legacies and complicated truths. The Economistes' history is now ours.

ACKNOWLEDGMENTS

I COULD NOT uncover centuries of history without the aid of many academics, writers, family members, and friends. I thank all of you for encouragement, insight, and patience. I have great respect for the historians and griots who preceded me. I am grateful for your devotion to the word.

The interdisciplinary nature of this book compelled me to reach out to experts in many areas, including history, music, economics, education, and New Orleans life. I am particularly indebted to those scholars and culture carriers who contributed to the content of this text. They include Caryn Cossé Bell, Shirley Thompson, Lester Sullivan, Roselyn Gregor, Connor Hartnett, Don Marquis, Michael White, Brian Mitchell, Mildred Boissiere, Rhonda Blache, Adrienne Blache, Ernestine Josephine Landry Jones, Anne Regina Joseph Bradshaw, Keith Medley, Nick Douglas, Barbara Trevigne, Mark Roudané, Virgie Robichaux, Debra Chapman, Rev. Phillip L. Flott, Devin Rafferty, Karl Alorbi, Jonathan Pritchett, James Etienne Viator, Richard Campanella, Walter C. Stern, Mishio Yamanaka, and Mark DeStephano, S.S.J. In addition is a long list of authors and publications, which are listed in my bibliography.

I cherish those who read the *Economy Hall* manuscript in early drafts and gave feedback, including Marie Brown, Lisa Bergson, Susan Kuklin, Elizabeth Levy, Carol Banks, Rhona Whitty, Marlene Veloso, Diane Simmons, Pamela Tabb, and Elizabeth Moore Rhodes. Thank you also to Gwendolyn Midlo Hall, Mary Frances Berry, Brenda Billips Square, Ellis Marsalis, Lolis Eric Elie, Nancy Milford, and Mitchell Zuckoff for commenting on the book's qualities and significance.

My appreciation also extends to the curators and staff at the following institutions, who helped me find documents and led me to further research, including the Mariners' Museum in Newport News, Virginia; the Historical Society of Pennsylvania; the New Orleans Public Library, especially the Louisiana Division and the Nora Navra branch; the New York Public Library, in particular the Schomburg Center for Research in Black Culture and the Library for the Performing Arts; Louisiana State Museum Library; the Law Library of Louisiana; the Bibliothèque nationale de France; Daisy DeCoster and the entire staff at the O'Toole Library at Saint Peter's University; Bruce Boyd Raeburn and Charles Chamberlain at the Hogan Jazz Archive, Tulane University, and the staff at the Amistad Research Center, also at Tulane, where I began my research many years ago; Florence M. Jumonville and Connie Phelps at the Louisiana and Special Collections division of the Earl K. Long Library at the University of New Orleans; Sally Kittredge Evans and Siva Blake at the New Orleans Notarial Archives Research Center; Robert Skinner at the Xavier University of Louisiana Library; Alexandre Vialou at the Alliance Française; and Alfred E. Lemmon and Rebecca Smith at the Williams Research Center of The Historic New Orleans Collection.

The following institutions and their representatives also have my deep appreciation. Two organizations—the John Anson Kittredge Fund and the Louisiana Endowment for the Humanities—provided vital funding to support my research. I am also grateful to Eugenia M. Palmegiano, John Walsh, Elizabeth Nelson, David Surrey, Eugene J. Cornacchia, Marylou Yam, Lauren Fleites, Kimberly Jaramillo, Natalie Kita, the office of Faculty Research and members of the Departments of English and of Communication at Saint Peter's University; Richard Petrow, Roscoe C. Brown, Manthia Diawara, and the staff of the Institute of African American Affairs and the Faculty Resource Network at New York University; and Donna Brodie at The Writers Room. Thank you to the board and members of the Louisiana Creole Research Association, especially Ingrid Stanley and Pat Schexnayder, and CreoleGen's Lolita Villavasso Cherrie and Jari Honora. For opportunities and encouragement: Andrew Solomon and Suzanne Nossel at PEN America; Thomas and Judith Bonner, Mary Gehman, Ralph Adamo,

Antonio Aiello, Gaiutra Bahadur, Kavery Kaul, Susan Larson, Vera Warren Williams, Jennifer Turner, Beverly McKenna, and Deni Béchard. Thank you to Scott Manning and Abigail Welhouse for publicity.

This book would not have been possible without Cathe Mizell-Nelson, who came to my short story reading at Xavier University of Louisiana, heard my aside about Economy Hall, and invited me to submit the manuscript. Her meticulous and patient editing for THNOC greatly increased the historical value of this book, and I am happy to know her.

Also at THNOC, Director of Publications Jessica Dorman offered me immense encouragement during the creation of the book. Her confidence in my research, documentation, and thesis paved the road to *Economy Hall*'s release. Editors Mary Garsaud and Margit Longbrake dedicated countless hours to research, with vital support from Marie B. Morris, Dorothy Ball, Heather Green, and Roxanne Guidry. Melissa Carrier, Tere Kirkland, and Keely Merritt took great care to photograph the Economie record books. Teresa Devlin, Rachel Gaudry, Eli Haddow, Kendric Perkins, Jenny Schwartzberg, and Dave Walker in marketing and education endeavored to bring this book to the widest possible audience. President and CEO Daniel Hammer and his predecessor, Priscilla Lawrence, provided steady support for the project. I could not have asked for a better team.

My husband James has my love and my thanks for listening to the story of Economy Hall for the last two decades, modeling artistic focus and discipline, and incorporating my accumulation of books, files, and technology into our lifestyle. Thank you for my writing porch. I am grateful to my daughters Celeste and Sophia, who received my divided attention many evenings and accompanied me to the libraries for recreation. You have been my inspiration for many books. I want you to know the history of your ancestors.

Finally, my mother, father, aunts, and uncles are the spirits around me. In addition to their comforting presence, they left an intellectual legacy—my father's thesis and files, the poems and plays of my mother and aunts, the echoes of my uncle's multiple languages at a time when the mainstream marked them as inferiors due to their race. I thank them for teaching me to believe nothing on face value.

NOTES

Abbreviations

ESM   Economy Society Minutes
NONA   New Orleans Notarial Archives
NOPL   New Orleans Public Library
THNOC The Historic New Orleans Collection

All quotations from primary sources have been faithfully transcribed, though some obvious errors of spelling and punctuation were silently corrected for clarity. All translations from the original French are by the author, unless otherwise noted.

INTRODUCTION

Vous nous voyez: The quotation reads, in full, "'You who see us, write—the friends are always there!' the ghost of Victor Lacroix and the others." These words appear in the notes from an 1871 séance recorded by Economie member Henry Louis Rey and other Spiritualist mediums who were active in New Orleans before and after the Civil War. Spiritualist register 85-32, February 9, 1871, 118, René Grandjean Collection, Earl K. Long Library, University of New Orleans (hereafter Grandjean Collection). Lacroix, a former soldier in the Union Army, was killed in the 1866 Mechanics' Institute massacre.

one of the biggest and most important urban centers: The city's population stood at 17,242 in the 1810 census, with 10,911 (63.3 percent) counted as "Black." Of these, 5,961 were enslaved, while 4,950 were free. Gibson and Jung, "Historical Census Statistics," table 19.

Approximately one-seventh of the nation's Black population was free at the time of emancipation (Woodson, *Free Negro Owners*, v). In New Orleans, this percentage was significantly higher through the first six decades of the nineteenth century. Census data shows that free people of color accounted for 45 percent of the city's Black population in 1810, 46 percent in 1820, 44 percent in 1830, 45 percent in 1840, 37 percent in 1850, and 44 percent in 1860. For more comprehensive data on Louisiana's enslaved population, see Gwendolyn Midlo Hall, *Databases for the Study of Afro-Louisiana History and Genealogy, 1699–1860*.

"natives" and "Negroes": In 1862, stationed at Camp Strong in Gentilly, Henry L. Rey observed that white Creoles who had once called free people of color friends were now calling them "Natives" as a sign of disrespect and were disparaging their fighting ability. "Our fathers will not be ashamed of Natives," Rey wrote, "a name which the Creoles have given us, the flatterers, and which they change now that they have no need of us." "Correspondance," *L'Union*, October 18, 1862.

"Everything 'that is good'": *The Picayune's Guide to New Orleans*, 75. The historical inaccuracy of the statement is readily apparent in primary sources from the antebellum period.

Lionel Dupart Sr. and his family: The 1930 federal census shows Lionel Dupart and family living at 2327 Lapeyrouse Street; a quarter of a century later, according to the 1956 New Orleans city directory, the family was living at 1023 N. Tonti. Unless otherwise specified, my source for individual census records has been the US Federal Census Collection, 1790–1940 (hereafter USFCC) on Ancestry.com. The data for this note is in USFCC, *Fifteenth Census of the United States* (1930), New Orleans, Ward 7, Ancestry.com.

Pierre Joseph deLisle, *dit* Dupart: Conrad, *First Families*, 2:45.

Jacques Dupart: Conrad, *First Families*, 1:6.

Nos hommes: Desdunes's original French edition, *Nos hommes et notre histoire*, published in 1911, can be accessed through Project Gutenberg. The English-language translation by Sister Dorothea Olga McCants was published in 1973 as *Our People and Our History*.

"the upper class": Desdunes, *Our People,* 29.

"The above title": "Local Intelligence," *New Orleans Tribune*, February 17, 1867. I received this article from Mark Charles Roudané in February 2019, after he informed me that the Boston Athenæum holds issues of the *Tribune* that are not available on microfilm. For more information about the paper, see Roudané, Roudanez: History and Legacy.

a relative from Africa: The 1850 census listed Esthere Dupart, 83, from Africa, as living with Martial, 60, and Victor, 15, both born in Louisiana. USFCC, *Seventh Census of the United States* (1850), New Orleans, Municipality 3, Ward 1, Ancestry.com.

"should be able to receive Jews": ESM, June 15, 1880. The members were contemplating a Catholic ceremony to bless the society's new banner when Rey said that the society should not be prejudicial to any religion: "*Le frère H. Rey fait un point d'ordre que les questions religieuses ne peuvent être entretenues, et qu'on peut recevoir des Juifs et des Chinois.*"

Joseph Daniel Warburg: ESM, February 19, 1872.

Walter L. Cohen: ESM, March 2, 1896; Ingham, "Cohen."

"to help one another": ESM, January 24, 1836.

daughters of Economistes: Mildred Meilleur Boissiere (age 82) and Adrienne Woods Blache (age 83), interviews by author, December 2003. Mildred's husband, Lambert Boissiere, was Economie vice president in 1948 and a friend of Lionel Dupart, an Economie member whose father joined in 1909. Adrienne's father, Numa Woods, also joined the Economie in 1909. Ernest Blache, the great-grandfather of Adrienne's husband, Fabian P. Blache Sr., joined in 1857.

The first was purchased: Unless otherwise noted, citations for property transactions and labor contracts are drawn from the records of the New Orleans Notarial Archives (henceforth NONA) and comprise the name of the notary public and the date of the act. Because New Orleans streets have been renumbered (often more than once) since the nineteenth century, approximate present-day addresses are supplemented by references to the 1883 *Robinson's Atlas of the City of New Orleans, Louisiana*, a standard locator for historical addresses within the city. Some plates on NONA's copy of the atlas have been annotated, permitting cross-referencing with present-day street numbers and lot configurations on the City of New Orleans Property Viewer.

The first Economy Hall appears as 219 Ursuline, one of three small, identical buildings on the Robinson atlas (plate 7, square 170); the present-day street address would be between 1421 and 1427 Ursulines Avenue (square 171, lot B, City of New Orleans Property Viewer). For the purchase, see Louis T. Caire, notary public, February 25, 1836, NONA. ESM, December 15, 1836, includes a statement from member Pierre Duhart, explaining that although he bought the land from Pierre Crocker, it doesn't belong to him but rather to the Société d'Economie, and that Duhart was merely representing the society in the transaction.

The members purchased the land for a new meeting place in July 1853 (Alexandre Emile Bienvenu, notary public, July 20, 1853, NONA), and the hall was built under a contract with Economie member William Belley (Joseph Lisbony, notary public, April 25, 1857, NONA). This second and most well-known Economy Hall was completed in July 1857 and inaugurated in December 1857. The hall is identified by name on the Robinson atlas (plate 7, square 169); the present-day address, 1422–26 Ursulines Avenue, is occupied by the schoolyard of Joseph A. Craig Elementary (square 170, lot 12, City of New Orleans Property Viewer).

In 1911 the society purchased a third property, at present-day 1428 Ursulines Avenue (square 170, lots M and 13, City of New Orleans Property Viewer), which it continued to maintain into the 1940s. Later scholarship, notably Roulhac Toledano and Mary Lou Christovich's *Faubourg Tremé and the Bayou Road*, a volume in the New Orleans Architecture series, provides incorrect data about the history of Economy Hall.

"We are compelled": "Local Intelligence," *New Orleans Tribune*, February 17, 1867.

"which stands on Ursuline street": Throughout the nineteenth century, the street was known interchangeably as "Ursuline" or "Ursulines." The name was formalized as "Ursulines Avenue" by city ordinance in 1894 (Amos, "Alphabetical Index").

displaced 272,000 African Americans: Gabe et al., "Hurricane Katrina," 16. The 2010 census recorded a drop of 118,526 in the Black population of New Orleans (Plyer, "What Census 2010 Reveals," 1). While some of the Katrina diaspora has returned, and while some population loss may be due to other factors, the storm's impact on the city's demographic makeup and neighborhood settlement patterns remains profound.

1873 workers' cooperative meeting: "Workers Cooperative Club Formed in Economy Hall," *Tägliche Deutsche Zeitung*, July 1, 1873.

"a gentle and peaceful brother": ESM, January 17, 1879. "*Le frère Engle Barthe a été parmi nous, un frère doux et paisible, vieillard respecté, et a été celui qui a supporté avec courage les misères et les vicissitudes de l'Existence.*"

PROLOGUE: The People Who Disappeared

Divine Providence: ESM, July 15, 1857. Pierre Casanave spoke these words over new member J. L. Populus.

grand opening party: ESM, December 7, 1857.

Boguille faced the building: Moellhausen, *Norman's Plan of New Orleans*; Robinson atlas plate 7; *Sanborn Fire Insurance Map from New Orleans*, map 62; building contract filed between the members of the Economie and William Belley, member/contractor (Joseph Lisbony, notary public, September 4, 1856, NONA).

Bamboula: Gottschalk, *Bamboula*.

ten thousand free colored people: Gibson and Jung, "Historical Census Statistics," table 19.

Comonfort had recently invited: ESM, July 8, 1857, discusses the portraits of Pétion and Comonfort in the hall.

The philharmonic: ESM, December 1, 1857. "Brother R. Angelain observed that there is no longer a Philharmonic Society, but that by sending a letter to Mr. Liautaud, he will be able to gather amateurs who will perform some pieces for the occasion." The concert program for "Identity, History, Legacy: La Société Philharmonique," presented in 2011 by The Historic New Orleans Collection and the Louisiana Philharmonic Orchestra, notes that the Société Philharmonique was already playing concerts by 1840.

"supposed to embrace the negro race": *Dred Scott v. Sandford*, 60 U.S. 393 (1856).

"May our behaviors": ESM, December 15, 1857.

THE AGE OF HOPE

In the Beginning: Haiti

The president talked: ESM, March 1, 1866.

district of Croix-des-Bouquets: For more information about the free colored community of Croix-des-Bouquets at the start of the revolution, see Geggus, *The Haitian Revolution*, 65–71. François Boguille's death certificate identifies his birthplace as Croix-des-Bouquets; his marriage contract says he is a native of Port-au-Prince, about eight miles away. Death certificate of François Boguille, January 15, 1845, New Orleans (La.) Board of Health Death Certificates, 1804–1915, microfilm FF650, vol. 10: 298, NOPL; hereafter F. Boguille death certificate. Marriage contract of François Boguy [*sic*] and Suzanne Butel (Marc Lafitte, notary public, September 27, 1820, NONA; hereafter Boguille-Butel marriage contract). Ludger's death certificate identifies his father as a native of Italy, an intriguing note possibly explained by administrative error, or possibly by erroneous oral history that the descendants repeated to the undertaker. Death certificate of J. B. Ludger Boguille, January 18, 1892, Orleans Parish Death Index-B, Death Index Reel 2, 1877–1895, vol. 101: 7, NOPL; hereafter L. Boguille death certificate.

The revolution began: Rainsford, *Historical Account*, 121, 125; James, *Black Jacobins*, 73–75.

His mother was dark-skinned: The Boguille-Butel marriage contract identifies François as a free man of color and the natural son of Charlotte, a *négresse décédée* (deceased negress). The term *négresse* indicates that Charlotte was an enslaved woman with dark skin color.

the threat of their alliance: Geggus, *Haitian Revolution*, 68–69.

a declaration of war: Geggus, *Haitian Revolution*, 65–68, 71. See also Bell, *Revolution*, 2, 3, 20, 21 for a discussion of Ogé and the transmission of revolutionary ideas to Louisiana.

François's friend Charles Joseph Savary: Bell, "Savary." In early publications, Bell referred to the elder Savary as "Joseph Charles," but her later research revealed that both he and his son were named Charles Joseph Savary (email message to author, March 18, 2018).

Savary retreated: Schomburg Center, "Haitian Immigration."

Jacmel and Jérémie: Saint-Rémy, *Pétion et Haïti*, 192.

Jérémie, a coastal town: Manuel, "Slavery, Coffee, and Family," 13.

Indigo, cocoa, cotton, and coffee: Remy, "Infiltrating the Colonial City," 198–200.

the port was busy: Manuel, "Slavery, Coffee, and Family," 11; Remy, "Infiltrating the Colonial City," 185. An engraving by Nicolas Ponce, originally published in *Recueil de vues des lieux principaux de la colonie françoise de Saint-Domingue* (Paris, 1791), depicts the bustling Jérémie harbor, while an eighteenth-century plan by Georges de Maillard de Bois Saint Lys delineates the street grid.

its most famous mixed-race resident: Reiss, *The Black Count*, 43, 44, 54–55, 58.

Their population had increased: Manuel, "Slavery, Coffee, and Family," 9.

the colored elite of Jérémie: Manuel, "Slavery, Coffee, and Family," 16–17, 31.

at least eleven racial categories: Moreau de Saint-Méry, *Description topographique*, 73–75.

citizens of Jérémie did too: Léger, *Haiti*, 57; Manuel, "A Guide to the Jérémie Papers."

on a plantation she owned: The Boguille-Butel marriage contract lists a habitation (house or plantation) in Fertel (or Tertel), Saint Domingue, as part of the property Suzanne Butel brought to the union.

Butel's new home: Boguille-Butel marriage contract.

Butel received 500 *piastres*: The record of sale (Marc Lafitte, notary public, August 23, 1813, NONA) identifies Marie Noel as one of Butel's "properties" in Saint Domingue but leaves some questions unanswered. Her reported birth year (1794) could suggest that the two women emigrated to Louisiana later in the decade. It is also possible that Marie Noel was older than the deed of sale suggests, and that Butel altered the date in an attempt to make the sale more attractive to the buyer, Bernard Marigny.

***Our militia will never be worth*:** Carter, *Territorial Papers*, 9:503.

Some of Savary's men: Bell, "Savary."

While the ships: Remini, *Battle of New Orleans*, 6–9.

"noble-hearted, generous": McConnell, "Louisiana's Black Military History," 41. In *Revolution*, Bell writes that Black soldiers were promised the same payment as whites, "$124 in cash and 160 acres of land" (53).

Charles Joseph Savary *père*: McConnell, *Negro Troops*, 70. Descriptions of the Savary family's service are informed by Caryn Cossé Bell's research in the Edward Livingston Papers at Princeton University Library (email message to author, March 18, 2018). See also "War Leader Profile" for speculation about D'Aquin's possible mixed-racial heritage.

joined a coalition: Schomburg Center, "Haitian Immigration."

Savary *fils*, Belton, and a few other members: Bell, "Savary."

Jackson later wrote a letter: Robarts, "Napoleon's Interest," 361. Jackson identified the likely sharpshooter as a "famous rifle-shot . . . from the Atakappas region of Louisiana."

Belton died: Christian, *Negro Soldiers*, 44.

In February 1815: McConnell, *Negro Troops*, 94; Bell, *Revolution*, 59.

Two months later: Bell, email message to author, March 18, 2018, citing Jackson correspondence in the Edward Livingston Papers at Princeton University Library.

a pension of eight dollars: "An Act for the Relief of Charles Savary," February 27, 1826, in Moreau Lislet and Brown, *General Digest*, 2:233.

an application for land: The application is recorded as "rejected" in the Bounty-Land Warrant Applications Index at the National Archives, under warrant numbers 50-178068 (as "Francois Boguille") and 55-255564 (as "Francis Boguille"). For these and other records related to military service, I have utilized the online database Fold3.com; these applications are found in the War of 1812 (United States) collection. McConnell, *Negro Troops*, 110, notes that the bounty applications for land began with laws passed in 1850, 1852, and 1855—all after François Boguille's death. It is possible that Ludger made the application, as he was an advocate of the Société des Vétérans de 1814–15, which met in the Economie's hall.

***Love is a beautiful dream*:** ESM, March 21, 1858.

held at the Washington Ballroom: This same venue, under previous ownership, was one of the earliest in the city to host balls for New Orleans's free colored community. See the entry for "St. Philip Street Ballroom" on NOPL's online exhibition *Que la fête commence! The French Influence on the Good Life in New Orleans*.

"*Chère, mo lemmé toi*": New Orleanian Camille Nickerson—pianist, folklorist, and longtime professor of music at Howard University—included this piece in her 1942 compilation *Five Creole Songs*.

François was forty-two: Although their precise birth dates are unknown, the couple's death records show that François was born about 1778, Suzanne about 1777. F. Boguille death certificate; Suzanne Buthel Boquille [*sic*] death certificate, January 1, 1855, Louisiana, Statewide Death Index, 1819–1964, Ancestry.com.

The contract notarized by Marc Lafitte: She lived on Washington Square in the Faubourg Marigny at the time of the marriage; he lived on Rue Condé, the section of present-day Chartres Street running from St. Louis Cathedral to the edge of Faubourg Marigny. The 1822 city directory lists François Boguil [*sic*], a cabinetmaker with a shop at 33 Rue Condé and a domicile at the corner of Union and Amour. The directory also lists François Bogie [*sic*], a carpenter, at 81 Union near Bon Enfants (Good Children). I believe Boguille worked on Condé, lived at Union and Amour, and owned 81 Union. Boguille-Butel marriage contract; 1822 New Orleans city directory.

now eight years old: According to his death certificate, Ludger Boguille was born in September 1812. Boguille-Butel marriage contract; L. Boguille death certificate.

His name was recorded: Boguille-Butel marriage contract. "Heludger" appears on no other official documentation. Boguille's death certificate identifies him as "J. B. Ludger Boguille"; "J. B." (presumably "Jean Baptiste") could be a confirmation name. These initials do not appear on his military records, where he is documented as "Ludgere Boguille" (records of the First Native Guards, Militia, 1861, Civil War Service Records (CMSR)—Confederate— Louisiana, Fold3.com).

The Early Life of Ludger Boguille

Before deposition of your votes: ESM, March 1, 1836.

His father's cabinetmaking shop: 1822 city directory.

Within a few years he would gain: *Boguille, f.m.c, Administrator, v. Faille, f.w.c.*, 1 La. Ann. 204 (1846) 01142, at 01162 names Ludger Boguille's siblings Elizabeth Boguille, Marie Charlotte Boguille, and Jean G. Boguille.

Parents in this community: "Miss Valframbert," *Courrier de la Louisiane*, May 6, 1822.

his mother went to court: Suzanne Butel emancipated Collinette on April 16, 1817. Emancipation petitions, 1813–43, microfilm reel 98-3, frame 801, NOPL.

François and his mother, Dauphine: Boguille-Butel marriage contract. At the time of the marriage, Butel owned the following people: Lecroix, 26; Choile, 24; Desiree, 22; Dauphine, 23; Sophia, 11; and François, 7; Dauphine was a *blanchisseuse* (laundress).

resided the editor: J. B. Maureau, the editor of *Le Louisianais et ami des lois / The Louisianian and Friend of the Laws*, is identified as a Frenchman in the *Courrier de la Louisiane*, August 16, 1822.

his paper ran many ads: 1822 New Orleans city directory; "$20 Reward," "Twenty Dollars Reward," "Parish of Placquemines District Court," *The Louisianian and Friend of the Laws*, May 3, 1823.

They carried ads: *L'Abeille de la Nouvelle-Orléans*: July 7, 1829 (leeches); July 30, 1829 (beaver hats); September 29, 1829 (shoes and wet nurses).

No more than four houses: Pinistri, *New Orleans General Guide*.

"Mentor then called my attention": Fénelon, *Adventures of Telemachus, the Son of Ulysses*, 20–21.

The town is divided: Murray, *Travels in North America*, 186.

The city separated: Richard Campanella, "Culture Wars Led to New Orleans' Most Peculiar Experiment in City Management," *Times-Picayune,* March 7, 2016.

lived in the old city: In 1836 Boguille was living with Andrénette Lamy and their children, most likely on Ursuline Street between Burgundy and Rampart Streets, where she died a decade later. Her death certificate, dated June 29, 1846, is appended to her succession record (Louisiana, Second District Court [Orleans Parish] succession records, 1846–80, VSB290, box 35, NOPL; hereafter A. Lamy succession).

Chitimacha, Chawasha, Houma: See the entry for "American Indians: The First Families of Louisiana on the Eve of French Settlement" in the Louisiana State Museum's online exhibition *The Cabildo: Two Centuries of Louisiana History.*

In 1732 there were fewer than ten: Maduell, *Census Tables,* 123–41; Vidal, *Caribbean New Orleans,* 201. The 1732 census identifies only two people of color—Xavier, a mulatto, and Marie, a "negress"—as free (133). Six more unnamed mulattos are enumerated as living with white householders, but they are not specifically listed as being free or enslaved.

By 1836 this population: Census data shows 16,710 free people of color in Louisiana in 1830, with 11,562 of them resident in New Orleans. The city's total had increased to 19,226 by 1840. *Abstract of the Returns of the Fifth Census,* 33; Gibson and Jung, "Historical Census Statistics," table 19.

the lullaby: "Fais Do-Do," sometimes "Fait Dodo" or "Dodo Titit," is a common Haitian lullaby. For lyrics and interpretation, see Chery, "Dodo Titit." A haunting rendition is included on the 1963 Smithsonian Folkways album *Lullabies of the World.*

His sister Elizabeth: *Boguille v. Faille,* at 01162 names Louis Clement Sacriste, spouse to Elizabeth Boguille. The death record of Marie Louise Frere, mother of Louis Clément Sacriste, indicates her birthplace as Croix-des-Bouquets (Marie Louise Frere death record, March 5, 1840, Louisiana, Orleans Parish Death Records and Certificates, 1835–1954, FamilySearch.org). Marie's relationship to Louis is confirmed in the will of Jean Sacriste, June 25, 1827, Louisiana, Wills and Probate Records, 1756–1984, Ancestry.com.

their son Henry L. Rey: Daggett, *Spiritualism,* 40–41.

a circle of writers: Desdunes, *Our People,* 29.

"Divine one": Desdunes, *Our People,* 85–86; Sullivan, "Edmond Dédé"; Trotter, *Music and Some Highly Musical People,* 341. Born in 1827, Dédé published "Mon Pauvre Cœur," his first major success—and the earliest known New Orleans sheet music by a Creole of color—in 1852. In the original French, the lyrics are *"Divine enfant chaque jour je t'implore / Avec ardeur / De partager la flamme qui dévore / Mon pauvre cœur."*

they had their first child: Suzette Boguille was born September 15, 1832; Fénelon Boguille was born May 17, 1834; and Florian Joseph Boguille was born February 15, 1836 (New Orleans, Louisiana, Birth Records Index, 1790–1915, Ancestry.com). The elder two were baptized on June 27, 1836, as the "fils légitime" and "fille légitime" of Ludger and Andrénette (A. Lamy succession).

a verse from the scriptures: Luke 12:34 (KJV).

At no distant day: These comments, attributed to the Hon. Henry Adams Bullard at the January 1839 meeting of the Louisiana Colonization Society, were reported in the *New Orleans Observer* and subsequently reprinted in the *African Repository and Colonial Journal,* 15:89.

the ACS was formed: See the entry on "Colonization" in *The African-American Mosaic,* a Library of Congress online exhibition.

The colored businessmen: To understand the Economistes' evolving attitude toward the emigration plans of the American Colonization Society, consider the letters of J. B. Jordan, an accountant in New Orleans who began writing to the ACS for ship's passage to Liberia as early as 1849. In an October 1, 1850, letter to Dr. J. W. Lugenbeel, a physician in Monrovia,

he said, "For the last nine years, I have been extolling the advantages of emigration to
Liberia. At first I was laughed at and rudely treated by those colored people who profiting
by the good times many years ago, made money and invested it in property here. About
five years ago the dislike to Colonization seems to have passed away. Some few would
talk of it whilst others in their timidity would only listen. Now there are few persons who
hesitate to speak of Colonization and of their intention or desire to emigrate to Liberia
in a few years." Quoted in Woodson, *Mind of the Negro*, 119.

"Louisiana in Africa": An 1839 report from the Mississippi Colonization Society observed
that "a territory for the purposes of a colony has been, we presume, . . . secured for this
purpose, and we look forward with pleasing anticipations to the hour, when 'Louisiana in
Africa' shall be as familiar to our ears, and pleasing to our minds, as the names of kindred
separated from us only by distance." *African Repository and Colonial Journal* 15:88.

guided them around the city: 1834 New Orleans city directory.

bière créole: Read, *Louisiana-French*, 11.

"destined . . . to be the greatest": Colton, *Manual for Emigrants to America*, 91.

In 1837, Louisiana banks: Trufant, *Review of Banking in New Orleans*, 9. See also Bodenhorn,
"Antebellum Banking in the United States," for more information on banking in Louisiana in the 1830s.

François Boisdoré: *Boisdoré and Goulé, f.p.c., v. Citizens' Bank of Louisiana*, 9 La. Ann. 506
(1836). Boisdoré's coplaintiff Goulé bought 150 shares, worth $15,000.

more than 58,000 enslaved people: *A Century of Population Growth*, 133, table 60.

a planter with an eight-hundred-acre farm: *Louisiana Gazette*, September 19, 1806, quoted
in Follett, *Sugar Masters*, 18.

"for feeling so indifferent": Garrison, "Exposure of the American Colonization Society," 14–15.

THE AGE OF AWARENESS

The Awakening of Ludger Boguille

Always remember: ESM, July 15, 1857.

fanciful descriptions: Florian, *History of the Moors*, 146–47.

"It is painful to quit": Florian, *History of the Moors*, 148.

The systems of taxation: Richard Campanella, "The Turbulent History behind the Seven
New Orleans Municipal Districts," *Times-Picayune*, October 9, 2013.

Ludger could see the notices: The December 9, 1835, issue of *L'Abeille de la Nouvelle-Orléans*
featured calls to the "Legion de Luisiana," "Garde Urbaine, No.1," "Chasseurs à Cheval
Louisianais," and "Cavalerie de Nlle-Orleans 1814–15."

The organizers did not call: Not until 1851 would the public celebration include the colored
battalions, as documented in "The Free Colored Veterans," *Daily Picayune*, January 9, 1851,
and discussed in Luxenberg, *Separate*, 91–95.

David Walker: WGBH Educational Foundation, "David Walker."

"There is a great work": Walker, *Walker's Appeal*, 35.

They lived near his house: The members of the Société des Vétérans de 1814–15 held banquets
and meetings in the Economie's hall. See, for instance, ESM January 4, 1858, March 1,
1869, and January 2, 1873.

Louisiana regulated writing and thinking: In 1806 the territorial legislature of Louisiana
passed a comprehensive Black Code governing the behaviors of enslaved and free colored

people. For origins of the code and adaptations during the early decades of statehood, see Schafer, "Roman Roots," 413–16, and Pearson, "Imperfect Equality," 191–210.

The courts threatened hard labor: Greiner, *Louisiana Digest*, 1:521.

"Wrong'd, persecuted, and proscrib'd": Florian, "The Philosopher and the Owl," in *Fables of Florian*, 60–61.

West African tales: The stories of Bouki and Lapin are part of a Western African tradition of trickster tales that were brought to the United States by enslaved people. Bouki and Lapin were the names used in the French colony of Louisiana. Joel Chandler Harris heard many of the same stories from enslaved people in Georgia when he was growing up and published them during the late nineteenth century in the Uncle Remus stories of Br'er Rabbit.

"Look at that mulatto": Allen, Ware, and Garrison, *Slave Songs of the United States*, 113.

to refer to a mulatto: Jones, *Strange Talk*, 121. The song "Mister Bainjo" was passed orally through the Creole community in New Orleans before folklorists put it in print. Although the words "mulet" and "mulatto" were known to be pejoratives, they were sung satirically in the way that contemporary words with negative connotations for Blacks are implemented in rap and hip-hop music.

"Hail Mary": Allen, Ware, and Garrison, *Slave Songs of the United States*, 45. See Flake, "Sing Two Stanzas and Rebel in the Morning," for more information on music as an act of free expression among the enslaved.

He possessed a dual consciousness: In *The Souls of Black Folks*, W. E. B. Du Bois would memorably theorize that Black Americans—simultaneously belonging to and excluded from American society—possess, and are continuously aware of, dual identity.

Ludger married Andrénette: The marriage of Andrénette Lamy and Ludger Boguille is recorded in her succession as an extract from the registers of the St. Louis Cathedral, June 27, 1836 (A. Lamy succession).

signing the marriage certificate: See McKee, *Exile's Song*, 38–40, for information on Edmond Dédé's relationship to Basile Dédé, the witness at the wedding.

David Walker died unexpectedly: David Walker Memorial Project, "Death of David Walker"; "Deaths," *Boston Recorder*, August 11, 1830; Garnet, *Walker's Appeal*.

All the civilized peoples: ESM, November 2, 1838.

Etienne Ludger, their fourth child: Etienne Ludger was born May 3, 1838, and died May 13, 1839. François Boguille (also known as Lespoir), died December 4, 1840. THNOC, Survey of Historic New Orleans Cemeteries, series VIII, St. Louis Cemetery No. 1, MSS 360.8.

"a joiner by trade": *Boguille v. Faille*, at 01200.

"scars from his head to his feet": *Boguille v. Faille*, at 01199.

The doctor came: *Boguille v. Faille*, at 01199–01200.

In the last two weeks: *Boguille v. Faille*, at 01201.

Finally at peace: François Boguille died on January 11, 1845, aged sixty-seven (F. Boguille death certificate). François lived at Union and Love Streets; Ludger's residence was on Ursuline Street, between Rampart and Burgundy. To pinpoint important sites, I used Pinistri's *New Orleans General Guide*, the Robinson atlas, early city directories, real estate sales records at the New Orleans Notarial Archives, and Freedmen's Bureau tax records (Records of the Superintendent of Education and of the Division of Education, 1865–1872, FamilySearch.org).

"It is all over!": "Necrologie," *L'Abeille de la Nouvelle-Orléans*, January 14, 1845.

The extended family: The Economie minutes include well over one hundred mentions of funerals and ceremonies.

François Boguille was interred: Boguille is buried in St. Louis Cemetery No. 2, square 3; THNOC, Survey of Historic New Orleans Cemeteries. Twenty-first-century photographs of Boguille family tombs can be found in Montana et al., "St. Louis No. 1 and 2," appendix A.

And furthermore: *Boguille v. Faille*, at 01190.

Neither his mother: The year before he died, François Boguille transferred five lots on the corner of Union and Virtue Streets in square 98 of Faubourg Marigny to Ludger (Charles V. Foulon, notary public, November 24, 1843, NONA). The Boguille-Butel marriage contract also named Ludger as inheritor of all François's money and property, including enslaved people. When his father's succession was opened in probate court, Ludger was appointed to serve as administrator of François's estate (*Boguille v. Faille*, at 01162).

The sheriff frequently seized property: *Boguille v. Faille*, at 01161–62. In 1842 François Boguille borrowed $2,510.20 from Elizabeth Faille at a rate of 10 percent interest to purchase a property at the corner of Union and Good Children Streets. Faille's suit says that until his death two years later, Boguille had only paid interest on the debt.

He got an injunction: *Boguille v. Faille*, at 01147–48. Williamson and Cain, "Seven Ways to Compute the Relative Value" estimates the value of the $500 bond in 1845 to be $17,600 in 2020. The value of the property at Union and Good Children would be $88,900 in 2020.

his father had written an X: *Boguille v. Faille*, at 01163.

Ludger asked for a new trial: *Boguille v. Faille*, at 01157–58.

could sell for about $550: Kotlikoff, "Structure of Slave Prices," 498. See also Williamson and Cain, "Measuring Slavery," which estimates the average price of an enslaved person in 1850 as $400, or about the same value as a house.

sold to Bernard Marigny: Marc Lafitte, notary public, August 23, 1813, NONA.

contract housekeepers and seamstresses: Manuel, "Slavery, Coffee, and Family," 19.

breakfast cakes made of rice: Godoy, "Meet the Calas."

too young to be free: Louisiana's Civil Code of 1825 extended provisions of earlier colonial and territorial codes prohibiting the manumission of enslaved people under thirty years of age. See Schafer, "Roman Roots," 415–16.

Butel legally emancipated her: The petition to emancipate Collinette, filed by Suzanne Butel on April 16, 1817, before Orleans Parish Judge James Pitot, said she was "over the age of 30, has honest conduct, and has not committed any crime or run away" (Emancipation petitions, 1813–43, microfilm reel 98-3, frame 801, NOPL).

One of Ludger's neighbors: In 1842 Martial Dupart was living in Boguille's neighborhood, at Union and Great Men Streets (1842 New Orleans city directory).

baptized them in the St. Louis Cathedral: Born in February 1790, Martial was brought by his mother, Marguerite, to be baptized on August 1, 1790 (St. Louis Cathedral, New Orleans, Baptism 1786–1792, part 2, 170, Archdiocese of New Orleans, Church Records, nolacatholic.org/church-records). Both mother and infant are documented as free mulattos, contradicting the record of their manumission in 1793. Perhaps their legal status was added later—or perhaps, per a phenomenon discussed in Neidenbach, "'Mes dernières volontés,'" par. 22, this notation represented the owner's intention to free enslaved family members.

"much love and affection": In September 1793, Joseph Dupart acknowledged paternity of Martial, Augusto, and Pedro and freed them and their mother, Marguerite (Pedro Pedesclaux, notary public, September 23, 1793, NONA). Dupart's signature is not on the document; it is signed by his representative Santiago Lemair.

Fearing God more than the law: Clark, *Strange History*, 84.

nearly fifty residents: Mills, "Isle of Canes," 165. See also Auguste Metoyer Papers and Norbert Badin Papers in the collaborative digital collection Free People of Color in Louisiana: Revealing an Unknown Past, hosted by LSU Libraries.

began to purchase enslaved workers: Ochs, *Black Patriot*, 45; Walker, "Negro Benevolent Societies," 37. Referring to the Société des Artisans and the Economie, Walker says, "The tradition among many of its members is, that many of these associations were founded by free Negroes for the purpose of raising money to purchase the freedom of the slaves." My research has not proved that unequivocally true, but I would not doubt that funds were used that way, considering the secrecy of the Economie. There is no outright accounting of funds for purchasing the enslaved, but individual members did buy and free enslaved people, and there are several funds and committees in the Economie that could be investigated. Walker quotes a member of Dieu Nous Protégé, founded in 1844, who said, "Its sole object was primarily to obtain the liberation of the other unfortunate members of their race held in subjugation and with this object in view it was possible to obtain the freedom of many of their own people." I have found no similar testimony from an Economiste.

thirty-five-year-old Marie Eglé: Emancipation petitions, 1813–43, microfilm reel 98-2, frame 37H (October 27, 1825), NOPL. Also cited in the Race and Slavery Petitions Project, hosted by the University of North Carolina at Greensboro Libraries (petition 20882551). Pierre Crocker's April 3, 1803, baptismal record lists his maternal grandmother as Ysavel (Isabel) Beauregard (St. Louis Cathedral, New Orleans, Baptism 1802–04, 906, Archdiocese of New Orleans, Church Records, nolacatholic.org/church-records).

Justine was liberated: Louis T. Caire, notary public, September 26, 1837, NONA.

had not forced any emancipated person: Schafer, "Forever Free," 143–46.

fickle legal system: As the plantation system grew, the state got involved in manumission: "The courts had to develop the idea that there could be no such thing as private manumission, although such had been frequently indulged in by masters during the earlier period. Manumission became a matter of the sovereign power of the state. The master could not of his own authority make with the slave a contract by which he could obtain his freedom" (Woodson, *Free Negro Heads of Families*, xv–xvi). Neither Boguille nor Butel are listed as slave owners in the 1830 census as compiled in Woodson, *Free Negro Owners*, 6–15.

"She was bought at St. Iago": *Boguille v. Faille*, at 01194. "St. Iago" is most likely the court reporter's rendition of Santiago. Around 18,000 refugees from the Haitian Revolution fled to Santiago, Cuba, in 1803; after Napoleon's army invaded Spain, the refugees were ejected from Cuba in 1809, and about 10,000 of them settled in New Orleans. See Scott and Hébrard, "Rosalie of the Poulard Nation," 125–27.

notary recorded six people: According to the Boguille-Butel marriage contract, Boguille brought no enslaved people into the marriage, and the enslaved people whom Butel brought were named Lespoir, Choisi, Desiree, Dauphine, François, and Sophia.

We find our hearts full: ESM, March 15, 1836.

advertisements from Beard, Calhoun & Co.: "Auction Sales," *Daily Picayune*, January 2, 1846.

while Black women cooked: For descriptions of the sociology of slave owners, see Johnson, *Soul by Soul*.

nankeen cotton imported from China: Johnson, *Soul by Soul*, chap. 3.

volume of poetry titled *Les Cenelles*: "It is well to remember that the poems found in *Les Cenelles* were composed during the era of slavery," Desdunes observed in *Our People*, "and that those who contributed to the collection did not enjoy the same advantages as other men of their day because the writers were restricted by law and by social prejudice. From a philosophical point of view, *Les Cenelles* represents the triumph of the human spirit over the forces of obscurantism in Louisiana that denied the education and intellectual advancement of the colored masses" (10).

family of Joseph Charles Dupart: USFCC, *Seventh Census of the United States* (1850), New Orleans, Municipality 3, Ward 1, Ancestry.com. After Victor's name, the census taker added a note: "goes to school!"

his "*cinco hijos lehitimos y naturals*": The last will and testament of Pierre Joseph Delille, *dit* Dupart notes that he has a wife named Jacqueline Michel and five legitimate and natural children (Juan B. Garic, notary public, September 17, 23, and 30, 1775, NONA). The Pierre Joseph named in the will may be the same person as the Pierre Joseph deLisle, *dit* Dupart mentioned in the Introduction.

Everyone knew: Augustin Macarty (mayor from 1815 to 1820) and Denis Prieur (mayor from 1828 to 1838 and again in 1842–43) lived with free women of color. On Macarty's relationships, see Clark, *Strange History*, 111–12. The abolitionist Benjamin Lundy, on his travels through the South, observed in June 1834 that the "present mayor of the city [Denis Prieur] has a coloured family, and no other, and is very friendly to the coloured people" (*Life, Travels and Opinions*, 114).

marriage or "concubinage" relationships: See *Digest of the Civil Laws in Force in the Territory of Orleans*, book 1, title IV, article 8, and Morgan, *Civil Code of the State of Louisiana*, book I, title IV, article 95.

the *Isaac Franklin*: "Inward Slave Manifests," entries 292–95. The AfriGeneas website (www.afrigeneas.com/) features transcriptions of several hundred records from a much larger collection of shipping manifests housed at the National Archives and Records Administration in Washington, DC, which document the transshipment of enslaved people along the eastern coastal waterways stretching from Boston to New Orleans. One of the consignees receiving some of the enslaved people from the *Isaac Franklin* was Theophilus Freeman, the trader who sold Solomon Northup, a free Black man from New York who would later write the well-known memoir *Twelve Years a Slave*.

sided with Faille: *Boguille v. Faille*, at 01211.

"gravest consequences" for the heirs: Court records show that Boguille appealed the probate court's decision (*Boguille v. Faille*, at 01210), but that the judgment of the district court was affirmed (01212). Boguille appealed again, questioning the court's jurisdiction and asserting that the decision would create the "gravest consequences" for the heirs (01215). The records contain the title page of a June 26, 1846, application for rehearing (01216). At this point the document trail ends. The case never went to court again, possibly because the application for a rehearing was denied and because the June 29, 1846, death of Andrénette may have directed Boguille's attention elsewhere.

auction of the property: Records kept by the sheriff's office show the advertisement from the newspaper and $1,600 received from the sale, plus the costs of the sale at $129.60 (Orleans Parish Sheriff's Office, Sales Books, 1846–63, vol. 1: 184, NOPL).

where the auctioneers sold people: The hotel was on St. Louis Street between Chartres and Royal Streets.

She disappeared from the court records: There is no record of Denise after the case, nor is Suzanne Butel Boguille listed independently or in her children's households. The only documentary trace of Suzanne is her death record, which notes the passing of a 78-year-old colored female on January 1, 1855 (Suzanne Buthel Boquille [*sic*] death certificate, January 1, 1855, Louisiana, Statewide Death Index, 1819–1964, Ancestry.com). Vendor indexes 41–87 in the Land Records Division of the Office of the Clerk of Civil Court for the Parish of Orleans show no record of any sales of the enslaved by the Boguilles or Butels from 1846 through emancipation. The sales and purchaser indexes indicate separate sales of real estate and people that were brought before notaries between April 1, 1827, and October 8, 1864. None of Butel's enslaved people are listed in the sales throughout this period. François Boguille, however, appears in these records as a seller of people on three occasions: before J. Cuvillier, notary public, on May 9, 1836, he sold Valentin, about 26 years old, to James Ferel; before Charles Foulon, notary public, on July 3, 1838, he sold Issac, mulatto, to Etienne Cassard; and before Cuvillier on June 23, 1843, he sold a 23- or 24-year-old mulatto woman to Pascaline Cassou, representing Charles Lamarque.

she unexpectedly died: Lamy died at her home on Ursuline Street between Burgundy and Rampart Streets on June 29, 1846. Her death certificate, which is appended to her succession record, says she is "married to Ludger Boguille, her surviving consort" but lists no cause of death (A. Lamy succession). She is interred in St. Louis Cemetery No. 2, square 3, in the Famille Boguille tomb (no. 57). THNOC, Survey of Historic New Orleans Cemeteries.

Boguille Finds Support in the Economie Brotherhood

Considering all the advantages: ESM, inside cover of the first journal (1836).

one of the Economie's founders: Boyer's signature (in French, "Adolphe Bouyer") appears alongside those of other founders in the society's 1836 journal.

disappeared with the minute books: The book or books containing the minutes between March 1, 1842, and March 2, 1857, are missing. They could have been destroyed in the rain just before my father brought the collection home, or perhaps lost or destroyed at an earlier date. An 1877 membership book notes that Boguille became a member on August 1, 1852, and was dismissed on February 1, 1877, after owing three dollars in dues for more than six months, along with a suspension tax of five dollars. The minutes note that Boguille was ill during this period.

He hung up his coat: ESM, February 20, 1836, describes the furnishings.

"presume to conceive themselves": These proscriptions were included in section 40 of Louisiana's Black Code of 1806 (*Acts Passed at the First Session of the First Legislature of the Territory of Orleans*, 188–91). Compiled by Louis Moreau Lislet and James Brown and published in 1808 as *A Digest of the Civil Laws Now in Force in the Territory of Orleans*, Louisiana's civil code established distinct categories for slaves, manumitted slaves, and "those who have preserved their natural liberty," without making explicit reference to race (book 1, title 1, chap. 2, articles 13–15). Many free people of color took this to mean they had equality with whites, while others were more cautious. See Palmer, *Through the Codes Darkly*, 116–20, and Scott, "She . . . Refuses," 131–35.

served in the First Battalion: Pierson, *Louisiana Soldiers*, 22, 86, 93.

He was the father: A plaque on the house at 1801 Dauphine identifies it as having been built for "Charles Laveaux, a free man of color said to be the father of the voodoo queen, Marie Laveaux."

The Dupart house sat: ESM, January 24, 1836, identifies Dupart's home as the location of the meeting. Dupart's store, at 25 Great Men, and home, at 23 History, are now united as a single house with the address of 1801 Dauphine.

The names that are mentioned: ESM, January 24, 1836.

"when the faith of the State": *Boisdoré and Goulé v. Citizens' Bank*, at 00733. Boisdoré had purchased 200 shares of stock (worth $20,000) and Goulé had purchased 150 shares (worth $15,000) when the bank was chartered by the legislature on April 1, 1833 (at 00723).

The bank had to keep: *Boisdoré and Goulé v. Citizens' Bank*, at 00881–84.

Wherever civilization carries: ESM, March 15, 1836.

there was debate: In the succession record, Andrénette and Ludger are identified as free people of color; documentation of their marriage, at St. Louis Cathedral, makes no reference to race. Andrénette's death certificate identifies her as a free woman of color; her father is identified as a colored man, while the race of her mother is not given, which usually means white (A. Lamy succession).

Because of the structure: Sachse, "Evolution of the Regime of Tutorship," 418.

"if the candidate is elected": ESM, March 17, 1858.

The Economie members brought: ESM, February 1, 1841. An accounting of funds from a ball held on January 10 shows the profits going to the Dames de la Charité—possibly the Daughters of Charity, a religious order whose members had begun working in a local hospital in 1834. Another group with a similar name, the Dames Hospitalier, or Ladies of Charity, founded a school for free colored girls in 1823 with the support of the Black community (Bell, *Revolution*, 28).

They rejected some people: ESM, September 15, 1857. The members discuss the candidacy of Joseph Smith, whom they describe as "un vicieux" and "un jouer."

whom they called *gentilshommes*: ESM, July 1, 1912.

Boguille carried himself: See Stewart, "Fashioning Frenchness," especially 544–46, for a discussion of the free colored community as exemplars and purveyors of high fashion in New Orleans. At one meeting a few years after Boguille's initiation, the membership was asked to spend less money on clothing so they could provide more support for the building fund (ESM, October 1, 1857).

creating a *"signe mystérieux"*: ESM, January 2, 1837.

One of the deputies: Although the minutes of Boguille's initiation are lost, the ceremony followed the same procedure for decades.

At one initiation: ESM, July 15, 1857.

"Divine Providence, bless our new Brother": ESM, December 15, 1857.

twenty-five dollars: ESM, March 15, 1836.

about a month's salary: For contemporary wages, see Margo, "North-South Wage Gap," 37, table 2, which sets $1.00 as the average daily wage for a common laborer in the south-central US during the period 1851–55.

He received a certificate: References to the tradition of greeting new members with a blessing, diploma, and official accolade appear regularly in the minutes.

Gentlemen, the committee: ESM, November 15, 1837.

an entire library: Among the books rescued by my father, Mohamed J. Shaik, PhD, and held privately by the Shaik-Little family are Charles van Tenac, *Histoire générale de la marine*, vol. 1 (Paris, 1847); Etienne Bézout, *Cours de mathématiques, à l'usage des gardes du pavillon et de la marine* (Paris, [1796]); *Procès des Ministres de Charles X, compte rendu littéral, et séance par séance, des débats à la Chambre des Pairs* [...] (Paris, 1830); and Philippe Le Bas (with Charles Weiss), *Précis d'histoire des temps modernes, depuis la formation du système d'équilibre des États européens jusqu'à la Révolution française* (Paris, 1842).

"the mulatto seems": Saint-Rémy, *Pétion et Haïti*, 28.

"It is thus that the colored population": Saint-Rémy, *Pétion et Haiti*, 27.

The son of Haitian president: The travels of a man, considered to be President Boyer's son, are described in Freund, *Gustav Dressel's Houston Journal*, 54.

Boguille Teaches His Own

Education . . . would become equally dangerous: Drayton, *South Vindicated*, 68–69.

Beginning in 1840: The 1840 census lists Boguille as the head of a fifty-one-person establishment whose occupants are broken out by race (all free people of color) and age cohort. USFCC, *Sixth Census of the United States* (1840), New Orleans, Ward 3, Ancestry.com. Additional documentation of Boguille's career as a teacher appears in the 1851, 1852, 1854, 1857, and 1861 New Orleans city directories. The neighborhood's residential and commercial fabric emerges in city directories from the 1820s, 30s, 40s, and 50s; the *New Orleans General Guide and Land Intelligence* map of 1841 by S. Pinistri; and property records in the New Orleans Notarial Archives. Additional information about the school's location was gleaned from Stern, *Race and Education* (34–35), and from the author's conversation with geographer Richard Campanella (August 10, 2018).

The Economie's library included: An 1806 edition of Stéphanie Félicité de Genlis's *Les annales de la vertu, ou histoire universelle, iconographique et littéraire* is another of the books rescued by my father.

"As soon as children arrive": Fénelon, *Fénelon's Treatise on the Education of Girls*, 29–30.

"When fortune threatens": Fénelon, *Adventures of Telemachus: In English Verse*, 36.

Fénelon's epic: There are no descriptions of Boguille's classroom. But because he named his son François Fénelon, I believe that he knew and admired the poet's famous *Adventures of Telemachus.*

"Vice alone is low": Desdunes invokes these lines in his portrait of poet and educator Armand Lanusse (*Our People*, 15).

One day, the free father: When Boguille taught the enslaved boy, he exploited a technicality in the law that allowed a master to request an education for his slave, conceivably to use the person to work in a business. An 1866 *Harper's New Monthly Magazine* article on educational opportunities for Louisiana's "colored population" cited Boguille's experience as an example of the biases still present in postwar New Orleans. In some private schools, the author reported, the children needed to be "bleached with an admixture of Caucasian blood" to be admitted, while in others the students' color was not so important as their class: "the great majority of the Professors make the social condition of the parents the only criterion. The majority of these schools are open to all pupils who were born free, and whose parents can afford to pay the monthly stipend required" (Willey, "Education," 247).

Boguille could not afford: Willey, "Education," 247.

I bequeath and order: Medley, "Will," 16.

In 1848, a school opened: Bell, *Revolution*, 123–26.

"for any literary": Bell, *Revolution*, 124.

Economiste François Lacroix: Bell, *Revolution*, 123–24.

Land for a school: Neidenbach, "'Mes dernières volontés'"; Desdunes, *Our People*, 102–6.

The school's first principal: Ochs, "Rock of New Orleans"; Desdunes, *Our People*, 104; Bell, *Revolution*, 125.

she married André Cailloux: Marriage record of Félicie Coulon and Andre Cailloux, June 22, 1847, New Orleans, Louisiana, Marriage Records Index, 1831–1964, Ancestry.com; Ochs, "Rock of New Orleans."

"prided himself": Brown, *The Negro*, 168–69: "One of the most efficient officers was Capt. André Cailloux, a man whose identity with his race could not be mistaken; for he prided himself on being the blackest man in the Crescent City."

Armand Lanusse: Desdunes, *Our People*, 14.

"he made no distinctions": Desdunes, *Our People*, 18.

Nelson Fouché: Secondary sources have long conflated the father and son of this name. Desdunes identifies the elder Nelson Fouché as one of the "patriots" whose oversight established the Couvent Institute on a firm footing in its early decades (*Our People*, 21). Born in Jamaica, he was fifty years old at the time of the 1850 census. It may have been he rather than his son—born in 1824 and commonly referred to as "Louis Nelson" in the Economy minutes—who served on the school's faculty. USFCC, *Seventh Census of the United States* (1850), New Orleans, Municipality 3, Ward 1, Ancestry.com.

Basile Crocker: Desdunes, *Our People*, 66. A January 30, 1879, death notice in *L'Abeille de la Nouvelle-Orléans* states Crocker's age as seventy-nine, which would have made him older than his brother Pierre.

only about 15 percent: Roser and Ortiz-Ospina, "Literacy."

I am happy to inform you: Rev. C. K. Marshall to Dr. Samuel Cartwright, October 23, 1854, Samuel A. Cartwright and Family Papers, Louisiana State University Libraries.

the decorated physician: Biographical/Historical Note, Samuel A. Cartwright and Family Papers, Louisiana State University Libraries.

Local physicians: See Cartwright, "Diseases and Peculiarities," 64.

Later critics: See Breeden, "States-Rights Medicine," for an overview.

Professor of Diseases of the Negro: Postell, "Principles of Medical Practice," 196.

"Dysaesthesia Aethiopis": Cartwright, "Diseases and Peculiarities," 333–36; Haller, "The Negro and the Southern Physician," 249–50.

"A remarkable ethnological peculiarity": Cartwright, "Ethnology of the Negro," 10, 14.

"whether educated or not": Cartwright, "Ethnology of the Negro," 13.

"conclusions were incorrect": Marshall, "Samuel Cartwright," 77–78.

THE AGE OF PRIDE

Boguille Takes His Place in the Economie Leadership

Conforming to article 19: ESM, March 2, 1857.

the Economistes' generosity: ESM, December 5, 1840; February 1, 1841.

a significant sum: The task of calculating the value of $369 relative to the wages of "the average Louisiana worker" in the 1840s is complicated by the fact that a significant portion of the state's manual labor was performed by the enslaved. While a robust body of scholarship has examined the economics of slavery, and the effects of an enslaved labor force on the pay scale for free workers, those broader questions are outside the purview of this note. Historical wage data is sparse for the early 1840s, but by 1850, paid agricultural laborers in Louisiana were earning $12.80 per month (Lebergott, "Wage Trends," 453). That same year, the daily wage for a carpenter in the "south central" portion of the US was $1.66 (Margo, "North-South Wage Gap," 34). And the annual pay for unskilled labor in 1850, nationally, was $82.50 (Officer and Williamson, "Annual Wages"). The sum of $369, while holding different value for different individuals, would nonetheless represent a significant amount of money for the average Louisiana worker—anywhere from three-quarters of a year's salary for a skilled laborer to more than four years' earnings for an unskilled laborer.

one member proposed: ESM, February 1, 1841; June 17, 1841.

They accomplished it: The land for the new hall was purchased from Elizabeth Conty, a free woman of color (A. E. Bienvenu, notary public, July 20, 1853, NONA).

Member William Belley: For the building contract with William Belley, see Joseph Lisbony, notary public, September 4, 1856, NONA.

Its railing would be smooth: The railing appears in photographs of the wreckage of the hall taken in 1965, in the aftermath of Hurricane Betsy (William Russell Jazz Collection at THNOC, 92-48-L.331.1266, 92-48-L.331.1271).

Belley's plans specified: ESM, August 3, 1857.

gumbo, pâté, and liquor: ESM, August 3, 1857. The *gardienne* had been selling refreshments both before and during meetings, until she was asked to halt sales fifteen minutes before meetings started.

gold lettering spelled out: ESM, May 4, 1857. Boguille made the motion, which was approved, to collect 20 cents from each member "pour réalise le montant qui sera réclamé pour graver l'inscription . . . en lettres d'or sur le promont de la Nouvelle Salle, du titre de la Société d'Economie ainsi que la ruche qui est notre allégeance" ("to gather the amount needed to engrave the name of the Economie Society in gold letters on the pediment of the new hall, along with the beehive to which we are devoted").

real estate valued at $15 million: Willey, "Education," 248.

a literacy rate: *Seventh Census*, "Statistics of Louisiana, Table 1—Population by Parishes—Age, Color, and Condition—Aggregates," 468–70, and "Statistics of Louisiana, Table 9—Adults in the State Who Cannot Read or Write," 480.

Even in New York: *Statistical View*, "Occupations of Free Colored Males over Fifteen Years, Distinguishing Blacks and Mulattoes—1850," 80–81, table 70.

"offering to the society as a gift": ESM, October 1, 1838.

"Always observe with veneration": ESM, October 15, 1838. Jonau had received the portrait from the estate of Charles Laveaux, whose house at Great Men and History Streets was where the Economie men held their first meeting. The president complimented the deceased Laveaux for "his liberalism and his veneration" of the Haitian president.

Yes, brother Economistes: ESM, April 15, 1857.

The president told the members: ESM, April 15, 1857.

"The society has contracted debts": ESM, October 1, 1857. Boisdoré gave the $2,000 loan on April 15, 1857 (ESM). This impassioned plea from Lanna took place months later, while the members were still paying off debts. I have condensed the action for the sake of the narrative.

master carpenters and plasterers: See Hankins and Maklansky, *Raised to the Trade*, for the long history of Creole craftsmanship in New Orleans. The history of the trades was passed father to son in New Orleans. My cousin, his father, and his grandfather talked history in this way as they worked in the 1960s.

"well-bred carpenter": ESM, July 15, 1857.

mahogany stairs placed just inside the entrance: A closeup of the staircase is among the images preserved in the William Russell Jazz Collection at THNOC, 92-48-L.331.1278.

"Let us prove to Europe": ESM, March 26, 1858.

"The achievement of our new building": ESM, April 15, 1857.

One great cause of the declension: *Population of the United States in 1860*, Introduction, x–xi.

"Gentlemen, the Société d'Economie": ESM, August 15, 1857.

"Dysæsthesia Æthiopis is a disease": Cartwright, "Diseases and Peculiarities," 333.

"cruel and superstitious, so ignorant": "Model Negro Empire," 204, 207.

equal accounting of the barbarism: Haiti was not formally recognized by the United States until 1862 and did not pay off its debt to France until 1947. See Matthewson, "Jefferson and the Nonrecognition of Haiti," for an assessment of the damaging effects of US diplomatic policy on the fledgling nation. See also Podur, *Haiti's New Dictatorship*, 6, 12–13.

"Such is the present condition": "Model Negro Empire," 211.

Proslavery advocates began to dominate: These writers "produced a voluminous literature critical of Haiti and its post-emancipation society. Demonizing the new Republic of Blacks, they offered Haiti as their chief objective argument against emancipation; they insisted that the Haitian violence arose from the character of Afro-Americans, not out of slavery itself" (Matthewson, "Jefferson," 37).

"The desire and yearning": Stowe, *Uncle Tom's Cabin*, 463–64.

"*the negro is not a white man*": "Dr. Cartwright's Letter to the Hon. Daniel Webster," *Concordia Intelligencer*, August 16, 1851, morning edition.

"a slave by Nature": "Dr. Cartwright's Letter to the Hon. Daniel Webster," *Concordia Intelligencer*, August 16, 1851, morning edition.

Among them was Solomon Northup: Northup's memoir, *Twelve Years a Slave,* originally published in 1853, was reissued by Louisiana State University Press in 1968 and adapted as a feature film in 2013.

European immigrants replaced: Reinders, "Free Negro," 276–77, 283.

the Louisiana legislature approved: "An Act Relative to Slaves and Free Colored Persons" was passed on March 15, 1855. See *Acts Passed by the Second Legislature*, 376–91, for the full, bilingual text. Section 88 (p. 389) addresses the right to carry weapons; section 91 (p. 390) prohibits bringing free people of color into Louisiana and passing them off as slaves; sections 92–98 (pp. 390–91) address travel.

Additional laws required: See Schafer, *Becoming Free*, chap. 6.

John Brown: See Bordewich, "John Brown's Day of Reckoning," for a cogent retelling of the events leading up to the raid on Harpers Ferry.

"The St. Domingo negro": Miles, *The Relation between the Races*, quoted in Hunt, *Haiti's Influence on Antebellum America*, 141.

"their association and example": "The Governor's Message," *Daily Picayune*, January 21, 1857.

similar resolutions across the nation: "Removal of Free Negroes from Missouri," *Daily Picayune*, December 14, 1855; "Removal of Free Negroes" (a report from the North Carolina legislature), *Daily Picayune*, November 19, 1852; "The Maryland Slaveholders' Convention," *Daily Picayune*, June 15, 1859; "Oregon Constitution," *Daily Advocate*, December 3, 1857.

By 1850 immigrants: Fussell, "Constructing New Orleans," fig. 1, "Population of New Orleans by Race, Legal Status, and Nativity, in Percentages, 1769–2000," 847.

"The community has a right": "Free Negroes," *Daily Picayune*, January 17, 1859, afternoon edition.

"genmen of color": Reddick, "The Negro in the New Orleans Press," provides a list of derogatory terms for people of color, both free and enslaved, used in the 1850s (205–6, 256).

"A lot of Creoles, and Spaniards": "Two Brief Lectures," *Daily True Delta*, December 11, 1859, supplement.

Slander is terribly cruel: ESM, June 8, 1857. This observation, from member Porée, came in reference to gossip about admitting Adolph Plique as a member.

Jean Guillaume: Death record of Jean Guillaume Boguille, March 5, 1852 (New Orleans, Louisiana, Death Records Index, 1804–1949, Ancestry.com).

Their daughter arrived: Therese Antoinette Boguille was born to Marie Françoise Filliette Marchand and Ludger Boguille on June 5, 1852 (New Orleans, Louisiana, Birth Records Index, 1790–1915, Ancestry.com). Although a firm identification is impossible, it appears highly likely that the Marie Françoise listed as the mother of Therese Antoinette was married to another man, Louis Marsden Davidson, during much of the pregnancy. According to many Marsden and Davidson family trees on Ancestry.com, Davidson died on April 1, 1852, but I was unable to find any documentation of this death date. In the 1892 city directory, Marie Davidson is listed as the widow of Louis M. Davidson. The 1860 census finds an eight-year-old girl named Angella Davidson living with four older Davidson children and a "Mrs. Marchand" (age forty-three and a washerwoman) in New Orleans's Fifth Ward. Ten years later, an eighteen-year-old Angela Boguille is living with fifty-three-year-old Mary Davidson, also in the Fifth Ward. The concordant ages and familiar names could be coincidence, but it seems more likely that Marie/Mary raised her daughter within the Davidson household and called her by a name less freighted than the one bestowed upon her by her birth father. USFCC, *Eighth Census of the United States* (1860), New Orleans, Ward 5, Ancestry.com; USFCC, *Ninth Census of the United States* (1870), New Orleans, Ward 5, Ancestry.com. Angela Boguille next appears in the archival record in 1876, upon her marriage to Ulysses M. Lartigue, a cigarmaker. The Lartigue and Davidson families are registered together in early twentieth-century Economy Society records—perhaps not conclusive proof that Angela Davidson, Angela Boguille, and Therese Antoinette Boguille are one and the same, but suggestive nonetheless. Marriage contract of Angela Boguille and Ulysses M. Lartigue, October 7, 1876 (New Orleans, Louisiana, Marriage Records Index, 1831–1964, Ancestry.com); 1875 New Orleans city directory; ESM, January 2, 1913.

"Poor little girl": Nagel, *Marie-Therese*, 23.

Mary Ann Taff was an English teacher: The 1850 census shows Mary Ann as twenty-eight years old and Ludger as thirty-eight; USFCC, *Seventh Census of the United States* (1850), New Orleans, Ward 7, Ancestry.com. The city's death records show her year of birth as 1815, which would mean she was thirty-five in 1850 (New Orleans, Louisiana, Death Records Index, 1804–1949, Ancestry.com). The 1860 census lists Mary Ann as forty years old and Ludger as forty-eight (USFCC, *Eighth Census of the United States* [1860], New Orleans, Ward 6, Ancestry.com). The records surrounding Mary Ann's maiden name are similarly inconsistent. In the 1850 census, her last name is listed as Jeffe. In the marriage certificate for her son Pierre Butel Boguille (listed as Butelle Boguille), she is identified as Mary A. Wise (Louisiana, Orleans Parish Marriages, 1837–1957, FamilySearch.org). Her death records all provide the last name Taff (New Orleans, Louisiana, Death Records Index, 1804–1949; Louisiana, Statewide Death Index, 1819–1964; and Louisiana, Wills and Probate Records, 1756–1984, all on Ancestry.com). Although the 1850 census says she was born in New York, I was unable to locate any record of Mary Ann in New York under any of the spellings of her last name. I have settled on using Taff as Mary Ann's maiden name.

By 1851 Mary Ann was teaching: 1851 New Orleans city directory.

But she was also white: In the 1850 census, Mary Ann is listed as mulatto, along with everyone else in the household. But in the 1860 census, her race is not listed, while Ludger and the couple's children are listed as mulatto. It was not uncommon for a census taker to designate everyone in a household as mulatto if he wasn't sure of the races, but he would not give the white designation (by omitting any race notation) to a woman in the household unless that information was clear. USFCC, *Seventh Census of the United States* (1850), New Orleans, Ward 7, Ancestry.com; USFCC, *Eighth Census of the United States* (1860), New Orleans, Ward 6, Ancestry.com.

two minor children: Alida and Zephir (sometimes called Pierre Zephir or P. Z.) appear to be the children of Mary Ann Taff and Zephir Canonge. P. Z. Canonge marriage record, February 23, 1876, Louisiana, Orleans Parish Marriages, 1837–1957, FamilySearch.org.

Mary Ann and Ludger were listed: 1851, 1852, 1854, 1857 New Orleans city directories.

Pierre Butel: Pierre Butel Boguille birth record, December 23, 1857, New Orleans, Louisiana, Birth Records Index, 1790–1915, Ancestry.com.

Jean Horace: Jean Horace Boguille birth record, June 29, 1859, New Orleans, Louisiana, Birth Records Index, 1790–1915, Ancestry.com.

In 1861 the family moved: 1861 New Orleans city directory.

The location of the new Boguille home: Boguille's address at 198 Esplanade Street is annotated on the Robinson atlas (plate 7, square 172). By cross-referencing the lot size and house configuration with the drawing in Toledano and Christovich's *Esplanade Ridge* (70–71), I was able to determine that the current address is 1322 Esplanade Avenue. The structure that presently stands at 1322 Esplanade was built in the 1880s, so it is not the house in which the Boguilles lived.

"the arbiter of the destiny": ESM, August 15, 1857.

Do not offer fodder: ESM, July 15, 1857.

a twenty-three-page pamphlet: A notice in the July 1857 issue of the *African Repository and Colonial Journal* mentions the pamphlet, "Facts in Regard to Colonization: A Memorial Addressed to the Citizens of Louisiana by the Louisiana Colonization Society: New Orleans" (315).

"I am forced to say": ESM, March 24, 1857.

Secretary Boguille wrote: ESM, March 24, 1857.

Tempers flared again: ESM, June 8, 1857.

"What is this, my brothers?" ESM, June 8, 1857.

"He has no children": ESM, July 27, 1857.

"When you push away an honest man": ESM, July 27, 1857.

a lecture about brotherhood: ESM, August 3, 1857. The eloquent victim, described in the minutes as Jh. Rousseau, was undoubtedly Joseph Colastin Rousseau, an author and attorney who emigrated to Haiti prior to the Civil War. Desdunes, *Our People*, 81; Sollors, *Multilingual America*, 30.

the members voted the same night: ESM, August 3, 1857.

the *New Orleans Bee* reported: "The Dred Scott Case," *New Orleans Bee*, March 14, 1857.

the French edition of the paper: "La Cour Suprême des États-Unis et l'esclavage," *L'Abeille de la Nouvelle-Orléans*, March 16, 1857.

The men who framed: *Dred Scott v. Sandford*, 60 U.S. 393 (1856), at 410.

police durant la séance: ESM, March 2, 1857; March 24, 1857; April 15, 1857. Boguille continued to document the presence of police through December 1857. Then, as suddenly as the notes had appeared, they were gone. The reason for the police visits, perhaps, was the city's new law that every gathering of colored people needed white supervision. For the Economistes, that wouldn't have been an insurmountable problem. They could secure a relative. Another reason may have been that the Economistes began to pay the police to provide security at the hall's dances.

"any free black man": Desdunes, *Our People*, 110–11.

Alfred Noel and Joseph Abélard: ESM, March 20, 185[7].

The night he entered the hall: ESM, May 18, 1857.

By June 1857: ESM, May 18, 1857.

Boguille had read a letter aloud: ESM, August 3, 1857.

Brother Fouché presents a portrait: ESM, July 8, 1857.

Choctaw from across Lake Pontchartrain: Gregory, "Indians and Folklife in the Florida Parishes."

Fouché's mission: ESM, July 8, 1857. Louis Nelson Fouché's mission was discussed at the society's first meeting in its new hall.

The Fouchés were well suited: The 1850 census documents two individuals named Nelson Fouché sharing a New Orleans residence. The elder, born in Jamaica and aged 50, is

identified as a beer merchant. The younger, born in Louisiana and aged 26, is identified as
an architect (USFCC, *Seventh Census of the United States* [1850], New Orleans, Municipality 3, Ward 1, Ancestry.com). It appears that father as well as son had experience in
the building trades: a "Nelson Fouché" appears as a bricklayer in the 1832 New Orleans
city directory, at a time when the son would have been a mere eight years old. The elder
Fouché is also identified as a builder in Toledano and Christovich, *Creole Faubourgs*, 107.

Doresmond Crocker went to court: In *Becoming Free*, Schafer discusses the case, identifying
Dominique Petit, the children's owner, as a free man of color (61–62). According to his
will, Petit was a native of Hautes-Pyrénées, in France; the document does not indicate
his race, although the absence of such notation is telling. Petit owned seven slaves when
he died, including Doresmond Crocker's nephews. Will of Dominigue [Dominique]
Petit, January 4, 1831, Louisiana, Wills and Probate Records, 1756–1984, Ancestry.com.

Jim Bowie: Bowie's trade in enslaved people is referenced in Bailey, "Jim Bowie," and his
alcoholism in Austerman, "Aguardiente at the Alamo," 74, 77–80.

When Comonfort became president: Enacted in June 1856, the Lerdo Law (authored by
Comonfort's finance minister, Miguel Lerdo de Tejada) was a profound challenge to the
authority of the clergy.

The Proprietors of the Hacienda: Veracruz-Llave, *Documens (traduits) relatifs à la colonie
d'Eureka*, 3.

All of the Economistes could go: Veracruz-Llave, *Documens (traduits) relatifs à la colonie
d'Eureka*, 8.

"My brothers, I ask": ESM, July 8, 1857.

Let us prove: ESM, March 26, 1858.

Pierre Crocker came to the meeting: ESM, July 1, 1857.

he ran a brokerage: Pierre Crocker is listed in the 1855 New Orleans city directory at 292
St. Philip Street, domicile, and 65 Exchange Place, brokerage.

"Money—Money—Money": *Daily Picayune*, August 6, 1858.

Commerce bustled: *Daily Delta*, February 6, 1858; *Daily Picayune*, August 6, 1858; *Daily
Picayune*, February 24, 1858.

At the real estate exchange: "Lease of the Merchants' and Auctioneers' Exchange," *Daily
Picayune*, May 2, 1866, describes the scene on Saturdays.

Crocker had recently brokered: Long, *New Orleans Voudou Priestess*, 80–82.

eleven real estate transactions: The transactions are indexed among the conveyance office
records now held in the Land Records Division of the Office of the Clerk of Civil District
Court for the Parish of Orleans. See conveyance office books 7/323, 7/519, 19/568, 19/553,
20/223, 21/437, 21/621, 21/622, 22/87, 22/465, and 22/685.

on the night of July 1: ESM, July 1, 1857.

Boguille read it aloud: ESM, July 8, 1857. Crocker's letter was dated July 7, 1857.

an apparent suicide: Crocker's letter confessing his guilt and shame supports the supposi-
tion that his death was a suicide. Daggett reaches a similar conclusion in *Spiritualism in
Nineteenth-Century New Orleans* (52), noting that Crocker's ghost appeared at a séance
to discuss having "succumbed to a weakness" (Spiritualist register 85-34, November 30,
1871, 104, Grandjean Collection).

The Economie minutes did not mention: ESM, July 15, 1857.

met at St. Augustine Church: *Courrier de la Louisiane*, July 10, 1857.

Secretary Boguille recorded a dispute: ESM, July 15, 1857.

printed on the front page: "Lettre de Pierre Crocker à Mme Héloise Glapïon," *L'Abeille de
la Nouvelle-Orléans*, July 14, 1857.

The essence of fraternity: ESM, June 15, 1857.

the *Daily Picayune* reported: "The City: Police Matters," and "The Courts," *Daily Picayune*, July 4, 1857.

"A great misfortune came": "Lettre de Pierre Crocker à Mme Héloïse Glapion," *L'Abeille de la Nouvelle-Orléans*, July 14, 1857.

A free carpenter would need: In Louisiana, a free carpenter's day wages, circa 1850, were $2.36, necessitating nearly two-and-a-half years to earn $1,700 (*Statistical View*, "Table 175—Average Wages, 1850," 164). A great deal of the carpentry performed in Louisiana, of course, was the work of enslaved laborers.

Marie Héloïse Euchariste Glapion: Long, *Voudou Priestess*, 51–56.

Rose, Marie Elizabeth, Henriette, and Mathilde: Long, *Voudou Priestess*, 240.

Joseph Ernest and Joseph Eugene died as infants: For Joseph Eugene, Héloïse Glapion's son, see Ward, *Voodoo Queen*, 71–72, and Long, *Voudou Priestess*, 66–67, 163. For Joseph Ernest, Rose Gignac's son, see Long, *Voudou Priestess*, 240.

His message to "Eucarice": "Lettre de Pierre Crocker à Mme Héloïse Glapion," *L'Abeille de la Nouvelle-Orléans*, July 14, 1857.

"My God. By tomorrow": ESM, July 15, 1857.

and locked the book away: I was in the New Orleans Public Library looking at the letter from Pierre Crocker to "Eucarice" when I saw a neighborhood acquaintance, historian Barbara Trevigne. I asked her whether she knew these people. She told me they were her ancestors.

Boguille Takes the High Road

All the get-togethers must be composed: ESM, December 28, 1857.

Now Boguille wrote in the journals: ESM, March 26, 1858.

on the night of October 19: ESM, October 19, 1857.

the preparations for inauguration day: ESM, December 1, 1857.

Liautaud was the former head: In the classic late-nineteenth-century survey *Music and Some Highly Musical People*, James Monroe Trotter describes Adolphe Liautaud as "one of the best performers on the cornet in New Orleans" and observes that Sidney Lambert "became conspicuous for brilliant execution on the piano-forte, and as a composer of music for that and other instruments" (339, 346).

Boguille recorded a deliberation: ESM, December 7, 1857.

"The president urges them": ESM, December 15, 1857.

Come to the hall at a good hour: ESM, December 18, 1857.

"Let us love one another": ESM, March 24, 1858, quoting the December 20, 1857, blessing.

Adolphe Liautaud directed the orchestra: ESM, December 28, 1857.

Resolution to show gratitude: ESM, December 28, 1857.

the men felt good about themselves: ESM, December 28, 1857.

Boguille noted in the week's minutes: ESM, December 22, 1857 (rules for children's balls); April 1, 1858 (rules broken at children's balls).

The members made other rules: ESM, December 28, 1857.

The Economie installed gaslights: ESM, December 25, 1857. The cost of installing the gas was $185.65.

a minimum of four guests: ESM, December 22, 1857.

the society sent $54.74: ESM, December 28, 1857. According to Boguille's meticulous accounting, ticket sales brought in $89.75, of which $35 went to cover expenses. The balance was given to charity: "To brother Martinez for L'Institution des Orphelins $10.00. To [Martinez] for John, blind, in Monsieur Frank Vidal's house $2.00. To Martinez for Jean, blind, in the house of Madame Henriette Macarty $2.00. Totaling $14; To Martinez for the Sister of Ferrand, Mlle. Fsy, mute $2.00. To Casanave for the daughter of Constance daughter of Manine $4.00. To [Casanave] for a blind girl on Ursulines Street $1.50. To F. Galle for Madame Chauchoute $1.50. To Fournier for Mr. Valentin, who fell during the construction of our Hall $4.75. To A. Angelain for Mr. Bélisaire $2.00. To Frilot for Mme. B. Beaulieu and her family $4.00; To [Frilot] for Mme. Emélie $2.00. To Dussuau for Narcisse and Fillette Dauphin $4.00. To Capla for [?] André Esclavon $2.00. To Casanave for Mournais $2.00. To Boguille for Rose Martin $2.00.; To Boisdoré Jr. for Francis Hazeur $2.00. To Casanave for Paulin $2.00. To Jolypère for Edouard, blind, and his sisters $5.00. Total $54.74."

at a time when the price: The costs of goods and entertainments are drawn from the advertising supplement pages of the December 23, 1857, issue of the *Daily True Delta*.

"Brothers, Economistes": ESM, March 21, 1858.

Boguille copied his speech word for word: ESM, March 21, 1858. The meeting's minutes capture the voices of several speakers, along with Boguille's poem, in the original French:

> Frère Lanna, je reçois ces conserves
> Que l'amitié me donne sans réserves;
> Elles feront ma vive admiration
> En avançant mon humble éducation
> Par les moyens de cultiver l'étude,
> Ce digne Ami de notre solitude!
> Votre présent est un gage d'amour,
> Que mon franc cœur conservera toujours.
> Lorsque, mes yeux verront par vos lunettes
> Mes facultés seront des plus complètes.
> Recevez donc, mes frères, par mes yeux,
> Les doux souhaits venus du-haut des cieux!!

The Further Erosion of Rights

The color of the slave: Drayton, *South Vindicated*, 113.

"Have you ever asked yourself": ESM, March 26, 1858.

"My great aim has been": Josiah Clark Nott to Ephraim G. Squier, May 4, 1850, quoted in Brace, "'Ethnology' of Josiah Clark Nott," 514. See also Erickson, "Anthropology of Josiah Clark Nott," for an overview of Nott's career.

"Man is free": ESM, May 10, 1858.

"This African blood": ESM, March 26, 1858.

some 15,000 people: Reinders, *End of an Era*, 27, quoted in Spain, "Race Relations and Residential Segregation," 85.

The condition of the negro: "The African Importation Scheme," *New Orleans Bee,* March 16, 1858. See also chap. 3 of Schafer, *Becoming Free,* which discusses the increased restrictions against manumission before the Civil War, and "Labor in the French Colonies," *Daily True Delta*, February 28, 1858, which obliquely suggests that planters should import "coolie" laborers from Africa to circumvent the law banning the international slave trade.

"In every Southern State": "The Slave Trade Project," *New York Times*, March 13, 1858.

fueled the nation's prosperity: For data and cost analyses, see Rhodes, *History of the United States*, 305–7; Fogel, "New Economic History," 279; Calomiris and Pritchett, "Betting on Secession," 13; and Foust and Swan, "Productivity and Profitability," 44, 57. As Williamson and Cain observe in "Measuring Slavery," the average price of an enslaved person in 1850 "was roughly equal to the average price of a house, so the purchase of even one slave would have given the purchaser some status."

"I've known him": ESM, January 25, 1858. I am suggesting that "Mulâtre Américain" in this context refers to the offspring of an Anglo- or Anglo-American white person and a free person of color or enslaved person.

"Let us beat down egoism": ESM, May 10, 1858.

The building sparkled: ESM, January 4, 1858; June 18, 1858.

"What are the sentiments": ESM, May 10, 1858.

The members chanted: ESM, May 10, 1858.

he resigned his position: ESM, May 10, 1858. "On the motion of brother Bernard, seconded by brother Davis and acclaimed by the group, the demission was accepted. Brother Boguille informed the assembly that he had begun to copy the minutes into a new book for the society, and if the society would give him time, he would be able to transcribe them."

Persac painted idyllic scenes: Bacot et al., *Marie Adrien Persac*, 65, 71, 104.

their plan to emigrate: ESM, July 8, 1857. Plans for the settlement are outlined in Veracruz-Llave, *Documens (traduits) relatifs à la colonie d'Eureka*.

"the only man of political eminence": "The Latter Days of the Mexican Republic," *New York Times,* February 17, 1858.

He came to New Orleans: A *New York Times* dispatch datelined February 10, 1858, documented Comonfort's approach to New Orleans: "The steamer *Tennessee* from Vera Cruz is coming up the river and Generals Comonfort and Garcia Conde are passengers. The *Tennessee* will be up at 5 p.m." ("Highly Important from Mexico," February 11, 1858).

"Remember that we have brothers": ESM, March 21, 1858.

Yellow fever was raging: NOPL, "Yellow Fever Deaths."

"Brother Frilot announced": ESM, August 9, 1858.

Comonfort left New Orleans: The former president's "deportment in the [train] cars on the route from New-Orleans was not such as to render him popular with those who traveled with him," observed the *Times* correspondent in an August 22, 1878, dispatch ("Affairs in Virginia," *New York Times*, September 1, 1858).

"That the people of the United States": "The Tribune on Mexico," *New York Times*, March 16, 1858. The *Times*'s advocacy of empire was not a universal sentiment; other contemporary dailies expressed concerns about US interventions abroad, as noted in "Mexico and the Tribune," *New York Times,* April 20, 1858. For additional discussion of the emigration of Louisianans to Veracruz, see Bell, *Revolution*, 86, and Gehman, "Louisiana Creoles."

THE AGE OF COURAGE

From the Militia to the Meeting

In spite of this unforeseen dismemberment: ESM, January 24, 1836. The Economie grew out of a schism in the Société d'Epargnes.

twenty new members: ESM, March 1, 1864. While the Economie minutes from August 1858 to March 1861 are missing, there is a book of expenses, titled "Caisse 1854," that shows receipts to 1860. This book documents that the Economie's members were still active in New Orleans during this period.

meeting on Sunday nights: The Economie minutes of June 1, 1858, record the Spiritualists' request to meet on Sundays in the Economie's hall.

Cercle Harmonique: Daggett, *Spiritualism*, 27–29. Daggett notes that Rey apparently derived the name of his Spiritualist group from A. J. Davis's Harmonial philosophy, which focused on ideals of unity and harmony.

figures like abolitionist John Brown: Grandjean Collection, series IX.1, book 85-32: 118; Daggett, *Spiritualism,* 52, 88–89, 124.

"Throw away the thoughts": quoted in Bellegarde-Smith, *Haiti*, 37–41.

"Each man in his sphere": quoted in Bell, *Revolution,* 220.

"Baptism of Blood": "Baptism of Blood," *Daily Picayune,* April 22, 1861.

"If . . . our independence": "Letter from Plaquemines Parish," *Daily Picayune*, April 21, 1861.

the Mounted Guards of Jefferson: *Daily Picayune,* April 21, 1861 (column 3 lists many units organizing). The *New Orleans Daily Crescent* reported that the "organization of the Confederate Guards was completed on Saturday night" ("The Confederate Guards," *New Orleans Daily Crescent,* April 22, 1861).

"to devise means": "Public Meeting," *Daily Picayune,* April 22, 1861.

"our oldest and most influential merchants": "Public Meeting at the Merchants' Exchange," *Daily Picayune,* April 23, 1861.

"uttered treasonable language": "Arrest under the Charge of Black Republicanism," *Daily Picayune,* April 23, 1861.

About half of the whites: *Ninth Census,* vol. 1, *Statistics of the Population of the United States,* table 2, "Population by Counties—1790–1870," State of Louisiana, 34. Whites increased from 77 percent of the population in 1850 to 85 percent in 1860, while the Black population decreased from 23 percent in 1850 to 15 percent in 1860.

Just under 20 percent: On the percentage and distribution of the ownership of enslaved persons in the United States in the nineteenth century, see Williamson and Cain, "Measuring Slavery."

large group of whites met: "Defenders of the Native Land," *Daily Picayune,* April 22, 1861.

"to repel any enemy": "The Colored Population Ready for the Fray," *Daily Picayune*, April 21, 1861.

"offer their services": "Meeting of the Free Colored Population," *Daily Picayune,* April 23, 1861. The Couvent School's Armand Lanusse, who Desdunes wrote was without prejudice, called together the meeting. Arnold Bertonneau, who would later meet with Frederick Douglass and William Lloyd Garrison, was also on the standing committee. Boguille is not listed but was undoubtedly present at the Couvent School meeting, since the school was his workplace and he later formed one of the militia units. Also see Hollandsworth, *Louisiana Native Guards*, 2.

a militia regiment of free people of color: Berry, "Negro Troops," 167.

On June 11, 1861: Minutes of the Economy Hall Native Guards, June 11, 1861, are on the back pages of the 1861 journal in the Grandjean Collection, series IX.1, book 85-30.

Boguille organized a company: For the military service records of Boguille and Zephir Canonge, see *Compiled Service Records of Confederate Soldiers Who Served in Organizations from the State of Louisiana,* Civil War Service Records (CMSR)—Confederate—Louisiana, Fold3.com. Boguille's rank is recorded as captain, Canonge's as lieutenant.

More than half of the eligible free men of color: According to Bergeron, "some fifteen hundred or more New Orleans free blacks made up the First Regiment Louisiana Native Guards" ("Free Men," 247). The 1860 census counted 10,939 free people of color in New Orleans. Of these, 2,338 were males aged 15 to 49—suggesting that more than half, and perhaps as many as two-thirds, of eligible individuals enlisted. *Population of the United States in 1860,* State of Louisiana, table 1, "Population by Age and Sex," 190–91.

"What will the Northerners": "Meeting of the Free Colored Population," *Daily Picayune*, April 23, 1861. On free people of color in the Confederate militia, see Stauffer, "Yes, There Were Black Confederates"; Nystrom, "African Americans"; Hollandsworth, *Louisiana Native Guards*, 3–6.

he had never sold anyone: Sales of enslaved people are included in the real estate transactions documented in the Land Records Division of the Office of the Clerk of Civil District Court for the Parish of Orleans. The conveyance records include indexes of vendors and vendees. I went through the names of every seller recorded in the index of vendors from the earliest of these compiled records (April 1, 1827) to October 8, 1864, when the sales ended. Boguille is not listed as having participated in any sales of people.

Henry, a man with no last name: USFCC, *Eighth Census of the United States* (1860), New Orleans, Ward 6, Ancestry.com.

remove any male of fourteen years or older: *Acts and Resolutions*, 16.

On November 22, 1861: "The Grand Review," *Daily True Delta*, November 22, 1861.

"If we had not volunteered": quoted in Hollandsworth, *Louisiana Native Guards,* 16.

The Native Guards have seen: "Our New Orleans Correspondence," *New York Times*, November 5, 1862.

leaving the Native Guards behind: Nystrom, "African Americans."

Adolphe Duhart, a gunsmith: USFCC, *Seventh Census of the United States* (1850), New Orleans, Municipality 3, Ward 1, Ancestry.com. The 1850 census lists an A. Duhart, gunsmith, mulatto, 40 years old, born in Cuba. In the 1851 city directory A. Duhart is listed as a gunsmith and lightning rod maker at 99 Elysian Fields.

Two of the hiding places: Desdunes, *Our People*, 118.

they couldn't have done any differently: Bell, *Revolution*, 231; Hollandsworth, *Louisiana Native Guards*, 16–18.

"Now, therefore, the Commanding General": quoted in "Department of the Gulf," *New York Times*, February 7, 1863.

had departed from their enslavers: Hollandsworth, *Louisiana Native Guards*, 17–18; Terry L. Jones, "Free Men of Color Go to War," *New York Times*, October 18, 2012.

"the number was too few": Desdunes, *Our People*, 120.

fifteen men of African descent: Terry L. Jones, "Free Men of Color Go to War," *New York Times*, October 18, 2012.

The Second Regiment: Berry, "Negro Troops," 174.

officers in the Union regiment: "Louisiana Native Guards."

"several were, to all superficial appearance": "Our New Orleans Correspondence: The First Louisiana Colored Regiment," *New York Times*, November 5, 1862.

"their line of march was marked by crowds": "Department of the Gulf," *New York Times*, February 7, 1863. The article notes that the First Native Guards were created on September 27, 1862, and that on October 27, 1862, they marched through the streets from the Louisiana racecourse (slightly northeast of the city) to Algiers.

"white complexion": "François Lacroix was of white complexion," according to the testimony of Thomy Lafon, a prominent Black businessman and philanthropist, in Lacroix's succession papers. Lafon's assessment was corroborated by John R. Clay, a New Orleans businessman (Succession of François Lacroix, Louisiana, Civil District Court [Orleans Parish] succession records, 1890–1903, docket no. 9804, VT290, City Archives, NOPL). For more information on Lacroix and his business partner Etienne Cordeviolle, see the online exhibition *The World of François Lacroix*, created by the New Orleans Public Library.

"coppery" colored with "crispy" hair: This description, by a French neighbor named DuBoys, appears on the second page of the English translation of the succession of

Etienne Cordeviolle, Louisiana, Civil District Court (Orleans Parish) succession records, 1890–1903, docket no. 3744, VT290, box 48, City Archives, NOPL. Cordeviolle died in Paris in 1868. His succession papers—written in French, English, and Italian—were originally held in the records of Louisiana's Second District Court but were moved to the Civil District Court when the succession was contested.

Writing from Camp Strong: Capt. H. L. R. [Henry L. Rey], "Correspondence, Camp Strong, Gentilly," *L'Union*, October 18, 1862.

Capt. Cailloux, of the First Louisiana: "Our Port Hudson Correspondence," *New York Times*, June 13, 1863.

joined the Union attack: National Park Service, "Port Hudson National Cemetery."

"On going into action": "Our Port Hudson Correspondence," *New York Times*, June 13, 1863.

born into bondage downriver: For a description of the early life and manumission of Cailloux, see Ochs, *Black Patriot*, 26–29.

member of Les Amis de l'Ordre: Mobley, "Crafting."

Thirty-six societies: "Our New-Orleans Correspondence," *New York Times*, August 8, 1863.

Cailloux's was the largest: For descriptions of the funeral procession, see "Funeral of Captain Andre Cailloux," 551; "Our New-Orleans Correspondence," *New York Times*, August 8, 1863; and Ochs, "Rock of New Orleans."

"justice, freedom and good government": "Our New-Orleans Correspondence," *New York Times*, August 8, 1863. On Maistre, see Logsdon and Bell, "Americanization," 233.

"To fall for our country": Dumas and Varney, "Les Girondins."

"Immense crowds of colored people": "Our New-Orleans Correspondence," *New York Times*, August 8, 1863.

"loved and respected" . . . "gallant bearing": The quotes from *L'Union* were included in the *New York Times* correspondent's August 8 report on Cailloux's funeral. The *Times's* article was excerpted in "Atlantic Intelligence," *Sacramento Daily Union*, September 1, 1863.

"A Defunct Darkey Canonized": The *New York World's* derisive article is quoted in the *New York Times's* pro-Cailloux rebuttal as an example of "unutterable baseness" and a "foul . . . spirit," akin to "a ghoul drag[ging] from the grave the body pierced by the bullets of the rebels" ("Capt. Andre Cailloux," *New York Times*, August 9, 1863).

If the love of the fatherland: Edouard Tinchant, quoted in "Assemblée a la Salle d'Economie," *L'Union*, June 30, 1863.

American flag to hang outside the door: "Assemblée a la Salle d'Economie," *L'Union*, June 30, 1863. On the Union League, see Rogers, "Union League."

The league's second resolution: ESM, May 2, 1864. The Economistes long continued to honor Cailloux's memory. A year after her husband's death, the society received a letter from "la Veuve Caillou" (the widow Cailloux), asking for the use of the hall for a "bal." Usually this word indicated a party or fundraiser, for which the hall was frequently used, rather than a grand ball. One member suggested the widow should be allowed to use the hall without charge because she had many children. Joseph Jean Pierre Lanna added a specific second to the motion, "not because she has children, because if it were for that, you have received many other petitioners. But she carries the name of André Caillou[x], and he has erased the dark stain we had on our foreheads. The society has always honored courage and bravery, which is why we must honor her request."

"Citizens, the world is watching us": "Assemblée a la Salle d'Economie," *L'Union*, June 30, 1863. On Tinchant, see Scott and Hébrard, "Rosalie of the Poulard Nation," 117.

"unquestionably one of the most important": "Department of the Gulf: Important Meeting of Colored People," *New York Times*, November 19, 1863. While the *New-Orleans Times* reported that an address "read in French . . . created the wildest excitement," the speech's contents were not specified, and the default language at the meeting appears to have been English ("A Meeting of the Free Colored Citizens at Economy Hall," *New-Orleans Times*, November 6, 1863).

Josiah Fisk: "A Meeting of the Free Colored Citizens at Economy Hall," *New-Orleans Times*, November 6, 1863; "Obituaries—Mrs. Vashti Harkness Fisk," 26.

Boisdoré's grandfather François Dubuisson: Honora, "Boisdoré"; Ingrid Stanley, interview by author, July 5, 2020. Stanley is a Louisiana Creole Research Association member and a Boisdoré descendant.

"contained more white American blood": "A Meeting of the Free Colored Citizens at Economy Hall," *New-Orleans Times*, November 6, 1863.

light-colored, mixed-raced people: Schafer, *Becoming Free*, 100.

included Jews: Among the mixed-race Jewish members were the Warburgs; the Cordeviolles, Azarettos, and Lucianis originated in Italy; and the Dupart and Couvent families had members born in Africa.

all Haitian citizens: Moreau de Saint-Méry, *Description topographique*, 73–75.

"vast amount of prejudice": "A Meeting of the Free Colored Citizens at Economy Hall," *New-Orleans Times*, November 6, 1863.

"I am not a speaker": "A Meeting of the Free Colored Citizens at Economy Hall," *New-Orleans Times*, November 6, 1863; "New Orleans Correspondence," *New-York Freeman's Journal and Catholic Register*, November 28, 1863.

The younger Boisdoré consistently attended: There are no minutes of the Economie meetings from 1858 to 1864. The August 19, 1858, meeting ends suddenly, and the remainder of the page is left blank. The reverse side of the same journal page begins with the March 1, 1864, meeting.

"When our fathers fought": "A Meeting of the Free Colored Citizens at Economy Hall," *New-Orleans Times*, November 6, 1863.

"When the Federals came to New Orleans": "A Meeting of the Free Colored Citizens at Economy Hall," *New-Orleans Times*, November 6, 1863.

"The assembly, composed of the elite": "Grande Assemblée à l'Economie. Immense Enthousiasme," *L'Union*, November 28, 1863.

If the United States has the right to arm us: "A Meeting of the Free Colored Citizens at Economy Hall," *New-Orleans Times*, November 6, 1863.

Durant had encouraged the free men of color: Bell, *Revolution*, 249, 251.

"having the restoration of the Union": "The President and a Colored Delegation from New-Orleans. Colored Petitions from Louisiana," *New York Times*, March 5, 1864.

Possibly moved by the delegation: Rodrigue, *Lincoln*, 82.

"My dear Sir": Lincoln's original letter is available online through the Shapell Foundation. The March 1864 letter was published in the *New York Times* the following year ("The Late President Lincoln on Negro Suffrage: A Letter from Him to Gov. Hahn of Louisiana," June 23, 1865).

Whether Hahn was sympathetic: Simpson and Baker, "Michael Hahn," 243–46.

The seventy-two men present: ESM, March 1, 1864.

they called him the *cherman*: ESM, May 16, 1864.

Boguille Steps Forward

Slavery . . . can never again exist: "Interesting Occasion," *Massachusetts Spy*, April 20, 1864.

William Henry Hire: Wetta, "The Louisiana Scalawags," 74–75. Hire would later provide eyewitness testimony on the Mechanics' Institute massacre, as documented in *Report* *of the Select Committee on the New Orleans Riots,* Testimony of Dr. Wm. Henry Hire, December 22, 1866, 64–68.

"Permit me to introduce to your notice": William Henry Hire to Isaac G. Hubbs, April 5, 1864, United States, Freedmen's Bureau, Records of the Superintendent of Education and of the Division of Education, 1865–1872, FamilySearch.org.

"Mrs. Boguille began alone": Inspection report received by the board of education, June 16, 1864, United States, Freedmen's Bureau, Records of the Superintendent of Education and of the Division of Education, 1865–1872, FamilySearch.org. See also *Report of the Select Committee on the New Orleans Riots,* Testimony of Ludgier Boquille [Ludger Boguille], January 1, 1867, 383, 385. Boguille's testimony was provided through an interpreter, J. F. Mollere.

she had 78 students: Statistical report, May 12, 1865, United States, Freedmen's Bureau, Records of the Superintendent of Education and of the Division of Education, 1865–1872, FamilySearch.org.

class sizes ranging from 13 to 182: Statistical report, May 12, 1865, United States, Freedmen's Bureau, Records of the Superintendent of Education and of the Division of Education, 1865–1872, FamilySearch.org.

Some were New Englanders: For an overview of the teachers' origins and motivations, see Hunt, "It Takes Great Nerve."

"ruddy complexion": "Georgia," *New York Times,* November 16, 1866. For examples of reprints, see "The Yankee School Teacher at the South," *Vermont Journal,* December 8, 1866, and "Yankee School Marms in the South," *Janesville Gazette,* December 19, 1866.

making John Brown into a martyr: "Yankee School Marms," *Daily Constitutionalist,* June 17, 1866.

"unfit him for his station": Drayton, *South Vindicated,* 69.

"We know that they come here": "Yankee School Marms," *Daily Constitutionalist,* June 17, 1866.

draw the rebel flag: *Report of the Select Committee on the New Orleans Riots,* Testimony of L. J. P. Capla, December 24, 1866, 122–23.

eight public schools for colored students: Christian and Dillard, "Negro in Louisiana," chap. 31, 2.

Bertonneau spoke to the audience: "Interesting Occasion," *Massachusetts Spy,* April 20, 1864.

add more Black schools: Stern, *Race and Education,* 40.

"I never will be so dishonest": Christian and Dillard, "Negro in Louisiana," chap. 31, 4.

"I simply offer this resolution": *Debates in the Convention,* 547–48.

"with a fair and rosy complexion": *Debates in the Convention,* 548.

We want labor, education, and progress: "The Meeting at Economy Hall (Proceedings Continued)," *New Orleans Tribune,* March 19, 1865.

Lanna told the others: ESM, May 16, 1864.

Tickets cost fifty cents: "A Grand Ratification Dinner," *New Orleans Tribune,* September 27, 1864.

The price was much less: See Margo, "North-South Wage Gap," 34.

L'Union **published frequent advertisements:** "Grande Assemblée," *L'Union,* May 28, 1864. See also *Grand Celebration in Honor of the Passage of the Ordinance of Emancipation,* in which Boguille (misspelled "Poguille") is identified as a grand marshal.

When the day arrived: "Emancipation Celebration in New-Orleans," *Era,* June 12, 1864, reprinted in *New York Daily Tribune,* June 20, 1864.

"as strong and hearty": "Emancipation Celebration in New-Orleans," *Era,* June 12, 1864, reprinted in *New York Daily Tribune,* June 20, 1864.

Governor Hahn . . . "had not come there": "Emancipation Celebration in New-Orleans," *Era*, reprinted in *New York Daily Tribune*, June 20, 1864.

François Boisdoré *fils* addressed the crowd: "Emancipation Celebration in New-Orleans," *Era*, reprinted in *New York Daily Tribune*, June 20, 1864.

"You will see by this little book": Willey, "Education," 249–50.

The day of the meeting: Editorial, *New Orleans Tribune*, January 15, 1865. The proceedings of the convention, along with the *Tribune* editorial, are available at coloredconventions.org/items /show/271, part of the University of Delaware's Colored Conventions Project.

Frederick Douglass convened: Proceedings of the Syracuse convention, University of Delaware, Colored Conventions Project, coloredconventions.org/items/show/282.

"seated side by side": Editorial, *New Orleans Tribune*, January 15, 1865.

who had been a soldier: For Henry Chevarre, see US, War of 1812 Pension Application Files Index, 1812–1815; for François Boisdoré *fils*, see US, Confederate Soldiers Compiled Service Records, 1861–1865; for François Boisdoré *père*, see Louisiana, Soldiers in the War of 1812; all accessed through Ancestry.com.

"Speakers in the French Language": Editorial, *New Orleans Tribune*, January 15, 1865. Economie founder Charles Martinez, whose parliamentary knowledge is singled out for praise, would become a city notary. His acts, dated from December 1, 1868, to August 31, 1869, are held in the New Orleans Notarial Archives.

Ingraham was the president: Hollandsworth, *Louisiana Native Guards*, 105, 120.

"I should say that the city cars": "Our New-Orleans Correspondence," *New York Times*, November 5, 1862.

"a procession, composed of all shades": "Our New-Orleans Correspondence," *New York Times*, June 26, 1864.

"We hope this fact": "Our New-Orleans Correspondence," *New York Times*, November 5, 1862.

"We declare that all men": Proceedings of the Syracuse convention, University of Delaware, Colored Conventions Project, coloredconventions.org/items/show/282.

The Louisiana convention also promoted: Introduction to the proceedings of the Louisiana convention, University of Delaware, Colored Conventions Project, coloredconventions .org/items/show/271.

The *Tribune*, reporting on the convention: Editorial, *New Orleans Tribune*, January 15, 1865.

the School of Liberty: Blokker, "Education in Louisiana," 18.

"He must infuse into their minds": Fénelon, *Dialogues Concerning Eloquence in General*, 40.

only a short paragraph: "Reunion à l'Ecole de Liberte," *La Tribune de la Nouvelle-Orléans*, January 11, 1865.

It is, unfortunately, a policy: "Freedmen's Aid Association of New Orleans," *New Orleans Tribune,* July 11, 1865.

Boguille had joined: "Officers of the Freedmen's Aid Association," *New Orleans Tribune*, May 11, 1865. The organization's mission, as stated in the *Tribune*, was to "develop the agriculture of the State of Louisiana by means of the Freedmen, to afford them aid, assistance and counsel, by the means of loans of money or of other objects, by means of education and the diffusion of useful information, and by such other means as the needs and requirements of the Freedmen may, in the judgement of the Association, demand."

"should be better known": "Freedmen's Aid Association," *New Orleans Tribune,* July 11, 1865.

The similarity of names and goals: For a discussion of the proliferation of aid organizations, see Eggleston, "The Work of Relief Societies."

"They are now cultivating": "Officers of the Freedmen's Aid Association," *New Orleans Tribune*, May 5, 1865.

Their appeal was reprinted: "Office of the Freedmen's Aid Society," 183.

contracts for planting and harvesting: See "The Freedmen's Bureau," *Daily Picayune*, December 17, 1865, for an itemized list of "rules for the interpretation of contracts between employers and freedmen."

Some employers then complained: "Freedmen's Aid Association," *New Orleans Tribune*, July 11, 1865.

"regular weekly cash payments": "Freedmen's Aid Association," *New-Orleans Times*, December 1, 1865.

the association had purchased mules: "Freedmen's Aid Association," *New Orleans Tribune*, July 11, 1865.

fourteen farms: "Land for the Freedmen," *New Orleans Tribune*, November 14, 1865.

"It has been shown": "Freedmen's Aid Association," *New Orleans Tribune*, July 11, 1865.

former plantation of Pierre A. Rost: The bureau's efforts are described in Knight, "Rost Home Colony." Rost married into the prominent Destrehan family, and the site of the former Rost Home Colony is open to the public today as Destrehan Plantation, in St. Charles Parish. A permanent exhibition explores the bureau's activities.

He inscribed the names: Descriptions of bureau operations and finances draw upon Knight, "Rost Home Colony," and my visits to the former plantation.

planters could hold wages: "Short Contracts," *New Orleans Tribune*, December 12, 1865.

a Freedmen's Bureau announcement: "To the Freedmen of Louisiana. Headquarters Bureau of Refugees Freedmen and Abandoned Lands. New Orleans," *New-Orleans Times*, October 22, 1865.

"Compulsion is nothing short": "Short Contracts," *New Orleans Tribune*, December 12, 1865.

a Confederate ambassador: Rost's failed diplomatic career is described in White and Baylen, "Pierre A. Rost's Mission." See also Knight, "Rost Home Colony," and Baldwin and Baldwin, *Baldwin's Guide*, 85.

God damn them: *Executive Documents*, vol. 10, no. 68, "New Orleans Riots," Testimony of Peter Crocker [Pierre Crocker Jr.], August 15, 1866, 242.

He and society member Charles Martinez: "Executive Board of the League," *New Orleans Tribune*, January 20, 1865.

white Republican Thomas Durant: "National Equal Rights League," *New Orleans Tribune*, February 3, 1865. For Durant's earlier speech, see "Mr. Durant's Address at Economy Hall," *Daily True Delta*, December 4, 1864.

a new organization: "Universal Suffrage," *New Orleans Tribune*, June 16, 1865; "Universal Suffrage," *New Orleans Tribune*, June 18, 1865; "Notice: To the Friends of Universal Suffrage," *New Orleans Tribune*, August 1, 1865. The Friends of Universal Suffrage and Freedmen's Aid Association were based at 49 Union Street.

joined the Friends of Universal Suffrage: See *Proceedings of the Convention of the Republican Party*, 2–3, 8, for a discussion of the registration efforts, and 10–12 for committee membership and delegate names.

Boguille was one of the commissioners: See, for instance, the September 7, 1865, voter registration certificate for Jules Jean-Baptiste, with Boguille's signature as commissioner. The certificate is filed with other documentation related to the military service of William Joseph, whose widow, Mary Baptiste Joseph, received a government pension (*Case Files of Approved Pension Applications of Widows and Other Dependents of Civil War Veterans, ca. 1861–ca. 1910*, Civil War "Widows' Pensions," Fold3.com).

Registration also took place: Mitchell, "Oscar James Dunn," 75.

"This pamphlet will be a useful manual": *Proceedings of the Convention of the Republican Party*, ii.

The booklet suggested: *Proceedings of the Convention of the Republican Party*, iv.

There were two important factions: Bell, *Revolution*, 256–59.

tallied 15,605 Black votes: Mitchell, "Oscar James Dunn," 79.

the November elections: Bell, *Revolution*, 259–60; Eakin, "James Madison Wells."

the radicals wanted to wait: Desdunes, *Our People*, 131.

Republican moderates decided to go ahead: Bell, *Revolution*, 260–61.

Lucien Capla: *Report of the Select Committee on the New Orleans Riots*, Testimony of L. J. P. Capla, 119–20. According to Lucien's testimony, his son was sixteen, but this must have been an error. All available records of Arnold's life say he was born sometime between 1858 and 1860. Arnold appears in the 1880 census, domiciled with his grandfather, brothers, and mother; he died July 18, 1883, at the age of 25. USFCC, *Tenth Census of the United States* (1880), Orleans Parish, Ward 6, Ancestry.com; Louisiana, Statewide Death Index, 1819–1964, Ancestry.com.

he saw a crowd of police officers: *Report of the Select Committee on the New Orleans Riots*, Testimony of Boguille, 384.

the same events: "Notice to the Public: Three Concluding Exhibitions," *New Orleans Tribune*, March 19, 1865; "A Fair for the Benefit of Orphans of Freedmen," *New Orleans Tribune*, April 4, 1865; "Patriotic and Literary Lecture," *New Orleans Tribune*, April 2, 1865; "Madam de Mortie's Lecture," *New Orleans Tribune*, April 6, 1865.

a band and some marchers: *Report of the Select Committee on the New Orleans Riots,* Minority Report, 50–51; Testimony of J. B. Jourdain, December 27, 1866, 204; Testimony of Boguille, 384.

"I saw a colored man killed": *Report of the Select Committee on the New Orleans Riots*, Testimony of Boguille, 384.

Capla "saw policemen firing": *Report of the Select Committee on the New Orleans Riots*, Testimony of Capla, 120.

Boguille told of his escape: *Report of the Select Committee on the New Orleans Riots*, Testimony of Boguille, 384.

Capla grabbed his son: *Report of the Select Committee on the New Orleans Riots*, Testimony of Capla, 120.

"Do not go out": *Report of the Select Committee on the New Orleans Riots*, Testimony of Sylvester Edward Planchard, December 31, 1866, 341.

"One-third of the way down stairs": *Report of the Select Committee on the New Orleans Riots*, Testimony of Demosthenes Charles Azaretto, December 31, 1866, 356. Azaretto's testimony was provided through an interpreter, J. F. Mollere.

"I was up in the hall": *Executive Documents*, Testimony of Crocker, 242–43.

slippery with blood: "The Riot in New-Orleans," *New York Times*, August 5, 1866.

Lacroix "was a young man": *Report of the Select Committee on the New Orleans Riots,* Testimony of Boguille, 384.

"My brothers, you all know": ESM, September 1, 1866.

"Patience, because your recompense": Spiritualist register 85-31, February 21, 1869, 101–3, Grandjean Collection (author's translation). See Bell, *Revolution*, 263, and Daggett, *Spiritualism*, 76 and 130, for more about visits to the séances by the spirit of Victor Lacroix. Many men from the Economie are quoted in the Grandjean Spiritualist registers.

Boguille, the Radical

I then tried to withdraw: *Report of the Select Committee on the New Orleans Riots*, Testimony of Boguille, 384–85.

Durant later told the congressional committee: *Report of the Select Committee on the New Orleans Riots*, Testimony of Thomas J. Durant, December 12, 1866, 8–9.

all who arrived: The names and ages of children documented by the bureau on December 24 and 31 appear on the Freedmen's Bureau Online, "List of Orphans."

the children came in like ghosts: Freedmen's Bureau Online, "List of Orphans," December 24 and 31, 1866.

rooms full of children: Freedmen's Bureau Online, "List of Orphans," December 31, 1866.

One educator at a colored freedmen's school: Alvord, *Sixth Semi-Annual Report*, 38.

"What is the state of feeling": *Report of the Select Committee on the New Orleans Riots*, Testimony of Charles S. Souvinet [Sauvinet], December 22, 1866, 45.

quite European in appearance: Testifying before the American Freedmen's Inquiry Commission on November 28, 1863, Gen. Benjamin F. Butler commented on Sauvinet's complexion, calling him "hardly a mulatto" (quoted in Hollandsworth, *Louisiana Native Guards*, 15).

questions that probed: *Report of the Select Committee on the New Orleans Riots*, Testimony of Sauvinet, 45.

"By words, by cross looks": *Report of the Select Committee on the New Orleans Riots*, Testimony of Sauvinet, 46.

continued to meet at the Economie's hall: "Meeting in the Sixth Ward," *New Orleans Tribune*, December 24, 1867.

"the cradle of the equal rights party": "What Right the Tribune Claims," *New Orleans Tribune*, July 3, 1867.

met on Tuesday nights: "Meeting of the Ward Clubs," *New Orleans Tribune*, April 17, 1867; "Meeting of the Sixth Ward Club," *New Orleans Tribune*, May 8, 1867.

"to carry dismay in the ranks": "Public Demonstration," *New Orleans Tribune*, May 11, 1867.

Fifteen thousand men marched: "Grand Torchlight Procession of the Republican Party," *New Orleans Tribune*, May 25, 1867; "The Procession of the Radicals," *New Orleans Tribune*, May 30, 1867; "La Grande Manifestation: Republicaine d'Hier Soir," *La Tribune de la Nouvelle-Orléans*, May 30, 1867.

"Taking the census of 1860": "Registration at the South—Louisiana and Alabama," *New York Times,* September 7, 1867.

Let those men who were with us: "Who Served the Republican Party" *New Orleans Tribune*, May 8, 1867.

Ludger Boguille ran for the office: "The Election: Full Returns," *Daily Picayune*, April 23, 1868. Boguille, listed as a Radical Republican, was one of two aldermen elected to represent the Second District. The other was a Democrat named Prados.

On the night of October 26: "Democratic Outrages," *New Orleans Republican,* October 27, 1868; "The Murder of an Innocent," *New Orleans Republican*, October 28, 1868. For the location of Armand Belot's cigar store, see 1867 New Orleans city directory. Belot filed suit to recoup his losses, totaling almost $27,000, claiming that the city failed to protect his home and business. He won the case, but the city appealed to the state supreme court. The claim was finally paid in August 1871. "Mayor Conway last evening transmitted to the council," *New Orleans Crescent*, November 18, 1868; "The City Council," *Daily Picayune*, August 31, 1870; "[P]aying a Judgment," *New Orleans Republican*, August 2, 1871.

hung an American flag: "Assemblée a la Salle d'Economie," *L'Union*, June 30, 1863, discusses a public meeting at the Economy Hall when a decision was made to hang the American flag ("un drapeau national"). Boguille is secretary at the meeting.

displayed the story on the front page: "More Mob Violence," *New Orleans Republican*, October 28, 1868.

at least $1,800: At a meeting on February 28, 1870, the board of aldermen forwarded to the city's finance committee a resolution to reimburse the Economy Society $1,800 for the 1868 damages to the hall. In early April, the board of aldermen approved a payment to the society of $1,694. "The City Council. Board of Aldermen," *Daily Picayune*, March 1, 1870; "The Common Council. Board of Aldermen," *New-Orleans Commercial Bulletin*, April 4, 1870. More than a year later, the funds had not yet come through—and Boguille was charged with pursuit of payment (ESM, May 25, 1871).

equivalent to six years' pay: In 1869, according to labor statistics compiled by the US Treasury Department, an agricultural laborer in Louisiana could expect to earn $6 per week. Assuming steady employment—fifty weeks per year—it would take that laborer a year to earn $300, and six years to cover the cost of the damage to the hall (Young, *Special Report on Immigration*, 212).

Octave Belot served as a representative: Poynter, *Membership in the Louisiana House of Representatives*, 187–90.

a Democratic newspaper: "A Case of Pistols," *Pomeroy's Democrat*, December 8, 1869.

Henry L. Rey: Foner, *Freedom's Lawmakers*, 181.

Henry's brother, Octave: Foner, *Freedom's Lawmakers*, 181.

nominated Francis Ernest Dumas: "The Nominating Convention," *New Orleans Republican*, January 14, 1868.

"I only wish to spend": Hollandsworth, *Louisiana Native Guards*, 27.

He told the investigating committee: *Report of the Select Committee on the New Orleans Riots*, Testimony of H. C. Warmouth [Henry Clay Warmoth], December 22, 1866, 40–43.

Warmoth took Oscar Dunn: For the definitive study of Dunn's life and political career, see Mitchell, Edwards, and Weldon, *Monumental*. See also Vincent, "Oscar Dunn"; Perkins, "Oscar James Dunn"; and Kinshasa, *African American Chronology*, 55, 58.

The *Tribune* faction: Connor. "Reconstruction Rebels," 179–80. See also Roudané, *Roudanez: History and Legacy*, for more information about the *Tribune*.

***Prejudice! does not the very word imply*:** "The Colored Race—The Present and the Future," *New Orleans Tribune*, August 18, 1864.

the most progressive constitution: Louis. Const. of 1868, art. I, II.

at least 210 Black officeholders: Foner, *Freedom's Lawmakers*, xiii–xiv, 249–51. Foner includes ten members of the Economy Society on his list—but the absence of Boguille suggests that other names might also be missing.

Charles Sauvinet had joined: "National Freedman's Savings and Trust Company," *New Orleans Tribune*, September 4, 1866. The bank was located at 114 Carondelet Street.

"The society, which has at all times": ESM, August 1, 1865.

Among the depositors: New Orleans deposit records 373, 454, 978, 999, United States, Freedman's Bank Records, 1865–1874, FamilySearch.org.

deposits totaled more than $1,300: "We Are Indebted to the Hon. C. S. Sauvinet," *New Orleans Tribune*, October 26, 1867.

a network of local branches: Blassingame, *Black New Orleans*, 67.

Individual Economie members: New Orleans deposit records 319, 456, 868, 7608, 8384, 4675, United States, Freedman's Bank Records, 1865–1874, FamilySearch.org.

Sauvinet confidently opened an account: New Orleans deposit records 468, 3054, United States, Freedman's Bank Records, 1865–1874, FamilySearch.org.

the Economie's thirty-third anniversary: ESM, March 1, 1869.

Sauvinet became the civil sheriff: Nystrom, *New Orleans after the Civil War*, 96.

Sauvinet stopped into a coffeehouse: Filleul, *C. S. Sauvinet vs. J. A. Walker*, 2–3, 6–9.

"under the Constitution and laws": "Damage Suit by the Civil Sheriff," *Daily Picayune*, January 28, 1871.

In the Eighth District court: Foner, *Freedom's Lawmakers*, 59. A procedural challenge to Sauvinet's suit delayed the awarding of damages to 1875. See *Walker v. Sauvinet*, 92 U.S. 90, 23 L.Ed. 678 (1875). According to the Bureau of Labor Statistics, a Louisiana bricklayer could expect to earn $2.50 a day in 1871 (*History of Wages in the United States*, 154). Assuming steady employment—six days per week, fifty weeks per year—it would take some sixteen months to earn $1,000.

Boguille and the Economistes Move toward Social Equity

Let us hope: ESM, September 3, 1838. Henry Chevarre's first inquiry into membership in the Economie was December 1, 1836, as noted in the minutes. The association installed him at the meeting of December 15, 1836. By September 1838, he was the president of the society.

"Your arrival among us": ESM, February 23, 1871.

"This ode impressed the society": ESM, February 23, 1871. The Economiste who signed the 1871 minutes as "P. A. Duhart" is likely Pierre Adolphe Duhart, born in New Orleans in 1830—and, despite the slight discrepancy in age, possibly the same individual as an Adolph Duhart, 37, listed as a teacher in the 1870 census. Pierre Adolphe Duhart birth record, February 1, 1830, New Orleans, Louisiana, Birth Records Index, 1790–1915, Ancestry.com; USFCC, *Ninth Census of the United States* (1870), New Orleans, Ward 5, Ancestry.com.

"morsel of English poetry": ESM, February 23, 1871.

he called them "réunions": ESM, March 1, 1872.

A people is no less a member: Fénelon, "Socrate et Alcibiade," in *Dialogues des morts* (1718), quoted in Hazard, *Crisis of the European Mind*, 282.

A French opera company: "The French Opera at the Economy Hall," *Weekly Louisianian*, May 15, 1875. See Sullivan, "Composers of Color," 63–68, for additional biographical information about Barès.

more than 56,000 "mulattos": *Ninth Census*, vol. 1, *Statistics of the Population of the United States*, table 22, "The Table of Sex," 608.

Mulattos had made up: Census data shows an increase of mulattos in the southern slaveholding states from 348,895 in 1850 (10.14% of blacks) to 518,360 in 1860 (12.3% of blacks). *Population of the United States in 1860*, Introduction, x.

the Scorsa family: See Vincent Scorsa, customhouse inspector, and Pepe Rodriguez, fisherman, USFCC, *Ninth Census of the United States* (1870), New Orleans, Ward 6, Ancestry.com.

An 1870 Dupart home: See Delphine Dupart, USFCC, *Ninth Census of the United States* (1870), New Orleans, Ward 7, Ancestry.com.

"it is only natural": "Miscegenation," *New Orleans Tribune*, October 25, 1866.

"Negro equality": "Ohio Democratic Platform," *Tri-Weekly Advocate*, August 17, 1866.

"It is unfortunate": ESM, January 2, 1872.

"to change this Aristocracy": ESM, December 2, 1872.

He modeled acceptance: According to the 1840 census, Jules Déjean [Sr.] was white, while the other members of his household were either free people of color or enslaved. In the

1850 census, Déjean's mother is identified as Marguerite Doubrère, a mulatto woman from the West Indies. Both father and son were employed as clerks. The younger Déjean is listed as Jules Dejan Jr., accountant, in the 1861 city directory. USFCC, *Sixth Census of the United States* (1840), New Orleans, Ward 1, Ancestry.com; USFCC, *Seventh Census of the United States* (1850), New Orleans, Municipality 1, Ward 4, Ancestry.com.

In typical Economie fashion: Lists of food purchased for banquets are found in ESM, March 1, 1872; March 6, 1882; April 1, 1886; March 8, 1889; March 1, 1893; and March 3, 1902.

Only a couple of months earlier: ESM, January 16, 1872.

"the most exquisite wines": ESM, March 1, 1872.

He wrote a song: ESM, March 1, 1872.

"Déjean, your presidency": ESM, March 1, 1874.

"It must be said": ESM, March 1, 1872.

THE AGE OF TREACHERY

The Former Rebels Push Back

They have managed: "The Oppressed Race," *Daily Picayune*, June 14, 1874.

As early as 1866: Freedmen's Bureau Online, "Miscellaneous Reports."

"at least 100 colored men murdered": "Romance of Politics in the Backwoods," *New Orleans Republican*, February 1, 1874.

But the most shocking death: Perkins, "Oscar James Dunn," 105–18; Brian K. Mitchell (Oscar Dunn relative and scholar), interview by author, December 19, 2017; "Death of Oscar J. Dunn," *New Orleans Republican*, November 23, 1871; "Fearful Suspicion," *Weekly Louisianian*, January 11, 1872; Christian, "Theory of the Poisoning of Oscar J. Dunn," 54–66.

Two days after Dunn's death: ESM, November 24, 1871.

"The square was illuminated": "Commemoration Meeting," *Daily Picayune*, December 5, 1871.

"Africanize Louisiana": Warmoth, *War, Politics, and Reconstruction*, quoted in Perkins, "Oscar James Dunn," 107.

Madame: Letter from Boguille to the widow of Joseph S. Soudé, ESM, May 1, 1872.

One of the newer members: "Branch Club No. 1, 7me Ward," *La Tribune de la Nouvelle-Orléans*, October 24, 1867.

a US Custom House officer: "The Vendetta," *Daily Picayune*, April 21, 1872.

Boguille also knew Soudé: "Gen. Howard at the Orleans Theater," *New Orleans Tribune*, November 6, 1865; "Ligue Caillou No. 8," *La Tribune de la Nouvelle-Orléans*, May 12, 1865; "Equal Rights Club," *New Orleans Tribune*, February 21, 1869; "Elections de wards pour le choix des delegues a la convention republicaine," *La Tribune de la Nouvelle-Orléans*, June 6, 1867; "Convention of the Radical Republican Party. Session of June 10," *New Orleans Tribune*, June 11, 1867; "The Radical Republican Convention," *New Orleans Tribune*, June 13, 1867; *Proceedings of the Convention of the Republican Party of Louisiana*, 11, appendix.

Soudé also rented the hall: "Bal Patriotique," *La Tribune de la Nouvelle-Orléans*, November 19, 1865.

"Brothers, I thank you": ESM, July 15, 1871.

"operations were cut short": "Les Frères-Unis," *La Tribune de la Nouvelle-Orléans*, February 17, 1867. Thanks to Mark Roudané for providing a copy of this issue, which hasn't been microfilmed or digitized.

The *Daily Picayune* reported: "Gallatin Street," *Daily Picayune*, September 8, 1873.

"whisky resort": "Knife and Cards," *New Orleans Republican*, April 7, 1868.

the port lost business: Ross, "Resisting the New South," 60, 63–64, 70, 72.

"This morning": "The Vendetta," *Daily Picayune*, April 21, 1872.

an "accidental death": ESM, May 1, 1872.

"at this time": Desdunes, *Our People*, 115.

All of the members: "The Double Murder," *Daily Picayune*, April 23, 1872.

The Italian community: "It is understood that the Italians…," *Daily Picayune*, April 24, 1872.

"the members silently": ESM, April 24, 1872.

Although the First District Court: "First District Court," *Daily Picayune*, May 19, 1872.

Today the society: ESM, March 1, 1874.

St. Barbara Society: ESM, December 4, 1873.

Société de Cigariers: ESM, October 15, 1874.

Société des Vétérans de 1814–15: ESM, August 21, 1873; September 22, 1873.

Many of Boguille's society brothers: For the death record of Cordeviolle, see Succession of Etienne Cordeviolle, Louisiana, Civil District Court (Orleans Parish) succession records, 1890–1903, docket no. 3744, VT290, box 48, City Archives, NOPL. For Casanave, Lanna, and Dupart, see Louisiana, Statewide Death Index, 1819–1964, Ancestry.com.

Raoul and Doresmond Crocker: ESM, December 15, 1873 (Raoul Crocker petitions for admission); March 12, 1874 (Doresmond Crocker is admitted). Raoul and Doresmond were the children of Economiste Doresmond Crocker (USFCC, *Seventh Census of the United States* [1850], New Orleans, Municipality 1, Ward 4, Ancestry.com).

François Tervalon *fils*: ESM, 1874. Many new members were added throughout 1874. Antonio Luciani is also referred to as Antoine in the minutes and membership book of 1877.

On St. Joseph's Day: ESM, August 1, 1872, reports on expenses and income from the March 19, 1872, ball.

almost seven weeks of work: The average daily wage for a carpenter working six days per week in Louisiana in 1872 was $2.86, or $17.16 per week (*History of Wages in the United States*, 161).

Les Amis de l'Équité: ESM, August 21, 1873. The Economie president created an exploratory committee to contact "the Société des Jeunes Amis as well as l'Équité to deliberate on the means that could be adopted to the satisfaction of all the parties in order to make our association and theirs one single and identical organization." The Economie accepted at least fifty-seven new members between December 1873 and December 1874. (Some were rejected.) I have no record of a unification with the Jeunes Amis. But a letter regarding the merger with l'Équité was entered into the Economie minutes on November 16, 1874: "The Société Les Amis de l'Équité, having two and a half years of existence, 66 active members, and a cashbox [with] all dues paid of $515.50, want to fuse with the Société d'Economie, composed of about 85 members, having a building, a debt of $1200 and in the cash box, $140."

Joseph sued the theater: *Joseph v. Bidwell*, 28 La. Ann. 382 (1876).

For the anniversary banquet: ESM, March 1, 1874.

The society assessed members twenty-five cents: ESM, June 25, 1874.

To overthrow this domination: "The Oppressed Race," *Daily Picayune*, June 14, 1874.

William Pitt Kellogg: National Governors Association, "Gov. William Pitt Kellogg."

An armed group: "The New-Orleans Mob," *New York Times*, March 7, 1873.

"The railing of Jackson-square": "The New-Orleans Mob" *New York Times*, March 7, 1873.

On April 13: Lewis, "1873 Colfax Massacre"; Keith, "Colfax Massacre."

Finally, on September 20, 1873: National Governors Association, "Gov. William Pitt Kellogg."

the White League formed: Schafer, "Battle of Liberty Place."

Knights of the White Camellia: Nystrom, "Knights of the White Camellia."

"Therefore we enter": Schafer, "Battle of Liberty Place."

"dearest rights": Schafer, "Battle of Liberty Place."

The armed battle: Schafer, "Battle of Liberty Place."

Captain Octave Rey escaped: ESM, October 8, 1874.

"honorable and brave men": "The Citizens' Victory," *Daily Picayune*, September 18, 1874.

no colored citizens: "The Slanders Against Our People and Cause," *Daily Picayune*, September 19, 1874.

In 1882 the outgoing city council: "The Final Session," *Daily Picayune*, November 16, 1882. During the monument's approximately one-hundred-year occupancy at the foot of Canal Street, near the US Customhouse, city commemorations took place—ranging from annual parades celebrating the post-Reconstruction victory to twentieth-century gatherings by members of the Ku Klux Klan using the site to promote their causes. In 1993 the monument was moved to a less conspicuous location between a parking garage and the back of the Aquarium of the Americas, at the corner of Iberville and Badine Streets. The plaque commemorating the white supremacist fighters was removed, and the names of Republicans who died in the struggle were added to the monument's base. The city finally removed the Battle of Liberty Place monument in April 2017 and placed it in storage for possible exhibition in a museum that would present it in its historical context.

"in memory of Brother Edouard Simon": ESM, September 15, 1874.

"Madame": ESM, October 8, 1874.

The second Economie casualty: ESM, October 8, 1874.

"Madame Widow Aristide Rivard": ESM, October 8, 1874.

"Sirs, since the death": ESM, October 15, 1874.

less than a week's pay: The average daily wage for a carpenter working six days per week in Louisiana in 1874 was $2.80, or $16.80 per week (*History of Wages in the United States*, 161).

Violence Escalates and Boguille's Health Fades

You call these measures: "The Rebels Triumphant," *New York Times*, April 4, 1879.

The funeral column: Boguille's letter to Soudé's widow states that her husband's name will be inscribed on the funeral column in the "salle d'audience" (ESM, May 1, 1872).

"*Apprends á vivre*": ESM, November 2, 1871.

"If you want land": "Grand Democratic Barbecue at Lake Joseph," *New-Orleans Times*, September 12, 1868.

General Philip Henry Sheridan: Woodson, *A Century of Negro Migration*, 128.

The Economie members had a plan: ESM, March 5, 1875.

He was Myrtil Piron: Some sources spell his first name as Myrthil, but the Economie's minutes use the Myrtil spelling.

Octave taught music: Douglas, "How New Orleans' Creole Musicians"; Trotter, *Music and Some Highly Musical People*, 349.

These ritual processions: *Report of the Select Committee on the New Orleans Riots*, Testimony of J. D. O'Connell, December 24, 1866, 77–86.

"make his vows": ESM, November 3, 1876.

The society paid bands: ESM, March 5, 1875.

"After a long discussion": ESM, March 5, 1875.

Pay the insurance: ESM, November 15, 1872.

the Freedman's Bank: Washington, "Freedman's Savings and Trust."

Henry L. Rey: US, Freedman's Bank Records, 1865–1874, Ancestry.com.

The bank had thirty-seven branches: Gordon, "Freedman's Bank."

"married to a corpse": Washington, "Freedman's Savings and Trust."

held a public auction: "Public Sale of Valuable Real Estate," *Evening Star*, April 3, 1877.

would be lucky to get 10 percent: "The Freedman's Savings Bank," *Weekly Louisianian*, March 20, 1875. This article predicted that the depositors would get 10 percent or, at most, 15 percent of their deposits returned. In fact, across the nation about half of the depositors received three-fifths of their money, but some people never received any compensation (Washington, "Freedman's Savings and Trust"; United States, Freedman's Bank Records, 1865–1874, FamilySearch.org).

"The fraudulent voters": "The City: Fraudulent Voters," *Daily Picayune*, November 4, 1874.

In the same roundup: "The City: A Well-Merited Tribute," *Daily Picayune*, November 4, 1874.

a group of eighteen investors: "State of Louisiana," *New-Orleans Commercial Bulletin*, April 21, 1870.

City School Board treasurer: "The City School Board," *New Orleans Republican*, April 23, 1870; Act of Incorporation, Economy Mutual Aid Association (notary Andrew Hero Jr., April 12, 1870, NONA).

advertised the purchase: "The Economy Mutual Aid Association," *New Orleans Republican*, July 2, 1870.

agents traveled around the state: "Local Items," *Weekly Advocate*, July 23, 1870.

Two years later: "That Tin Box Case," "The Civil Courts," and "The Custodian of a Corrupt Stake," *Daily Picayune*, March 6, 1872; "The Bee as Legal Advisor," *New Orleans Republican*, March 6, 1872.

Perhaps the members: ESM, April 20, 1874.

"The Economy Society": "The Economy Society," *Daily Picayune*, April 25, 1874.

"announced that the Act of Incorporation": ESM, June 25, 1874. The act of incorporation signed by Governor William Pitt Kellogg is included in the Economie's minutes (Act of Incorporation, Laws of the State of Louisiana, Publication by Authority No. 153, An act to incorporate the Association d'Economie and of Mutual Assistance in New Orleans, Louisiana).

a problem with the hall: ESM, July 1, 1874.

To the respective Assessors: Lusher, *Report of the State Superintendent*, appendix, circular 3, quoted in M. Shaik, "The Development of Public Education," 45.

"Of what use": Fénelon, *Dialogues Concerning Eloquence*, 32.

"Old men": *Report of the Select Committee on the New Orleans Riots*, Testimony of Sauvinet, 45.

a New Orleans school "of niggers": Alvord, *First Semi-Annual Report*, 6.

Henry L. Rey sent his children: School register, Millard Filmore School, item 3, book 1, John McDonogh No.16 boxes, Orleans Parish School Board Collection, MSS 147, book 3, Louisiana and Special Collections Department, Earl K. Long Library, University of New Orleans.

Albert's recitation: "Our Public Schools," *New Orleans Republican*, June 24, 1876. Rey recited "Young America." Information on Albert Rey thanks to Mishio Yamanaka, Doshisha University, Kyoto.

white boys at the Central High School: Christian and Dillard, "Negro in Louisiana," chap. 31, 24–25.

Eugene Duclos-Lange: Breaux, "William G. Brown," 158.

"a Negro of fair reputation": "A Promiscuous Row: An Unfortunate Sequel to the School Boys Raid on the Mixed Schools a Melee at The Keller Market," *New-Orleans Times*,

December 18, 1874. For more information on the incidents at the Keller School, see *Annual Report of the State Superintendent*, lxxx–lxxxvi.

The *New-Orleans Times* newspaper satirized: "The Regulators," *New-Orleans Times*, December 19, 1874.

"We know, without urging": "Mixed Schools," *New Orleans Bulletin*, December 16, 1874.

"A 'mixed school'": "The Public Schools," *Daily Picayune*, December 16, 1874, quoted in M. Shaik, "The Development of Public Education," 72.

"young ladies": "The Color Line," *New-Orleans Times*, December 18, 1874.

Later the White League learned: "The Week," *Weekly Louisianian*, December 26, 1874.

Charles Sumner: United States House of Representatives. "The Civil Rights Act of 1875."

"Mixed schools": "New-Orleans Schools," *New York Times*, December 23, 1874.

It even put a Black mathematician: Breaux, "William G. Brown," 162.

"nothing but 'a nigger'": "Protesting Pupils," *New-Orleans Times*, September 14, 1875.

It sometimes happened: Willey, "Education," 246.

he interviewed Ludger Boguille: Willey, "Education," 247.

Zephir Canonge: USFCC, *Eighth Census of the United States* (1860), New Orleans, Ward 6, Ancestry.com; 1868 New Orleans city directory.

chairman of the *secours*: ESM, March 23, 1875.

By November he was so ill: ESM, November 15, 1875; December 1, 1875; January 15, 1876. Boguille remained absent until March 15, 1876.

Equality, as applied: "The Color Line," *New-Orleans Times*, December 18, 1874.

"No such unwise": Christian and Dillard, "Negro in Louisiana," chap. 31, 37.

"The injunction recently issued": "Affairs in Louisiana," *New York Times*, October 24, 1877.

"the demand of a few colored": "The Color-Line in New-Orleans," editorial, *New York Times*, November 17, 1877.

"the colored fathers": P. B. S. Pinchback, letter to the editor, "The Southern Color Line," *New York Times*, November 30, 1877.

Out of nineteen thousand students: Stern, *Race and Education*, 78, table 2.3; Breaux, "William G. Brown," 179–80.

At noon on April 24, 1877: Bennett, "Louisiana."

"It grieves me": "The Louisiana Surrender," *New York Times*, April 26, 1877.

"We bulldozed": Editorial, *Daily States*, July 25, 1899, quoted in Wilds, *Afternoon Story*, 58.

Nil Desperandum: Never Despair

We observe that many: "Bulldoze," *New-Orleans Times*, November 16, 1876.

The worthless: "Here and There," *Weekly Louisianian*, December 20, 1879.

"is still sick": ESM, January 15, 1876.

"softening of the brain": Mrs. Ludger [Mary Ann Taff] Boguille death certificate, January 4, 1875, Louisiana, Death Records Index, 1804–1949, Ancestry.com.

"Who can harm us": ESM, March 26, 1858.

Louis Nelson Fouché came back: Louis Nelson Fouché was still sitting in the bimonthly meetings of the Economie society as late as 1875.

Etienne Cordeviolle: Succession of Etienne Cordeviolle, Louisiana, Civil District Court (Orleans Parish) succession records, 1890–1903, docket no. 3744, VT290, box 48, City Archives, NOPL.

Joseph Colastin Rousseau: Desdunes, *Our People*, 81.

members discussed regular business: ESM, May 1, 1876.

"honest persons": ESM, December 2, 1872.

building's construction and maintenance: ESM, March 2, 1857, includes discussions about paying the contractor and the treasurer's accounting. The "Caisse 1854" account book lists payments and balances, including taxes (January 1857), insurance (August 1857), gas (December 25, 1857), the banner (August 9, 1858), and mosquito nets (August 1, 1859).

He knew the *gardienne*'s salary: ESM, August 3, 1857. The name of the first *gardienne*, a woman, has not been preserved in the Economie records. Other individuals—all men, and all members of the society—served in custodial roles in subsequent decades, as documented in New Orleans city directories: Doresmon Crocker (218 Ursulines, 1861), Ovide Gaillardet (218 Ursulines, 1868), Albert Meilleur (216 Ursulines, 1890), and Joseph Tureaud (1422 Ursulines, 1921). Joseph Dias appears in the 1871 directory as a bartender at 218 Ursulines.

dates of the balls: ESM, January 15, 1858, and February 24, 1858 (ball receipts); April 1, 1858 (children's ball discussion).

No more despair: Horace, *Odes*, 10.

"*notre chef bien ami*": ESM, September 22, 1881.

citywide memorial march: For an overview of the city's memorial parade honoring President James Garfield, see *A History of the Proceedings in the City of New Orleans*.

"bearing three neat looking flags": "The Garfield Obsequies," *Daily Picayune*, September 27, 1881. Each division in the September 26 memorial parade was headed by a brass band (Schafer and Allen, *Brass Bands*, 13).

forty-sixth anniversary: ESM, March 1, 1882; March 6, 1882.

an even more extravagant party: ESM, February 1, 1883; March 1, 1883. Octave Rey was elected president in 1880, 1881, and 1883. He was elected president again in 1886 and 1889.

Scottish Rite Masonic Hall: The March 1, 1883, minutes refer to the Maçonic Hall Ecossaise (Scottish Rite Masonic Hall) being located on St. Peter Street, but it actually stood at the corner of Dumaine and St. Claude at the time. St. Claude Avenue ran parallel to Rampart Street as far as the New Basin Canal. Most of the buildings in the surrounding blocks were razed to create Louis Armstrong Park in the 1970s, but the Scottish Rite Masonic Hall, now called Perseverance Hall, still stands, one of a handful of buildings that make up part of the New Orleans Jazz National Historical Park (Armagost, "New Orleans Jazz Sites").

twenty-six dollars: The average daily wage for a carpenter working six days per week in Louisiana in 1883 was $2.54, or $15.24 per week (*History of Wages in the United States*, 162).

"the president ordered": ESM, March 1, 1883.

Some of the men and women: ESM, March 1, 1883; March 5, 1883.

"Dames and Demoiselles": ESM, March 1, 1883. The minutes state "*musique au frais des danceurs*" (music at the expense of the dancers).

In October 1885: "The American Exposition," *Daily Picayune*, October 29, 1885; "William M. Burwell," *Daily Picayune*, March 6, 1888; "The American Exposition," *Daily Picayune*, August 2, 1885; "The Exposition," *Daily Picayune*, June 14, 1885.

A colleague of Martinet: Louis Martinet was a vice president and Pierre Butel Boguille was a member of the Crescent City Arthur Republican Central Club ("Crescent City Arthur Republican Central Club," *Weekly Louisianian*, May 27, 1882).

Our young friend: "Personal Mention," *Weekly Pelican*, April 16, 1887.

create a political club: "Crescent City Arthur Republican Central Political Club," *Weekly Louisianian*, May 27, 1882.

signed into law the Pendleton Act: "Pendleton Act (1883)."

"the bounteous meal": "Consul Astwood at Home," *Weekly Pelican*, May 21, 1887.

L. J. Joubert: Medley, *We as Freemen*, 125.

George G. Johnson: *Official Register* (1879), 217; *Official Register* (1883), 172.

the presence of Butel: "Consul Astwood at Home," *Weekly Pelican*, May 21, 1887.

"If these enterprises": "Consul Astwood at Home," *Weekly Pelican*, May 21, 1887.

Separate Car Act: Boyd, *Separate or "Jim Crow" Car Laws*, 22–27.

On September 5, 1891: Desdunes, *Our People*, 141. Desdunes states, "It was in 1890 that the Citizens' Committee was formed," and then "the group organized itself in New Orleans, September 5, 1891. This committee, in an address published in the columns of the *Crusader*, made itself publicly known, explained its purpose and determination, and asked the public for donations to help it in its patriotic enterprise." From these statements, I made the conclusion that the committee was an informal, possibly private, political group in 1890 and began its public life in 1891.

"the question is whether to contribute": ESM, October 1, 1891.

In an "extraordinary" meeting: ESM, October 1, 1891; October 15, 1891.

one and one-half weeks' wages: The average daily wage for a carpenter working six days per week in Louisiana in 1891 was $2.35, or $14.10 per week (*History of Wages in the United States*, 163).

On February 24, 1892: Luxenberg, *Separate*, 425–26. See Medley, *We as Freemen*, for more information on Daniel Desdunes and the Comité des Citoyens.

THE AGE OF TRANSFORMATION

An Ode for Boguille

Amis Inséparables: ESM, August 1, 1892.

Magnolia Gardens: "Auction Sales," *Daily Picayune*, March 8, 1885; see also "Magnolia Gardens."

a smaller brick building with a kitchen: "Auction Sales," *Daily Picayune*, March 8, 1885.

the Economie paid $40: ESM, August 2, 1880.

The society purchased twelve gallons: ESM, May 2, 1880; August 2, 1880; May 2, 1881.

W. C. Handy: Grosvenor and Toll, "Blackface."

Clarence Williams: Songwriters Hall of Fame, "Clarence Williams."

Armand Piron, the nephew: Burlingame, "Clarence Williams."

a rental for a minstrel show: ESM, September 1, 1890.

Alfred Jourdain's installation: ESM, March 1, 1891.

I declare that the truth above: Goldthwaite, *Life and Labors of Henry W. Grady*, 188.

annual count of Negro lynchings: Wells-Barnett, *Mob Rule*.

seventeen thousand Sicilians: Saucier, "From Dago to White," 39.

Etienne Cordeviolle's father: Nolan, *Sacramental Records*, 11:98, identifies Stefano Cordeviola as a native of Genoa in the baptisms of Etienne Cordeviolle's sisters Eugenia Francisca and Maria Rosa.

the grandfather of Demosthenes Azaretto: Will of Jean Baptiste Azaretto ("Azareto"), April 17, 1843, Louisiana, Wills and Probate Records, 1756–1984, Ancestry.com.

shoemaker Ernest Luciani: ESM, March 12, 1874 (reception for Antonio Luciani); February 10, 1875 (reception for Ernest Luciani). Ernest Luciani's father was born in Italy (USFCC, *Tenth Census of the United States* [1880], Orleans Parish, Ward 7, Ancestry.com).

church of St. Augustine: ESM, June 15, 1871; September 15, 1871; October 1, 1872; April 1, 1875; November 22, 1880.

opened its parish to the immigrants: Feldman, "Why African American Churches"; Persica, "Oldest Parish"; Branley, "NOLA History."

Sicilians' patron saint: Feldman, "Why African American Churches."

"young and old men": "Chief Hennessy Avenged," *New York Times*, March 15, 1891.

"were visited at their homes": "The Lynchers Justified," *New York Times*, May 6, 1891.

a grand jury to look into the mob violence: "Blaine Answers Rudini," *New York Times*, April 16, 1891; "In Congo Square," *Daily Picayune*, April 14, 1891.

"the negro must be led to know": Goldthwaite, *Life and Labors of Henry W. Grady*, 186.

The young people imagined: Gates and McKay, *Norton Anthology*, 149–51.

"representative young colored": *A History of the Proceedings in the City of New Orleans*, 251.

Sauvinet killed himself: "Affection and Despair, Suicide of an Ex-Civil Sheriff," *Daily Picayune*, July 24, 1878.

lived at the corner: "Death notice of M. C. S. Sauvinet," *L'Abeille de la Nouvelle-Orléans*, July 24, 1878.

Samuel Wakefield: "An Ex-Senator's Suicide," *Daily Picayune*, February 2, 1883.

died by his own hand: "Suicide in a Cemetery," *Daily Picayune*, October 4, 1882.

among the first Black detectives: Ross, *Great New Orleans Kidnapping Case*, 25–26, 216–17.

walked to his family tomb: "Suicide in a Cemetery," *Daily Picayune*, April 6, 1888.

would shoot himself: "Killed Himself," *New Orleans Item*, May 15, 1893.

"When life becomes a burden": "In Congo Square," *Daily Picayune*, April 14, 1891.

taken care of his doctor bills: ESM, June 1, 1881; January 16, 1882; March 1, 1882; March 6, 1882.

had joined the society: ESM, April 1, 1874; April 20, 1874; September 15, 1874; May 15, 1879; May 2, 1880; February 1, 1881.

Fifteen out of one hundred: *Mortality Statistics: 1910*, 15.

About 3.5 percent: "Colored Persons Poor Risks," *New York Times*, April 24, 1893. The death rate for New Orleans in 1891 was 35.01 colored people per 1,000 and 23.97 white people per 1,000.

Mansion charged sixty dollars: ESM, December 15, 1880.

Every man attended every funeral: ESM, November 3, 1876. During A. Dégeorge's initiation, he said his job would not allow him to "be absent on a moment's notice" to attend funerals. The president told him he must either commit to attending the funerals or end his initiation. "This man reflected for a moment, put the money into the hands of the treasurer for his initiation and made his vows," according to the minutes.

"through the miseries": ESM, January 17, 1879. At his funeral, Engle Bart was characterized as "a respected elder . . . who supported with courage the miseries and vicissitudes of existence." (Members of the Bart and Boguille families later intermarried.)

As a unit, the members: ESM, September 1, 1880 (musicians); March 1 and 2, 1888 (Eagle Brass Band).

Jourdain's letter was in transit: "In Congo Square," *Daily Picayune*, April 14, 1891.

"pulling the trigger": "Another Suicide," *Times-Democrat*, April 14, 1891.

"As life is very uncertain": "Another Suicide," *Times-Democrat*, April 14, 1891.

"In Congo Square": "In Congo Square," *Daily Picayune*, April 14, 1891.

They lived to be very much: ESM, November 2, 1871.

approximately 2,528 Negroes lynched: Wells-Barnett, *Mob Rule*. A more contemporary figure from the Equal Justice Initiative's *Lynching in America* report says 4,048 African Americans were lynched between 1880 and 1930.

"to form a solid chain": ESM, November 2, 1871.

"Messieurs," read the entry: ESM, May 1, 1891.

My prayers were scant: Horace, *Odes*, 34.

"He can lowliest change": Horace, *Odes*, 35.

"sublime charity toward all": Spiritualist register 85–39, February 25, 1872, Grandjean Collection.

"a mother one loves": ESM, October 1, 1857.

"All wars are civil wars": Fénelon, *Moral and Political Writings*, 45.

the United States census: Pew Research Center, "What Census."

"The spiritual life is acquired": Spiritualist register 85–39, February 25, 1872, Grandjean Collection.

Ludger Boguille died: L. Boguille death certificate. The cause of death listed on Ludger's death certificate was senile debility.

Transformation

***Henceforth nothing else could*:** Desdunes, *Our People*, 145.

He may have been interred: THNOC's Survey of Historic New Orleans Cemeteries documents members of the Lacroix, Lanna, Rey, and Boisdoré families interred in St. Louis No. 2, square 3, which is also the location of the Société de Silence, Société Les Amis de l'Equité, and other benevolent society tombs.

Homer Plessy to challenge: "The Jim Crow Cars," *Daily Picayune*, October 29, 1892. Plessy was one-eighth white.

the year the Louisiana state legislature: Wells-Barnett, *Mob Rule*.

The *Daily Picayune* reported: "The Jim Crow Cars," *Daily Picayune*, October 29, 1892.

"seven-eighths Caucasian": Urofsky, "Homer Plessy."

"The object of the amendment": *Plessy v. Ferguson,* 163 U.S. 537 (1896).

"In my opinion": *Plessy v. Ferguson*, 163 U.S. 537 (1896).

***Before the killing*:** "Still Pursuing Murderer Julian," *Daily Picayune*, September 21, 1893.

***[The race issue] has aroused*:** "The Black Spectre," editorial, *Daily Advocate*, March 8, 1896.

***No certainty of death*:** "Punishment for an Outrageous Crime," *Daily Picayune*, June 22, 1899.

***Crusader* newspaper, which took up:** Greater New Orleans Louis A. Martinet Legal Society, "History."

"Seeing that the friends": Desdunes, *Our People,* 147.

"[T]he opportunity here afforded": History Matters, "Booker T. Washington."

"It is more noble and dignified": Desdunes, *Our People,* 147.

for being "suspicious": Wells-Barnett, *Mob Rule*.

Pierce surrendered to an officer: Hair, *Carnival of Fury*, 119–20.

"the Negro desperado": "Negro Kills Bluecoats and Escapes," *Times-Democrat*, July 25, 1900, quoted in Wells-Barnett, *Mob Rule*.

The mayor offered a \$250 reward: Hair, *Carnival of Fury*, 146.

"and there was no plan": "Negroes Hunted All Night by Mobs Made Up of Boys," *Daily Picayune*, July 26, 1900.

They injured and killed: Hair, *Carnival of Fury*, 149.

"in the melee a man": "Mob Anger Is Vented at Random," *Times-Democrat*, July 26, 1900, quoted in Wells-Barnett, *Mob Rule*.

"A vicious kick directed": "Mob Anger Is Vented at Random," *Times-Democrat*, July 26, 1900, quoted in Wells-Barnett, *Mob Rule*.

"I understand that he is still": "Negroes Hunted All Night by Mobs Made Up of Boys," *Daily Picayune*, July 26, 1900.

By Saturday, he was dead: "Two More Die," *Daily Picayune*, July 28, 1900.

They pulled the shutters off: Wells-Barnett, *Mob Rule*.

he ported baskets of fish and meat: "Negroes Hunted All Night by Mobs Made Up of Boys,"
    Daily Picayune, July 26, 1900.
They left him where he fell: "At Mercy of a Mob," *Daily Advocate*, July 27, 1900.
"squad of special police": "Charles Killed After Slaying Four Others," *Daily Picayune*, July
    28, 1900.
Charles weaved throughout the building: "Charles Killed After Slaying Four Others," *Daily
    Picayune*, July 28, 1900.
in a "thrilling climax": "Charles Is No More but His Deadly Aim Claims New Victims,"
    Times-Democrat, July 28, 1900, quoted in Wells-Barnett, *Mob Rule*. The calendar dates
    of the day of Charles's death are wrong in Wells-Barnett's report. She writes that the
    Times-Democrat published Charles's shootout on July 26, the day following his death,
    but the correct date of the standoff was July 27.
riled-up mobs in other parts: "Charles Killed After Slaying Four Others," *Daily Picayune*,
    July 28, 1900.
"The negroes are not subdued": "News and Notables at Local Hotels," *Daily Picayune*,
    October 15, 1900.
They had a song out: Monrovia Sound Studio, "Library of Congress Narrative."
Walter Cohen: Ingham, "Cohen, Walter L." A ten-year-old Walter is listed in the 1870
    census along with his brothers, sister, and parents; the family name is recorded as "Coin."
    USFCC, *Ninth Census of the United States* (1870), New Orleans, Ward 4, Ancestry.com.
after his brother Edward: ESM, June 15, 1880.
earlier than his brother Bernard: ESM, June 2, 1884.
Walter had substituted briefly: ESM, October 1, 1886; December 1, 1896.
The hall now hosted many organizations: ESM, October 1, 1896 (Phillis Wheatley); April 1,
    1903 (Colored Industrial Home and School); October 2, 1909 (Francs Amis and La
    Candeur).
"Rapporté par le comité": ESM, May 1, 1899.
"took the gavel and gave": ESM, December 9, 1909.
Cohen encouraged the society to buy: ESM, October 1, 1909; November 3, 1909. Victor
    Adams was the person who rented the hall and did not want to change the date. "The man
    who rented the Hall does not want to come to a compromise regarding the November 1st
    date. So the president will have to find the mayor of the city and get the permit revoked
    by the mayor. . . . A motion made to thank the president."
Cohen and lawyer J. Madison Vance: Moore, *I Fight for a Living*, 81. The Orleans Athletic
    Club opened as a sports venue in 1892 and was located at 1023 Bienville (1912 New
    Orleans city directory). Cohen and Vance's club is not to be confused with the nearby,
    present-day New Orleans Athletic Club at 222 N. Rampart Street, which was "organized
    in 1872 as the Independent Gymnastic Club, changing to the Young Men's Gymnastic
    Club in 1883 and to the present name in 1929, when it completed a fine new building"
    (1947 New Orleans city directory).
Orleans Athletic Club's advertisements: ESM, February 1, 1910; December 14, 1915. Posters
    exhibiting the Orleans Athletic Club dances are in the Hogan Jazz Archives' online exhibit
    Early New Orleans Jazz Posters.
"I know nothing against": Harlan and Smock, *Booker T. Washington Papers*, 129.
"one of the most lucrative": "Negro Gets $5,000 Office," *New York Times*, November 5, 1922.
the average annual salary: *Annual Report for the Louisiana State Department of Education*,
    23–24; there were 132,597 students enrolled. The average net per capita income for Loui-
    siana in 1922 was $3,041.04 (*Statistics of Income*, 4).

The upper class, composed: Desdunes, *Our People*, 29. In the original French: "La classe aisée, composée des gens de profession, voulant se distinguer, avait formé la Société d'Economie, qui renfermait dans son cadre tous les Créoles aux tendances exclusivistes" (*Nos hommes*, chap. 3).

Another twentieth-century assessment: Daggett, *Spiritualism*, xv.

"It was the duty of those": Grandjean's poem, bearing the French title "La Floraison—de 1848 à la guerre," is included in the Spiritualist register 85–83, Grandjean Collection.

"The memory of people": "La Floraison," Spiritualist register 85–83, Grandjean Collection.

[Members will consist of]: Urquhart, "Seventy Years," 10.

"a person too black to be": Louis. Const. of 1913, art. 248.

Light-skinned men and women: "Negroes Married to Octoroons Must Leave Louisiana," *Chicago Defender*, May 7, 1910. "Throughout the length and breadth of the State there has never been such unrest as there is to-day since the days of the Civil War," the article stated.

"25 *sous* for a souper": The word "souper" appears in the Economie minutes of March 2, 1890, which note the charge of "25 sous par a souper (banquet)." The French word "banquet" was added parenthetically to explain to the new term. The charge increased to 50 sous on February 5, 1893, but alternated between 25 sous and 50 sous through 1912. According to the Bureau of Labor Statistics, a Louisiana carpenter earned $0.29 an hour in 1890 and $0.40 an hour in 1912, making the cost of the banquet roughly equivalent to an hour's pay (*History of Wages in the United States,* 166).

The 1913 banquet consisted: ESM, February 5, 1913.

more than ninety thousand: According to federal census figures, there were approximately 89,000 Negroes in New Orleans in 1910; 101,000 in 1920; 149,000 in 1940; and 182,000 in 1950. Gibson and Jung, "Historical Census Statistics," table 19.

One report from the: ESM, July 15, 1885.

"one of the finest types": "Heard Guns Roar on Chalmette: Angele Soude Dies at 108 Years," *Times-Picayune*, March 16, 1917.

"nos jeunes beautés": "Bal Patriotique," *La Tribune de la Nouvelle-Orléans*, November 19, 1865.

"I can't help it if I am": "Heard Guns Roar on Chalmette," *Times-Picayune*, March 16, 1917.

"At present all the slave states": Rev. C. K. Marshall to Dr. Samuel A. Cartwright, October 23, 1854, Samuel A. Cartwright and Family Papers, Louisiana State University Libraries. Wayland's *Elements of Moral Science* was controversial because it suggested that individual masters should free the enslaved. Neither abolitionists nor proslavery forces liked this position.

chose to largely ignore: Fortier, *Louisiana*, 366–67. According to federal census data, the Negro population in New Orleans increased from approximately 27 percent in 1900 to 32 percent in 1950. Gibson and Jung, "Historical Census Statistics," table 19.

"was first invented": Gayarré, *Creoles of History*, 1–2.

"was extended to cover animals": Fortier, *Louisiana*, 299.

The Carnegie Hall of Jazz

When you made Economy Hall: George "Pops" Foster, interview by William Russell, August 24, 1958, reel 1, track 2, Hogan Jazz Archive Oral Histories Collection.

The night before a dance: Emile Barnes, interview by William Russell, December 20, 1960, Hogan Jazz Archive Oral Histories Collection.

Sometimes the musicians would play: Alice Zeno, interview by William Russell, November 14, 1958, Hogan Jazz Archive Oral Histories Collection.

the "**sporting class**": Cassius Wilson, interview by Richard B. Allen and Marjorie Zander, April 5, 1962, Hogan Jazz Archive Oral Histories Collection.

or daybreak: Barnes, interview by Russell, Hogan Jazz Archive Oral Histories Collection.

The first volunteer: Medley, *We as Freemen*, 135–37.

Charles Dupart: 1891 New Orleans city directory.

Posters for balls: Economy Hall ball posters, February 1, 1909 (92-48-L.331.948), February 23, 1909 (92-48-L.331.942), April 17, 1909 (92-48-L.331.943), and March 19, 1910 (92-48-L.331.941), all in the William Russell Jazz Collection at THNOC.

George Filhe and drummer John Vigne: ESM, January 2, 1906. For the band rosters of the Imperial and Peerless Orchestras, see Rose and Souchon, *New Orleans Jazz*, 144, 158.

Léon Vignes: ESM, May 1, 1874 (initiation); February 1, 1905 (funeral).

President Cohen remained at the helm: ESM, February 5, 1930.

Raoul was eight months old: USFCC, *Twelfth Census of the United States* (1900), New Orleans, Ward 6, Ancestry.com; "City Tax Sales of Immovable Property," *New Orleans Item*, October 1, 1892.

Raoul Boguille was identified as Black: USFCC, *Twelfth Census of the United States* (1900), New Orleans, Ward 6, Ancestry.com; USFCC, *Fourteenth Census of the United States* (1920), New Orleans, Ward 5, Ancestry.com; USFCC, *Fifteenth Census of the United States* (1930), New Orleans, Ward 6, Ancestry.com.

"Economy Hall was high class": Foster, interview by Russell, August 24, 1958, reel 1, track 2, Hogan Jazz Archive Oral Histories Collection.

Clarinetist George Lewis: George Lewis, interview by Tom Bethell, November 1, 1968, Hogan Jazz Archive Oral Histories Collection.

musicians often use the words: Ricard Alexis, interview by William Russell and Richard B. Allen, January 16, 1959; George Justin, interview by William Russell, June 1, 1958; both in the Hogan Jazz Archive Oral Histories Collection.

"Cheapskate Hall": Rose and Souchon, *New Orleans Jazz*, 208. The jazz musician and historian Michael White suspects that the term "Cheapskate Hall" was used by musicians in an offhand way because from time to time they hadn't received pay commensurate with their work—but he is not familiar with Cheapskate Hall being used as a substitute for the name Economy Hall. Interview by author, December 20, 2017.

members of the Streckfus family: Verne Streckfus, interview by Richard B. Allen and Paul Crawford, September 22, 1960, Hogan Jazz Archive Oral Histories Collection.

the noun *party*: Rob Kyff, "Throw A Shindig, Festival, Carnival Over These Words." *Hartford Courant*, March 29, 2010.

saxophonist Harold Dejan: Roger Mitchell, interview by Jane Julian and Harold Dejan, January 19, 1972, Hogan Jazz Archive Oral Histories Collection.

EPILOGUE: The People Who Stayed

There are but few Historians: Fénelon, *Dialogues Concerning Eloquence*, 288.

Virgie Demas Robichaux: Virgie Demas Robichaux, interview by author, February 1, 1999.

They drowned at home: Elizabeth Mullener, "Katrina's Lives Lost," *Times-Picayune*, January 31, 2006.

Other elders: Boissiere and Blache, interviews by author, December 2003.

He "had the sweetest sound": Blache, interview by author.

"Oh. Yeah!": Ernestine Josephine Landry (age 103) and Anne Regina Joseph (93), interviews by author, April 26, 2007.

The music of the 1920s: Michael White, interview by author, December 20, 2017.

members tried to sell: November 8, 1928, was the first meeting at which members discussed selling the hall and the rental property (ESM).

The structure was named: Cherrie, "History of Joseph A. Craig School."

Cohen offered: ESM, February 14, 1929. The 1428 Ursulines property (square 170, lot M) was purchased in 1950 from the Globe Homestead Association by Henry Ellis (Elmer Flanders, notary public, July 10, 1950, NONA).

"Member Jos. Craig": ESM, January 2, 1931.

"Whereas on account": ESM, July 2, 1932. The resolution is written on a ledger page following the March 1, 1935, minutes and a list of burial committee members.

Only nineteen members: ESM, July 1, 1932.

the center of its community: ESM, December 3, 1928; May 1, 1929; September 2, 1930; July 1, 1932.

"that a gentleman": ESM, November 3, 1933.

Other organizations: "Negro Morticians to Convene Sunday," *Times-Picayune*, April 23, 1938; "Laundry Workers in City Organize," *New Orleans Item*, April 19, 1935.

banquet in 1933: ESM, February 10, 1933.

International Labor Defense: "Labor Body Plans Scottsboro Drive," *Times-Picayune*, October 19, 1934.

Workers Alliance of America: "Plan Mass Meeting on Relief Slash," *New Orleans Item*, January 25, 1939.

An FBI informant: "FBI Spy Identifies Nelson as Commie," *Times-Picayune*, September 5, 1956.

the Economie sold its hall: On November 2, 1945, the Economie sold 1422 Ursulines to the Ideal Savings and Homestead for $7,000, and Ideal resold it to Arthur James Alexander for $2,400 (Label A. Katz, notary public, November 2, 1945, NONA). In 1962, Alexander sold the property to the St. Mark Missionary Baptist Church for $3,313.97 (Melissa Norvell, notary public, April 6, 1962, NONA). In 1966, the church sold the property to the Orleans Parish School Board (Samuel I. Rosenberg, notary public, July 1, 1966, NONA).

the site had a special significance: William Russell notes on Economy Hall, October 9–12, 1965, Bars and Buildings vertical file, Local, Economy Hall, Hogan Jazz Archives.

In 1964 tornadoes: F. Shaik, "The Economy Society and Community Support for Jazz."

Jazz historian: William Russell notes on Economy Hall, October 9–12, 1965, Bars and Buildings vertical file, Local, Economy Hall, Hogan Jazz Archives. After the hurricane, the school board made an offer to Rev. Alexander to buy the property, but he was unwilling and wanted to rebuild. In the end, he did not rebuild at that site.

Bailey employed Lee Dorsey: Errol Bailey Jr., interview by author, November 3, 2020.

the 1948 vice president: Lambert Boissiere Sr. is among the officers listed on the inside cover of the society's 1948–49 *Constitution and By-Laws*, a booklet in the author's holdings.

BIBLIOGRAPHY

Selected Archives and Manuscript Collections

Samuel A. Cartwright and Family Papers. Louisiana and Lower Mississippi Valley
    Collections. Special Collections. Hill Memorial Library. Louisiana State University
    Libraries, Baton Rouge.

Earl K. Long Library, University of New Orleans.
    Marcus Christian Collection.
    René Grandjean Collection.
    Historical Archives of the Supreme Court of Louisiana.
    Orleans Parish School Board Collection. Louisiana and Special Collections
        Department.

Economy Society Minutes (ESM). Private collection of the author.

The Historic New Orleans Collection (THNOC).
    Survey of Historic New Orleans Cemeteries. Some records from this survey are
        available at hnoc.org/database/cemetery/.
    William Russell Jazz Collection.

Hogan Jazz Archive. Special Collections. Howard-Tilton Memorial Library, Tulane
    University, New Orleans, LA.
    Bars and Buildings vertical file. Local, Economy Hall.
    Oral Histories Collection. Some interview recordings and transcripts are available
        online at Music Rising, musicrising.tulane.edu/listen.

Land Records Division. Office of the Clerk of Civil Court for the Parish of Orleans.
    Conveyance office records.
    New Orleans Notarial Archives (NONA).

Edward Livingston Papers. Special Collections. Princeton University Library, Princeton, NJ.

New Orleans Public Library (NOPL).
    Emancipation petitions, 1813–43.
    Louisiana, Civil District Court (Orleans Parish) succession records, 1890–1903.
    Louisiana, Second District Court (Orleans Parish) succession records, 1846–80.
    Orleans Parish Sheriff's Office. Sales Books, 1846–63.

St. Louis Cathedral Baptism Records. Church Records. Archdiocese of New Orleans.

Newspapers Consulted

L'Abeille de la Nouvelle-Orléans / *The New Orleans Bee*
Boston Recorder

Chicago Defender
Concordia Intelligencer, Vidalia, LA
Le Courrier de la Louisiane / Louisiana Courier, New Orleans, LA
Daily Advocate, Baton Rouge, LA
Daily Constitutionalist, Augusta, GA
Daily Delta, New Orleans, LA
Daily Picayune, New Orleans, LA
Daily States, New Orleans, LA
Daily True Delta, New Orleans, LA
Era, New Orleans, LA
Evening Star, Washington, DC
Hartford Courant, Connecticut
Janesville Gazette, Wisconsin
Louisiana Gazette, New Orleans, LA
Le Louisianais et ami des lois / The Louisianian and Friend of the Laws, New Orleans, LA
Massachusetts Spy, Worcester, MA
New Orleans Bulletin
New-Orleans Commercial Bulletin
New Orleans Crescent
New Orleans Daily Crescent
New Orleans Item
New Orleans Observer
New Orleans Republican
New-Orleans Times
New Orleans Times-Picayune
New York Daily Tribune
New-York Freeman's Journal and Catholic Register
New York Times
New York World
Pomeroy's Democrat, New York, NY
Sacramento Daily Union
Tägliche Deutsche Zeitung, New Orleans, LA
Times-Democrat, New Orleans, LA
La Tribune de la Nouvelle-Orléans / New Orleans Tribune, New Orleans, LA
Tri-Weekly Advocate, Baton Rouge, LA
L'Union: mémorial politique, littéraire et progressiste / The Union: Political, Literary, and Progressive Record, New Orleans, LA
Vermont Journal, Windsor, VT
Weekly Advocate, Baton Rouge, LA
Weekly Louisianian, New Orleans, LA
Weekly Pelican, New Orleans, LA

City Directories

Cohen's New Orleans Directory for 1855. New Orleans, 1855.
Cohen's New Orleans and Lafayette Directory. New Orleans, 1851, 1852, 1854.
Edwards' Annual Director. New Orleans, 1871.
Gardner's New Orleans Directory. New Orleans, 1861, 1867, 1868.
Michel's New Orleans Annual and Commercial Register for 1834. New Orleans, 1833.
Mygatt and Co.'s Directory. New Orleans, 1857.

The New Orleans Directory. New Orleans, 1832.
The New-Orleans Directory and Register. New Orleans, 1822.
New Orleans Directory for 1842. New Orleans, 1842.
Polk's New Orleans Directory. New Orleans: R. L. Polk and Co., 1947, 1956.
Soards' New Orleans Directory. New Orleans: L. Soards, 1875, 1890, 1891, 1892, 1912, 1921.

Interviews by Author

Bailey, Errol, Jr. November 3, 2020.
Blache, Adrienne Woods. December 2003.
Boissiere, Mildred Meilleur. December 2003.
Campanella, Richard. August 10, 2018.
Joseph, Anne Regina. April 26, 2007.
Landry, Ernestine Josephine. April 26, 2007.
Mitchell, Brian K. December 19, 2017.
Robichaux, Virgie Demas. February 1, 1999.
Stanley, Ingrid. July 5, 2020.
White, Michael. December 20, 2017.

Online Databases

Ancestry.com
  Louisiana, Soldiers in the War of 1812.
  Louisiana, Statewide Death Index, 1819–1964.
  Louisiana, Wills and Probate Records, 1756–1984.
  New Orleans, Louisiana, Birth Records Index, 1790–1915.
  New Orleans, Louisiana, Death Records Index, 1804–1949.
  New Orleans, Louisiana, Marriage Records Index, 1831–1964.
  US, City Directories, 1822–1995.
  US, Confederate Soldiers Compiled Service Records, 1861–1865.
  US Federal Census Collection, 1790–1940.
  US, Freedman's Bank Records, 1865–1874.
  US, War of 1812 Pension Application Files Index, 1812–1815.
FamilySearch.org
  Louisiana, Orleans Parish Death Records and Certificates, 1835–1954.
  Louisiana, Orleans Parish Marriages, 1837–1957.
  United States, Freedman's Bank Records, 1865–1874.
  United States, Freedmen's Bureau, Records of the Superintendent of Education
    and of the Division of Education, 1865–1872.
Fold3.com
  Civil War Service Records (CMSR)—Confederate—Louisiana.
  Civil War "Widows' Pensions."
  War of 1812 (United States).

Works Consulted

*Abstract of the Returns of the Fifth Census, Showing the Number of Free People, the Number
    of Slaves, the Federal or Representative Number, and the Aggregate of Each County of
    Each State of the United States*. Washington, DC, 1832.
*Acts and Resolutions of the Third Session of the Provisional Congress of the Confederate States,
    Held at Richmond, Va*. Richmond, VA: 1861.

Acts Passed at the First Session of the First Legislature of the Territory of Orleans. New Orleans, 1807.

Acts Passed by the Second Legislature of the State of Louisiana, at its Second Session, Held and Begun in the Town of Baton Rouge, on the 15th January, 1855. New Orleans, 1855.

Allen, William Francis, Charles Pickard Ware, and Lucy McKim Garrison, comp. *Slave Songs of the United States.* 1867. Facsimile edition. Bedford, MA: Applewood, 1996.

Alvord, John W. *First Semi-Annual Report on Schools and Finances of Freedmen, January 1, 1866.* In *Semi-Annual Report on Schools for Freedmen*, Freedmen's Schools and Textbooks 1. New York: AMS Press, 1980.

———. *Sixth Semi-Annual Report on Schools for Freedmen, July 1, 1868.* In *Semi-Annual Report on Schools for Freedmen*, Freedmen's Schools and Textbooks 1. New York: AMS Press, 1980.

Amos, Gray B., comp. "Alphabetical Index of Changes in Street Names, Old and New Period 1852 to Current Date, Dec. 1st 1938." New Orleans Public Library, Louisiana Division. archives.nolalibrary.org/~nopl/facts/streetnames /namesa.htm.

———. "Corrected—Index, Alphabetical and Numerical, of Changes in Street Names and Numbers, Old and New, 1852 to Current Date [1938]." New Orleans Public Library, Louisiana Division. archives.nolalibrary.org/~nopl/info/louinfo /numberchanges/numberchanges.htm.

Annual Report for the Louisiana State Department of Education for the Session 1921–1922. Baton Rouge: Ramires-Jones Printing Company, 1923.

Annual Report of the State Superintendent, William G. Brown, to the General Assembly of Louisiana, for the Year 1874. New Orleans, 1875.

Armagost, Karen. "New Orleans Jazz Sites: Then and Now." National Park Service, May 2012. nps.gov/jazz/learn/historyculture/upload/New-Orleans-Jazz-Sites-Then -and-Now.pdf.

Austerman, Wayne R. "Aguardiente at the Alamo: Alcohol Abuse and the Texas War for Independence, 1835–1836." *US Army Medical Department Journal.* April–June 2010: 72–80.

Bacot, H. Parrott, Barbara SoRelle Bacot, Sally Kittredge Reeves, John Magill, and John H. Lawrence. *Marie Adrien Persac: Louisiana Artist.* Baton Rouge: Louisiana State University Press, 2000.

Bailey, Jeff. "Jim Bowie (1796–1836)." *CALS Encyclopedia of Arkansas.* Central Arkansas Library System, 2006–. Last revised November 18, 2011. encyclopediaofarkansas .net/entries/jim-bowie-2420/.

Baldwin, Jack, and Winnie Baldwin. *Baldwin's Guide to Museums of Louisiana.* Gretna, LA: Pelican, 1999.

Bell, Caryn Cossé. *Revolution, Romanticism, and the Afro-Creole Protest Tradition in Louisiana, 1718–1868.* Baton Rouge: Louisiana State University Press, 2004.

———. "Savary, Charles Joseph." In *African American National Biography*, edited by Henry Louis Gates Jr. and Evelyn Brooks Higginbotham. Vol. 7. New York: Oxford University Press, 2008.

Bellegarde-Smith, Patrick. *Haiti: The Breached Citadel.* Boulder: Westview Press, 1990.

Bennett, A. J. "Louisiana—The Withdrawal of the Federal Troops from the State House in New Orleans, at Noon, on April 24th." *Frank Leslie's Illustrated Newspaper*, May 19, 1877.

Bergeron, Arthur W., Jr. "Free Men of Color in Gray." *Civil War History* 32, no. 3 (September 1986): 247–55.

Berry, Mary F. "Negro Troops in Blue and Gray: The Louisiana Native Guards, 1861–1863." *Louisiana History* 8, no. 2 (Spring 1967): 165–90.

Blassingame, John W. *Black New Orleans, 1860–1880*. Chicago: University of Chicago Press, 1973.

Blokker, Laura Ewen. "Education in Louisiana." Louisiana Department of Culture, Recreation, and Tourism, May 15, 2012. crt.state.la.us/Assets/OCD/hp /nationalregister/historic_contexts/Education_in_Louisiana.pdf.

Bodenhorn, Howard. "Antebellum Banking in the United States." EH.net (Economic History Association). Accessed November 12, 2020. eh.net/encyclopedia /antebellum-banking-in-the-united-states/.

Boguille, FMC, Administrator, v. Faille, FWC. 1 La. Ann. 204 (1846) 01142. Historical Archives of the Supreme Court of Louisiana. Earl K. Long Library, University of New Orleans. dspace.uno.edu:8080/xmlui/handle/123456789/21237.

Boguille, François. Death certificate of François Boguille. January 15, 1845. New Orleans (La.) Board of Health Death Certificates, 1804–1915, microfilm FF650, vol. 10: 298. Louisiana Division, New Orleans Public Library.

Boguille, François, and Suzanne Butel. Marriage contract of François Boguy [*sic*] and Suzanne Butel. September 27, 1820, vol. 18: 67. Marc Lafitte, notary public. New Orleans Notarial Archives.

Boguille, Ludger. Death certificate of J. B. Ludger Boguille. January 18, 1892. Orleans Parish Death Index-B, Death Index Reel 2, 1877–1895, vol. 101: 7. Louisiana Division, New Orleans Public Library.

Boisdoré and Goulé, FPC, v. Citizens' Bank of Louisiana. 9 La. Ann. 506 (1836) 00722. Historical Archives of the Supreme Court of Louisiana. Earl K. Long Library, University of New Orleans. dspace.uno.edu:8080/xmlui/handle/123456789 /18067.

Bois Saint Lys, Georges de Maillard de. *Plan de la ville de Jérémie dans la partie sud de Saint-Domingue*. 18th century. Gallica, Bibliothèque nationale de France. gallica.bnf.fr/ark:/12148/btv1b8442523h/f1.item.zoom.

Bordewich, Fergus M. "John Brown's Day of Reckoning." *Smithsonian Magazine*, October 2009. smithsonianmag.com/history/john-browns-day-of-reckoning-139165084/.

Boyd, Richard Henry. *The Separate or "Jim Crow" Car Laws or Legislative Enactments of Fourteen Southern States, Together with the Report and Order of the Interstate Commerce Commission to Segregate Negro or "Colored" Passengers on Railroad Trains and in Railroad Stations*. Nashville: National Baptist Publishing Board, 1909.

Brace, C. Loring. "The 'Ethnology' of Josiah Clark Nott." *Bulletin of the New York Academy of Medicine* 50, no. 4 (April 1974): 509–28.

Branley, Edward. "NOLA History: St. Augustine Church in Faubourg Tremé." GONOLA, September 18, 2015. gonola.com/things-to-do-in-new-orleans/nola -history-st-augustine-church-faubourg-treme.

Breaux, Peter J. "William G. Brown and the Development of Education: A Retrospective on the Career of a State Superintendent of Public Education of African Descent in Louisiana." PhD diss., Florida State University, 2006.

Breeden, James O., "States-Rights Medicine in the Old South." *Bulletin of the New York Academy of Medicine* 52, no. 3 (March–April 1976): 348–72.

Brown, William Wells. *The Negro in the American Rebellion: His Heroism and His Fidelity.* Boston, 1867.

Bruce, Clint, ed. and trans. *Afro-Creole Poetry in French from Louisiana's Radical Civil War–Era Newspapers: A Bilingual Edition.* New Orleans: The Historic New Orleans Collection, 2020.

Burlingame, Sandra. "Clarence Williams." Naxos Records. Accessed November 12, 2020. naxos.com/person/Clarence_Williams_20074/20074.htm.

Calomiris, Charles W., and Jonathan Pritchett. "Betting on Secession: Quantifying Political Events Surrounding Slavery and the Civil War." *American Economic Review* 106, no. 1 (January 2016): 1–23.

Carter, Clarence Edwin, ed. *The Territorial Papers of the United States.* Vol. 9, *The Territory of Orleans, 1803–1812.* Washington, DC: Government Printing Office, 1940.

Cartwright, Samuel A. "Diseases and Peculiarities of the Negro Race." *De Bow's Review* 11, nos. 1–3 (1851): 64–69, 209–13, 331–36.

———. "Ethnology of the Negro or Prognathous Race." Lecture presented at the New Orleans Academy of Sciences, New Orleans, LA, November 30, 1857. US National Library of Medicine. archive.org/details/101168906.nlm.nih.gov.

A Century of Population Growth: From the First Census of the United States to the Twelfth, 1790–1900. Washington, DC: Government Printing Office, 1909.

Cherrie, Lolita V. "The History of Joseph A. Craig School." CreoleGen.com, January 5, 2015. creolegen.org/2015/01/05/the-history-of-joseph-a-craig-school/.

Chery, Dady. "Dodo Titit—Sleep Little One: Haitian Lullaby." Haiti Chery, March 26, 2012. dadychery.org/2012/03/26/dodo-titit-sleep-little-one-haitian-lullaby/.

Christian, Marcus B. *Negro Soldiers in the Battle of New Orleans.* New Orleans: Eastern Park and Monument Association Printers, 1991. First published 1965 by Battle of New Orleans, 150th Anniversary Committee of Louisiana (New Orleans).

———. "The Theory of the Poisoning of Oscar J. Dunn." *Phylon* 6, no. 3 (1945): 254–66.

Christian, Marcus B., and Dillard Unit of the Louisiana Writers' Project. "The Negro in Louisiana." 1942. Marcus Christian Collection. Earl K. Long Library, University of New Orleans, 2011. louisianadigitallibrary.org/islandora/object/uno -p15140coll42:collection.

City of New Orleans Property Viewer. City of New Orleans, Mayor LaToya Cantrell. Last updated May 23, 2018. nola.gov/onestop/property-viewer.

Clark, Emily. *The Strange History of the American Quadroon.* Chapel Hill: University of North Carolina Press, 2013.

Clark, Emily Suzanne. *A Luminous Brotherhood: Afro-Creole Spiritualism in Nineteenth-Century New Orleans.* Chapel Hill: University of North Carolina Press, 2016.

Colton, Calvin. *Manual for Emigrants to America.* London, 1832.

Connor, William P. "Reconstruction Rebels: The *New Orleans Tribune* in Post-War Louisiana." *Louisiana History* 21, no. 2 (Spring 1980): 159–81.

Conrad, Glenn R. *The First Families of Louisiana.* 2 vols. Baton Rouge: Claitor's, 1970.

Constitution Adopted by the State Constitutional Convention of the State of Louisiana, March 7, 1868. New Orleans, 1868.

Constitution of the State of Louisiana Adopted in Convention at the City of Baton Rouge, November 22, 1913. Baton Rouge, Ramires-Jones Printing Company, 1913.

Daggett, Melissa. *Spiritualism in Nineteenth-Century New Orleans: The Life and Times of Henry Louis Rey.* Jackson: University Press of Mississippi, 2016.

The David Walker Memorial Project. "The Death of David Walker." Accessed November 12, 2020. www.davidwalkermemorial.org/david-walker/death-of-david-walker.

Debates in the Convention for the Revision and Amendment of the Constitution of the State of Louisiana. New Orleans, 1864.

Dédé, Edmond. *Edmond Dédé: Mon pauvre coeur / Francoise et Tortillard / Méphisto masqué.* Naxos American Classics 8.559038, 2000, CD.

Desdunes, Rodolphe Lucien. *Nos hommes et notre histoire.* Montreal: Arbour and Dupont, 1911; Project Gutenberg, 2007. gutenberg.org/files/20554/20554-h/20554-h.htm.

———. *Our People and Our History.* Translated and edited by Sr. Dorothea Olga McCants. Baton Rouge: Louisiana State University Press, 1973.

A Digest of the Civil Laws in Force in the Territory of Orleans. New Orleans, 1808.

Douglas, Nick. "How New Orleans' Creole Musicians Forged the Fight for Civil Rights." AfroPunk, February 25, 2019. afropunk.com/2019/02/black-history-month-how -new-orleans-creole-musicians-forged-the-fight-for-civil-rights/.

Drayton, William. *The South Vindicated from the Treason and Fanaticism of the Northern Abolitionists.* Philadelphia, 1836.

Du Bois, W. E. B. *The Souls of Black Folk: Essays and Sketches.* Chicago: A. C. McClurg, 1903; Project Gutenberg, 2008. gutenberg.org/files/408/408-h/408-h.htm.

Dumas, Alexandre, *père,* and Alphonse Varney. "Les Girondins: Mourir pour la patrie. Revolutionary Song of '48." New York, 1848. Box 032, item 03, Levy Sheet Music Collection, Johns Hopkins University. jhir.library.jhu.edu/handle/1774.2/17172.

Eakin, Sue. "James Madison Wells." *64 Parishes Encyclopedia of Louisiana.* Louisiana Endowment for the Humanities, 2010–. 64parishes.org/entry/james -madison-wells.

Eggleston, G. K. "The Work of Relief Societies During the Civil War." *Journal of Negro History* 14, no. 3 (July 1929): 272–99.

Equal Justice Initiative. *Lynching in America: Confronting the Legacy of Racial Terror.* 3d ed. Montgomery, AL: Equal Justice Initiative, 2017. lynchinginamerica.eji.org/report/.

Erickson, Paul A. "The Anthropology of Josiah Clark Nott." *Kroeber Anthropological Society Papers* no. 65–66 (1986): 103–20.

Executive Documents Printed by Order of the House of Representatives during the Second Session of the Thirty-Ninth Congress, 1866–'67. Vol. 10. Washington, DC, 1867.

"Facts in Regard to African Colonization: A Memorial Addressed to the Citizens of Louisiana by the Louisiana Colonization Society." *The African Repository and Colonial Journal* 33, no. 10 (July 1857): 315.

Feldman, Nina. "Why African American Churches in New Orleans Celebrate a Sicilian Holiday." *The World.* PRI, March 16, 2016. pri.org/stories/2016-03-16 /why-african-american-churches-new-orleans-celebrate-sicilian-holiday.

Fénelon, François. *The Adventures of Telemachus: In English Verse.* Book 1. London, 1712.

———. *The Adventures of Telemachus, the Son of Ulysses.* Translated by John Hawkesworth. Manchester, UK, 1847.

———. *Dialogues Concerning Eloquence in General; and Particularly, That Kind Which Is Fit for the Pulpit: by the Late Archbishop of Cambray.* Translated by William Stevenson. London, 1722.

———. *Dialogues des morts anciens et modernes avec quelques fables, composez pour l'éducation d'un Prince.* Paris, 1718.

———. *Fénelon: Moral and Political Writings.* Translated by Ryan Patrick Hanley. New York: Oxford University Press, 2020.

———. *Fénelon's Treatise on the Education of Girls: Translated from the French, and Adapted to English Readers, with an Additional Chapter, "On Religious Studies."* Translated by Rev. Thomas Frognall Dibdin. Albany, NY, 1806.

Filleul, E. *C. S. Sauvinet vs. J. A. Walker: A Brief on Behalf of Plaintiff and Appellee.* New Orleans, 1871.

Flake, Marcella Monk. "Sing Two Stanzas and Rebel in the Morning: The Role of Black Religious Music in the Struggle for Freedom." Yale-New Haven Teachers Institute, 1997. teachersinstitute.yale.edu/curriculum/units/1997/5/97.05.07.x.html.

Florian, Jean-Pierre Claris de. *The Fables of Florian.* Translated by Gen. J. W. Phelps. New York, 1888.

———. *History of the Moors of Spain: Translated from the French Original of M. Florian: To Which Is Added, a Brief Notice of Islamism.* New York, 1840.

Fogel, Robert William. "The New Economic History: Its Findings and Methods." In *Foundations,* edited by Robert M. Burns, 276–92. Vol. 1 of *Historiography: Critical Concepts in Historical Studies.* New York: Routledge, 2006.

Fogel, Robert William, and Stanley L. Engerman. *Time on the Cross: The Economics of American Negro Slavery.* New York: W. W. Norton, 1995. Originally published 1974.

Follett, Richard. *The Sugar Masters: Planters and Slaves in Louisiana's Cane World 1820–1860.* Baton Rouge: Louisiana State University Press, 2005.

Foner, Eric. *Freedom's Lawmakers: A Directory of Black Officeholders during Reconstruction.* Rev. ed. Baton Rouge: Louisiana State University Press, 1996.

Foner, Eric, and John A. Garraty, eds. *The Reader's Companion to American History.* Boston: Houghton Mifflin, 1991.

Fortier, Alcée, ed. *Louisiana: Comprising Sketches of Parishes, Towns, Events, Institutions, and Persons Arranged in Cyclopedic Form.* Vol. 1. Madison, WI: Century Historical Association, 1914.

Foust, James D., and Dale E. Swan. "Productivity and Profitability of Antebellum Slave Labor: A Micro-Approach." *Agricultural History* 44, no. 1 (January 1970): 39–62.

The Freedmen's Bureau Online. "List of Orphans in Orphan Asylum, New Orleans, Louisiana, 1866." freedmensbureau.com/louisiana/orleansorphans.htm.

———. "Miscellaneous Reports and Lists Relating to Murders and Outrages, March 1867–November 1868." Records of the Assistant Commissioner for the State of Louisiana, Bureau of Refugees, Freedmen and Abandoned Lands, 1865–1869. National Archives and Records Administration, Microfilm M1027, Roll 34. freedmensbureau.com/louisiana/outrages/outrages4.htm.

Freund, Max, ed. and trans. *Gustav Dressel's Houston Journal: Adventures in North America and Texas, 1837–1841.* Austin: University of Texas Press, 1954.

"The Funeral of Captain Andre Cailloux." *Harper's Weekly,* August 29, 1863.

Fussell, Elizabeth. "Constructing New Orleans, Constructing Race: A Population History of New Orleans." In "Through the Eye of Katrina: The Past as Prologue?," edited by Clarence Mohr and Lawrence Powell, special issue, *Journal of American History* 94, no. 3 (December 2007): 846–55.

Gabe, Thomas, Gene Falk, Maggie McCarty, and Virginia W. Mason. "Hurricane Katrina: Social-Demographic Characteristics of Impacted Areas." Washington, DC: Library of Congress, 2005. gnocdc.s3.amazonaws.com/reports/crsrept.pdf.

Garnet, Henry Highland. *Walker's Appeal, with a Brief Sketch of His Life, and Also Garnet's Address to the Slaves of the United States of America.* New York, 1848.

Garrison, William Lloyd. "Exposure of the American Colonization Society." Extract from "Thoughts on African Colonization: or an Impartial Exhibition of the Doctrines, Principles and Purposes of the American Colonization Society" (Boston, 1852). Uncle Tom's Cabin and American Culture. Institute for Advanced Technology in the Humanities, University of Virginia. utc.iath.virginia.edu/abolitn/abeswlgbt .html.

Gates, Henry Louis, Jr., and Nellie Y. McKay, eds. *The Norton Anthology of African American Literature.* 2nd ed. New York: W. W. Norton and Company, 2003.

Gayarré, Charles. *The Creoles of History and the Creoles of Romance: A Lecture Delivered in the Hall of the Tulane University, New Orleans.* New Orleans, 1885.

Geggus, David, ed. and trans. *The Haitian Revolution: A Documentary History.* Indianapolis: Hackett, 2014.

Gehman, Mary. "Louisiana Creoles Who Emigrated to Mexico Mid-to-Late 19th Century." DVille Press, 2000. dvillepress.com/LCMC.php.

Gibson, Campbell, and Kay Jung. "Historical Census Statistics on Population Totals by Race, 1790 to 1990, and by Hispanic Origin, 1970 to 1990, for Large Cities and Other Urban Places in the United States." Working Paper no. 76, Population Division, US Census. February 2005. www.census.gov/content/dam/Census /library/working-papers/2005/demo/POP-twps0076.pdf.

Godoy, Maria. "Meet the Calas, a New Orleans Tradition That Helped Free Slaves." *The Salt: What's on Your Plate.* National Public Radio, February 12, 2013. npr.org /sections/thesalt/2013/02/10/171663336/meet-the-calas-a-new-orleans-treat-that -helped-free-slaves.

Goldthwaite, Wm. M., ed. *Life and Labors of Henry W. Grady, His Speeches, Writings, Etc.* New York, 1890.

Gordon, John Steele. "The Freedman's Bank." *American Heritage* 44, no. 8 (December 1993). americanheritage.com/freedmans-bank.

Gottschalk, Louis Moreau. *Bamboula: Danse des nègres.* Paris, n.d.

Grand Celebration in Honor of the Passage of the Ordinance of Emancipation, by the Free State Convention, on the Eleventh Day of May, 1864. New Orleans, 1864.

Greater New Orleans Louis A. Martinet Legal Society. "History." Accessed November 12, 2020. gnomartinet.com/history/.

Greene, Harlan, Brian E. Hutchins, and Harry S. Hutchins. *Slave Badges and the Slave-Hire System in Charleston, South Carolina, 1783–1865.* Jefferson, NC: McFarland, 2004.

Greenwald, Erin M., ed. *New Orleans, the Founding Era.* New Orleans: The Historic New Orleans Collection, 2018.

Gregory, H. F. "Pete." "Indians and Folklife in the Florida Parishes of Louisiana." In *Folklife in the Florida Parishes.* Baton Rouge: Louisiana Department of Culture, Recreation, and Tourism, 2000. louisianafolklife.org/LT/Virtual_Books/Fla _Parishes/book_florida_indians.html.

Greiner, Meinrad. *The Louisiana Digest: Embracing the Laws of the Legislature of a General Nature, Enacted from the Year 1804 to 1841.* Vol. 1. New Orleans, 1841.

Grosvenor, Edwin S., and Robert C. Toll. "Blackface: The Sad History of Minstrelsy." *American Heritage* 64, no. 1 (Winter 2019). americanheritage.com/blackface -sad-history-minstrel-shows.

Hair, William Ivy. *Carnival of Fury.* Baton Rouge: Louisiana State University Press, 1976.

Hall, Gwendolyn Midlo. *Databases for the Study of Afro-Louisiana History and Genealogy, 1699–1860.* Baton Rouge: Louisiana State University Press, 2000, CD-ROM. Data

available online at Afro-Louisiana History and Genealogy, 1718–1820, ibiblio.org
/laslave/, and Slave Biographies: The Atlantic Database Network, slavebiographies
.org/.

Haller, J. S., Jr. "The Negro and the Southern Physician: A Study of Medical and Racial
Attitudes 1800–1860." *Medical History* 16, no. 3 (1972): 238–53.

Hankins, Jonn Ethan, and Steven Maklansky, eds. *Raised to the Trade: Creole Building Arts
of New Orleans*. New Orleans: New Orleans Museum of Art, 2002. Exhibition
catalog.

Harlan, Louis R., and Raymond W. Smock, eds. *The Booker T. Washington Papers*. Volume
10, *1909–11*. Urbana: University of Illinois Press, 1981.

Hazard, Paul. *The Crisis of the European Mind, 1680–1715*. New York: New York Review
Books, 2013.

The Historic New Orleans Collection and the Louisiana Philharmonic Orchestra.
"Identity, History, Legacy: La Société Philharmonique." New Orleans: The
Historic New Orleans Collection, 2011. hnoc.org/sites/default/files/file_uploads
/IdentityHistoryLegacyProgram_reduced.pdf.

History Matters. "Booker T. Washington Delivers the 1895 Atlanta Compromise Speech."
Accessed November 12, 2020. historymatters.gmu.edu/d/39/.

*A History of the Proceedings in the City of New Orleans, on the Occasion of the Funeral
Ceremonies in Honor of James Abram Garfield, Late President of the United States,
which Took Place on Monday, September 26th, 1881*. New Orleans, 1881.

*History of Wages in the United States from Colonial Times to 1928. Revision of Bulletin No.
499 with Supplement, 1929–1933*. Washington, DC: US Government Printing
Office, 1934.

Hogan Jazz Archive. *Early New Orleans Jazz Posters*. Special Collections, Howard-Tilton
Memorial Library, Tulane University, New Orleans, LA. Accessed November 12,
2020. exhibits.tulane.edu/exhibit/jazz-posters/.

Hollandsworth, James G., Jr. *The Louisiana Native Guards: The Black Military Experience
during the Civil War*. Baton Rouge: Louisiana State University Press, 1995.

Honora, Jari Christopher. "Boisdoré—A Quintessential Creole Family." CreoleGen.com,
August 8, 2012. creolegen.org/2012/08/08/boisdore-a-quintessential-creole
-family/.

Horace. *The Odes and Carmen Saeculare of Horace*. Translated by John Conington, 5th ed.
London, 1872.

Hunt, Alfred N. *Haiti's Influence on Antebellum America: Slumbering Volcano in the
Caribbean*. Baton Rouge: Louisiana State University Press, 1988.

Hunt, Sarah. "It Takes Great Nerve to Walk Here: Yankee Schoolmarms and
Southern Belles in Post-Bellum Freedman's Schools—1860–1870." *Journal of
Interdisciplinary Undergraduate Research* 9 (2017): article 4.

Ingham, John N. "Cohen, Walter L." In *American National Biography*. New York: Oxford
University Press, 2000. doi.org/10.1093/anb/9780198606697.article.1001933.

"Inward Slave Manifests for the Port of New Orleans: Roll 12, 1837–1839." Transcribed by
Alma McClendon. In "A Partial Transcription of Inward Slave Manifests: Port
of New Orleans, Record Group 36, United States Customs Service, Collector of
Customs at New Orleans. Microfilm rolls 1–3, 12 of 25 rolls." AfriGeneas.com,
December 27, 1999. afrigeneas.com/slavedata/Roll.12.1837-1839.html.

James, C. L. R. *The Black Jacobins: Toussaint L'Ouverture and the San Domingo Revolution*.
2nd ed., rev. New York: Vintage, 1989.

Johnson, Walter. *Soul by Soul: Life inside the Antebellum Slave Market*. Cambridge: Harvard University Press, 2001.

Jones, Gavin. *Strange Talk: The Politics of Dialect Literature in Gilded Age America*. Berkley and Los Angeles: University of California Press, 1999.

Keith, LeeAnna. "Colfax Massacre." *64 Parishes Encyclopedia of Louisiana*. Louisiana Endowment for the Humanities, 2010–. 64parishes.org/entry/colfax-massacre.

Kinshasa, Kwando Mbiassi. *African American Chronology: Chronologies of the American Mosaic*. Westport, CT: Greenwood, 2006.

Kmen, Henry A. *Music in New Orleans: The Formative Years, 1791–1841*. Baton Rouge: Louisiana State University Press, 1966.

Knight, Michael F. "The Rost Home Colony, St. Charles Parish, Louisiana." *Prologue* 33, no. 3 (Fall 2001): 214–20. archives.gov/publications/prologue/2001/fall/rost-home-colony.html.

Kotlikoff, Laurence J. "The Structure of Slave Prices in New Orleans, 1804–1862." *Economic Inquiry* 17, no. 4 (October 1979): 496–518.

Lamy, Andrénette. Succession record of Andrénette Lamy (Mrs. Ludger Boguille). June 1853. Louisiana, Second District Court (Orleans Parish) succession records, 1846–80, VSB290, box 35. New Orleans Public Library.

Lebergott, Stanley. "Wage Trends, 1800–1900." In *Trends in the American Economy in the Nineteenth Century*, edited by the Conference on Research in Income and Wealth, 449–500. Princeton, NJ: Princeton University Press, 1960.

Léger, Jacques Nicolas. *Haiti: Her History and Her Detractors*. New York: Neale, 1907.

Lewis, Dany. "The 1873 Colfax Massacre Crippled the Reconstruction Era." *Smithsonian Magazine*, April 13, 2016. smithsonianmag.com/smart-news/1873-colfax-massacre-crippled-reconstruction-180958746/.

Library of Congress. "Colonization." *The African-American Mosaic*. 1994. loc.gov/exhibits/african/afam002.html.

Lincoln, Abraham. Letter to Gov. Michael Hahn. March 13, 1864. Shapell Foundation. shapell.org/manuscript/reconstruction-suffrage-for-louisiana-blacks/#transcripts.

Logsdon, Joseph, and Caryn Cossé Bell. "The Americanization of Black New Orleans, 1850–1900." In *Creole New Orleans: Race and Americanization*, edited by Joseph Logsdon and Arthur R. Hirsch. Baton Rouge: Louisiana State University Press, 1992.

Long, Carolyn Morrow. *A New Orleans Voudou Priestess: The Legend and Reality of Marie Laveau*. Gainesville: University Press of Florida, 2006.

"The Louisiana Native Guards." Excerpted and submitted by Jim Hollandsworth from *Freedom's Lawmakers: A Directory of Black Officeholders during Reconstruction*, edited by Eric Foner. Baton Rouge: Louisiana State University Press, 1996. USGenWeb Archives. files.usgwarchives.net/la/state/military/afriamer/natguard.txt.

"Louisiana State Colonization Society." *The African Repository and Colonial Journal* 15, no. 5 (March 1839): 89.

Louisiana State Museum. *The Cabildo: Two Centuries of Louisiana History*. Louisiana Department of Culture, Recreation and Tourism, 2018. crt.state.la.us/louisiana-state-museum/online-exhibits/the-cabildo/index.

LSU Libraries. Free People of Color in Louisiana: Revealing an Unknown Past. A Collaborative Digital Collection. Accessed November 12, 2020. lib.lsu.edu/sites/all/files/sc/fpoc/collections.html.

Lundy, Benjamin. *The Life, Travels, and Opinions of Benjamin Lundy, Including His Journeys to Texas and Mexico.* Compiled by Thomas Earl. Philadelphia, 1847.

Lusher, Robert M. *Report of the State Superintendent of Public Education, to the General Assembly of the State of Louisiana.* In *Documents of the Second Session of the Second Legislature of the State of Louisiana.* New Orleans, 1867.

Luxenberg, Steve. *Separate: The Story of* Plessy v. Ferguson*, and America's Journey from Slavery to Segregation.* New York: W. W. Norton, 2019.

Maduell, Charles R., comp. and trans. *The Census Tables for the French Colony of Louisiana from 1699 through 1732.* N.p.: Clearfield, 1993. First published 1972 by Genealogical Publishing (Baltimore).

"Magnolia Gardens." In *Resorts of New Orleans.* BasinStreet.com. Accessed November 20, 2020. basinstreet.com/wp-content/uploads/2016/09/complete-magnolia -gardens.pdf.

Manuel, Keith A. "A Guide to the Jérémie Papers." With contributions by Andrée-Luce Fourcand and Lesley Futterknecht. University of Florida Smathers Libraries, Special and Area Studies Collections, October 2007. web.uflib.ufl.edu/spec /manuscript/guides/jeremie.htm.

———. "Slavery, Coffee, and Family in a Frontier Society: Jérémie and its Hinterland, 1780–1789." Master's thesis, University of Florida, 2005.

Margo, Robert A. "The North-South Wage Gap, Before and After the Civil War." Working Paper 8778. Cambridge, MA: National Bureau of Economic Research, 2002. nber.org/papers/w8778.

Marshall, Mary Louise. "Samuel Cartwright and States' Rights Medicine." *New Orleans Medical and Surgical Journal* 93, no. 2 (August 1940): 74–78.

Matthewson, Tim. "Jefferson and the Nonrecognition of Haiti." *Proceedings of the American Philosophical Society* 140, no. 1 (March 1996): 22–48.

McConnell, Roland C. "Louisiana's Black Military History, 1729–1865." In *Louisiana's Black Heritage,* edited by Robert R. Macdonald, John R. Kemp, and Edward F. Haas, 32–62. New Orleans: Louisiana State Museum, 1979.

———. *Negro Troops of Antebellum Louisiana: A History of the Battalion of Free Men of Color.* Baton Rouge: Louisiana State University Press, 1968.

McKee, Sally. *The Exile's Song: Edmond Dédé and the Unfinished Revolutions of the Atlantic World.* New Haven: Yale University Press, 2017.

Medley, Keith Weldon. *We as Freemen: Plessy v. Ferguson.* Gretna, LA: Pelican, 2003.

———. "The Will of the Widow Couvent." *Preservation in Print* 26, no. 2 (March 1999): 16–17.

Miles, James Warley. *The Relation between the Races at the South.* Charleston, SC, 1861.

Mills, Elizabeth Shown. "'Isle of Canes' and Issues of Conscience: Master-Slave Sexual Dynamics and Slaveholding by Free People of Color." In "Between Two Worlds," special issue, *Southern Quarterly: A Journal of the Arts in the South* 43 (Winter 2006): 158–75.

"Mississippi Colonization Society." *The African Repository and Colonial Journal* 15 (1839): 85–89.

Mitchell, Brian K. "Oscar James Dunn: A Case Study in Race and Politics in Reconstruction Louisiana." Master's thesis, University of New Orleans, 2011.

Mitchell, Brian K., Barrington S. Edwards, and Nick Weldon. *Monumental: Oscar Dunn and His Radical Fight in Reconstruction Louisiana.* New Orleans: The Historic New Orleans Collection, 2021.

Mobley, Sue. "Crafting a Transparent Process for Championing Public Art and
    Monuments." *Lens*, November 27, 2017. thelensnola.org/2017/11/27/crafting-a
    -transparent-process-for-championing-public-art-and-monuments/.
"The Model Negro Empire." *DeBow's Review* 24, no. 3 (March 1858): 203–11.
Moellhausen, Henry, surveyor. *Norman's Plan of New Orleans & Environs*. 1845. Shields
    and Hammond, engraver; Benjamin Moore Norman, publisher. The Historic
    New Orleans Collection, The L. Kemper and Leila Moore Williams Founders
    Collection.
Monrovia Sound Studio. "Library of Congress Narrative: Jelly Roll Morton and Alan
    Lomax." Transcribed by Michael Hill, Roger Richard, and Mike Meddings. 2003.
    doctorjazz.co.uk/locspeech1.html.
Montana, Angele, Brandon Peltier, and Erica Plaisance. "St. Louis No. 1 and 2 Cemetery
    Documentation, New Orleans, Orleans Parish, Louisiana," Appendix A.
    New Orleans: EarthSearch, July 2013. Choice Neighborhoods Initiative New
    Orleans. cnineworleans.org/wp-content/uploads/docs/Appendix_A_-_06.03
    .13.pdf.
Moore, Louis. *I Fight for a Living: Boxing and the Battle for Black Manhood, 1880–1915*.
    Urbana: University of Illinois Press, 2017.
Moreau Lislet, Louis. *A General Digest of the Acts of the Legislature of Louisiana: Passed
    from the Year 1804, to 1827, Inclusive*. 2 vols. New Orleans, 1828.
Moreau Lislet, Louis, and James Brown. *A Digest of the Civil Laws Now in Force in the
    Territory of Orleans*. Baton Rouge: Claitor's, 2008. First published 1808.
Moreau de Saint-Méry, Médéric Louis Élie. *Description topographique, physique,
    civile, politique et historique de la partie française de l'isle Saint-Domingue*.
    Philadelphia, 1797.
Morgan, Thomas Gibbes, ed., *Civil Code of the State of Louisiana: With the Statutory
    Amendments, from 1825 to 1853, Inclusive*. New Orleans, 1861.
Mortality Statistics: 1910. Washington, DC: Government Printing Office, 1912.
Murray, Charles Augustus. *Travels in North America during the Years 1834, 1835, 1836:
    Including a Summer Residence with the Pawnee Tribe of Indians, in the Remote
    Prairies of the Missouri, and a Visit to Cuba and the Azore Islands*. Vol. 2.
    London, 1839.
Nagel, Susan. *Marie-Therese, Child of Terror: The Fate of Marie-Antoinette's Daughter*.
    New York: Bloomsbury, 2010.
National Governors Association. "Gov. William Pitt Kellogg." Accessed November 12,
    2020. nga.org/governor/william-pitt-kellogg/.
National Park Service. "Port Hudson National Cemetery." Accessed November 12,
    2020. nps.gov/nr/travel/national_cemeteries/Louisiana/Port_Hudson
    _National_Cemetery.html.
Neidenbach, Elizabeth C. "'*Mes dernières volontés*': Testaments to the Life of Marie
    Couvent, a Former Slave in New Orleans." *Transatlantica* 2 (2012).
    transatlantica.revues.org/6186.
New Orleans Public Library. *Que la fête commence! The French Influence on the Good Life
    in New Orleans*. Accessed November 12, 2020. nutrias.org/exhibits/french
    /french.htm.
———. *The World of François Lacroix*. Accessed November 12, 2020. nutrias.org/exhibits
    /lacroix/lafon.htm.
———. "Yellow Fever Deaths in New Orleans, 1817–1905." Louisiana Division, revised
    2003. nutrias.org/facts/feverdeaths.htm.

Nickerson, Camille. *Five Creole Songs*. Boston: Boston Music, 1942.

Ninth Census. Vol. 1, *The Statistics of the Population of the United States*. Washington, DC, 1872.

Nolan, Charles E., ed. *Sacramental Records of the Roman Catholic Church of the Archdiocese of New Orleans*. Vol. 11, *1813–1815*. New Orleans: Archdiocese of New Orleans, 1996.

Northup, Solomon. *Twelve Years a Slave*. Edited by Sue Eakin and Joseph Logsdon. Baton Rouge: Louisiana State University Press, 1968.

Nystrom, Justin A. "African Americans in the Civil War." *64 Parishes Encyclopedia of Louisiana*. Louisiana Endowment for the Humanities, 2010–. 64parishes.org/entry/african-americans-in-the-civil-war/.

———. "Knights of the White Camellia." *64 Parishes Encyclopedia of Louisiana*. Louisiana Endowment for the Humanities, 2010–. 64parishes.org/entry/knights-of-the -white-camellia/.

———. *New Orleans after the Civil War: Race, Politics, and a New Birth of Freedom*. Baltimore: Johns Hopkins University Press, 2010.

"Obituaries—Mrs. Vashti Harkness Fisk." *Northwestern Christian Advocate* 50, no. 52 (December 31, 1902): 26.

Ochs, Stephen J. *A Black Patriot and a White Priest: André Cailloux and Claude Paschal Maistre in Civil War New Orleans*. Baton Rouge: Louisiana State University Press, 2006.

———. "The Rock of New Orleans." *Opinionator* (blog). *New York Times,* July 31, 2013. opinionator.blogs.nytimes.com/2013/07/31/the-rock-of-new-orleans/?_php= true&_type=blogs&_r=0.

"Office of the Freedmen's Aid Society for the City of New Orleans." *Anti-Slavery Reporter*, 3rd ser., 13 (1865): 183.

Officer, Lawrence H., and Samuel H. Williamson. "Annual Wages in the United States: Unskilled Labor and Manufacturing Workers, 1774–Present." MeasuringWorth.com, 2020. measuringworth.com/datasets/uswage/.

Official Register of the United States, Containing a List of Officers and Employés in the Civil, Military, and Naval Service on the First of July, 1883. Vol. 1. Washington, DC, 1883.

Official Register of the United States, Containing a List of Officers and Employés in the Civil, Military, and Naval Service on the Thirtieth of June, 1879. Vol. 1. Washington, DC, 1879.

O'Neill, Charles Edwards. "Fine Arts and Literature; Nineteenth-Century Louisiana Black Artists and Authors." In *Louisiana's Black Heritage*, edited by Robert Macdonald, John Kemp, and Edward Haas, 63–84. New Orleans: Louisiana State Museum, 1979.

Palmer, Vernon Valentine. *Through the Codes Darkly: Slave Law and Civil Law in Louisiana*. Clark, NJ: Lawbook Exchange, 2012.

Pearson, Ellen Holmes. "Imperfect Equality: The Legal Status of Free People of Color in New Orleans, 1803–1860." In *A Law unto Itself? Essays in the New Louisiana Legal History*, edited by Warren M. Billings and Mark Fernandez, 191–210. Baton Rouge: Louisiana State University Press, 2001.

"Pendleton Act (1883)." *Our Documents*. National Archives and Records Administration. Accessed November 22, 2020. ourdocuments.gov/doc.php?flash=false&doc=48.

Perkins, A. E. "Oscar James Dunn." *Phylon* 4, no. 2 (1943): 102, 105–18, 121.

Persica, Dennis. "Oldest Parish Created by African-Americans Celebrates 175 Years." *NCR Today* (blog). *National Catholic Reporter*, September 29, 2016. ncronline.org /blogs/ncr-today/oldest-parish-created-african-americans-celebrates-175-years.

Pew Research Center. "What Census Calls Us." February 6, 2020. pewresearch.org/interactives/what-census-calls-us/.

The Picayune's Guide to New Orleans. 5th ed. New Orleans: The Picayune, 1903.

Pierson, Marion John Bennett, comp. *Louisiana Soldiers in the War of 1812*. Baton Rouge: Louisiana Genealogical Historical Society, 1963.

Pinistri, S. *New Orleans General Guide and Land Intelligence*. May 1841. The Historic New Orleans Collection.

Plyer, Allison. "What Census 2010 Reveals about Population and Housing in New Orleans and the Metro Area." Greater New Orleans Community Data Center, March 7, 2011. gnocdc.s3.amazonaws.com/reports/GNOCDC _Census2010PopulationAndHousing.pdf.

Podur, Justin. *Haiti's New Dictatorship: The Coup, the Earthquake and the UN Occupation*. London: Pluto Press, 2012.

Ponce, Nicolas. *Vue de la Ville de Jérémie*. In *Recueil de vues des lieux principaux de la colonie françoise de Saint-Domingue*. Paris, 1791. John Carter Brown Library. jcb. lunaimaging.com/luna/servlet/detail/JCBMAPS~1~1~789~100072:-top--No--11 --Veu--sic--du-Port-de-.

Population of the United States in 1860: Compiled from the Original Returns of the Eighth Census, under the Direction of the Secretary of the Interior. Washington, DC, 1864.

Postell, William Dosité. "The Principles of Medical Practice in Louisiana during the First Half of the Nineteenth Century." *Bulletin of the Medical Library Association* 30, no. 3 (1942): 191–97.

Poynter, David R. *Membership in the Louisiana House of Representatives, 1812–2024*. Baton Rouge: Legislative Research Library, 2020.

Proceedings of the Convention of the Republican Party of Louisiana, Held at Economy Hall, New Orleans, September 25, 1865, and of the Central Executive Committee of the Friends of Universal Suffrage of Louisiana. New Orleans, 1865.

Rainsford, Marcus. *An Historical Account of the Black Empire of Hayti: Comprehending a View of the Principal Transactions in the Revolution of Saint Domingo; with its An[c]ient and Modern State*. London, 1805.

Read, William Alexander. *Louisiana-French*. Louisiana State University Studies 5. Baton Rouge: Louisiana State University Press, 1931.

Reddick, Lawrence Dunbar. "The Negro in the New Orleans Press, 1850–1860: A Study in Attitudes and Propaganda." Part of PhD diss., University of Chicago, 1939.

Reinders, Robert C. *End of an Era: New Orleans, 1850–1860*. New Orleans: Pelican, 1965.

———. "The Free Negro in the New Orleans Economy, 1850–1860." *Louisiana History* 6, no. 3 (Summer 1965): 273–85.

Reiss, Tom. *The Black Count: Glory, Revolution, Betrayal, and the Real Count of Monte Cristo*. New York: Broadway Books, 2013. First published 2012 by Crown (New York).

Remini, Robert V. *The Battle of New Orleans: Andrew Jackson and America's First Military Victory*. New York: Penguin, 2001. First published 1999 by Viking (New York).

Remy, Avonelle Pauline. "Infiltrating the Colonial City through the Imaginaries of Metissage: Saint-Louis (Senegal), Saint-Pierre (Martinique) and Jeremie (Haiti)." PhD diss., University of Iowa, 2015.

Report of the Select Committee on the New Orleans Riots. Washington, DC, 1867.

Rhodes, James Ford. *History of the United States from the Compromise of 1850 to the Final Restoration of Home Rule at the South in 1877*. Vol. 1, *1850–1854*. New York, 1896.

Robarts, William Hugh. "Napoleon's Interest in the Battle of New Orleans. With a Description of the Battle by General Jackson." *Century Magazine*, January 1897.

Robinson, Elisha, and Roger H. Pidgeon. *Robinson's Atlas of the City of New Orleans, Louisiana*. New York, 1883. New Orleans Notarial Archives.

Rodrigue, John C. *Lincoln and Reconstruction*. Carbondale: Southern Illinois University Press, 2013.

Rogers, Brittany. "Union League (1863–)." BlackPast, February 26, 2009. blackpast.org/african-american-history/union-league-1863/.

Rose, Al, and Edmond Souchon. *New Orleans Jazz: A Family Album*. Baton Rouge: Louisiana State University Press, 1967.

Roser, Max, and Esteban Ortiz-Ospina. "Literacy." Our World in Data, last revised September 20, 2018. ourworldindata.org/literacy/.

Ross, Michael A. *The Great New Orleans Kidnapping Case: Race, Law, and Justice in the Reconstruction Era*. New York: Oxford University Press, 2015.

———. "Resisting the New South: Commercial Crisis and Decline in New Orleans 1865–85." *American Nineteenth Century History* 4, no. 1 (Spring 2003): 59–76.

Roudané, Mark Charles. Roudanez: History and Legacy, 2015. roudanez.com/.

Sachse, Henry R. "The Evolution of the Regime of Tutorship in Louisiana." *Louisiana Law Review* 16, no. 2 (February 1956): 412–30.

Saint-Rémy, Joseph. *Pétion et Haïti, étude monographique et historique*. Paris, 1864.

Sanborn Fire Insurance Map from New Orleans, Orleans Parish, Louisiana. Vol. 3. New York, 1887. Library of Congress. loc.gov/item/sanborn03376_003/.

Saucier, H. Denise LoPresto. "From Dago to White: The Story of Sicilian Ethnic Evolution in New Orleans Amidst the Yellow Fever Epidemic of 1905." Master's thesis, University of Southern Mississippi, 2018.

Schafer, Judith Kelleher. "The Battle of Liberty Place." *64 Parishes Encyclopedia of Louisiana*. Louisiana Endowment for the Humanities, 2010–. 64parishes.org/the-battle-of-liberty-place.

———. *Becoming Free, Remaining Free: Manumission and Enslavement in New Orleans, 1846–1862*. Baton Rouge: Louisiana State University Press, 2003.

———. "Forever Free from the Bonds of Slavery: Emancipation in New Orleans 1855–1857." In *A Law unto Itself? Essays in the New Louisiana Legal History*, edited by Warren M. Billings and Mark F. Fernandez, 141–77. Baton Rouge: Louisiana State University Press, 2001.

———. "The Roman Roots of the Louisiana Law of Slavery: Emancipation in American Louisiana, 1803–1857." *Louisiana Law Review* 56, no. 2 (1996): 409–22.

Schafer, William John, and Richard B. Allen. *Brass Bands and New Orleans Jazz*. Baton Rouge: Louisiana State University Press, 1977.

Schomburg Center for Research in Black Culture. "Haitian Immigration: Eighteenth and Nineteenth Centuries." Motion: The African-American Migration Experience. Accessed November 12, 2020. inmotionaame.org/migrations/landing.cfm?migration=5.

Scott, Rebecca J. "'She . . . Refuses to Deliver Up Herself as the Slave of Your Petitioner': Émigrés, Enslavement, and the 1808 Louisiana Digest of the Civil Laws." *Tulane European and Civil Law Forum* 24 (2009): 115–36.

Scott, Rebecca J., and Jean M. Hébrard. "Rosalie of the Poulard Nation: Freedom, Law, and Dignity in the Era of the Haitian Revolution." In *Assumed Identities:*

The Meaning of Race in the Atlantic World, edited by John D. Garrigus and Christopher Charles Morris, 116–43. College Station: Texas A&M Press, 2010.

The Seventh Census of the United States: 1850, Embracing a Statistical View of Each of the States and Territories, Arranged by Counties, Towns, Etc. Washington, DC, 1853.

Shaik, Fatima. "The Economy Society and Community Support for Jazz." *Jazz Archivist* 18 (2004): 1–9.

Shaik, Mohammed J. "The Development of Public Education for Negroes in Louisiana." PhD diss., University of Ottawa, 1964.

Simpson, Amos E., and Vaughan Baker. "Michael Hahn: Steady Patriot." *Louisiana History* 13, no. 3 (Summer 1972): 229–52.

Smithsonian Folkways Recordings. *Lullabies of the World*. Collected and edited by Lilian Mendelssohn. Folkways Records, 1963.

Sollors, Werner, ed. *Multilingual America: Transnationalism, Ethnicity, and the Languages of American Literature*. New York: New York University Press, 1998.

Songwriters Hall of Fame. "Clarence Williams." Accessed November 12, 2020. songhall.org/profile/Clarence_Williams.

Spain, Daphne. "Race Relations and Residential Segregation in New Orleans: Two Centuries of Paradox." *Annals of the American Academy of Political and Social Science* 441 (January 1979): 82–96.

Statistical View of the United States: Embracing its Territory, Population—White, Free Colored, and Slave—Moral and Social Condition, Industry, Property, and Revenue. Washington, DC, 1854.

Statistics of Income from Returns of Net Income for 1922. Washington, DC: Government Printing Office, 1925.

Stauffer, John. "Yes, There Were Black Confederates. Here's Why." *The Root*, January 20, 2015. theroot.com/yes-there-were-black-confederates-here-s-why-1790858546.

Stern, Walter. *Race and Education in New Orleans: Creating the Segregated City, 1764–1960*. Baton Rouge: Louisiana State University Press, 2018.

Stewart, Whitney Nell. "Fashioning Frenchness: *Gens de Couleur Libres* and the Cultural Struggle for Power in Antebellum New Orleans." *Journal of Social History* 51, no. 3 (Spring 2018): 526–56.

Stowe, Harriet Beecher. *Uncle Tom's Cabin: A Tale of Life Among the Lowly*. London, 1852.

Sullivan, Lester. "Composers of Color of Nineteenth-Century New Orleans: The History behind the Music." *Black Music Research Journal* 8, no. 1 (1988): 51–82.

———. "Edmond Dédé (1827–1901)." Hot Springs Music Festival, November 18, 2011. hotmusic.org/442/edmond-dede/.

Toledano, Roulhac, and Mary Louise Christovich. *The Creole Faubourgs*. New Orleans Architecture 4. 2nd ed. Gretna, LA: Pelican, 1996.

———. *The Esplanade Ridge*. New Orleans Architecture 5. Gretna, LA: Pelican, 1977.

———. *Faubourg Tremé and the Bayou Road: North Rampart Street to North Broad Street to St. Bernard Avenue*. New Orleans Architecture 6. Gretna, LA: Pelican, 2003.

Trotter, James Monroe. *Music and Some Highly Musical People*. New York: Johnson Reprint Corp., 1968. First published 1878 by Lee and Shepard (Boston).

Trufant, Samuel A. *Review of Banking in New Orleans, 1830–1840: History of the Panic of 1837*. [New Orleans?], [1918?].

Ulentin, Anne. "Shades of Grey: Slaveholding Free Women of Color in Antebellum New Orleans, 1800–1840." PhD diss., Louisiana State University, 2012.

United States House of Representatives. "The Civil Rights Act of 1875." History, Art and
    Archives. Accessed November 13, 2020. history.house.gov/Historical-Highlights
    /1851-1900/The-Civil-Rights-Act-of-1875/.

University of Delaware. Colored Conventions Project, 2012–2020.
    coloredconventions.org/.

University of North Carolina at Greensboro Libraries. Race and Slavery Petitions Project.
    Accessed November 16, 2020. library.uncg.edu/slavery/petitions/.

Urofsky, Melvin I. "Homer Plessy." In *Encyclopaedia Britannica*. Encyclopædia Britannica,
    2014–. Article last modified March 13, 2020. britannica.com/biography
    /Homer-Plessy.

Urquhart, Kenneth Trist. "Seventy Years of the Louisiana Historical Association."
    Louisiana History 1, no. 1 (Winter 1960): 5–24.

Veracruz-Llave (Mexico: State). *Documens (traduits) relatifs à la colonie d'Eureka, dans
    l'état de Veracruz, République Mexicaine*. New Orleans, 1857. Louisiana Research
    Collection. Howard-Tilton Memorial Library, Tulane University.

Vidal, Cécile. *Caribbean New Orleans: Empire, Race, and the Making of a Slave Society*.
    Williamsburg, VA: Omohundro Institute of Early American History and Culture;
    Chapel Hill: University of North Carolina Press, 2019.

Vincent, Charles. "Oscar Dunn." *64 Parishes Encyclopedia of Louisiana*. Louisiana
    Endowment for the Humanities, 2010–. 64parishes.org/entry/oscar-dunn-2/.

Wainwright, James E. "William Claiborne and New Orleans's Battalion of Color,
    1803–1815: Race and the Limits of Federal Power in the Early Republic." *Louisiana
    History* 57, no. 1 (Winter 2016): 5–44.

Walker, David. *Walker's Appeal, in Four Articles; Together with a Preamble, to the Coloured
    Citizens of the World, but in Particular, and Very Expressly, to Those of the United
    States of America, Written in Boston, State of Massachusetts, September 28, 1829*.
    Boston, 1830.

Walker, Harry Joseph. "Negro Benevolent Societies in New Orleans: A Study of Their
    Structure, Function and Membership." Master's thesis, Fisk University, 1937.

Ward, Martha. *Voodoo Queen: The Spirited Lives of Marie Laveau*. Jackson: University Press
    of Mississippi, 2004.

"War Leader Profile: Joseph Savary." *Journal of the War of 1812* 12, no. 1 (Spring 2009): 6.

Warmoth, Henry Clay. *War, Politics, and Reconstruction: Stormy Days in Louisiana*.
    New York: Macmillan, 1930.

Washington, Reginald. "The Freedman's Savings and Trust Association and African
    American Genealogical Research." *Prologue* 29, no. 2 (Summer 1997). archives.gov
    /publications/prologue/1997/summer/freedmans-savings-and-trust.html.

Wayland, Francis. *The Elements of Moral Science*. New York, 1835.

Wells-Barnett, Ida B. *Mob Rule in New Orleans: Robert Charles and His Fight to Death, the
    Story of His Life, Burning Human Beings Alive, Other Lynching Statistics*. Chicago:
    Ida B. Wells-Barnett, 1900; Project Gutenberg, 2005. gutenberg.org/files/14976
    /14976-h/14976-h.htm.

Wetta, Francis Joseph. "'Bulldozing the Scalawags': Some Examples of the Persecution
    of Southern White Republicans in Louisiana during Reconstruction." *Louisiana
    History* 21, no. 1 (Winter 1980): 43–58.

———. "The Louisiana Scalawags. (Volumes I and II)." PhD diss., Louisiana State
    University, 1977.

WGBH Educational Foundation. "David Walker, 1796–1830." Africans in America, 1998,
    1999. pbs.org/wgbh/aia/part4/4p2930.html.

White, William W., and Joseph O. Baylen. "Pierre A. Rost's Mission to Europe, 1861–1863." *Louisiana History* 2, no. 3 (Summer 1961): 322–31.

Wilds, John. *Afternoon Story: A Century of the New Orleans States-Item.* Baton Rouge: Louisiana State University Press, 1976.

Willey, Nathan. "Education of the Colored Population of Louisiana." *Harper's New Monthly Magazine* 33, no. 194 (July 1866): 244–50.

Williamson, Samuel H., and Louis P. Cain. "Measuring Slavery in 2016 Dollars." MeasuringWorth.com, 2020. Measuringworth.com/slavery.php.

———. "Seven Ways to Compute the Relative Value of a U.S. Dollar Amount, 1790 to Present." MeasuringWorth.com, 2020. measuringworth.com/calculators /uscompare/.

Wong, Eddie. "In the Shadow of Haiti: The Negro Seaman Act, Counter-Revolutionary St. Domingue, and Black Emigration." In *The Haitian Revolution and the Early United States*, edited by Elizabeth Maddock Dillon and Michael J. Drexler, 162–88. Early American Studies. Philadelphia: University of Pennsylvania Press, 2016.

Woodson, Carter G. *A Century of Negro Migration.* Washington, DC: The Association for the Study of Negro Life and History, 1918.

———. *Free Negro Heads of Families in the United States in 1830, Together with a Brief Treatment of the Free Negro.* Washington, DC: Association for the Study of Negro Life and History, 1925.

———. *Free Negro Owners of Slaves in the United States in 1830: Together with Absentee Ownership of Slaves in the United States in 1830.* 1924. Reprint, New York: Negro Universities Press, 1968.

———. *The Mind of the Negro as Reflected in Letters during the Crisis, 1800–1860.* Mineola, NY: Dover, 2013. First published 1926 by the Association for the Study of Negro Life and History (Washington, DC).

Young, Edward. *Special Report on Immigration; Accompanying Information for Immigrants Relative to the Prices and Rentals of Land, the Staple Products, Facilities of Access to Market, Cost of Farm Stock, Kind of Labor in Demand in the Western and Southern States.* Washington, DC, 1871.

Zaborney, John J. *Slaves for Hire: Renting Enslaved Laborers in Antebellum Virginia.* Baton Rouge: Louisiana State University Press, 2012.

INDEX

Page references for illustrations appear in italics.

The Historic
New Orleans Collection
MUSEUM · RESEARCH CENTER · PUBLISHER